Israeli Women's Studies

Israeli Women's Studies

A Reader

ESTHER FUCHS, EDITOR

RUTGERS UNIVERSITY PRESS
New Brunswick, New Jersey and London

Library of Congress Cataloging-in-Publication data

Israeli women's studies : a reader.
    p.   cm.
    Compiled and edited by Esther Fuchs.
    Includes bibliographical references and index.
    ISBN 0-8135-3615-4 (hardcover : alk. paper). — ISBN 0-8135-3616-2 (pbk. :
alk. paper)
    1. Women—Israel—Social conditions.   2. Women—Legal status, laws, etc.—
Israel.   3. Jewish women—Israel—Social conditions.   4. Women's studies.   5.
Feminism—Israel.   I. Fuchs, Esther, 1953–
HQ1728.5.I88   2005
305.42'095694—dc22

2004023484

Manufactured in the United States of America

For my students—past and present

Contents

Acknowledgments

Dafna N. Izraeli, "The Zionist Women's Movement in Palestine, 1911–1927: A Sociological Analysis." *Signs: Journal of Women in Culture and Society* 7 (1) ©1981 The University of Chicago. Shulamit Reinharz, "Manya W. Shohat and the Winding Road to Sejera." Reprinted by permission from *Pioneers and Homemakers: Jewish Women in Pre-State Israel*, Deborah S. Bernstein, ed., The State University of New York Press ©1992. The State University of New York. All Rights Reserved. Deborah S. Bernstein, "Daughters of the Nation: Between the Public and the Private Spheres in Pre-State Israel." *Jewish Women in Historical Perspective*, Judith Baskin, ed. © 1998, with permission of Wayne State University Press. Tamar Mayer, "From Zero to Hero: Masculinity in Jewish Nationalism." In *Gender Ironies of Nationalism: Sexing the Nation*, 283–308, Tamar Mayer, ed., Routledge, 2000 ©Tamar Mayer. Nira Yuval-Davis, "The Bearers of the Collective: Women and Religious Legislation in Israel." © *Feminist Review* 4 (1980):15–27. Tamar El-Or, "Educated and Ignorant: Ultra-Orthodox Jewish Women and Their World." Preprinted from *Educated and Ignorant* by Tamar El-Or, Haim Watzman, trans., © Lynne Rienner Publishers, Inc. Reprinted with permission of the publisher. Susan Sered, "The Ritualized Body: Brides, Purity, and the Mikveh." In *What Makes Women Sick: Maternity, Modesty and Militarism in Israeli Society.* © Brandeis University Press; 104–121 reprinted by permission. Judith Buber Agassi, "The Status of Women in the Kibbutz." Judith Buber Agassi, "The Status of Women in Kibbutz Society." In *Integrated Cooperatives in the Industrial Society*, 118–130, Klaus Bartolke, Theodor Bergmann, and Ludwig Liegle, eds. Assen: Van Gorcum,1980. © Judith Buber Agassi. Manar Hassan, "Growing Up Female and Palestinian." In B. Swirsky and M. Safir, eds., *Calling the Equality Bluff: Women in Israel*, 66–74. Reprinted by permission of Teachers College Press © 1991 Teachers College, Columbia University, all rights reserved. Yael Yishai, "Between the Flag and the Banner: Women in Israeli Politics." In *Between the Flag and the Banner: Women in Israeli Politics* by Yael Yishai. Reprinted by permission of the State University of New York Press, © 1997, State University of New York; all rights reserved. Hanna Herzog, "Homefront and Battlefront: The Status of Jewish and Palestinian Women in Israel." *Israel Stud-*

ies 3 (1):61–84, Indiana University Press, © Simona Sharoni, "Homefront as Battlefront: Gender, Military Occupation and Violence against Women" in *Women and the Israeli Occupation*, Tamar Mayer, ed., Routledge, 1994, 121–137. Ayala Emmett, "Citizens of the State and Political Women." In *Our Sisters' Promised Land*, University of Michigan Press, 1996, 19–41, © Ayala Emmett. Orna Sasson-Levy, "Gender Performance in a Changing Military: Women Soldiers in 'Masculine' Roles." ©*Israel Studies Forum* 17, 1 (2001):7–22. Esther Fuchs, "Amalia Kahana-Carmon and Contemporary Hebrew Women's Fiction," *Signs: Journal of Women in Culture and Society* 13 (2):299–310, ©1988 The University of Chicago. Ella Shohat, "Making the Silences Speak in the Israeli Cinema." In B. Swirski and M. Safir, eds, *Calling the Equality Bluff: Women in Israel*, 31–40. Reprinted by permission of Teachers College Press; ©1991 Teachers College, Columbia University; all rights reserved. Orly Lubin, "The Woman as Other in Israeli Cinema." Laurence J. Silberstein and Robert Cohn, eds., *The Other in Jewish Thought and History: Constructions of Jewish Culture and Identity* ©1994, New York University Press. Yael Feldman, "Feminism under Siege: The Vicarious Selves of Israeli Women Writers." In Judith Baskin, ed., *Women of the Word: Jewish Women and Jewish Writing*, 323–342; ©1994 reprinted with the permission of Wayne State University Press.

Preface

This book was inspired by the course "Israeli Women" which I have been teaching at the University of Arizona in Tucson for several years. What began as a segment in my survey course "Women in Judaism," had, by 2001, far outgrown the limits, in readings and assignments, of a mere segment. I, therefore, proposed a new course that would be entirely devoted to this particular topic. However, I soon found that the only available reader in English was somewhat dated, having been published in 1991. Nevertheless, I continued to assign it as the main text. To supplement this text, students were expected to read articles on electronic reserve. In 2003, in response to repeated student requests for a book they could hold in their hands, I finally sent off a proposal to Rutgers University Press, noting the pedagogic urgency for a reader on a topic that lacked serious representation in the academic marketplace. My main challenge, as is often the case with readers, was selection. Half the articles I normally recommend for reading had to be omitted for technical considerations. I include references to these important materials in my endnotes. I encourage readers to consult these notes, and the notes and references in respective chapters as sources for further research and further reading. Students should keep in mind that what they read is merely a small sampling of a growing literature that is becoming available. An entire section in my course on otherness and difference had to be omitted since the manuscript already exceeded the usual number of pages allotted for specialized readers. This section offered personal and subjective voices of women, among them, lesbian, Mizrahi, and Palestinian voices, as well as my own piece on growing up as a daughter of Holocaust survivors in Israel. I also omitted my essay on gender and war in Israeli literature, a piece I usually include in my required reading list.

Although editors of readers often include several of their own pieces, my aim here is to offer an overview of an evolution of a body of knowledge. In the last two decades gender has become a central topic in Israeli Studies, and in this book I make the case that the growing diversity and complexity of knowledge on Israeli Women's Studies justifies its constitution as an autonomous academic field. A field is not merely a collection of the most recent work on a particular subject, but rather a context that recognizes the importance of both cutting-edge work and pioneering work that has laid the epistemological foundations for current developments. Students are, therefore, encouraged to follow not just the notes and references, but the dates of publication that provide the logic of internal organization of each of the disciplinary sections that comprise this reader.

I thank my students for inspiring me and for insisting that Israeli women deserve a textbook of their own. Their questions and responses alerted me to the need for this book, which I dedicate to them in the hope that it will, in turn, inspire them to keep searching for answers and to consult additional sources on this and related subjects. I want to thank the contributors for their pioneering, groundbreaking essays, and especially Hanna Herzog and Shula Reinharz for their support as well as Orly Lubin for her advice on the book cover. I thank as well Pnina Lahav, Yael Zerubavel, and Ella Shohat for their warm responses to the idea of the book at its inception. I thank Marilyn Safir for her gracious and reliable assistance and for having co-edited one of the earliest interdisciplinary anthologies on this subject. I am grateful to Ronit Lentin for being a colleague and friend, for her support, advice, and wisdom. I want to mention those who wrote to me in the course of this project for information, ideas, and advice: Rachel Giora, Edna Erez, Uta Klein, Dafna Lemish, Beverly Mizrachi, Smadar Lavie, Pnina Motzafi-Haller, Judith Tydor Baumel, Tovi Fenster, Anita Shapira, and Yaffa Berlovitz. I thank Esther Hertzog for her hospitality, colleagueship, and advice. I thank as well Gershon Shafir of the department of sociology at the University of California in San Diego for his interest in the project, and Ilan Peleg, the editor of *Israeli Studies Forum* for his assistance. I thank Yael Dayan for her inspiring discussion of the topic during her visit to Tucson in 2004. I thank the panelists of the Future of Israeli Women's Studies, Hannah Naveh, Shula Reinharz, Hanna Herzog, Melanie S. Rich, Henriette Dahan-Kalev, and Khawla Abu-Baker. Their anticipated participation assures me that this book is only the beginning of a long and productive collaboration across geographic, institutional, and disciplinary boundaries. I thank Rachel Brenner for her colleagueship and Joel Migdal for his assistance with the conference of the Association of Israel Studies in Tucson. I am grateful to Liz Kennedy, director of women's studies at the University of Arizona for being my colleague and mentor. I thank my colleagues at the department of Near Eastern studies, notably Leila Hudson, Samira Farwaneh, and Kari McBride, and Miranda Joseph of the women's studies department for helping to broaden the frame of reference and for their contributions to our course on gender issues in Middles Eastern studies. I also thank Racheli Guy of the Tucson chapter of Women in Black and Penny Rosenwasser of the Jewish women's caucus of the National Women's Studies Association for their excellent presentations in my class on Israeli women. At Rutgers, I thank as well the anonymous readers, of the manuscript, Kristi Long, my acquisitions editor, Adi Hovav, the associate editor, and Brigitte Goldstein, the copyeditor.

In addition, I want to thank the electronic reserves staff, the inter-library loan staff at the University of Arizona library, especially Scott Cossel and Linda Dols. I thank the Center for Computing and Information Technology, especially Laura Roth-Sheperd, and the Learning Center, especially Gary Forger. Much goes into the making of a book in addition to academic and technical expertise and professional support. I, therefore, want to thank Janet MacGregor and Karen Fox for their wisdom and Lynn Jubilier and Dick Altes for being my friends, Yael for being my sister, and Revital for being my niece. Finally, as always, I thank Shelley for being my devoted partner and companion and for reminding me never to look back.

Israeli Women's Studies

Introduction

Israeli Women's Studies

Defining the Field

When I published my monograph *Israeli Mythogynies: Women in Contemporary Hebrew Fiction* in 1987, there was only one book-length scholarly anthology in Hebrew on Israeli women.[1] While a few edited volumes have appeared since then, in both Hebrew and English, mostly in the social sciences, the first, and so far only, interdisciplinary anthology of feminist essays *The Equality Bluff* was published in 1991.[2] Since then, numerous book-length studies and scores of essays in the fields of social sciences and the humanities have appeared in journals, special volumes, and anthologies. Three anthologies by and about Israeli women were published only in the last three years.[3] The quantity, quality, diversity, and international scope of these works suggest that within two decades that Israeli women's studies has evolved into an academic field of its own. The purpose of the present anthology is to bring together, select, and organize the significant work that has been done in the last two decades. The idea is to highlight current state of the art essays and point to an evolutionary trajectory from the earlier pioneering essays to the voices that define the field today. My selections were not only guided by a scholarly principle, but a pedagogic one as well. When I began teaching a course on Israeli women in 1995, most resources were in Hebrew, a language inaccessible to most of my students, and those available in English were far too specialized for this kind of course. Anthologies in English were special issues of academic journals, mostly in the social sciences, that were not suitable for classroom use. I, therefore, decided to assign articles that would provide a general discussion of background issues. The students showed great interest in the articles I assigned, and so the following year I proceeded to add a few articles. My electronic reserve list soon expanded to more than twenty articles. Despite avid interest in the materials I had them read, everyone agreed that it would be nice to have a textbook, something we could "hold in our hands." As I collected the texts for my class, I discovered that work done in one discipline is rarely mentioned in another.

Discourses employed in the social sciences differed greatly from those in literary and cultural studies. I realized that the insight and knowledge contained in the scattered essays and books I collected had to be brought together somehow. True to the original title of my course, I selected scholarship by and about Israeli women. Israeli women are both the subject of inquiry as a group and the individual actors constructing the research. Among the actors are Israeli scholars who teach in Israel as well as in Europe and the United States, they are residents of Israel and expatriates. As I explained in class, the essays I selected are significant either historically, substantively, or theoretically. They begin new lines of inquiry, make connections between disparate bodies of knowledge, offer innovative methodologies, or shed light on uniquely Israeli configurations. For the most part, I opted for essays that are nontechnical and not overly theoretical and may be valued by scholars and students in women's studies in general, as well as in Israel studies, Jewish studies and Middle Eastern studies. Therefore, though all the articles have gone through a refereeing process, I believe they will appeal to students, scholars, activists, and nonspecialists.

FEMINIST THEORY

If nationality is one criterion for selection, theory and method are two more. The essays I collected challenge traditional, objective scientific discourses about women and explore women's experience, and women's ways of knowing or epistemologies. While not partisan, they are political in the profoundest sense of the word: they seek to expose power relations in surface descriptions of women's realities.[4] To the extent that this scholarship is committed to changing what we know, it engenders a kind of "engaged" knowledge, rather than the descriptive, authoritative, and objective knowledge that characterizes traditional representations of Israel. In this regard it shares much with what is known as the new Israeli sociology and post-Zionist theories.[5] Thus, Israeli women's studies is not merely a field that studies women as topics, to be added to other fields of knowledge. It is a field of critical studies using gender—that is, the asymmetrical, hierarchical definition of sexual difference—as an analytic category.[6] Whether the object of critical inquiry is society or literature, politics or culture—Israeli feminist scholarship challenges the status quo rather than describing it. Despite their great variety of viewpoints, the critical essays included here challenge traditional knowledge about women. In this regard they share a methodology of "re-vision"— the ability to see anew, to look at things differently—which defines the broader field of women's studies.[7] Feminist critical revision focuses on patriarchal structural dichotomies—for example, public/private; national/feminist; majority/minority; male/female; Jew/Arab— that have hindered gender, racial, and ethnic equality. Though critique is at the very center of this academic enterprise, scholars are equally interested in reconstructing the neglected social and literary history of Israeli women. Produced in both the social sciences and the humanities, Israeli feminist scholarship is both empiricist and poststructuralist. It seeks to reveal the truth or reality underlying popular representations, as well as to expose the gendered narratives, or meta-narratives, through which truths and realities are constructed. In this reader I included both pioneering work that laid the foundation for contemporary inquiries, and cutting-edge work that informs major scholarly work today. As the American example has shown, the field of women's studies derives its energy from generational dialogue as well as from contemporary debates.[8] Rather than create hierarchies of knowledge, dismissing the first phase as too empiricist or ethnocentric, this reader seeks to highlight both the pioneering phase and the more recent developments as they are linked in an evolving process of scholarly inquiry.

The earliest essays, published in the 1970s, argued that gender disparity is a social and legal problem that could somehow be remedied through appropriate change and reform.[9] Based on this research, Anglo-American feminist publications and the work of the Israeli feminist movement, popular publications began to criticize the Israeli myth of equality.[10] As we shall see, in the 1980s scholars sought to exemplify and document the manifestations of inequality in the workplace, the legal system, the kibbutz, the army, and the family. The first critiques of Israeli cultural representations of women and the first anthologies of women's creative work began to appear.[11] The first phase of Israeli women's studies sought to open a space in academic discourse for feminist analysis, both in Israel and the United States.[12] In the 1990s the concern was to explain *how* and *why* inequality works, linking it to fundamental social structures and cultural processes that could not be easily changed. While the early phase focused on society, the second focused on the nation, moving from a reformist vision to a more radical one. The compass in the 1990s was broadened from a concern with state apparatus to national ideologies—though both continue to be foci of concern. If the Yom Kippur War of 1973 inspired the contemporary phase of the feminist movement in Israel, the Lebanon War in (1982–1985) and the Intifada, or Palestinian uprising (1987–1992) reconfirmed the feminist emphasis on war and peace as critical to understanding the unique predicament of Israeli women. A growing awareness of the interconnections between the discourse of war and the gendering of the nation found expression in the late 1980sand burgeoned into comprehensive monographs in the 1990s.[13] Yet, as Israeli feminist scholarship increased in volume and its scope broadened, it became increasingly self-conscious, turning the lens of critical inquiry on itself, its own theories and scholarly practices.[14] Though Israeli feminism—both the contemporary feminist movement and women's studies in Israel—allied itself, at least in theory, with racial and ethnic struggles for equality in Israel, it has come under increasing criticism for failing to put its theory into practice.[15] The challenge of Israeli women's studies will be to generate and promote scholarship by and about *all* Israeli women, Jewish Israelis —Ashkenazi (European and American descent) and Mizrahi (Asian and North African descent)—as well as Arab Israeli citizens and Palestinians. The recent expressions of self-criticism testify to the resilience and promise of the field rather than to any incipient decline.

INTERDISCIPLINARITY

The following organization of the works into topical areas of inquiry aims at linking and crossing disciplinary boundaries. Although several of the sections analyze the relationship of war and gender, I devote a thematic section to this important topic, which continues to preoccupy feminist researchers across the disciplines. These dual topics link common objects of inquiry and deconstruct and reconstruct the boundaries that separate them. For example, history, a discipline that reconstructs past events, causalities, and facts, is combined with myth, the overarching meta-narrative, produced by historians to legitimize the nation's current policies. Law, the system created by the modern secular state to enforce civic discipline is juxtaposed with religion, the mythic system that feeds the nation's collective imagination. Politics, the symbolic procedures and institutional justifications of the state's power relationships with other states, is juxtaposed with society, the various communities and constituencies that make up the nation.[16] Literary studies, which focus on fictional accounts by individual authors, literary canons, and systems of critical evaluations, are juxtaposed with film studies which focus on the political implications of fictional constructions of gender, ethnicity, and the nation.[17] Needless to say, these disciplinary juxtapositions are also meant to highlight complementarities; the topical dualisms feed each other and are deeply interdependent as they highlight and transgress each other's boundaries. The discussion of gender in the following articles straddles the modern and postmodern divide, as some scholars tackle the issue of sexual politics—power relations between "real" men and women—while others focus on textual politics, or the hegemony of masculinity as repressive power in cultural scripts and national discourse.[18] As is common in feminist theory, gender is a term of debate and multiple definitions, and here too it is discussed as the social construction of sexual difference and as the discursive control of women's bodies, activities, and subjectivities.[19] Masculinity figures as a performance of toughness and virile superiority, as a discourse that shapes the subjectivity of individual men, who nevertheless can also participate in dismantling it.[20] The essays I included here reflect the critical investigation of woman as Other, as the devalued side of the gender binary and as a marginal discourse that can subvert masculine epistemologies.[21] "Woman" here is understood as a historical subject creating social change, whose entry into the social system—including the military system—is both crucial and fraught with danger.[22] Even though critique has emerged as a central method in the social sciences, the re-construction of women's histories and texts pursued by historians and literary critics is of central importance. These procedures complement each other as part of the effort to introduce women's experiences and perspectives so as to make them visible and interrupt the silences surrounding them in traditional scholarship.

Despite their diverse approaches, most of the essays grapple with the deeper roots of gender asymmetries in Israel. While social scientists see the root of the problem in social processes and political constructions, cultural critics find it in the masculine hegemony inscribed in representational and symbolic systems, in the structure of the literary and cinematographic canons, and in nationalist mythologies. The section on myth and history deals with the mythological interdependence of Zionism and masculinity in the late nineteenth century and with the social structures and political pressures that pushed women and feminism to the periphery in the early decades of the twentieth century. The next section on law and religion traces the causes of disparity back even further to Halakhah (Jewish religious law) and its imbrications with the secular legal system in Israel. The section on society and politics exposes the social and political constructions of gender, the ways in which relations of center and periphery in society and politics are maintained and reproduced by patriarchal dichotomies—for example, public versus private; national versus feminist—that determine and define the collective behavior of men and women. The section on war and peace exposes the ways in which the Arab-Israeli conflict exacerbates gender hierarchies—in both society and literature—and how, in response, women politicize their marginal status to counter both militarism and sexism. The section on literature and culture delineates the exclusion of women from privileged representations and analyzes work of contemporary women authors and film producers who are claiming their own space and voice.

Myth and History

Women as subjects and agents of change are glaringly missing from popular and critical historical accounts on Israel.[23] Canonic accounts of pre-Israeli Zionist thought and ideology rarely include women's names.[24] Histories of modern Israel rarely devote space to women's leadership or contributions to nation building.[25] In the last decade serious questions have been raised about Israeli historiography, the ideologies and methodologies that shape the writing of Israeli history.[26] National themes in historical accounts of the distant past and of the Yishuv, the pre-state period (1881–1948), have been deconstructed as ideological narratives, or myths.[27] While the scholars included here agree that gender equality in the period of the Yishuv was one such myth, they argue that women's contributions have been marginalized. While it is recognized that the Yishuv was a gendered society, the efforts of the first feminist movement to change this reality have been mostly forgotten. The most balanced portrayal of the pre-state woman takes note of both her revolutionary and traditional aspects.[28] In order to restore this former aspect to memory, it is vital to retrace the history of the first women's movement and to recover the stories of individual women. But are the memory and history of the few exceptional women who carved a space in Zionist history—Rachel (1890–1931), Sara Aharonson (1890–1970), Manya Shohat (1880–1959), Hannah Senesz (1921–1944)—enough to make a dent in traditional and current Zionist historiographies? Furthermore, if we agree that the Zionist meta-narrative is masculine in its fundamental orientation would not the new recoveries and rediscoveries re-inscribe women's marginality in Zionist history?

The contributors to this volume exemplify four distinct approaches to the question of gender and Zionist history. Each approach helps explain present gender disparities by casting a look back to earlier stages and processes that have shaped the power relations between feminism and Zionism. Dafna Izraeli considers the history of the Zionist women's movement by illuminating the specific personalities and factors that gave precedence to accommodation and pragmatism over the principle of equality endorsed by the radical feminists. Izraeli implies that the past may offer a clue for current political decisions. Just as the Zionist Women's Movement in the early 1920s was virtually coopted by the male leadership, the contemporary feminist movement in Israel runs the risk of being co-opted as well unless it forges a separate leadership with its own agenda. This approach makes it clear that the loss of the feminist momentum in the early decades of the twentieth century was by no means inevitable, and that specific political decisions could have been avoided had the early feminist leaders had the benefit of the kind of hindsight we have today. Rather than focusing on a missed opportunity, Shulamit Reinharz highlights the contributions of women Zionists to the national enterprise, and the extent to which their behavior and thought may be considered feminist. Her reconsideration of Manya Shohat suggests that it is up to us to re-read and re-interpret the history of women in Zionism, women who have been taken for granted, and either largely forgotten or neglected by the official record of the past. Deborah Bernstein is less optimistic. She considers not so much what individual women or women's groups have done, but how certain inevitable political and social conditions have led to their restriction to the private sphere, to domesticity and thus to a secondary role within the Zionist settlement. Politically, since the British Mandate was in control of Palestine since the 1920s, it imposed on the Jewish immigrants the gender codes, mores, and ethos that prevailed in England at the time. Women were seen as wives and mothers, not as self-sufficient, economically independent citizens in spite of the suffragist movement and the granting of voting rights to women. Socially, most of the Jewish population in Palestine in the early decades, in both the religious and the sectors, was organized around male-dominated families. Thus the social history of the Zionist movement laid the foundation for present gender inequities in Israel. The fourth approach to Zionist history suggests that male supremacy was not an external factor imposed by European culture or by Jewish traditionalism, but by masculinist notions of supremacy embedded in the doctrines of the earliest Zionist thinkers. Thus, a solution to gender disparity in the present requires not merely social re-organization, greater tolerance for diverse family structures, or a reformulation of feminist agendas in Israel, but a radical, comprehensive reconsideration of fundamental Zionist concepts and orientations.

In her essay "The Zionist Women's Movement in Palestine, 1911–1927: A Sociological Analysis," Dafna Izraeli offers a detailed reading of the rise and decline of the first Zionist Women's Movement in Palestine in the first two decades of the twentieth century, notably during the socialist-Zionist immigration waves known as the second and the third Aliyah. The immigrants who came to Palestine then were no doubt dedicated to the ideal of class and gender equality. However, years of traditional gender segregation could not apparently be swept aside over night, despite the fervor of these idealistic nationalists. Even in the early *kvutzot*, or agrarian communes, women found themselves in the communal kitchen and laundry, occupied with service jobs that were considered secondary in the hierarchy of pioneering values. The first women's farm, established by Hanna Meizel, was one in a series of efforts to train women for productive labor. The period of frustration (1904–1911) led to the creation of the Women's Workers' Movement which oversaw training programs for women in agriculture and urban construction. This was a separatist movement that realized that women's goals could not be achieved within the existing organizational structures of the Zionist Labor movement in Palestine. In 1921 the Women's Workers' Council was established and led by radicals like Yael Gordon and Ada Maimon. Its charge was to protect women's right to work, to create employment opportunities for women and to help them compete for the few available jobs. . From the perspective of the Histadrut, the largest labor organization, the women's movement represented a threat that subverted its legitimacy as the representative of all Jewish workers in Palestine. David Ben-Gurion, who went on to become Israel's first prime minister, discounted the significance of the women's movement as a particularistic or partisan group in competition with the collective goals of the workers' union. This viewpoint deepened the rift between the radicals and the loyalists within the women's movement. Loyalists, like Golda Meir, did not want to be perceived as a special interest group. Golda Meir was favored and promoted by the Zionist leadership, while the Women's Workers' Council was coopted by the Histadrut and, by 1927, lost its organizational autonomy. Izraeli suggests that the collapse of the first feminist movement in Palestine was due, in part, to the political pressure, intervention and cooptation efforts of the male leadership of the Yishuv and, in part, to the tension between loyalists and radicals within the movement itself.

Despite the constraints imposed on them by a gendered society, some women pioneers not only contributed to the nation building effort, but may have even shaped one of its lasting legacies.[29] In her essay "The Winding Road to Sejera," Shulamit Reinharz credits Manya Shohat with having invented and established the first self-reliant, truly egalitarian, agricultural collective, a prototype of the kibbutz, one of the greatest legacies of the socialist Zionist movement in Palestine. Manya Shohat's transformation from socialist revolutionary and anti-Tsarist terrorist, who had been subjected to interrogation by the Russian secret police, to Zionist pioneer is traced here with great detail. Reinharz points out that Manya Shohat's belief in activism, self-labor, and collectivism were revolutionary ideals in 1904, when most Jewish settlers were landowners dependent on Jewish philanthropy and Arab labor. Manya's idealism did not obstruct her view for realistic economic and financial planning. She met with numerous leaders and patrons to raise money for her experimental cooperatives. True to socialist Zionist ideals, she stipulated that the Hebrew workers must abolish the class system, abolish private property, and avoid competition with Arabs, or takeover of Arab employment. Furthermore, she insisted that people be free to leave the commune at any time and that work hours be limited so as to permit and promote cultural activities. Sejera was subsequently transformed into the nucleus of Hashomer, the first Jewish defense organization in Palestine, led by Manya's husband, Israel Shohat. Manya Shohat then can be credited for creating in Sejera two of the most significant institutions of the Zionist Yishuv. Her most important contribution from a feminist standpoint is her successful creation of the first and only egalitarian framework where women could demonstrate their ability for arduous agricultural work equal to their male comrades.

In "Daughters of the Nation: Between the Public and the Private Spheres in Pre-State Israel," Deborah Bernstein reminds us that for the most part, the pre-state Yishuv was a gendered society. Bernstein highlights three major factors that contributed to the restriction of women to the private or domestic sphere: the immigration policy of the British authorities, the familistic structure of the mostly urban and middle class Yishuv, and the economic recession and competitive labor market in the 1920s and 1930s.[30] The British mandatory authorities relegated most women immigrants to a class of dependents, wives, or elderly mothers, who could not be expected to find employment on their own. This gendered system of immigration foreclosed opportunities for equal status in the labor force. Bernstein also reminds us that the Yishuv was a society largely composed of families. The traditional family unit expected women to be responsible for childbearing, socialization, and daily sustenance. While paying lip service to women's domestic duties, the Yishuv leadership elevated men's service in the public sphere to the status of greater significance and a true contribution to the national weal. If women were not recognized for their nation-building efforts at home, their efforts to find employment and participate in the labor market were often a bitter struggle against great odds. Most employed women were young and single and were concentrated in either domestic service or in the textile industry. Upon getting married most—both Sephardi and Ashkenazi women—dropped out of the labor market. Bernstein emphasizes that even married middle class women struggled to break out of traditional feminine roles by joining voluntary and welfare organizations. Until recently, the memoirs and diaries these women left behind have widely been neglected and forgotten.[31]

Tamar Mayer's "From Hero to Zero" locates the roots of exclusion in the Zionist meta-narrative, the national mythos, created to counter European anti-Semitic representations of Jewish men as effeminate.[32] The Zionist dream, as expressed in the writings of Theodor Herzl and Max Nordau, was freedom and manliness. This legacy was reinforced in the memorial culture that was created in Palestine, celebrating male fallen heroes and sanctifying (male) self-sacrifice. The representation of feminine symbols (for example, the land) is strikingly analogous to the construction of Arab-Palestinian nationalism.[33] Mayer's postmodernist foregrounding of gender in her analysis of Zionism suggests that the reasons for continued masculine hegemony in Israel are not merely historical. Because they are deeply rooted in the very fabric of national myth–making, they may require a more radical solution than the socioeconomic changes advocated by liberal feminists.

Law and Religion

While historians and cultural critics look to narratives of the past in an effort to identify the causes of perduring gender hierarchies, legal scholars look to Israel's legal system, notably to its problematic interdependence with religious law as one of the fundamental obstacles in the way of gender equality. On the one hand, Israel was one of the first states to have inscribed sexual equality in its declaration of independence: "The State of Israel will maintain equal social and political rights for all citizens, irrespective of religion, race or sex." This egalitarian principle was reiterated in 1949 as a "basic law" and again in 1951 as the "women's equal rights law." On the other hand, Israel enforces biblical laws, based on a vision of women's segregation and subordination, following an ancient patriarchal system derived from ancient Near Eastern codes.[34] Israel's legal system is based on so-called basic laws which lack constitutional power. Many of the progressive laws that have been passed in the 1980s and 1990s are rarely tested in court. The Supreme Court as a secular body does not have jurisdiction over domestic law—including divorce and marriage—that are controlled by Jewish Rabbinic, Muslim, or Christian courts. The non-separation of religion and state is the legacy of the Ottoman "millet" system which provided juridical autonomy to its diverse religious groups. Its persistence in the state of Israel is the result of the status-quo agreement between David Ben-Gurion, Israel's first prime minister, and the Orthodox parties in 1947.[35] While the religious parties see this nexus as vital to the Jewish identity of the state, secular Jews condemn it as a violation of their civil rights. While scholars disagree about the extent and scope of the religious-secular divide, the exclusive jurisdiction of religious courts over marriage and divorce continues to define Israeli women—be they Jewish, Christian or Muslim—as second-class citizens.[36] Feminist scholars are divided on the question of litigation as a mechanism for change.[37] While some progress was made in the late 1980s and 1990s, the case of "The Women of the Wall," a feminist group is a glaring example of the Supreme Court's unwillingness to enforce equality laws. The group's challenge to the Orthodox rabbinate's authority by insisting on the rights of women to public worship at the Western Wall, including the use of Torah (reading from the scroll), Tallit (wearing of prayer shawls), and Teffilin (wearing of phylacteries), was rejected by the Supreme Court not on grounds of legality, but because it would disturb the public peace.[38] Rather than choosing detailed scholarly articles on Israeli law and jurisprudence, I decided to focus on the paradoxical influence on women's lives of the non-separation of religion and state. The essays in this section do not take issue with the gendered aspects of Jewish religious law or tradition as such, but with its rigid, repressive interpretation, application, and imposition on secular and religious women in Israel. The pieces I included here focus on cultural processes of "disciplining" Jewish women—both secular and religious—into conduct that is in keeping with the patriarchal interests of the state and of certain rabbinic leaderships. Whether the cultural message relates to reproductive duties or to women's corporeality, it is circulated through the mechanism that combines religious and political hegemonies. While Nira Yuval-Davis and Susan Sered are interested mostly in the "embodiment" (the symbolic construction of women as bodies, or corporeal beings) of secular women, Tamar El-Or is interested in the daily lives of religious women, as determined, controlled, and supervised by local ultra-Orthodox (male) leaders. Both El-Or and Sered focus on the repressive effect of religious culture on women. While El-Or's focus is primarily on intellectual repression, Sered's is on the daily social and physical oppressions of women. It is the invisible, symbolic processes of patriarchal control that the following pieces explore as it finds expression in the strange collusion of religion and secular culture.

In her essay "The Bearers of the Collective: Women and Religious Legislation in Israel," Nira Yuval-Davis offers an overview of the abusive excesses of Israel's religious courts. She touches on the fate of the *agunot* (literally anchored or chained women), wives whose spouses refuse to grant them a divorce. Since only a man can grant his wife a *get* (bill of divorcement), a woman is liable to languish for years without recourse to civil marriage. Because she belongs to her husband, such a woman is unable to remarry and have children. Any such children are considered *mamzerim* (bastards) who will not be able to marry Jews for ten generations. A divorced woman who is married to a *kohen* (believed to be descended from the priestly caste), is liable to be divorced by her husband without any claim to alimony or any other protection.[39] Yuval-Davis, however, goes beyond cataloguing some of the most censorious cases of legal discrimination.[40] She points to the connection between religious legislation and the cultural promotion of women's reproductive roles. The demographic race against citizen and noncitizen Palestinians defines Israeli women as the "bearers of the collective." Women's loyalty to the state is not measured by their military or civic contributions, but by their procreative conduct. Yuval-Davis argues that women constitute the symbolic means by which the state polices the boundaries of the Jewish national collective. She notes that according women special accolades for having reproduced numerous children is not unique to Israel, suggesting that in addition to traditional and religious legacies that continue to shape modern reproductive policies, the nation-state as such uses women as reproductive agents for either economic or military goals.[41] Religious legislation in Israel thus consolidates the definition of women as reproductive workers, as it naturalizes the gendered division of (national) labor assigning soldiering to men and motherhood to women.[42]

In "Paradoxes and Social Boundaries: Ultra-Orthodox Jewish Women and Their World" based on her larger study of the lives of Israeli *haredi* (ultra-Orthodox) women, Tamar El-Or examines the social and symbolic repression of women in the Ashkenazi, hasidic *Gur* sect in Bnei Brak.[43] Even though its members tend to segregate themselves from the secular population, the haredi community relies on the Israeli government for subsidies and for privileges (for example, exemption from military duty) that enables haredi men to devote themselves to the study of Torah.[44] Much of the burden of daily existence falls on the shoulders of haredi women who are responsible for domestic and parenting work, and often as well for daily sustenance. Nevertheless, women who seek employment in the secular sector are suspect.[45] Women who seek to ease their domestic and reproductive work through recourse to modern amenities are castigated or frowned upon, even though the community in general does not forbid the use of electrical appliances. The battle to restrict consumption is organized as a campaign against women, who are accused of greed or lack of modesty. This repressive policy complements the ambivalent attitude of the male authorities toward women's education. The long years of education in all female institutions prepare women neither for leadership positions in their own community nor for economic independence. The gendered regime of knowledge in the haredi community insures that the most coveted achievement, the enlightened practice of Judaism, will remain the monopoly of men. It insures that despite long years of learning, haredi women will continue to depend on male authorities for instruction and continued guidance on both daily observance and on more complex spiritual concepts and religious principles.[46] The ambivalent attitude toward women's education is inscribed in and circulated through

brochures, lectures, classes, newspapers, and pamphlets, which the women consume and reproduce. Gradually, the women themselves begin to police the communal boundaries that separate them from and bind them to the secular population.
Nevertheless, El-Or points out that haredi women also question the system and
resist it as they point to the gaps, contradictions, and inconsistencies in the
knowledge they are made to consume and in the scripts they are made to follow.

Susan Sered's piece "The Ritualized Body: Brides, Purity, and the Mikveh"
argues that in certain institutional settings religious rituals are interpreted in
ways that authorize and validate male control of female bodies. All brides, including secular brides must show proof of immersion in the *mikveh*, or ritual bath, before
they can receive a marriage license. Beyond the question of religious coercion, Sered
analyses the objectification of the bride's body as it is inspected and scrutinized
through ritual performance. In addition to objectifying the bride, the *mikveh* discourse implies that her body is naturally impure.[47] Mikveh folklore implies that
immersion grants women health, fertility, and successful children. The symbolic
moment of transition from autonomy to marriage signals the woman's incorporation into the national collective through marriage. But women cannot become
part of the collective unless they entrust their bodies to the inspection of religious
authorities. If religious culture implies that the bride's body is naturally impure,
secular-national discourses emphasizing maternity and reproduction construct it
as weak and dependent on medical (that is, male expert) care. While religious culture attempts to purify women's bodies, secular abortion laws control them by transferring the decision-making process to the state, submitting women to physical
and psychological scrutiny.[48] Sered suggests that Israeli culture as a whole embodies women. The cultural emphasis on women's corporeal functions transfers discursive and social control over their bodies to male authorities whereby women's
autonomy is undermined and they are literally made physically sick.

Society and Politics

Sociologists observed as far back as the 1970s that, despite their growing numbers
in the workforce, Israeli women, when compared with men, earned less, were less
often promoted, and less likely to attain managerial positions.[49] Researchers
found that even educated and qualified women preferred part-time jobs because
such jobs allowed them to fulfill their domestic duties as wives and mothers.[50] In
the 1990s, researchers found that Ashkenazi women had higher educational
achievements and workforce participation than Mizrahi women. In the mid
1990s, two-thirds of Ashkenazi women were employed compared to more than half
of their Mizrahi counterparts, while Israeli-Palestinian women showed an employment rate of less than 20 percent. This state of affairs has not changed much in
the last decade. Women made up a majority of the unemployed population, and

were poorly represented in the upper echelons of business, management and academia.[51] These results spurred researchers to examine the gendered nature of the workplace as such, finding that women often colluded with the unequal distribution of economic power because they were reluctant to act "aggressively," to act like men—demanding equal pay, financial parity, and negotiating for better conditions. Research into the political behavior of women yielded similar results. The limited representation of women in the Knesseth (Israeli parliament)—about 10 percent on average since the establishment of the state—and the tendency to relegate them to so-called soft committees, those dealing with domestic issues rather than foreign policy and security issues, has been noted.[52] The limited participation of women in successive governments, in decision-making committees within multiple parties, and in local politics has also been noted, as has been the lower participation in politics of Mizrahi women, and the very limited participation of citizen Palestinian women. This state of affairs has been linked to a deeper association of the public sphere as such with masculinity. Researchers in the late 1990s concluded that politics as such is perceived by both men and women as a masculine domain, where women are hard pressed to reassure voters they are feminine, that is, traditional, women who are not overly ambitious and who give priority to family and domesticity just as normal women are expected to do.[53]

In "The Status of Women in Kibbutz-Society," Judith Buber Agassi points up the impact of what is called "familism," the traditional domestic definition of women on a society, that originally—at least in theory—set out to undo traditional patriarchal arrangements. The kibbutz, an agrarian egalitarian collective, was touted as a social experiment specifically designed to liberate women from childrearing and family duties by establishing communal kitchens and childcare facilities. In the 1950s women began to reclaim their maternal and domestic roles, demanding more time with their infants and greater attention to family needs. The return to the nuclear family generated biosocial theories regarding women's natural reproductive and mothering nature, and the kibbutz was held up as a proof that, contrary to feminist notions of women's liberation, when given a choice, women prefer domestic and maternal occupations to the workplace.[54] These biosocial theories were based on the assumption that the kibbutz had achieved sexual equality and that the women who reclaimed their domestic roles did have a choice. Buber Agassi challenges this assumption and argues that occupational segregation and polarization defined the kibbutz from its very inception. Women were relegated to less prestigious service jobs in the kitchen, laundry, childcare and early education, while men were employed and trained in mostly industrial and agricultural so-called productive branches.[55] This suggests that women's return to domestic and individual parental roles was not a choice, but an attempt to reclaim the prestige and status that were denied them. Buber Agassi claims that familism as such, or the return to familial living quarters, does not in and of itself undermine women's status. More than anything it is sex-typing, or occupational segregation, that is the issue. She further suggests that occupational segregation and familism have hindered women from joining decision-making committees and taking on leadership and management positions within individual kibbutzim and in the kibbutz movement at large.[56] Because the kibbutz has undergone dramatic changes since the 1980s, due to an attempt to adjust to the demands of an industrialized and capitalistic national economy, it is less insulated from the broader society.[57] The kibbutz then may not serve as an appropriate test case for gender equality because, in effect, historically this equality has never quite been achieved.[58]

In "Growing up Female and Palestinian in Israel," Manar Hassan emphasizes the difference of having to shoulder a double burden, living as a woman in a traditional Muslim family and community and as a Palestinian in the State of Israel. Her analysis collapses the private/public, personal/political and sexual/cultural dichotomies and insists on the validity of the individual narrative by highlighting biographical and anecdotal detail of specific women's lives. She describes the repression of Muslim girls, who are taught from birth that they are a liability to their families and that they ought not to set their sights on what their brothers should—for example, careers, success outside the home. Discouraged from seeking education and economic independence, women are often exploited by their fathers who deem themselves their proprietors. Restricted socially, girls are also constricted physically, socialized to be supportive of and obedient to their family, notably the men, and prohibited from any conduct that may suggest a violation of the strict code of sexual conduct. The suspicion of inappropriate sexual conduct may lead to honor killing or the killing of a girl by her agnatic relatives to protect the honor of the family.

Needless to say, the threat of killing functions as a mechanism of social control.[59] This type of social control is enhanced by the political control exercised by Israeli authorities over its Arab citizenry. Hassan argues that Israeli police are reluctant to punish the male perpetrators because they are interested in consolidating their own authority over a traditional, patriarchal leadership, divided into hamulahs (extended families).[60] By returning run-away girls who seek asylum from their families, Israeli authorities bear responsibility for the ritualistic sacrifice of the weakest and most expendable element in Palestinian society, its unprotected women.[61]

In "Between the Flag and the Banner," Yael Yishai argues that Israeli women have been forced into a difficult dilemma of having to choose between nationalism, the flag, and feminism, the banner. This dilemma is related to the political character of Israel, which is a visionary rather than a service democracy. Because in Israel democratic procedures are secondary to overarching national interests (for example, security, immigration), women's interests are perceived as partisan and as such competitive and even incongruent with the interest of the nation.

This may explain why Israeli women traditionally prefer the strategy of integration, working within existing structures, to mobilization, creating separatist, alternative feminist groups. Although they have increasingly been radicalized by feminist ideology, the largest women's associations continue to advocate women's traditional roles within the family and traditional volunteering activities in public.[62] As voters, Jewish Israeli women tend to be relatively hawkish on issues of security. The author suggests that these gestures of adherence to the flag at the expense of the banner are an attempt to compensate for their lesser participation in the military and political life.[63] Yishai contrasts Jewish women's oscillation between the flag and the banner with what she considers an opposite trend among Israeli-Palestinian women, whose political organizations usually combine nationalist and feminist agendas[64] Nevertheless, Yishai suggests that Israel does not fare too badly when compared with other Western democracies. The women's party, which was dissolved in the late 1970s, metamorphosed into numerous feminist groups—for example, rape crisis centers, shelters for battered women, lesbian culture clubs, advocacy groups, peace coalitions. An active umbrella organization, the Women's Network was established in the mid 1980s and a Women's Committee in the Knesset, dating from the early 1990s, oversees progressive and egalitarian legislation.

In "Homefront and Battlefront: The Status of Jewish and Palestinian Women in Israel," Hanna Herzog examines the deeper social structures that frustrate and hinder the achievement of gender equality. She links the higher status of men in the workforce to their higher status in political life and suggests that both are related to men's greater participation in the military. Men who serve longer, and in more prestigious jobs, in the military often convert the human and symbolic capital they accumulate into managerial positions in business and industry and into leadership positions in politics. Because of their military experience male, rather than female, leaders are perceived as best qualified to engage in discourse about security issues and to shape Israel's foreign policy and defense doctrines. These factors have engendered and reproduced male dominance in the public sphere. Israel's perpetual state of war with its Arab neighbors also has furthered entrenchment of the institution of the heterosexual, patriarchal family in Israel. The demographic race creates pressure on women to marry young and have children. As part of the home front, women are expected to give full support to sons or husbands in the army and to subordinate their own goals to those of the men. The same public policy that curtails women's access to public power, promotes their familial roles by providing maternity leaves and daycare facilities to working mothers, and natal care and subsidies to large families.[65] Thus women are included in the national process of coping with security, and by extension in public life, by adhering to traditional roles in the private sphere. This gendered division of labor dilutes protest and obstructs the rise of an effective feminist movement. Though the

Palestinian community finds itself on the other side of the Arab-Israeli conflict, Herzog finds a similar gendered organization there as well. Barriers to integration within Jewish society strengthen the status of the Arab family as the locus of solidarity and nationalism. Upholding traditional values and cultural distinctiveness means tightening of social supervision over women. Thus life in the shadow of the security threat has created barriers between Israeli and Palestinian women, while keeping them subordinated within their respective patriarchal communities, unable to cooperate despite much common ground.

War and Peace

Much has been written about Israel's military conflict with its Arab neighbors including the 1948 War of Independence, the 1956 Sinai Campaign against Egypt, the 1967 Six Day War during which it gained control over Palestinian populated territories in the West Bank and the Gaza Strip, and the 1982–1985 Lebanon War waged in Southern Lebanon against the Palestine Liberation Organization, the 1992 Gulf War, and the two Intifadas, or Palestinian uprisings, from 1987 to 1992 and 2000 to the present.[66] Yet, the critical examination of individual wars, of the history of Israel's military engagement with the Arabs, and of Israel's military culture has only recently begun to include gender as a relevant analytic concept.[67] The essays included here argue that gender is vital to a broader understanding of the military and militarism in Israel. War, in general, often constructs women as needing male protection, thus justifying the military enterprise as such.[68] War is fundamental to the definition of Israeli manhood and to the identification of courage with self-sacrifice.[69] Militarism—the culture of war—glorifies male sacrifice and martyrdom and tends to construct women as a source of danger.[70]

In the growing body of scholarship on gender and Israeli militarism two approaches seem to emerge. One approach, typical of the 1980s, argues for the egalitarian inclusion of women in the army as a means toward achieving civil equality. This approach tends to question the special protections and exclusions of women from prestigious positions and responsibilities. Women's shorter military service (two years versus the three required of men), the exemption of mothers, wives, and religious women, the exemption of women from reserve duty, and the overwhelming number of women in auxiliary (safer) roles—as clerks, instructors, communications specialists, drivers—have been criticized as symptoms of disparity, subordination, and disempowerment.[71] In 2000 legislation was passed in the Knesset that opened up a large number of military positions heretofore closed to women. This egalitarian approach posits that women's more active participation in the military will eliminate, or at least moderate, the power asymmetries between men and women in Israel's social and political life. This approach highlights the centrality of the military in the social and cultural construction of national identity and citizenship. It questions the traditional feminization and embodiment of soldier girls as sexual objects and morale boosters with the argument that such policies make women in the army more vulnerable to sexual harassment and rape.[72] It highlights the erasure of women's experiences from national discourses and representations of Israel's wars.[73] The pacifist viewpoint on the other hand, one that seems to have predominated in the 1990s, challenges the centrality of war in the national meta-narrative and questions the institutional and cultural hegemony of the army. It condemns the use of women in the army as a means of domesticating the military and highlights the nefarious influence of military aggression on heterosexual marital and domestic relationships. Military activity is seen as a destructive and primitive expression of masculine competitiveness.[74] This viewpoint places in opposition to the militaristic, agonistic, either/or, self/other dichotomizations a cultural tradition of "maternal thinking" that refuses confrontation in favor of dialogue, compromise, empathy, and alliance.[75] Feminist pacifism endorses women's traditional exclusion from the military as morally valid and vital for bringing together women from opposite sides of national divides.[76]

In "Homefront as Battlefield: Gender, Military Occupation and Violence against Women," Simona Sharoni links the forceful suppression of the first Intifada (1987–1992) to the rise in domestic violence during the same period in Israel.[77] The military violence in the territories, often against Palestinian women who became increasingly active and vocal in their political resistance efforts has led to an increase in Jewish domestic violence. Rather than incidental examples of human rights violations, Sharoni sees individual cases of sexual harassment of Palestinian political prisoners as a symptom of a culture of militarism, sexism, and racism. Sharoni links the militarist culture that authorizes the occupation of enemy territory to the sexist Israeli discourse that often constructs a woman's body as a territory to be sexually possessed and occupied.[78] The sexist culture that led to the physical abuse of Palestinian women was combined with a toughening of military culture leading to violent assaults on (Jewish) women on the home front. The same ideology that constructs every Israeli man as a soldier also constructs every Israeli woman as an occupied territory.[79] Sharoni links women's resistance in the occupied territories to Jewish women's feminist responses.[80] Just as Palestinian women have begun to organize in women's political resistance committees, Israeli women have created protest groups, including Women's Organizations for Women Political Prisoners whose goal it was to insure that Palestinian women are protected from abuse during their incarceration. Across the border, women's alliances, conferences, and dialogue groups have begun to challenge the entire edifice of the national conflict over contested territories.[81]

In "Citizens of the State and Political Women" Ayala Emmett examines the symbolic war for peace waged by Women in Black (Nashim beshahor), a feminist peace organization founded in 1987 in the wake of the first Intifada. Even though

Women in Black did not differ in essence from the pro-peace camp that endorsed the two state solution—a sovereign Palestinian state free of Israeli rule—a position which became the formal policy of the Labor government led by Yitzhak Rabin (1992–1995), the organization came under severe attack from its political opponents, followers of the right-wing Likud party, who believe that the West Bank—Judea and Samaria—are Jewish territory.[82] Emmett suggests that the verbal assaults and symbolic harassment of Women in Black reveal a profoundly misogynous denial of women's right to exercise publicly their civil rights and duties as citizens of the state. The verbal taunts, threats, intimidation and abuse ("Arafat's whores" or "go back to the kitchen") denigrate women as a group, suggesting that women who leave the private space and assert their public status are transgressors, or prostitutes, who betray both their husbands and their nation. Ironically, the onlookers' emotionalism and rage disclosed precisely the kind of irresponsible and irrational behavior that the onlookers attributed to women, who despite the violent attacks carried on their vigils with restraint and dignity. Emmett reads the vigils as both a pacifist protest against all loss of life, and as a feminist assertion of solidarity with Middle Eastern cultural traditions of mourning. Emmett emphasizes that the symbolic use of protective motherhood, the new definition of women as protectors is a symbolic strategy for forging a transnational, maternal solidarity, not a neoconservative promotion of women's reproductive roles.[83] Despite considerable ideological, cultural, and class divisions among Orthodox and secular, Mizrahi and Ashkenazi, and Palestinian and Israeli women, she suggests that feminist discourse can serve as a unifying strategy for social (internal) and political (external) peace.[84]

In "Gender Performance in a Changing Military: Women Soldiers in Masculine Roles," Orna Sasson-Levy questions the premise that greater participation of women in combat duty will necessarily transform the gendered regime of the Israeli military as such. Rather than pursue a quantitative method of inquiry into the disproportionate number of men in higher command positions, she demonstrates that the women only enhance the gendered regime of the military culture. The combat soldiers Sasson-Levy interviewed tended to distance themselves from femininity, from women in general. They trivialized sexual harassment because complaints about such issues may be framed as an admission of vulnerability, which is anathema in the context of elite fighting troops. In an attempt to be accepted as equal "men" within their respective units, women soldiers tend to mimic male body language, tough posturing, sexual obscenities, and misogynous attitudes. As colonized subjects, the women soldiers hope their performance of masculinity will differentiate them from women in general and smooth their way to greater social acceptance within the misogynous context of the combat units. Upon discharge, these women soldier return to their domestic and reproductive roles, to an expected feminine performance. Socially and culturally then, the temporary inclusion of women in combat units does not challenge the deeper structures of the military gendered system, nor does it change the culture of misogyny and aggression that is associated with authentic masculinity.

Literature and Culture

Feminist criticism in the sense of cultural critique of literary texts, canons and traditions was launched in the mid 1980s. It targeted the Hebrew literary tradition that dichotomized and stereotyped women in texts dating back to biblical, medieval, Enlightenment and pre-state periods.[85] It targeted critical trends that ignored, devalued and tokenized women as authors, while exposing the politics of literary history and the literary canon.[86] Israeli mythogynies, or mythical representations of women, have been shown to present women as secondary characters lacking psychological complexity, as physical bodies, lacking consciousness and conscience, as embodiments of social and national deficits.[87] The suppression or erasure of the new Israeli woman as historical, public, and individual subject was exposed as a central trope of the fictional construction of the national narrative. Feminist critics have argued that the fabrication of texts and contexts of gender hierarchies were central to the project of narrating the nation that was undertaken by Israeli authors since the establishment of the state. The late 1980s saw also the evolution of a cultural critique that questions the exclusion and representation of Mizrahi Jews. The postcolonial theory introduced by Ella Shohat at this stage has become a central critical discourse in Israeli film studies.[88] Eurocentric representations of Mizrahim and the marginality of the Mizrahi experience in the nation's cultural discourse gave rise to critiques of Eurocentric exclusions of Mizrahi authors from the Israeli literary canon.[89] In the 1990s increasing attention is given to the literary representation of Palestinians and to the exclusion of Palestinian authors from the Israeli literary canon.[90] Voices of Mizrahi and Palestinian women authors and poets are beginning to be reconfigured as minority discourses central to an alternative literary canon.[91]

In a series of articles, published in Hebrew in the late 1980s, concerning the Israeli canon, the author Amalia Kahana-Carmon charged that women's literary voices were being ignored and devalued.[92] Subsequent publications have examined the reasons for the exclusion of women from literary discourse, including what was called the "masculinity" of Hebrew as a language appropriated by generations of male scholars and authors.[93] The role of the early poets—Elisheva, Rachel, Esther Raab, and Yocheved Bat Miriam—was debated and re-assessed, and the work of the first woman prose writer, Dvora Baron (1887–1956) was recovered and translated.[94] Anthologies of work by contemporary Israeli women authors and poets have been published in Hebrew and English.[95] More recently, an anthology of Hebrew women's poetry offering a reconstruction of women's poetic tradition dating back

to the Bible has been published, and the first literary history of Israeli women novelists were published.[96] Gynocriticism, the study of women's creative expression
and literary traditions, turned into a central preoccupation of literary critics in the
1990s.[97] Literary critics continue to search for ways to articulate the difference of
women's writing, and to construct an alternative female literary tradition—a
search that began in the late 1980s.[98]

This gynocritical approach guides my reading of Amalia Kahana-Carmon's
fiction. My essay questions the literary reception of the author who was embraced
by the male-dominated literary establishment for her aesthetics rather than for her
thematic focus on women's lives. I suggest that the author's focus on female protagonists is a deliberate response to the caricaturing of the female subject in
"malestream" literature. By constructing a complex feminine subjectivity, the author
fills the representational gaps that define mainstream Israeli fiction. Kahana-
Carmon's representation of women's intricate inner lives, their emotional, moral,
cognitive, intellectual, and artistic articulations challenge the embodied vacuities
constructed in mainstream fiction. I suggest, furthermore, that Kahana-Carmon's
feminine writing challenges the representational conventions of narrative as a genre,
of the linear plot progression, and the knowable protagonist, of a stable identity
or subjectivity that develops and grows over time. Her construction of feminine
subjectivity as a sort of unheard and undisclosed poetry of consciousness defies the
devaluation of the private sphere and shifts attention from the collective drama
of national crisis to the personal struggle of her heroines to live with dignity. From
the busy public sphere, dominated by male subjects, some of her heroines escape
into romance. Kahana-Carmon subverts the conventional plot of romance by using
intricate techniques that disrupt the plot of the euphoric and dysphoric romance
and suggests that heterosexual love is an illusion, temporary at best. In her novel
And Moon in the Valley of Ajalon, she constructs narrative analogies linking her
heroine to the lives of other women.[99] By alluding to a common female predicament and presenting the weak vulnerable woman as a hero, Kahana-Carmon challenges the national definition of public, male heroism. Her work thus constitutes
a counternarrative suggestive of previous women authors' work and is best understood within a generational context of a female literary tradition.

Ella Shohat's essay "Making the Silences Speak in the Israeli Cinema" considers both the Eurocentric hegemony of Israeli film, an industry almost entirely
controlled by Ashkenazi male producers and directors. Polarized into either a hard-
working saint or a selfish whore, the marginalized women of the early pioneer, nation-
alist-heroic genre, in the period of the 1930s to the 1950s, stood in sharp contrast
to the idealized Ashkenazi Sabra hero. Entirely silenced are Arab women who
embody the mute and powerless Orient, eager for redemption at the hands of the
Western male.[100] Silenced as well is the Mizrahi woman who is accepted only after
an act of ultimate self-sacrifice, usually for the Zionist cause. Films of the 1960s

continued the Eurocentric erasure and assimilation of Mizrahi culture by representing Mizrahi women as victims of the patriarchal tyranny of their own families. Shohat explains that by presenting the Ashkenazi male as savior, these films bolster the bias that attributes violence and patriarchal backwardness to Mizrahim alone.[101] In the 1970s, the comic *bourekas* genre gave expression to the dominant nationalist illusion that cultural and class differences can be eliminated by the younger generation, especially through marriage.[102] The decline of the mythic heroic Sabra in the 1970s gave rise to a personal genre and to the entry of women producers and directors as well. Shohat argues, nevertheless, that both Palestinian Arabs and Mizrahim constitute structuring absences, mere backdrops in this new genre, which is entirely centered in the West as it elaborates the alienated protagonists' search for identity. The superficiality and passivity usually associated with Middle Eastern women has, nevertheless, been challenged in films by producers of Middle Eastern origin. In such films Mizrahi women fight back within their limited means against an oppressive establishment rather than on a mythical monstrous Middle Eastern man.

In "The Woman as Other in Israeli Cinema," Orly Lubin considers the question of masculine cultural hegemony in both male and female produced films. She discusses the mechanism of the male penetrating gaze, a mechanism that reifies women as sexual objects—as Others. Though this mechanism is prevalent in Israeli film, it is not as dominant as the mechanism of social positioning that confines women to male related domestic, marital, and sexual roles. Within the larger Zionist project, sexuality and eroticism are subordinated to physical and mental work, usually assigned to male characters. Thus, when the female sexual body appears in Israeli film, it functions as a subversive sign. Israeli women filmmakers have used the discarded space of the sexual body both to express their artistic visions and to subvert the hegemonic project. At times, women filmmakers expose the penetrating gaze by placing the focus on a man looking at a naked woman's body. This exposure turns the power of the onlooker back, thereby undermining the illusion of a universal perspective and turning the observing subject into a visual object. Lubin analyzes several films in which the focus on the female sexual body and the visual subversion of the male gaze helps underscore attempts to question the power vested in an Israeli soldier in the occupied territories, or in a patriarchal husband who murders one of his wives. Lubin emphasizes, however, that subversive films are not necessarily revolutionary films. Except for rare Mizrahi experiments, most daring women filmmakers of the early 1990s have stopped short of constituting their heroines as autonomous social subjects, both sexual and social, corporeal and cultural.[103]

In "Feminism under Siege: Israeli Women Writers," Yael Feldman finds that contemporary women novelists have shied away from telling their life stories directly. Using the examples of Shulamith Hareven and Shulamit Lapid, she suggests that we look for the representation of the "self" of Israeli female authors in their historical novels. These historical novels reveal a contemporary feminist consciousness struggling with questions of female subjectivity and gender boundaries. By displacing their autobiographic retrospections to various historical contexts, Israeli women novelists negotiate more freely the conflict between broader political issues that always command public attention and feminist concerns that are officially relegated to the culture's margins. The vicarious representations of women's quests reveal feminist expectations that Israeli reality cannot satisfy. The pressure of national events does not seem to permit articulation of feminist concerns, nor personal introspection. Thus contemporary women novelists who wish to escape the historical, collective, and national siege must resort to literary strategies that, at times, hamper a deeper exploration of feminist paradoxes. The conflict between personal/feminist aspirations and the pressure of historical/national constraints is a central theme in other contemporary women novelists. This conflict may explain the curious absence of the New Hebrew woman even from the work of the contemporary women novelists who set out to explore this conflict.[104] This absence notwithstanding, Israeli women novelists manifest an ability to examine both nation and gender critically, as they reveal an androgynous consciousness that Feldman traces to the translated work of Virginia Woolf[105] Contemporary women novelists construct their own imagined nation, as they invest their heroines with the ability to shuttle between masculinity and femininity, challenging the borders and boundaries of gender.

The Future of Israeli Women's Studies

The multiplicity of approaches and the diversity of interpretations exemplify the best in Israeli women's studies, though at times, as is the case in other national and international contexts of women's studies, it can be overwhelming.[106] "Israeli" is increasingly becoming a term of multiple meanings. The growing recognition of the national difference of Palestinian Arabs and the ethnic difference of Mizrahi Jews has engendered analyses of the decline of Israeli identity.[107] "Israeli women" has become a contested term in the mid 1990s in the wake of Mizrahi critiques of the feminist movement and of Israeli feminist scholarship. Mizrahi feminist scholars have questioned the totalizing label based on their experiences of exclusion both from the leadership of the feminist movement and from Israeli feminist scholarship.[108] Increasingly, voices of Israeli Palestinian women scholars and activists inside and outside of Israel demand attention to the impact of the Arab-Israeli war on their lives.[109] Lesbian Israelis have also written personal narratives about the impact of homophobia and heterosexual familism on their lives.[110] Though still few in number, feminist analyses of immigrant women, notably from the former Soviet Union and Ethiopia, are assessing the impact of racism and xenophobia.[111] The identity politics of second generation Holocaust survivors, including daughters of Holocaust survivors, has become a subject of creative and scholarly inquiry.[112] Women's studies is increasingly an area of ambiguity, as feminist theories proliferate and methods of inquiry change, and as gender studies and men's studies are sometimes understood as competing with rather than complementing women's studies.

The challenge of Israeli women's studies in the future will be to integrate the new approaches into an already dynamic field of study. It remains to be seen whether the concept of sisterhood and mother-daughter paradigms of generational solidarity will retain their theoretical and academic meaning. Other areas of women's studies have come to recognize that the strength and vitality of women's studies depends not on discarding old feminisms, but on reading and applying them creatively to changing conditions of learning and teaching. The future of Israeli women's studies depends on an appropriate appreciation, revision, application, and critique of academic pioneering efforts and on the ability to transcend the old and current divide, as well as academic divisions between the disciplines.

The future of Israeli women's studies also depends on the willingness and ability of scholars to cooperate and encourage each other's efforts across geographic, political, and national boundaries. Work done by Israeli expatriates in the United States or Europe ought to be integrated into the Israeli curriculum, much as Israeli feminist work ought to be integrated into the Jewish feminist curriculum and US academic conferences ought to create shared discourses in which Jewish American and Israeli academicians can recognize their common concerns, juxtaposing and setting into some sort of interaction the American focus on history and theology and the Israeli focus on politics and society. Rather than declare this or that academic institution as the center rather than compete for academic prestige by creating insiders and outsiders, we ought to foster academic alliances that will replace old divisions of institutionalized knowledge.

The current crisis of factionalism and divisiveness within the Israeli feminist movement ought to be theorized and used as an opportunity for intellectual reflection. If unity and coherence are crucial for the success of political movements, disparity and debate are essential components in any academic environment. Thus Mizrahi and Palestinian or Lesbian interventions ought to be welcomed into what might be called the academic discourse, even as class, nationality, religion, race, and sexuality emerge as analytic paradigms. The academic challenge then is to clarify the lines of debate and disagreement and to create a context for a more heterogeneous and pluralistic Israeli women's studies program.[113]

In addition to the question of theory, pedagogy too ought to be included in the academic conversation. What kind of student do we hope to create? Israeli women's studies as it was institutionalized in the 1980s must not forget its indebtedness to political activism. Israeli feminist pedagogy must incorporate both a theoretical and an activist agenda in the curriculum.[114] On the other hand, the beginnings of Israeli women's studies, notably its serious indebtedness to Western, specifically American styles of feminist thinking, need not restrict it in the future. One of the challenges of Israeli women's studies is to create academic dialogues with transnational and Middle Eastern women's studies. The future challenge of Israeli women's studies then is to foster debate and dialogue within and without, among Israeli women's studies students and teachers and between them and other women's studies communities. The challenge for the future will be one of speaking to each other across theoretical, political, ethnic, and national divides and to consider our differences as sources of empowerment rather than impoverishment.

Notes

1. Esther Fuchs, *Israeli Mythogynies: Women in Contemporary Hebrew Fiction* (Albany: State University of New York Press, 1987); Dafna Izraeli et al, eds. *The Double Bind: Women in Israel* (Hebrew) (Tel Aviv: Hakibbutz Hameuchad, 1982).
2. Barbara Swirsky and Marilyn P. Safir, eds., *Calling the Equality Bluff: Women in Israel* (New York: Pergamon Press, 1991).
3. Yael Azmon, *Will You Listen to My Voice? Representations of Women in Israeli Culture* (Tel Aviv: Hakibbutz Hameuchad, 2001; in Hebrew); Kalpana Misra and Melanie S. Rich, eds., *Jewish Feminism in Israel: Some Contemporary Perspectives* (Hanover, N.H.: Brandeis University Press and the University Press of New England, 2003); Hannah Naveh, ed., *Israeli Family and Community: Women's Time* and. *Gender and Israeli Society: Women's Time*, 2 vols. (London: Vallentine Mitchell, 2003).
4. Teresa de Lauretis, *Feminist Studies, Critical Studies* (Bloomington: Indiana University Press, 1986); Judith Butler and Joan W. Scott, eds., *Feminists Theorize the Political* (New York: Routledge, 1992).
5. Uri Ram, *The Changing Agenda of Israeli Sociology: Theory, Ideology, and Identity* (Albany: State University of New York Press, 1995); Laurence J. Silberstein, *The Post-Zionism Debates: Knowledge and Power in Israeli Culture* (New York: Routledge, 1999).
6. Kate Millet, *Sexual Politics* (New York: Doubleday, 1970); Joan W. Scott, *Gender and the Politics of History* (New York: Columbia University Press, 1988).
7. Liz Stanley, "Methodology Matters!" In Victoria Robinson and Diane Richardson, eds., *Introducing Women's Studies: Feminist Theory and Practice*, 2nd edition (New York: New York University Press, 1997), 198–219.
8. Marilyn J. Boxer, *When Women Ask the Questions: Creating Women's Studies in America* (Baltimore: The Johns Hopkins University Press, 1998); Robyn Wiegman, ed., *Women's Studies on Its Own: A Next Wave Reader in Institutional Change* (Durham, N.C., and London: Duke University Press, 2002).
9. Rivka Bar-Yosef, "The Position of Women in Israel." In S.N. Eisenstadt, R. Bar-Yosef, and C. Adler, eds., *Integration and Development in Israel* (Jerusalem: Israeli Universities Press, 1970); Pnina Lahav, "The Status of Women in Israel: Myth and Reality." *The American Journal of Comparative Law* 22 (1974):107–129; Judith Buber Agassi, "The Unequal Occupational Distribution of Women in Israel," *Signs: Journal of Women in Culture and Society* 6 (1977):403–420.
10. Lesley Hazleton, *Israeli Women: The Reality Behind the Myth* (New York: Simon and Schuster, 1977). Natalie Rein, *Daughters of Rachel: Women in Israel* (London: Penguin, 1979).

11. Myra Glazer, *Burning Air and a Clear Mind: Contemporary Israeli Women Poets* (Athens: Ohio University Press, 1979); Yaffa Berlovitz, *Literature of the Early Pioneer Women* (Tel Aviv: Tarmil, 1984; in Hebrew); Esther Fuchs, "The Beast Within: Women in Amos Oz's Early Fiction." *Modern Judaism* 4/3 (1984):311–321.

12. Marilyn P. Safir, Jessica Nevo, and Barabara Swirski, "The Interface of Feminism and Women's Studies in Israel." *Women's Studies Quarterly* 3 and 4 (1994):116–131.

13. Tamar Mayer, ed., *Women and the Israeli Occupation: The Politics of Change* (New York: Routledge, 1994); Simona Sharoni, *Gender and the Israeli-Palestinian Conflict* (Syracuse, N.Y.: Syracuse University Press, 1995); Ayala Emmett, *Our Sisters' Promised Land: Women, Politics, and Israeli-Palestinian Coexistence* (Ann Arbor: The University of Michigan Press, 1996).

14. Hanna Herzog, "Ways of Knowing: The Production of Feminist Knowledge in Israeli Social Science Research." *Israel Social Science Research*,12, 2 (1997):1–28; Pnina Motzafi-Haller, "Scholarship, Identity, and Power: Mizrahi Women in Israel." *Signs: Journal of Women in Culture and Society*, 26, 3 (2001):697–734; Yael S. Feldman, *No Room of Their Own Gender and Nation in Israeli Women's Fiction* (New York: Columbia University Press, 1999), 141–176.

15. Vicki Shiran, "Feminist Identity vs. Oriental Identity." In *The Equality Bluff*, 303–311; Marcia Freedman, *Exile in the Promised Land: A Memoir* (Ithaca, N.Y.: Firebrand, 1990).

16. Catherine MacKinnon, *Toward a Feminist Theory of the State* (Cambridge, Mass.: Harvard University Press, 1989); Nira Yuval Davis and Floya Anthias, eds., *Woman, Nation, State* (London: Macmillan, 1989); Virginia R. Dominguez, *People as Subject, People as Object-Selfhood and Peoplehood in Contemporary Israel* (Madison: University of Wisconsin Press, 1989); Tamar Mayer, ed., *Gender Ironies of Nationalism: Sexing the Nation* (New York: Routledge, 2000).

17. Elizabeth A. Flynn and Patrocinio P. Schweickart, eds., *Gender and Reading: Essays on Readers, Texts and Contexts* (Baltimore: The Johns Hopkins University Press, 1986); Robyn R. Warhol and Diane Price Herndl, eds., *Feminisms: An Anthology of Literary Theory and Criticism* (New Brunswick, N.J.: Rutgers University Press, 1997).

18. Toril Moi, *Sexual/Textual Politics* (London: Methuen, 1985); Linda Nicholson, *Feminism/Postmodernism* (New York: Routledge, 1990).

19. Linda Nicholson, ed., *The Second Wave: A Reader in Feminist Theory* (New York: Routledge, 1997); Wendy Kolmar and Frances Bartowski, eds., *Feminist Theory: A Reader* (London and Toronto: Mayfield Publishing Company, 2000).

20. Alice Jardine and Paul Smith, *Men in Feminism* (New York: Methuen, 1987); Judith Butler, *Gender Trouble: Feminism and the Subversion of Identity* (New York: Routledge, 1990).

21. Simone de Beauvoir, *The Second Sex* (New York: Vintage, 1974 [1952]); Luce Irigaray, *This Sex Which is not One* (Ithaca, N.Y.: Cornell University Press, 1985).

22. Virginia Woolf, *Three Guineas* (New York: Harcourt, Brace and Company, 1938).

23. Amos Elon, *The Israelis: Founders and Sons* (New York: Holt, Rinehart and Winston, 1971); Amnon Rubinstein, *From Herzl to Rabin: The Changing Image of Zionism* (New York: Holmes and Meier, 2000).

24. Shlomo Avineri, *The Making of Modern Zionism: The Intellectual Origins of the Jewish State* (New York: Basic Books, 1981); Gideon Shimoni, *The Zionist Ideology* (Hanover, N.H.: Brandeis University Press and University Press of New England, 1995).

25. Howard Sachar, *A History of Israel: From the Rise of Zionism to Our Time* (New York: Knopf, 1979); Walter Laqueur, *The History of Zionism* (London: Tauris Parke, 2003).

26. Laurence J. Silberstein, ed., *New Perspectives on Israeli History: The Early Years of the State* (New York: New York University Press, 1991); Nissim Rejwan, *Israel in Search of Identity: Reading the Formative Years* (Gainesville: University Press of Florida, 1999).

27. Yael Zerubavel, *Recovered Roots: Collective Memory and the Making of Israeli National Tradition* (Chicago and London: The University of Chicago Press, 1995); Nurith Gertz, *Myths in Israeli Culture: Captives of a Dream* (London: Vallentine Mitchell, 2000).

28. Margalit Shilo, "The Double of Multiple Image of the New Hebrew Woman." *Nashim* 1 (winter 1998):73–94.

29. For a more skeptical reconstruction of the biography of yet another Zionist heroine, see Judith Tydor Baumel, "The Heroism of Hannah Senesz: An Exercise in Creating Collective National Memory in the State of Israel." *Journal of Contemporary History* 31 (3):521–546.

30. Deborah Bernstein, *The Struggle for Equality: Urban Women Workers in Pre-state Israeli Society* (New York: Praeger, 1987).

31. Deborah Bernstein, ed., *Pioneers and Homemakers: Jewish Women in Pre-state Israel* (Albany: State University of New York Press, 1992); Mark A. Raider and Miriam B. Raider-Roth, eds., *The Plough Woman: Records of the Pioneer Women of Palestine: A Critical Edition* (Hanover, N.H., and London: Brandeis University Press, 2002).

32. Daniel Boyarin, *Unheroic Conduct: The Rise of Heterosexuality and the Invention of the Jewish Man* (Berkeley: University of California Press, 1997); Michael Berkowitz, *Zionist Culture and West European Jewry Before the First World War* (New York: Cambridge University Press, 1993).

33. See Sheila Hannah Katz, "*Adam* and *Adama, Ird* and *Ard*: En-gendering Political Conflict and Identity in Early Jewish and Palestinian Nationalisms." In Deniz Kandiyoti, ed., *Gendering the Middle East: Emerging Perspectives* (Syracuse, N.Y.: Syracuse University Press, 1966), 85–105.

34. Frances Raday, "Equality of Women Under Israeli Law." *The Jerusalem Quarterly* 27 (spring 1983):81–108.

35. Philippa Strum, "Women and the Politics of Religion in Israel." *Human Rights Quarterly* 11 (1989):483–503.

36. Eva Etzioni-Halevy, *The Divided People: Can Israel's Breakup Be Stopped?* (Lanham, Md.: Lexington Books, 2002); Charles S. Liebman and Elihu Katz, eds., *The Jewishness of Israelis: Responses to the Guttman Report* (Albany: State University of New York Press, 1997).

37. Frances Raday, "Women, Work and Law." In *Equality Bluff*, 178–186; Leora Bilsky, "Giving Voice to Women: An Israeli Case Study." *Israel Studies* 3, 2 (fall 1998):47–79.

38. Susan Sered, "Women and Religious Change in Israel: Rebellion or Revolution." *Sociology of Religion* 58, 1, 1–24; Pnina Lahav, "Up Against the Wall: Women's Legal Struggle to Pray at the Western Wall in Jerusalem." *Israel Studies Bulletin* 16,1 (fall 2000):19–22.

39. See Shulamith Aloni, *Women as Human Beings* (Tel Aviv: Mabat Publications, 1976; in Hebrew).

40. For a different perspective on Jewish domestic laws, see Rachel Biale, *Women and Jewish Law: An Exploration of Women's Issues in Halakhic Sources* (New York: Schocken Books, 1984); Judith Hauptman, *Rereading the Rabbis: A Woman's Voice* (Boulder, Colo: Westview Press, 1998).

41. Nira Yuval-Davis, "National Reproduction and 'the Demographic Race' in Israel." In Nira Yuval-Davis and Flora Anthias, eds., *Woman, Nation, State*, 92–109.

42. Nitza Berkovitch, "Motherhood as a National Mission: The Construction of Womanhood in the Legal Discourse in Israel." *Women's Studies International Forum* 20, 5/6 (1997):605–619.

43. *Educated and Ignorant: Ultraorthodox Jewish Women and their World*, trans. Haim Watzman (Boulder, Colo. and London: Lynne Rienner Publishers, 1994).

44. On the diverse ideologies and differences within the haredi community see Aviezer Ravitzky, *Messianism, Zionism and Jewish Religious Radicalism* (Chicago and London: The University of Chicago Press, 1996).

45. *Educated and Ignorant*, 149–176.
46. For a different view on literacy and knowledge among ultra-orthodox (Mizrahi) women, see Susan Sered, *Women as Ritual Experts: The Religious Lives of Elderly Jewish Women in Jerusalem* (New York: Oxford University Press, 1992).
47. For other views on the meaning and function of the mikveh see Rahel Wasserfall, ed., *Women and Water: Menstruation in Jewish Life and Law Water* (Hanover, N.H., and London: Brandeis University and the University Press of New England, 1999).
48. Susan Sered, *What Makes Women Sick? Maternity, Modesty and Militarism in Israeli Society* (Hanover, N.H., and London: Brandeis University Press, 2000), 22–40; Yael Yishai, *Between the Flag and the Banner: Women in Israeli Politics* (Albany: State University of New York Press, 1997), 205–230.
49. Dorit D. Padan-Eisenstark, "Are Israeli Women Really Equal? Trends and Patterns of Israeli Women's Labor Force Participation : A Comparative Analysis." *Journal of Marriage and the Family* (August 1973): 538–547.
50. Dafna N.Izraeli, "Women in the Workplace." In *The Double Bind: Women in Israel,* 113–171 (in Hebrew); "Women and Work: From Collective to Career." In *Equality Bluff*, 165–177.
51. Dafna N. Izraeli, "Gender in the Workplace." In *Sex, Gender, Politics: Women in Israel* (Tel Aviv: Hakibbutz Hameuchad, 1999; in Hebrew), 167–216; Nina Toren, *Hurdles in the Halls of Science: The Israeli Case* (Lanham, Md.: Lexington Books, 2000).
52. Judith Buber Agassi, "How Much Political Power Do Israeli Women Have?" In *Equality Bluff*, 203–212; Hanna Herzog, "Women in Politics and the Politics of Women," *Sex, Gender, Politics*, 307–355.
53. Hanna Herzog, *Gendering Politics: Women in Israel* (Ann Arbor: The University of Michigan Press, 2002).
54. Lionel Tiger and Joseph Shepher, *Women in the Kibbutz* (New York: Harcourt Brace Jovanovich, 1975); Melford E. Spiro, *Gender and Culture: Kibbutz Women Revisited* (New York: Schocken Books, 1979).
55. Rae Lesser Blumberg, "The Erosion of Sexual Equality in the Kibbutz: Structural Factors Affecting the Status of Women." In Joan I. Roberts, ed., *Beyond Intellectual Sexism: A New Woman, A New Reality* (New York: D. McKay Co, 1976), 320–329.
56. See also Michal Palgi, "Women Members in the Kibbutz and Participation." In *Integrated Cooperatives in the Industrial Society: The Example of the Kibbutz* (Assen: Van Gorcum, 1980), 107–117; Michal Palgi, "Kibbutz Women: Gender Roles and Status." *Israel Social Science Research* 8 (1993):108–121.
57. Amia Libelich, *Kibbutz Makom* (New York: Pantheon Books, 1981); Daniel Gavron, *The Kibbutz: Awakening from Utopia* (New York: Rowman and Littlefield, 2000).
58. Judith Buber Agassi, "Theories of Gender Equality: Lessons from the Israeli Kibbutz." In Judith Lorber and Susan A. Farrell, eds., *The Social Construction of Gender* (London: Sage Publications, 1991), 313–337.
59. On wife-beating as social control in Palestinian communities, see Nadera Shaloub-Kevorkian, "Wife-Abuse: A Method of Social Control." *Israel Social Science Research* 12, 1 (1997):59–72.
60. Elia Zureik, *The Palestinians in Israel: A Study in Internal Colonialism* (Boston: Routledge and K. Paul, 1979); Ian Lustick, *Arabs in the Jewish State: Israel's Control of a National Minority* (Austin: University of Texas Press, 1980).
61. But see on (non-Israeli) Palestinian women's political activism Philippa Strum, *The Women Are Marching: The Second Sex and the Palestinian Revolution* (Chicago: Lawrence Hill Books, 1992); Amal Kawar, *Daughters of Palestine: Leading Women of the Palestinian National Movement* (New York: State University of New York Press, 1996).
62. Yishai, *Between the Flag and the Banner*, 57–90.
63. Ibid., 109.
64. Ibid., 19–143.

65. See also Susan Martha Kahn, *Reproducing Jews: A Cultural Account of Assisted Conception in Israel* (Durham, N.C., and London: Duke University Press, 2000); Rhoda Ann Kanaaneh, *Birthing the Nation: Strategies of Palestinian Women in Israel* (Berkeley and Los Angeles: University of California Press, 2002).

66. Ilan Pappé, *The Israel/Palestine Question* (New York: Routledge, 1999); Avi Shlaim, *The Iron Wall: Israel and the Arab World* (New York: Norton, 2000); Benny Morris, *Righteous Victims: A History of the Zionist-Arab Conflict, 1881–1999* (New York: Knopf, 1999).

67. Edna Lomsky-Feder and Eyal Ben Ari, eds., *The Military and Militarism in Israeli Society* (New York: State University of New York Press, 1999).

68. Jean B. Elshtain, *Women and War* (New York: Basic Books, 1987).

69. Meira Weiss, *The Chosen Body: The Politics of the Body in Israeli Society* (Stanford, Calif.: Stanford University Press, 2002); Uta Klein, "Our Best Boys: The Gendered Nature of Civil-Military Relations in Israel," *Men and Masculinities* 2, 1 (July 1999): 47–65.

70. Esther Fuchs, "Images of Love and War in Contemporary Israeli Fiction: A Feminist Re-Vision." In Helen M. Cooper, Adrienne Auslander Munich, and Susan Merrill Squier, eds., *Arms and the Woman: War, Gender, and Literary Representation* (Chapel Hill and London: University of North Carolina Press, 1989).

71. Nira Yuval-Davis, "Front and Rear: The Sexual Division of Labor in the Israeli Army," *Feminist Studies* 11, 3 (1985):649–675; Anne Bloom, "Women in the Defense Forces." In *Equality Bluff*, 128–138; Dafna N. Izraeli, "Gendering Military Service in the Israel Defense Forces." *Israel Social Studies Research* 12, 1 (1997):129–166.

72. Sered, *What Makes Women Sick?*, 68–103.

73. Meira Weiss, "Engendering the Gulf War: Israeli Nurses and the Discourses of Soldiering." In *The Military and Militarism in Israeli Society*, 281–300; Yael Feldman, "Hebrew Gender and Zionist Ideology: The Palmach Trilogy of Netiva Ben Yehuda," *Prooftexts* 20, 1-2 (2000):139–157.

74. Betty Reardon, *Sexism and the War System* (New York: Teachers College Press, 1985).

75. Sara Ruddick, *Maternal Thinking: Toward a Politics of Peace* (Boston: Beacon Press, 1989).

76. Lois Lorentzen and Jennifer Turpin, eds., *The Women and War Reader* (New York: New York University Press, 1998).

77. On domestic violence in Israel see Barbara Swirsky, "Jews Don't Batter Their Wives: Another Myth Bites the Dust," in *Equality Bluff*, 319–327. See also Naomi Graetz, ed., *Silence is Deadly: Judaism Confronts Wifebeating* (Northvale, N.J., and Jerusalem: Jason Aronson, 1998).

78. Sharoni, *Gender and the Israeli-Palestinian Conflict*, 31–55.

79. Ibid., 90–109.

80. Ibid., 110–130.

81. Ibid., 131–149.

82. For further detail see Ehud Sprinzak, *The Ascendance of Israel's Radical Right* (New York: Oxford University Press, 1978); Yaron Ezrahi, *Rubber Bullets: Power and Conscience in Modern Israel* (Berkeley: University of California Press, 1997).

83. Emmett, *Our Sisters' Promised Land*, 199–209; Dafna Lemish and Inbal Barzel, "Four Mothers: The Womb in the Public Sphere." *European Journal of Communication* 15, 2 (2000):147–169.

84. Emmett, *Our Sisters' Promised Land*, 97–170.

85. Esther Fuchs, "The Representation of Biblical Women in Israeli Narrative Fiction: Some Transformations and Continuities." In Mark H. Gelber, ed., *Identity and Ethos* ed. (New York: Peter Lang, 1986), 343–360; Nehama Ashkenasy, *Eve's Journey: Feminine Images in Hebraic Literary Tradition* (Philadelphia: University of Pennsylvania Press, 1986).

86. Fuchs, *Israeli Mythogynies*, 87–122

87. Ibid., 1–86. But see also Anne G. Hoffman, "Bodies and Borders: The Politics of Gender in Contemporary Israeli Fiction." In Alan Mintz, ed., *The Boom in Contemporary*

Israeli Fiction (Hanover, N.H. and London: Brandeis University Press, 1997), 35–70.

88. Ella Shohat, *Israeli Cinema East/West and the Politics of Representation* (Austin: University of Texas Press, 1989); Yosefa Loshitzky, *Identity Politics on the Israeli Screen* (Austin: University of Texas Press, 2001).

89. Ammiel Alcalay, *After Jews and Arabs: Remaking Levantine Culture* (Minneapolis: University of Minnesota Press, 1993); Nancy Berg, *Exile from Exile: Israeli Writers from Iraq* (Albany: State University of New York Press, 1996).

90. Yerach Gover; *Zionism: The Limits of Moral Discourse in Israeli Hebrew Fiction* (Minneapolis: University of Minnesota Press, 1994); Hannan Hever, *Producing the Modern Hebrew Canon: Nation Building and Minority Discourse* (New York and London: New York University Press, 2002).

91. Ammiel Alacalay, *Keys to the Garden: New Israeli Writing* (San Francisco: City Lights Books, 1996); Smadar Lavie, "Border Poets: Translating by Dialogues." In Ruth Behar and Devorah A. Gordon, eds., *Women Writing Culture* (Berkeley: University of California Press), 412–427.

92. Amalia Kahana-Carmon, "The Song of Bats in Flight," trans. Naomi Sokoloff. In Naomi B. Sokoloff, Anne Lapidus Lerner, and Anita Norich, eds., *Gender and Text in Modern Hebrew and Yiddish Literature* (New York: The Jewish Theological Seminary, 1992), 235–245.

93. Dan Miron, *Founding Mothers, Stepsisters* (Tel Aviv: Hakibbutz Hameuchad, 1991; in Hebrew); Naomi Seidman, *A Marriage Made in Heaven: The Sexual Politics of Hebrew and Yiddish* (Berkeley: University of California Press, 1997).

94. Michael Gluzman, "The Exclusion of Women from Hebrew Literary History." *Prooftexts* 11/3 (1991):259–278; Dvora Baron, *The First Day and Other Stories*, trans. and ed. Naomi Seidman and Chana Kronfeld (Berkeley: University of California Press, 2001); Amia Lieblich, *Conversations with Dvora: An Experimental Biography of the First Modern Hebrew Woman Writer* trans. Naomi Seidman. (Berkeley and Los Angeles: University of California Press, 1991).

95. Lily Rattok, *The Other Voice: Women's Fiction in Hebrew* (Tel Aviv: Hakibbutz Hameuchad, 1994; in Hebrew); Risa Domb, ed., *New Women's Writing from Israel* (London: Vallentine Mitchell, 1996); Miriyam Glazer, *Dreaming the Actual: Contemporary Fiction and Poetry by Israeli Women Writers* (New York: State University of New York Press, 2000).

96. Shirley Kaufman, Galit Hasan-Rokem and Tamar Hess, eds., *The Defiant Muse: Hebrew Feminist Poems from Antiquity to the Present* (New York: The Feminist Press, 1999), 1–30; Yael Feldman, *No Room of Our Own: Gender and Nation in Israeli Women's Fiction* (New York: Columbia University Press, 1999).

97. Naomi Sokoloff, "The Impact of Feminist Research." In Lynn Davidman and Shelly Tenenbaum, eds., *Feminist Perspectives on Jewish Studies* (New Haven, Conn.: Yale University Press, 1994), 224–243.

98. Lily Rattok, *The Other Voice*, 261–346; Hannah Naveh, "Life Outside the Canon." In *Sex, Gender, Politics: Women in Israel*, 49–106 (Hebrew); Hannan Hever, "Gender, Body, and the National Subject: Israeli Women's Poetry in the War of Independence." *The Military and Militarism in Israel Society*, 225–260.

99. Esther Fuchs, "Amalia Kahana-Carmon's *And Moon in the Valley of Ajalon*" *Prooftexts* 8, 1 (1988):129–141.

100. Edward Said, *Orientalism* (New York: Vintage, 1977).

101. For more background on the social aspects of the ethnic division, see Sammy Smooha, *Israel: Pluralism and Conflict* (Berkeley and Los Angeles: University of California Press, 1978); Shlomo Swirsky, *Israel: The Oriental Majority* trans. Barbara Swirsky (London: Zed Books, 1989):115–178.

102. Ella Shohat, *Israeli Cinema: East/West and the Politics of Representation* (Austin: University of Texas Press, 1989).

103. Orly Lubin, "Body and Territory: Women in Israeli Cinema." *Israel Studies* 4, 1 (spring 1999): 175–187.
104. Yael Feldman, "From Feminist Romance to an Anatomy of Freedom: Israeli Women Novelists." In Alan Mintz, ed., *The Boom in Contemporary Israeli Fiction* (Hanover, N.H. and London: Brandeis University Press, 1977), 71–113.
105. Yael S. Feldman, *No Room of Their Own*, 91–110.
106. Dale Spender and Cheris Kramarae, *The Knowledge Explosion: Generations of Feminist Scholarship* (New York: Teachers College Press, 1992).
107. Baruch Kimmerling, *The Invention and Decline of Israeliness: State, Society, and the Military* (Berkeley and Los Angeles: University of California Press, 2001); Gershon Shafir and Yoav Peled, *Being Israeli: The Dynamics of Multiple Citizenship* (Cambridge, U.K.: Cambridge University Press, 2002).
108. Henriette Dahan-Kalev, "The Oppression of Women by Other Women: Relations and Struggle between Mizrahi and Ashkenazi Women in Israel." *Israel Social Science Research* 12, 1 (1997); Pnina Motzafi-Haller, "Scholarship, Identity, and Power: Mizrahi Women in Israel." *Signs* 26, 3 (2001):697–734.
109. Ronit Lentin and Nahla Abdo, *Women and the Politics of Military Confrontation: Palestinian and Israeli Gendered Narratives of Dislocation* (New York: Berghahn, 2002).
110. Tracy Moore, ed., *Israeli Lesbians Talk about Sexuality, Feminism, Judaism and their Lives* (London: Cassell, 1995); Freedman, *Exile in the Promised Land*, 204–234.
111. Dafna Lemish, "The Whore and the Other: Israeli Images of Female Immigrants from the Former USSR." *Gender and Society* 14, 2 (April 2000):333–349; Esther Hertzog, "Gender and Power Relations in a Bureaucratic Context: Female Immigrants from Ethiopia in an Absorption Center in Israel," *Gender and Development* 9, 3 (November 2001):60–69.
112. Ronit Lentin, *Israel and the Daughters of the Shoah: Reoccupying the Territories of Silence* (New York: Berghahn, 2000); Loshitzky, *Identity Politics on the Israeli Screen*, 1–71.
113. Esther Fuchs, "Jewish Feminist Scholarship: A Critical Perspective." In Leonard Greenspoon and Ronald A. Simkins, eds., *Studies in Jewish Civilization* (Omaha, Neb.: Creighton University Press, 2003), 225–246.
114. Esther Fuchs, "Feminism, Anti-Semitism, Politics: Does Jewish Women's Studies Have a Future?" In Elizabeth L. Kennedy and Agatha Beins, eds., *Women's Studies for the Future: Foundations, Interrogations, Politics* (New Brunswick, N.J.: Rutgers University Press, forthcoming).

Myth and History

DAFNA N. IZRAELI

The Zionist Women's Movement in Palestine, 1911–1927

A Sociological Analysis

THE ZIONIST WOMEN'S MOVEMENT in Palestine developed within the socialist Zionist movement as a reaction to the disappointment of a small group of women with the limited role they were assigned in the emerging society. From its beginnings in 1911, the movement aimed to expand the boundaries of the Jewish woman's role in Palestine and to secure her full and equal participation in the process of Jewish national reconstruction. Members of the movement were nationalists and idealists who had come as pioneers from Eastern Europe during the years 1904–1914, and they were joined by women who arrived in Palestine after World War I, from 1919 through 1923. These periods, known in the history of Zionism as the second and third waves of immigration (*aliyah*), are considered the formative periods of Israeli society. During the second wave the dominant values of the society were formulated and the rudiments of new organizational forms appeared. During the third wave goals were implemented and major institutional structures took shape.[1]

Because they were marked by social creativity, readiness for experimentation, and remodeling of institutional forms, these periods were also crucial for the status of women in the new society. Many of the obstacles to a restructuring of sex roles were reduced, and conditions were favorable for redefining traditional role relations between men and women. That equality of the sexes was achieved during the second wave and that women played a role of importance are two of the founding myths of Israeli society. Although the career of Golda Meir and the conscription of women into the army are often invoked to lend credence to these ideas, and to link the idealized past with the present, the facts of the case have never been subject to systematic investigation.

While this account is a study of a specific place, time, and circumstance, it highlights dilemmas that commonly confront women in socialist movements generally, especially during periods of economic and political upheaval. At such time the commitment of a movement's participants tends to be heavily taxed, and the demand for undivided loyalties is great. Identification with a larger movement creates a set of constraints on the development of feminist ideology and on the creation of a separate feminist organization, particularly when feminist dissatisfaction is directed toward the position of women within the movement itself.[2] These constraints, and their consequences for the career of the feminist movement in Palestine, are the major themes of this paper.

Background

Modern political Zionism developed in Europe and America in the last decades of the nineteenth century. The World Zionist Movement and its organizational arm, the World Zionist Organization, established in 1897, served as umbrella structures incorporating a variety of social and political ideologies for which the rebuilding of Zion was the binding element. The Palestinian women's movement developed within Labor Zionism, which was inspired by radical socialist ideas then gaining momentum in Russia. The Labor Zionist groups, based in the cities and towns of what was formerly the Russian empire, professed an egalitarian ideology. Women did not organize in separate groups nor were they assigned specialized roles, although they tended to be more active in cultural activities than in politics.[3] In contrast, women in the nonsocialist sector of the Zionist movement, both in Europe and North America, formed separate chapters that engaged in fund raising, education, and philanthropy.

Although Labor Zionism was ideologically committed to social equality, it did not concern itself with the issues of women's emancipation. One explanation may lie in socialist theory: if the elimination of exploitive relationships automatically results in women's emancipation, then within the new society in Palestine women's emancipation must be assured. A more persuasive explanation, however, is that the Zionist movement defined the problem of Jewish existence as the fundamental and overriding social issue to which all efforts had to be directed. As Eisenstadt suggests: "The Zionist ideology assumed that the Jews would not be able to participate fully in the new modern societies and would become, despite their assimilation, an alien element."[4] Jewish feminists were told that the Jewish woman "must bear in mind that even those [non-Jewish] women fighting for [feminist] emancipation view her first not as a woman, but as a Jewess."[5] But, for whatever reason, within the Labor Zionist movement sexual equality was taken for granted, and the value of equality between men and women in early political Zionist ideology was institutionalized in the socialist movement through the integration of the sexes in the various groups and activities prior to immigration to Palestine. Since the subordination of women in society was not defined as a condition requiring special action, no legitimation existed for specialized institutional arrangements for its change. Women's experience in Labor Zionist groups prior to immigration created a set of expectations that later conditioned their reaction to what they encountered in Palestine.

The pioneers of the second wave emigrated from Russia following the pogroms that took place in 1903 and after the October revolution in 1905. Many pioneers were infused with radical and socialist ideas prevalent in Russia at the time, but they had been disappointed by the social reform movement there and by its failure to solve the problems of the Jewish people.[6] The immigrants consisted primarily of middle class young, single people or young couples without children or parents. In a new country the usual restraints and obligations that bind women to domestic roles and traditional definitions of their domain were reduced, which allowed women freedom to experiment with alternative roles. Furthermore, there are indications that these women constituted a self-selected group that had "liberated" itself from the effects of traditional socialization. The move to Palestine required determination and idealism from all the immigrants, but even more so from the women. They had to combat the traditionally stronger social control exerted by parents over daughters, the stigma attached to a single woman leaving home (especially in the company of a group of men), as well as the physical hardship of the passage itself. It is not surprising that women constituted only about 30 percent of the total immigrants to Palestine, many of whom joined the religious communities in the holy cities. Among the minority who came to live productive lives as laborers—those whose initiative, energy, and ideological fervor were the dominant force for change in the structure of the Jewish community—the proportion of women was even smaller.[7]

Women came to Palestine ready to participate more fully in social life than they had been permitted to do in Jewish bourgeois circles in Russia. In the words of Sara Malchin, a founder of the women's movement: "These young women Zionists dreamed of engaging in battle and sacrifice for the ideal of redemption, even while still in the diaspora."[8] They did not expect to struggle for women's place; they thought equality would be an accompanying feature of their move to the new homeland.

Years of Incubation, 1904–1911

Ideas and ideology played an important role in shaping the character of the pioneering society, even though specific activities undertaken in the name of the ideology were redefined to suit the constraints of practical experience. A basic tenet of the ideology was the value attributed to the collective. The individual was expected to sacrifice personal interests to the welfare of the new Jewish society whose members included not only those who had already immigrated but also the multitudes of Jews who would return home in the future.

Among the two most important cultural creations of the second wave were the image of the ideal pioneer—the *halutz*—and the ideal form of social organization—the *kvutza* (forerunner of the kibbutz).[9] Halutz literally means a member of the vanguard, one who goes before the camp and fulfills its highest purposes. These include a readiness for personal sacrifice made necessary by the persistent dangers of working in the malaria-infested swamplands and of defending the young collectives from attack by Arab marauders, belief in a return to the biblical state of farming the land, and dedication to manual work. During the second wave physical work was idealized and elevated to a religious value.[10] These key elements of the halutz ideal had an essentially masculine character, which heightened the relevance of biological differences between the sexes.

The most urgent problem facing the new immigrants upon their arrival in Palestine was employment. In vain did they knock at the doors of the established farmers of the first wave (1881–1891), who were unwilling to substitute Jewish labor for the cheaper, more experienced, and amenable Arab labor. Women faced greater obstacles than men. The first-wave farmers considered their insistence on having men's jobs "unnatural." They stigmatized and ostracized the women and forbade their own daughters any contact with them.[11] Those who were less antagonistic feared for the women's safety. Any girl doing man's work in the vineyards might be considered easy prey by the Arab laborers, unaccustomed to such license from "respectable" women. Faced with unemployment and filled with a desire to establish a new type of Jewish society, the second wave rejected as unsuited to their purpose the existing socioeconomic structures developed by their forerunners. They moved north to the barren lands of the lower Galilee, drained the swamps, and established a new type of communal life—the kvutza—a small collective settlement in which everyone labored.

Two of the guiding principles of the new settlement were "conquering the land," that is, making it arable for Jewish farmers, and economic self-sufficiency.[12] The kvutza was a pragmatic solution for the pioneers who faced the problem of "how to organize some form of settlement for young people with strong socialist and nationalist aspirations, without capital and with little experience and know-how."[13] This form of living very quickly became a normative ideal.

In the kvutza the women were automatically assigned to the kitchen and the laundry.[14] It seems that among the men, and many of the women, the conscious rebellion against the traditional occupational structure of Jewish society did not extend to women's work. It remained part of the world taken for granted that domestic work was the woman's responsibility.[15] The attitude of the men is described by one of the women pioneers in an article that appeared in the socialist party newspaper at the time: "Many [of the workers] believed that the role of the young female idealist coming to Palestine was to serve them. The young women, who were still inexperienced, submitted to this view and believed that in cooking and serving they were solving most of our questions [concerning our role] in Palestine. The young woman who dared to doubt this assumption was considered strange."[16] It is ironic that the women should have been expected to perform domestic tasks, which in their former homes usually had been the responsibility of domestics. They were poorly equipped for the jobs they were expected to fill so "naturally" and doubly frustrated because the roles for which they had hoped were denied them. Although the men had been neither farmers nor watchmen prior to immigration, it was assumed natural for them to undertake these "manly" roles. Plowing and loading crops were considered too strenuous and even harmful for women, a situation reflected in the following statement: "My first six weeks in Palestine I worked in Degania [a kvutza established in 1909]. I listened with such admiration as the men spoke of their work tools and sounded the names of corn yields. My soul yearned to be in contact with the soil, to work the land, but that was not granted me, nor to any other women."[17]

Since the training men received from professional agronomists in Palestine was usually not extended to women, the ability gap between the sexes widened. Economic considerations also encouraged the perpetuation of a traditional division of labor between the sexes. The newly formed communes were dependent on the World Zionist Organization, which had yet to be convinced that agricultural collectivism was preferable to the previous system of farms under the direction of a professional agronomist in which the pioneers were paid a wage, women paid less than men.[18] The *halutzim* (plural of halutz) had to prove that the kvutza was economically viable. Viewing women as less productive, they feared that their participation in agriculture would result in a deficit, and so women were confined to more "suitable" jobs. The same men who had demanded that the farmers of the first wave overlook economic considerations on ideological grounds and prefer them to Arab laborers accepted only one to three women into a kvutza with between ten and thirty male members on the grounds that women were economically less productive. The fact that women were so few bound them even more strictly to domestic chores because it was impossible for them to rotate between kitchen and field work. In 1909 there were 165 Jewish workers organized in *kvutzot* [plural] or workers' collectives in the Galilee, only eleven of whom were women. In 1912 there were 522 Jewish workers in kvutzot in Judea, thirty of whom were women. During the war years, the number of workers rose to 1,500 while the proportion of women increased to over 13 percent (200 women).[19]

Domestic chores, although physical work, had low status among the pioneers who established a hierarchy of values according to both the conditions under which work was performed and the type of work engaged in. A member of a collective had higher status than someone who was an employee; productive work, work that produced marketable goods, was deemed more valuable than nonproductive work, such as services provided for the members of the collective. Thus, cooking, laundering, and mending were not considered productive work, and they ranked low among pioneering values. Cooking for a collective held greater prestige than cooking in a private household, but it was less worthy than tilling the soil. Within productive work, agriculture, specifically field crops (*falcha*), became the embodiment of the halutz endeavor, symbolizing economic self-sufficiency as well as rejection of the pattern set by the farmers of the first wave with their dependence on Arab labor and foreign markets.

One of the unintended consequences of this pioneering ideology as well as of the new forms of social organization was that they relegated women to secondary roles in the new society. The halutza (female form of halutz) had virtually no opportunity to become a bearer of the effective symbols of the halutz ideology. Thus, the women's dissatisfaction and growing sense of deprivation came to focus on three issues: formal status, participation, and attitudes in the kvutza.

In these early years, women were not accorded full membership; it was taken for granted that the kvutza was made up of male members and the few women were helpers doing domestic work. They were not included as members in the annual contracts with the Zionist Organization even though "they had shared the burden and dangers equally with the men." [20] As Maimon explains, "It was argued that in point of fact the women were working for them [members of the *kvutza*], not for the Palestine Office [of the Zionist Organization] which was concerned with the farm, not with the kitchen."[21]

In addition, the women felt deprived of the opportunity to "conquer new fields of work" through agriculture and to guard the kvutza as the men were doing, and they resented the restrictions placed on their participation in group decision making about the affairs of the kvutza. In an article, "On the Question of the Women Workers," which appeared in the workers' newspaper in 1913, Tchiya Liberson bemoaned the fact that "the men could not get used to thinking of them [the women] as real members. They did not want to come to terms with the fact that the women express their ideas freely about how matters should be handled and that they stand firm in their opinions."[22] The problem of women's participation in group meetings was exacerbated by the fact that relatively few knew Hebrew, the language of religious instruction in the Diaspora and of the pioneers in Palestine. A study of second-wave pioneers still living in Palestine in 1940 found that 60 percent of men, but only 30 percent of the women, knew Hebrew upon arrival.[23]

But the issue that most aroused the women's indignation is expressed in the Hebrew term *yachas*, which literally means attitude or relation. In the context of the second wave, it referred to what women deemed degrading treatment. It combined, women argued, expressions of disregard and even derision for their yearning to work equally in the building of the country. In the words of another female pioneer: "We young women did not encounter hardship in our work but rather in the humiliating treatment and apathetic attitude toward our aspirations. Even in the eyes of the [pioneer] laborers we were ludicrous; not only those of us who wished to destroy the natural barriers and take hold of the difficult occupations of agricultural work but even those who undertook work in which a woman is able to compete with men, even there we were ludicrous [in their eyes]."[24] The issue of yachas came up most frequently in the kitchens of the communes as well as of other workers' groups. Unaccustomed to cooking, particularly with primitive utensils and unfamiliar ingredients—which were, in addition, in very meager supply—the women very often produced unappetizing food. At times, when the workers preferred to be hungry rather than consume burned food, they would arrange their bowls like wagons in a train and push them along the table toward the kitchen chanting "train, train"—an act of protest on the part of the hungry pioneers but also a "degradation ceremony" for the cook.[25]

In spite of their disappointments, however, the women pioneers in the communes of the Galilee found new hope in occasional incidents. For example, in 1908 at Sejera, a small group of farm laborers decided to form an independent agricultural collective. Among the members was Manya Schochat, a radical labor leader and known activist prior to her immigration as well as the first to promote the idea of collective settlement in Palestine. She succeeded in persuading the agronomist who managed the farm to train women to plow with a pair of oxen. Though a successful experiment, this did not seem a workable solution to the women. An alternative was found in vegetable gardening. In 1909, under the initiative and guidance of one of the members, Hanna Meizel, a trained agronomist, the women secretly planted the first garden, hidden behind a distant hill.[26] The experience at Sejera, in which women proved themselves capable of plowing, provided a sense of efficacy and justified the claim for participation in physical work, while the gardening experiment supplied a suitable model. Women could become farmers by creating new agricultural branches compatible with their physical abilities.

A women's training farm at Kineret (on the Sea of Galilee) was founded in 1910 after Hanna Meizel had obtained funds from a women's Zionist group in Germany. The timing was propitious because a group of men at the Kineret farm had established an independent *falcha* collective. Five women under the leadership of Hanna Meizel were apportioned a courtyard, a plot of land, and minimum facilities for establishing their own collective. One of them describes the excitement: "And for us too the young women, this was the beginning of a new period. Our male comrades would be only our neighbors. Their life and ours would flow along separate paths. We are receiving a separate plot of land which will be solely for our use, worked according to our own wishes and abilities. A period of splendor, what emancipation!"[27]

For the time being, at least, these women gave up the idea that their equality could be achieved in the mixed group.

Beginnings of the Movement

The transformation of dissatisfied people into a social movement requires their awareness that they share a situation which is in some important respects unjust.[28] This process of change first manifested itself in 1911 in Kineret at a meeting initiated by Hanna Meizel for the purpose of explaining her plans for the women's training farm. Although only seventeen women attended, this meeting—providing as it did the first opportunity for the *halutzot* (female plural of halutz) to exchange experiences, share their individual grievances, and give each other moral support—laid the foundation for the emergence of a women's movement within the Labor Zionist camp in Palestine.[29] First, the problem of the woman worker emerged as a social reality and legitimized the establishment of a segregated organization. Once socially identified and labeled, the issue could become the basis for social action. Second, the meeting defined the goals of the movement's future, outlined the strategy for change, and identified a group of leaders among the second wave of pioneers. The ideological orientation first formulated at Kineret, and reiterated at every subsequent conference of women workers, emphasized the need for self-transformation. To achieve their goals, namely, equal participation, women had to change themselves. As they proclaimed: "We, the women laborers, like the men, aspire first and foremost to rehabilitate our spirit and bodies through work . . . in the field and in nature, and in this way we can rid ourselves of the habits, the way of life and even the way of thinking that we brought with us from the diaspora."[30]

Turner and Killian list three conditions as essential for a movement to follow the route of self-transformation rather than that of institutional change: a belief that widespread improvement is possible, a belief that "the state of the social order will reflect the integrity and character of individual man," and an acceptance by the people of responsibility "for their present unsatisfactory conditions."[31] Belief in the possibility for transforming the Jewish *Luftmensch* [a person living by fancies, ed.] of the Diaspora into a manual worker and tiller of the soil, as we have seen, was fundamental to Labor Zionism. In defining self-alteration as their major goal, the halutzot adopted a stance that fit well with the dominant ideology and was, therefore, attractive. The women believed that they had the same potential as men, though for historical reasons it had remained dormant. Through training as manual workers they would overcome their passive, dependent character. Once the halutza proved her skill, not only would she be accepted as a full member in the kvutza, but men would seek her out. "At the dawn of the movement we thought that we had only to overcome the barrier of occupational training, and as for equality, it would all follow automatically," wrote Ada Maimon, one of the leading figures in the struggle for women's equal participation.[32]

Men were not to be blamed for women's unhappy predicament since they, too, were conditioned by habitual ways of thinking and behaving. However, since they seemed unable to understand the problem of women workers, they could not be relied upon to bring about the necessary changes. Women would have to transform themselves.[33] An ideology oriented toward self-transformation rather than toward changing men and social institutions helped to legitimate the creation of a separate women's movement within Labor Zionism in that it avoided direct conflict with the male-dominated ideology and with the male pioneers. The network of social ties that linked the feminists of the second wave with the male leadership of the labor movement discouraged the development of a "we-they" dichotomy. A number of highly influential male comrades had encouraged the halutzot, and some of the women's leaders were members of the same political party and the same kvutza, or they shared backgrounds, friends, and relatives. These relationships put pressure on the women who feared that their desire for separate institutional arrangements would lead to accusations of lack of trust and even of the betrayal of their male comrades. The ideology of self-transformation mitigated this danger by emphasizing the common goals of male and female pioneers: women must be helped to change so that they could contribute more effectively toward the realization of shared values.

The Kineret meeting defined the operational goals of the women's movement. The strategy was to push for the development of new agricultural branches, such as vegetable gardening, poultry, and dairy farming, which were considered "suitable for women." The women also demanded a monopoly over these areas of work, since, they argued, men had many other jobs to do. Two main tactics were adopted. First, the farm at Kineret was to serve as a training center where women could learn technical skills and begin personal transformation within a supportive environment, unhampered by the presence of men. Second, in the future women would join only those kvutzot willing to accept at least ten of them, so that rotation between household and agriculture would be feasible.[34] The former tactic aimed at achieving the goal of self-transformation, the latter that of participation.

The women's desire for a separate organization resulted from their growing awareness that their goals could not be realized through the existing structures of Palestine's Labor Zionist movement. These consisted of two competing political parties, which were the most important organizations of the labor movement prior to World War I, the agriculturally oriented, leftist Hapoel Hatzair and the radical socialist Poalei Zion, as well as two unions of agricultural workers, one in the Galilee and one in Judea. The parties sent representatives to the unions, which negotiated with the Palestine Office of the World Zionist Organization on behalf of the agricultural communes and mobilized resources for new settlements.

Because very few women were influential or active in the labor parties, they hesitated to raise their particular problems. In addition, there were always "more important" problems of survival that took priority. Nevertheless, the disregard for women's problems struck even a male observer, who found it necessary to comment on the point in a labor newspaper: "I have been in the country five years and have taken part in many workers' meetings where every conceivable subject was discussed. To my complete surprise there was one subject that was never discussed, not even in passing; the situation of our women workers."[35] The failure to permit women to participate in the various decision-making forums of the labor movement organizations had a cumulative effect. When the agricultural union of the Galilee neglected to invite a woman representative to its fifth conference in 1914, the halutzot barged into their meeting and vociferously protested.[36] But a more important result was the women's decision to convene their own conference of women agricultural workers only three months later. Thirty delegates met representing 209 women workers.[37] Thus the organizational arm of the women's movement was established. In the war years the women's movement created two organizational structures: an annual conference, five of which were held between 1914 and 1918, and the women workers' committee to organize and coordinate the activities of the movement between the conferences. The leaders were not anonymous women but women linked to the inner circles of Palestine's emerging elites. Some had political experience, and according to the evidence none received monetary remuneration for their work in the women's movement.

The issues on the agenda of the various conferences were similar to those which had been raised at Kineret in 1911, though there were additions. When the halutzot gave birth to their first children, the problem of how to combine child care with public activities became urgent. If each woman had to care for her own children, she would have to give up many work tasks outside the home, and the gains made would be lost. Since women accepted childrearing as their primary responsibility, the demand that men share in the responsibilities, while occasionally voiced, was never seriously considered. The arrival of children threatened the women's status. Miriam Baratz, the first mother in the kvutza, describes her struggle against social pressure: "The general opinion was that I should devote all my time to my child. I objected to this with all my might. I knew that that way I would no longer be a part of the community and of everything that was happening in the group."[38] The solution adopted was collective child care with women in the collective rotating the responsibility.[39] Women's participation in the labor movement was another issue at consecutive conferences, as women came increasingly to realize that doing agricultural work did not automatically lead to participation in the decision-making bodies either of the labor movement as a whole or even of the commune.[40]

The most pressing general issue for all the pioneers of the time related to employment. During the war years, the movement achieved some important successes in providing work. Women were trained on the Kineret farm and then integrated into the kvutzot. The shift in economic policy within the agricultural communes between 1914 and 1918 from total reliance on grain crops toward greater diversification opened new branches and thus new opportunities for women. In 1919 a drop in the price of grain and a drought accelerated the process toward diversification and self-reliance.[41] Women joined grain-growing collectives and established a number of independent vegetable-growing collectives which successfully sold their produce in the markets.[42] The vegetable gardens were usually situated next to the workers' public kitchens, where the women were employed as cooks. Most of the projects received modest financial assistance from the agricultural union and, through the intervention of the women workers' committee, from Zionist women's groups abroad.

The change in women's self-image and in their status within the labor movement is reflected in the differences noticeable between the first meeting at Kineret in 1911 and later conferences. At Kineret the doors were closed to men. Those who showed up were accused of having come to ridicule or out of curiosity, and they were thought to be indifferent to the problems of the halutzot. At the opening session of the fifth conference held in Tel Aviv, apart from the seventy women delegates, there were a large number of invited guests, including several official male representatives of the parties and the agricultural union.[43] This change of policy manifests the increased self-confidence of the movement and its recognition by the pioneering community.

Although the women's movement brought about important cultural change in the nouns regarding woman's role, it did not institutionalize a social structure to serve as a power center in relation to other organizations in the Yishuv (Jewish community of Palestine) r the World Zionist Organization (the major source of funds for the pioneers in Palestine). The women gave relatively little attention to organizational activity, partly because they were so few and partly because they accepted as their major structural referent the agricultural unions, where they had gained official recognition. An important additional factor was that the women preferred doing to organizing others. A characteristic of the second wave as a whole was that it was oriented more toward the implementation of ideals through direct participation in grass-roots activities associated with Zionist fulfillment than toward political activity.[44] No organizational bodies were developed between the years 1914 and 1918, apart from the conferences and the elected committee. Whatever funds were obtained, whether from the agricultural union or from women's organizations abroad, were earmarked for specific employment and agricultural training projects. But these financial contributions were not institutionalized in a structural commitment of continuous support.

The Career of the Women's Movement, 1918–1927

The end of World War I ushered in a period of developments in the Yishuv, where new dilemmas for the women's movement emerged. Comparing the Yishuv before and after the First World War, Eisenstadt observes, "If the period of the second wave was the period of ideological emphasis, the [British] Mandate ushered in a period of stress on the formulation and practical implementation of the major goals of the Yishuv."[45] The ability of the women workers' movement to implement its goals was affected by two major developments: first, the arrival of the third wave of immigrants (1919–1923); second, the establishment of the Histadrut (the Jewish Federation of Labor).

The third wave, arriving after World War I, was encouraged by the Balfour Declaration, which affirmed the British government's support for the establishment of a Jewish homeland in Palestine. In many of its social and ideological characteristics the third wave was a continuation of the second. A sizable proportion of the immigrants were young socialist pioneers from Eastern Europe; and they too had been influenced by ideas prevalent at the time of the Russian Revolution. From the perspective of the women's movement, however, the third wave differed from the second in three respects. First, the proportion of women among all immigrants during the third wave was larger, 36.8 percent. Among the single immigrants the proportion was 17 percent in 1920, increasing to 30 percent in 1922. Among the more strongly nationalistic pioneers, women comprised some 17 to 18 percent, compared with approximately 10 percent during the second wave.[46] Second, the pioneers arrived as members of different pioneering groups and social movements, most notably Gdud Avoda (Work Battalion) and Hashomer Hatzair (The Young Watchman). These were created in the Diaspora and organized in communes committed to the principle of equality in production and consumption. Third, larger numbers of pioneers gravitated to the towns, where they formed part of the new urban proletariat. There, unemployment was particularly acute for women.

The period began ominously for the women's movement. The women's vegetable-growing collectives collapsed due to competition from British imports. The farm at Kineret was closed for lack of financial means. The settlement department of the Zionist Organization discontinued its support of women's farming collectives, believing that women would find their place in kibbutzim.[47] The women's committee had failed to gain the recognition granted to other institutions of the labor movement, particularly the political parties, by the World Zionist Organization. In other words, in 1918 on the eve of the arrival of the third wave, the women workers' movement lacked its own mechanisms for coping with the new problems of unemployment and for pursuing its goals.

The new sources of employment that developed after the establishment of the mandate, namely, rail and road construction and then building in the towns, did not welcome women. Nevertheless, women pressed for entry, and in 1922 they composed 16 percent of the total membership in construction collectives, although half of them supplied the domestic services such as cooking. The Construction Workers' Union in 1924 resolved to increase the number of women accepted into the work groups; train women in building crafts; establish work groups in the crafts suitable for women such as floor tiling, plastering, and painting; and put women in line for suitable jobs.[48] These resolutions, however, were never translated into a program of action.

Working in construction became the epic expression of the halutz ideal and a challenge to the women's movement seeking to conquer new fields, as agriculture had been for the halutzot of the second wave. Again, however, women faced strong opposition. Jobs were scarce. They were mainly allocated through the labor bureau of the political parties and, after 1920, through the Histadrut (General Federation of Labor). Since work contracts were assigned to groups, getting a job depended on being accepted to a work group, which was problematic for women. As Tchiya Liberson, a member of the Construction Workers' Union reported: "The men had quite a number of reasons for keeping us out. Some said the work was too strenuous for women. Others argued that if women were admitted to the building trade communes, which contracted for work as a group, the output would decrease and the pay with it."[49]

Faced with resistance to their acceptance by male groups, and indignant at being accused of causing financial deficits, women formed their own work communes and even competed with men for job contracts.[50] In the mid1920s there were two women's construction groups, several floor-tiling communes, as well as tobacco and laundry collectives. The women's organization established a half-dozen training farms modeled on the Kineret experiment. Women also formed havurot, small collectives based on a combination of vegetable gardening and outside employmen.[51] Organizing, encouraging, and financing these projects were the major activities of the executive committee of the Women Workers' Council, the organizational arm of the Women Workers' Movement within the newly established Histadrut (Jewish Federation of Labor).

After World War I, there had been a trend toward unification among the labor groups in the Yishuv which in 1920 led to the establishment of an umbrella organization, the Histadrut. The trade unions, the sick fund, the consumers' union, labor exchanges, immigration office, public works and building office, schools, and workers' public kitchens, which had been created by the political parties, were transferred to the Histadrut. The consolidation of these structures within a single organization, which controlled virtually all the resource-generating institutions of the labor movement, meant that the women's movement became dependent on the Histadrut.

Election of delegates to the founding convention of the Histadrut, held in December 1920, was by proportional representation of political parties. As the women's movement did not consider itself a political faction but viewed its goals as cutting across the ideological differences that segmented the labor movement, it did not submit a separate list of candidates and was not officially represented. Among eighty-seven delegates to the founding convention of the Histadrut, only four were women, all sent by the Achdut Haavoda party (an extension of the Poalei Zion party). The more committed feminists, such as Ada Fishman Maimon and Yael Gordon, leading members of the Hapoel Hatzair party, were among the thirty or so women who had been invited to attend the proceedings as guests. Restricted to passive participation, these guests objected strongly to the poor representation of women by the political factions and to the failure of the convention to deal with the special problems of the woman worker. In the last hours of the closing session, Ada Maimon, leader in the struggle for women's electoral rights in all institutions of Jewish self-government, declared that the female delegates, having been chosen by the parties and not by the women workers, did not and could not represent them. She announced that the women planned to form their own association within the Histadrut, and if refused representation on the Histadrut Council they "would feel forced to submit a separate electoral list to compete for representation on the Histadrut Council in the next election."[52] Maimon's proposal won the support of leading figures in the major parties and was accepted by the convention. Two places were reserved for representatives to be elected directly by the women workers.

The admission of the women's movement into the Histadrut stimulated a new wave of organizational activity among the women. The leadership set out to mobilize support among the new immigrants, particularly those pioneers who had arrived as part of organized ideological movements. They were potentially most cooptable. First, they were physically concentrated and thus more accessible than the mass of individual women employed primarily as seamstresses and domestics in private homes. Second, more than other women, their immigration had been motivated by aspirations similar to those of the feminists of the Second Aliyah, namely, realization of the pioneering goals of socialist Zionism. Third, they were the most predisposed to egalitarian ideals.

The meeting between the second- and third-wave pioneers may be analyzed in terms of an encounter between "sociological generations." The halutzot of the second wave had been excluded from full participation in the kvutzot, and their aspirations had been ridiculed. After a decade of struggle, they found that women were still discriminated against in all areas of public life. The halutzot of the third wave belonged to sexually mixed and strongly ideological socialist groups which provided work for their women members. They did not feel as deprived as did their forerunners. Although dissatisfaction with the sex division of labor and status existed even within such aggressively egalitarian groups as the Gdud Avoda, it was expressed, if at all, within the organization through its internal media and did not spark collective action across factional boundaries.[53] Loyalty to the group and its goals took priority over the issues that had united the women a decade earlier. Nonetheless, out of reverence for the women of the second wave, they attended the founding conference of the Women Workers' Council (WWC) held in 1921.[54] The 1921 conference, with forty-three delegates representing 485 workers, officially established WWC as the organizational arm of the women workers' movement within the Histadrut. The council elected an executive committee and representatives to each of the major departments within the Histadrut.[55]

By the time of the second conference in 1922, at which thirty-seven delegates represented six hundred women members, the underlying tensions within the women's movement had surfaced. Two major opposing factions emerged. I refer to them as the "radicals" and the "loyalists." The difference between them may be analyzed in terms of degrees of commitment to feminism and of trust put in the male leadership. The old leaders, joined by the disenchanted among the Third Aliyah, were the more radical. They put little trust in a male-dominated Histadrut to look after women's interests and advocated a strong, separate organization, free of party control and in contact with grass-roots members, which would initiate and monitor women's training and employment opportunities. The newly arrived third-wave pioneers held the loyalist position which recognized that women had special problems but believed there was no need for a separate women's organization to solve them. They argued that the newly constituted Histadrut should look after all workers alike. The WWC should concentrate on reeducating and activating women for participation in public life. In relation to the Histadrut it should limit itself to an advisory role and certainly not duplicate the services of the labor exchange and other bodies that generated and allocated resources. Organizational segregation was objectionable also because it implied lack of faith in the men which, the loyalists felt, was not deserved.[56]

The dispute over the WWC's role was not merely an internal matter. The positions defended, and the relative influence of the respective protagonists, were determined by the interests of the male leaders of the Histadrut, whose response to the WWC was a reflection of its general policy toward particular interest groups. Analysis of the events in the 1920s therefore requires some understanding of the wider sociopolitical context.

At that time the leadership of the Histadrut faced two major organizational problems. The first was how to safeguard the stability of the new, unifying institution, which had been forged from a variety of divergent ideological streams within Labor Zionism and incorporated a number of conflicting power groups. The second problem concerned the relationship of the political parties to the Histadrut. Although elements within Achdut Haavoda argued that after the establishment of the Histadrut political parties were no longer necessary and should be dissolved, those in their favor prevailed. The latter faction, furthermore, opposed a pluralistic structure and pressed for centralization of the party organization and for party control over the Histadrut.[57] Clearly, a women's organization independent of party control conflicted with the interests of Achdut Haavoda, which argued that separatist tendencies among particular interest groups would waste resources and weaken the Histadrut. At the same time the leadership was generally sympathetic toward the special problems and goals of the women pioneers. The decision to include the WWC in the Histadrut may be viewed as a form of cooptation, a mechanism of social control first defined by Selznick as "the process of absorbing new elements into the leadership of the policy determining structure of an organization as a means of averting threats to its stability or existence."[58]

As noted, in 1920 the Histadrut's control over the worker community was still tenuous. The leaders of the Achdut Haavoda party feared the separate organization of various factions among both the second and third waves. For Histadrut leaders at the 1920 convention, Maimon's threat that the women workers would submit an independent electoral list made it expedient to absorb the leadership into the council, especially since events outside the labor movement gave the threat greater credibility. The conflict over women's voting rights in the newly forming National Assembly, the Jewish parliament of the Yishuv, had made feminism a salient issue and a legitimate basis for organizational differentiation. By 1920, the Association of Hebrew Women for Equal Rights in Eretz Yisrael (Palestine) had been established and was mobilizing support outside the labor sector. The association was an umbrella organization for women's groups which formed after World War I in the urban centers and larger agricultural villages (moshavot). The members were mainly from the educated middle class and secular elements of the Jewish community.[59]

Not affiliated with any existing political party, the association's activities were directed to overcoming the religious sector's militant opposition to equal civil and political liberties for women and particularly to their right to active and passive representation on the local and national bodies of Jewish self-government which developed during the first and second decades under the British Mandate.[60] The WWC apparently viewed its commitment to the labor movement as precluding an alliance with this "bourgeois" women's rights party. In the elections to the National Assembly, some eight months before the founding convention of the Histadrut, the association submitted a separate women's list that won seven mandates—the same number as there were women elected by the two labor parties to the assembly. These developments influenced the response to the demand of the women workers for representatives and their incorporation in the Histadrut Council.

Transformation of the Feminist Movement, 1921–1927

From the perspective of the Histadrut and particularly that of the Achdut Haavoda party, which was struggling for dominance within the newly established superstructure, the women's movement posed a problem of social control. Its accusations of discrimination undermined the legitimacy of the Histadrut's claim to represent all workers. To offset the potential costs of such allegations, the WWC was defined as an embarrassment to the labor movement. This perspective emerges in the report presented by David Ben Gurion, then leader of Achdut Haavoda to the second convention of the Histadrut in 1923 in which he explained, "the very existence and need for the existence of a special institution in the form of the WWC to protect the interests of the women workers does not add to our honor."[61] This stance most affected those women in the WWC who were closely identified with the male leaders of Achdut Haavoda and committed to them. One such woman was Golda Meir, who at the same convention declared: "It is a sad and shameful fact that we are forced to create a special organization to deal with matters of the woman worker."[62]

The tactical aspect of this admission about the WWC is twofold. First, when viewed as a concession to an unfortunate and embarrassing reality, the organization became a vestige of some unresolved past rather than a positive creative force projected into the future and devoted to the creation of a better society. Second, presented as a kind of bastard child of the labor movement (unwanted and unplanned for by the father), the women's movement was discredited for exposing the labor movement's failure to live up to its own ideals. Another tactic employed to confine the amount of resources the Histadrut would be required to divert to satisfy the demands of the WWC was to understate the magnitude of the change aspired to. The women's goals were translated into specific objectives and defined in negative rather than positive terms. For example, describing women's aspirations for equality as the need to eliminate discrimination at work made fewer demands on the system than a definition that called for affirmative action in all walks of life. In the same address in 1923, Ben Gurion went on to explain: "There is no special Histadrut for women workers nor is there a need for such a Histadrut, but we cannot ignore the bitter truth that the matter of equality for women, which we accept as a first principle, is only formal . . . there is still a need for a special institution for the women workers which will stand guard and concern itself with the social and economic position of the female worker so that she not be discriminated against within the community of workers."[63]

Ben Gurion's interpretation of the role of the WWC discounts the importance of the movement in the ideology and activity of national rebirth. Instead of being depicted as a creator of a new cultural image for women in the emerging social-ist society, it was ascribed the role of watchdog guarding the interests of a minor-ity group. Its members are thus denied the right to pride in a mission whose importance for the labor movement is discounted. According to Ben Gurion, imple-mentation of the women's movement goals, such as creating employment oppor-tunities, was to be left to the Histadrut. His statement that no special union for women existed as it did, for example, for agricultural workers, was not merely a description of the facts. It was intended as a warning that separation would not be tolerated and that women would have to solve their problems through the exist-ing structures of the Histadrut.

The need for women workers to prove that they were indeed not "creating a separate platform" for women (the phrase used to accuse the WWC of separatism) put the movement on the defensive. On all public occasions, such as the Histadrut and WWC conventions, WWC leaders repeatedly declared their loyalty to the Histadrut and denied that, in demanding greater opportunities, women were seeking a separate platform for themselves.[64]

The election system, based on proportional representation, gave the politi-cal parties and particularly the dominant Achdut Haavoda considerable control over the Histadrut in general and over the WWC in particular. Each political fac-tion constructed its lists of candidates so that the voter elected a party rather than an individual. Representation was indirect, since the party members elected dele-gates to the national convention, the convention to the council, and the coun-cil to the central committee of the Histadrut. The party bosses constructed the lists of candidates to the convention, which meant that they virtually controlled the access to all important and paid positions within the Histadrut and secured control of the top leadership over the organization. Women candidates usually made up no more than 20 percent of the list.

What weakened women's bargaining position was first, that so few were politically active and second, that many, particularly the loyalists, experienced ambivalence regarding the definition of women as a special interest group. Sex as a basis for interest aggregation was unacceptable to those who wished to partici-pate as individuals and not as members of a category which, by implication, was in some way inferior. Willingly or not, however, women on a party list were almost inevitably perceived as representing women.

In the Histadrut, the political logic of party list construction was aimed at select-ing people who could claim to represent the respective interest groups but whose loyalty to the party was not in question. Selective sponsorship of leaders by the dominant coalition, according to Gamson, is a strategy of social control similar to cooptation.[65] Because only the loyal are sponsored, the strategy reduces the need for direct intervention and continuous monitoring by the establishment. The sponsorship strategy is evident in the Histadrut's intervention through the selection of the leadership of the WWC and in its control over the organization's election system.

The Histadrut leadership strengthened the position of some women and weakened that of others through its appointments to policymaking and resource-allocating committees of its various agencies. Although formally the executive committee of the WWC had the right to recommend representatives to these bodies, they required the approval of the Central Committee, which used its prerogative to appoint and depose committee members in accord with its political interests. For example, in 1925 Maimon, member of Hapoel Hatzair, was removed from the important immigration committee because she fought for 50 percent representation for women among those allocated immigration permits to Palestine. While the male leadership opposed her on this issue, they objected even more strongly to her independent behavior.[66] She was replaced by a male member of Achdut Haavoda.

There is also evidence that the Histadrut intervened and affected leadership recruitment within the WWC. Golda Meir records that in 1927 David Remez, influential member of the Achdut Haavoda faction in the Central Committee of the Histadrut, invited her to become secretary (equivalent to chairperson) of the WWC.[67] Golda Meir had immigrated in 1921from the United States, where she had been an active member of the Poalei Zion party, forerunner of the Achdut Haavoda party. The following year she was elected to the executive committee of the WWC, and in 1923 she and Maimon were elected to the Histadrut council.[68] Meir's qualifications for the post are not at issue, but it should be recognized that her election was initiated and engineered by the male leadership.

The process of centralization within the Histadrut was combined with the creation of a network of labor councils to implement Histadrut policy at the local level. Under the initiative of the WWC, committees of women workers were established within the councils in the cities and agricultural villages. The WWC defined their role as "activating" women workers and representing them in the various departments of the local labor council, such as the Offices of Public Works and Immigration, as well as in trade unions. Antagonism developed between the party functionaries of the local labor councils who controlled employment opportunities and other resources and the members of the women's committees whose direct election by the local female constituency weakened the former's control over them. Work was scarce, and the functionaries rejected the women's claim to special consideration, refusing to grant them privileges.[69]

The issue came to a head in a debate concerning the system to be employed for electing members of the women's committee. There were two camps in the WWC: the radical feminists, who favored direct elections by a general meeting of women workers at the local level without regard to women's party affiliation and free from party intervention, and the loyalists, who advocated that candidates be appointed by the party functionaries of the local council in cooperation with the WWC. The two views came to be known as "elected committees" and "appointed committees." The radical feminists, headed by Ada Maimon, Tova Yaffe, and other members of Hapoel Hatzair, argued that direct elections were essential to arouse women to active involvement in public life. The major concern of the radicals was that with appointed committees there would be no meaningful ties between the delegates and the women workers. Members would be selected on the basis of criteria such as compliance and party allegiance, and not on the basis of their ability and readiness to represent women's issues. Direct election of candidates, therefore, was essential to promote women's confidence in their representatives and to assure that the latter would be loyal first and foremost to the female constituency.

The loyalists argued that such low trust of the local labor council functionaries would result in conflicts, which would make the women's committee ineffective. It was, therefore, in the women's interest that the committees be appointed, with the advice of the WWC, by the local functionaries who would consequently feel more responsible for them.[70]

The issue was hotly debated during the meeting of the WWC in June 1926, at which Ben Gurion, representing the central committee of the Histadrut, commented: "There is no need to create a negative attitude toward the women's committees among the local labor councils from the start. A committee elected from among the community of women workers will create a negative attitude on the part of the local labor councils."[71] The implication that withdrawal of Histadrut support would be the price the WWC would have to pay for its independence and that by raising such demands they were intensifying interparty conflict within the Histadrut was intended to intimidate those who opposed appointed committees. These statements, however, do not reveal what appears to have been the deeper concern of the male leadership.

Achdut Haavoda feared that separate elections for women would set a dangerous precedent for other interest groups, such as the Orthodox and Yemenite communities, which could result in a weakening of the control of the center over the periphery.[72] Despite pressure from the male leadership, however, the executive council of the WWC decided twelve to eight in favor of elected committees at its November 1926 meeting. Women members of Hapoel Hatzair and other parties voted for them and those of Achdut Haavoda against them, and it is apparent that the division between the radicals and the loyalists more and more paralleled that between the two labor parties.[73] Because the struggle among political factions for control within the Histadrut had intensified the demand for party loyalty, party rivalries were penetrating the WWC. The Histadrut leadership, which by the mid-twenties was mainly in the hands of the centralist Achdut Haavoda, encouraged the loyalists. The leaders of the ideologically pluralist Hapoel Hatzair party, fearful of the growing control of its rival party, favored independently elected committees. At the third Histadrut convention in 1927, the majority of whose delegates came from the Achdut Haavoda party, the vote was ninety-seven to seventy-nine in favor of appointed women's committees. In 1926, election by proportional representation of political factions was introduced into the conference of the WWC as well. At the following conference held in 1932 all candidates were sponsored by the respective political factions, and proportional representation was officially implemented.[74] Thus, by the end of the 1920s, the struggle between the radicals and the loyalists had been determined in favor of the latter.

The Histadrut, while extending its control over the women's movement through selective sponsorship of leaders, was also under pressure to make concessions to the WWC. But, in terms of its original goals, the WWC was able to exact a small price from the Histadrut for its active support. It developed six agricultural training farms as well as a number of vocational training courses for women; however, these were financed almost entirely by Zionist women's organizations abroad. By 1926 the Histadrut had not yet assigned a budget to the WWC or determined salaries for its representatives on the major Histadrut committees.[75] The WWC conference of that year reports a list of abortive attempts to gain concessions from the local labor councils in the field of employment.[76] The economic crisis that hit Palestine, and especially the cities, in the years 1926 to 1929 resulted in large-scale unemployment for both women and men and intensified the competition between the sexes for scarce jobs. By 1930 the proportion of women in nontraditional jobs had dropped considerably. Only 0.4 percent of the urban female labor force was then employed in construction and public works, while 46.1 percent were employed in private homes.[77] In addition, the Histadrut made only insignificant concessions to the WWC's demands for power. A few token women were assigned to various Histadrut committees in the early twenties, but their numbers dwindled as the decade progressed. Apart from Maimon, who was a member of the economic council of Hevrat Haovdim (economic enterprises of the Histadrut), women were not found in any of the policymaking bodies of the economic organizations created by the Histadrut in the 1920s. No woman was represented on the fifteen-member committee which in 1925 negotiated the first collective agreement between the Histadrut and employers in the Yishuv. In this agreement, unskilled women workers employed in factories were officially discriminated against in wages-a situation that continued until the 1970s. A review of the minutes of the Histadrut Executive Council meetings held between 1921 and 1927 reveals that the problem of women was raised only four times, invariably by a woman and without response from other members.

The problem of the woman worker, which was an item on the agenda of the second Histadrut conference in 1923, was dropped from that of the third in 1927. It was argued that with the creation of the WWC the problem had been solved. Although the subject was returned to the agenda in later conferences and even became a permanent item, it was an issue to which only women gave their attention. The position of women within the new worker community was and remained the responsibility and concern of the WWC. Once the organization ceased to make unacceptable demands and its energies were harnessed to advance the interests of the Histadrut establishment, the sex division of labor and a large women's organization proved highly convenient. Looking after women's issues functioned as an outlet for the political energies of women while it freed the men for dealing with the "more important" issues of the day. Every woman who joined the Histadrut was automatically registered as a member of the WWC, a bureaucratic procedure that enabled the WWC in later years to boast of being the largest women's organization in the country.

The year 1927 marks the eclipse of radical feminism within the women workers' movement. Two events that year reflect the transformation that took place in the WWC and that led to the displacement of its original goals. The first was the decision in favor of appointed committees, which has already been discussed in some detail. The grass-roots organization was co-opted by the local councils. This discouraged sustained feminist pressure to give priority to women's emancipation since there were always more pressing problems that required attention. Pressing problems were usually those for which pressure could not be eliminated, and the silencing of the radical elements was as much a consequence of the WWC's weakness as a cause of it.

The second event was the replacement of Ada Maimon as secretary of the WWC by Golda Meir. In view of their very different conceptions of the role of the WWC, this change represents the culmination of the struggle for power between the old guard and the new generation.[78] Although Maimon was reelected to the WWC executive committee, after 1927, she and the old guard had lost ground. Power had shifted to the loyalist faction.

Meir's entrance into office symbolizes the succession of generations. The generation that had put women's self-transformation above party politics gave way to a cadre whose priorities were determined by the interests of the overall party organization. Meir, who was selected by the male leadership of Achdut Haavoda, was, according to her own report, attracted to the WWC not so much because it was concerned with the issue of women as such, but because she was "very interested in the work it was doing, particularly in the agricultural training farms they set up for immigrant girls."[79] For her, the WWC was a brief interlude in a long career within the male establishment of the labor party. The WWC was transformed into a social service organization, meeting the needs of women in their traditional roles of wives and mothers, albeit working mothers. It sponsored child day-care centers to free women to enter the labor market. Its occupational training prepared girls primarily for traditionally feminine roles as hairdressers, dressmakers, nursemaids, and the like. It turned its attention more and more to looking after welfare needs of mothers and children in the urban centers, leaving the political decisions, the trade union activities, and economic policy in the hands of the male establishment. In addition it served ancillary political functions, the most important of which was mobilizing female support for the party at elections.

Conclusion

From its inception, the Zionist women workers' movement avoided defining itself as engaged in a struggle against male oppression. Nonetheless, in the period between 1911 and 1927, the commitment of the women's movement to self-transformation and equal participation in the building of the new society united its members across the competing political factions within the labor movement. As a united front it pressed for greater equality in the allocation of scarce resources such as immigration certificates, job opportunities, and participation in decision-making bodies of the various organizations of the labor movement.

The structural integration of the WWC within the Histadrut as a separate, but not autonomous, part of the socialist movement brought it under the control of the emerging power centers. From the late 1920s two forces diverted the women's movement from a sustained struggle for sexual equality: first, the demands of the political parties within the Histadrut and particularly of the dominant Achdut Ha'avoda for the women's undivided commitment to the wider interests of the labor movement as these were defined by the party; and second, the party's failure to develop a real commitment to women's emancipation in the construction of the new economic, political, and social institutions of the Yishuv. These forces also shaped the course of the WWC for decades to come. The feminist movement, which had emerged in response to the wish of women pioneers to be equal partners in conquering new fields of work and building the nation, became the largest voluntary social service and, later, welfare organization in the Yishuv. In addition, the movement institutionalized and thus reinforced the categorical treatment of women at the same time it monitored their public careers. Women in the labor party, which dominated the country until 1977, were expected to rise through the ranks of the WWC, while its leadership acted as gatekeepers between the female enclave and the male establishment, allowing only a selected few, sponsored by them, to pass. Those who succeeded were rewarded with a seat in the Knesset (Israeli parliament) and other central bodies, and they provided the few tokens that bolstered public belief in the notion that capable women do make it. The lack of institutionalized rotation in the leadership, however, set stringent limits on the number who ever did.

Despite the WWC's shift in activities, the organization remained officially committed to the full participation of women in public life. Consequently, the existence of this powerful women's organization, which claimed to be the vanguard of women's interests, helped to perpetuate the myth of equality and to discourage the emergence of alternative definitions around which women could organize.

Notes

1. S. N. Eisenstadt, *Israeli Society* (London: Weidenfeld & Nicolson, 1967); A. Bein, *The History of Jewish Agricultural Settlement in Palestine*, 3rd ed. (Tel Aviv: Massada Press, 1954); Y. Shapiro, *Achdut Ha'avoda Party: The Power of Political Organization* (Tel Aviv: Am Oved, 1976; in Hebrew).
2. J. M. Slaughter, "Women and Socialism: The Case of Angelica Balabanoff," *Social Science Journal* 14, 2 (1977):57–65.
3. Katzir, *Source Readings for the Zionist Movement in Russia* (Tel Aviv: Massada Press, 1964; in Hebrew).
4. Eisenstadt, *Israeli Society*, 3.
5. From a manifesto prepared in 1897 by the Committee of Women Zionists in Stanislau, Galicia (Poland), quoted in N. Gelber, *The History of the Zionist Movement in Galicia 1875–1918* (Jerusalem: Histadrut Hazionit, 1958), 2:806.
6. Shapiro, *Achdut Ha'avoda*.
7. Y. Gorni, "Changes in the Social and Political Structure of the Second Aliya between 1904–1940." In D. Carpi, ed., *Zionism: Studies in the History of the Zionist Movement and the Jewish Community in Palestine* (Tel Aviv: Massada Press, 1975). Throughout this paper we are dealing with small numbers of people. According to Gorni some 35,000 to 40,000 persons came on the Second Aliyah, but most left the country or were deported by 1914. Only a fraction of those who remained formed the socialist pioneering element that gave the tone to the developments in the Yishuv (the Jewish community in Palestine) and influenced the course of its history. Eisenstadt, in describing the Second Aliyah, points out, "Although workers were in the minority . . . it is nonetheless considered as a labor immigration, since the workers' initiative and energy changed the whole structure of the Jewish community" (p. 11).
8. S. Malchin, "The Woman Worker in Kineret," *Hapoel Hatzair*, vol. 11 no. 13 11,13 (1912; in Hebrew). For an expression of similar aspirations, see the memoirs of women pioneers in B. Chabas, ed., *The Second Aliya* (Tel Aviv: Am Oved Ltd., 1947; in Hebrew); R. Katzenelson Shazar, ed., *The Plough Woman* (New York: Herzl Press, 1975); Y. Harari, *Woman and Mother in Israel* (Tel Aviv: Massada Press, 1959; in Hebrew).
9. Eisenstadt, *Israeli Society*, 17.
10. Bein, *Jewish Agricultural Settlements*, 31; W. Preuss, *The Labor Movement in Israel* (Jerusalem: Rubin Mass, 1965), 19; A. D. Gordon, "People and Labor." In A. Hertzberg, ed., *The Zionist Idea* (New York: Meridian Books, 1959), 373. Bein observes that the typical photograph of the second wave shows pioneers with their work tools.
11. Z. Even Shoshan, *The History of the Workers' Movement in Eretz Israel* (Tel Aviv: Am Oved Ltd., 1963; in Hebrew), 1:208–209.
12. Bein, *Jewish Agricultural Settlements*, 53.
13. Eisenstadt, *Israeli Society*, 20.
14. Chabas B. Katznelson, *Writings* (Tel Aviv: Mapai Publication, 1948; in Hebrew), 4:179.

15. Even Shoshan, *Workers' Movement*, 196–197.

16. T. Liberson, "On the Question of the Women Workers." *Hapoel Hatzair*, 27 (1913; in Hebrew).

17. A. Shidlovsky, "Kineret in His Jubilee" In R. Katznelson Shazar, ed., *With the Steps of the Generation* (Israel: Histadrut HaKlalit-Moetzet Hapoalot, 1964; in Hebrew).

18. M. Schochat, "The Collective." In Katznelson Shazar, *Plough Woman*; Bein, *Jewish Agricultural Settlements*, 73.

19. Even Shoshan, *Workers' Movement*, 213–214; Y. Shapira, *Work and Land—Fifty Years of the Histadrut of Agricultural Workers* (Tel Aviv: Am Oved, 1961), 1:226 (in Hebrew); A. Maimon (Fishman), *Women Workers' Movement in Eretz Israel* (Tel Aviv: Hapoel Hatzair, 1929), 37 (in Hebrew).

20. E. Becker, "From the Life of a Watchman's Family." In Chabas, *Second Aliyah*, 517; Bein, *Jewish Agricultural Settlements*.

21. Maimon, *Women Workers*, 91.

22. Liberson, "Question of Women Workers," 27; R. Yanait Ben Zvi, *We Ascend: Memoirs* (Tel Aviv: Am Oved, 1959; in Hebrew), 394.

23. Gorni, "Social and Political Structure." Gorni found that women tended to have somewhat more formal education than men but less Jewish instruction.

24. Malchin, *The Woman Worker*, 11.

25. Z. Liberson, "The Workers' Kitchen in Hadera." In Chabas, *Second Aliya*, 272–273.

26. R. Yanait Ben Zvi, *Manya Schochat* (Jerusalem: Yad Ben Zvi, 1976; in Hebrew); S. Krigser, "Our First Agricultural Training." In Chabas, *Second Aliya*, 506; Mamashi, "On the Question of the Women Workers." *Hapoel Hatzair* 27 (1913).

27. S. Blumstein, "Life in the Kineret Commune." In A. Ya'ari, ed., *Memoirs of Eretz Yisrael* (Jerusalem: Zionist Organization Youth Department, 1937; in Hebrew), 2:814–822.

28. N. J. Smelser, *Theory of Collective Behavior* (New York: Free Press of Glencoe, 1963).

29. Even Shoshan, *Workers' Movement*, 1:215.

30. Group of Women Workers, "In Answer to Mrs. Tahon." *Hapoel Hatzair* 26 (1913; in Hebrew).

31. R. H. Turner and L. M. Killian, *Collective Behavior*, 2d ed. (Englewood Cliffs, N. J.: Prentice Hall, hoc., 1972), 275.

32. A. Maimon, *Along the Way* (Tel Aviv: Am Oved, 1972; in Hebrew), 121.

33. "The First Women Workers' Conference." Hapoel Hatzair, 37 (1914; in Hebrew).

34. Maimon, *Women Workers' Movement*, 23.

35. Mamashi, "Question of Women Workers."

36. Maimon, *Women Workers' Movement*, 52; Shapira, *Work and Land*, 140.

37. "First Women Workers' Conference."

38. M. Baratz, "How I Conquered Work?" In Katznelson Shazar, *Steps of the Generation*.

39. R. Porat, *Education in the Collectives and Kibbutzim* (Tel Aviv: HaKibbutz Hameuchad, 1977; in Hebrew).

40. Harari, *Woman and Mother*, 492.

41. Bein, *Jewish Agricultural Settlements*, 55, 164.

42. Y. Etinger, "Cooperative Groups in the Year 1919." Kontres 12 (1919):5–6.

43. Maimon, *Women Workers' Movement*; Harari, *Woman and Mother*, 492.

44. Gorni ("Social and Political Structure") found that prior to immigration, 51 percent of the immigrants belonged to a political party; after immigration that figure declined to 33 percent. Among the 47 percent of the immigrants who had been active in parties abroad, only 14.7 percent continued in Palestine. Shapiro ("Power of Political Organization") suggests that the preference of the second wave for activities directly related to self-actualization explains these findings. This preference was probably stronger among women than among men.

45. Eisenstadt, *Israeli Society*, 24.

46. Even Shoshan, *Workers' Movement*, 1:400; Y. Erez, *The Third Aliya* (Jerusalem: Zionist Organization Youth Department, 1948), 43.

47. Bein, *Jewish Agricultural Settlements*, 157–158; *Histadrut Haklait—the Union of Agricultural Workers in Its Thirtieth Year* (Tel Aviv: Vaad Hapoel, 1951; in Hebrew), p. 549. Kibbutzim developed during the third wave. They differed from the kvutzot, which were restricted to twenty to thirty members and where social relations were modeled on the intimacy characteristic of family ties, primarily in that they were larger social units with one hundred and more members and consequently less selective and more open to individuals ready to share their way of life.

48. "Second Conference of the Construction Workers' Union." *Pinkas Hahistadrut*, special edition (1924), 27.

49. T. Liberson, "Women Build Houses." In Katznelson Shazar, *Plough Woman*, 176.

50. Erez, *Third Aliyah*.

51. "The Third Conference of the Women Workers' Council." *Pinkas Hahistadrut* (1926).

52. "Protocol of the First Convention of the Histadrut, December, 192."*Asufot* 1 (14) (December 1970):5–80. Maimon reports that it was Rachel Yanait, one of the official delegates of Achdut Ha'avoda at the conference, who had asked her to speak on behalf of the poalot (women workers). Yanait was a party leader and "it seems she felt it not appropriate nor in good taste for her to do the task; to demand elected representatives of the poalot, and therefore, she turned to me" (*Along the Way*, 105).

53. *Erez, Me'Chayieu* [From our life], newspaper of the Gdud Aavoda, no. 25 (1922):252 (in Hebrew).

54. Ch. Drori, "From Soviet Russia to the Conference in Haifa." in Katznelson Shazar, *Plough Woman*, 14–17. Drori recounts the report of the delegate to the 1922 WWC conference from Ein Harod-a kibbutz belonging to Gdud Avoda that she represented those who supported the WWC, while the second delegate represented those who opposed a separate Women's Movement. See also Even Shoshan, *Workers' Movement*, 2:199.

55. "The First Conference of the Women Workers' Council." *Pinkas Hahistadrut* (1921; in Hebrew).

56. Maimon, *Women Workers' Movement*; Minutes of the Second Meeting of the Executive Committee of the Women Workers' Council, June 1926, unpublished (Labor Archives, Tel Aviv, in Hebrew); hereafter cited as *Minutes*.

57. Shapiro, "Power of Political Organization."

58. P. Selznick, *TVA and the Grassroots* (Berkeley: University of California Press, 1949).

59. Dr. Rose Walt Stroim, founder and leader of the association, immigrated from the United States where she had been an activist in the women's suffrage movement and a founding member of the International Woman Suffrage Alliance.

60. S. Azaryahu, *The Association of Hebrew Women for Equal Rights in Eretz Yisrael*, 2d ed. (Haifa: Foundation for Women's Aid, 1977; in Hebrew).

61. "The Second Histadrut Convention." *Pinkas Hahistadrut* (1923): 22.

62. Ibid., 49.

63. Ibid., 22.

64. See, for example, ibid., 17 and 99; R. Katznelson, "The Participation of the Female Workers." *Kontres* 14 (1927):15-20 (in Hebrew).

65. W. A. Garrison, *Power and Discontent* (Homewood, Ill.: Dorsev Press, 1968), 135 ff.

66. Maimon, *Women Workers' Movement*, 252.

67. G. Meir, *My Life* (London: Futura Publications, 1975), 85.

68. "The Second Conference of the Women Workers' Council." *Pinkas Hahistadrut* (192; in Hebrew); "The Second Histadrut Convention."

69. "Report of the Second Conference of the Women Workers' Council." *Hapoel Hatzair* 37 (1922):12 (in Hebrew).

70. *Minutes*; B. S. Cheikin, "Protocol of the Third Histadrut Conventio.," *Pinkas Hahistadrut* (1927):337 (in Hebrew).

71. *Minutes.*
72. M. Sharet, "Protocol of the Third Histadrut Convention." *Pinkas Hahistadrut* (1927):328 (in Hebrew).
73. "The Women Workers' Council." *Hapoel Hatzair* 20, 9 (1926):13 (in Hebrew).
74. Even Shoshan, *Workers' Movement*, 3:165, ff.
75. *Minutes.*
76. Sharet, "Protocol."
77. Even Shoshan, *Workers' Movement*, 3:165.
78. In 1926, three months prior to the third WWC conference, a crisis arose within the executive committee of the WWC when Maimon was sharply criticized for ruling the organization with her "favorites" and neglecting others. Maimon resigned, the council disbanded, and the executive committee of the Histadrut appointed an interim committee to prepare for the third Histadrut convention. See "The Third Conference of the Women Workers' Council."
79. Meir, *My Life*, 88.

Manya Wilbushewitz-Shohat
and the Winding Road to Sejera

In 1907 on the Sejera training farm in the Lower Galilee, Manya Wilbushe-witz implemented a socio-economic plan on which she had been working for several years. Her goal was to organize a group of Jewish workers in a way that would enable them to support themselves in agricultural labor, without exploiting anyone and without being dependent on charity. Her hope was that if her project succeeded, it could become a model for other groups of Jews in Palestine and eventually a model for large-scale settlement and employment. Whether or not her group at Sejera actually achieved that goal is a matter of continuous debate (see Frankel 1981; Near 1983). The purpose of this essay, however, is to focus on the origins of her ideas and the winding road she took to put them into practice with the men and women at Sejera.

Manya Wilbushewitz was born in 1880 on an estate in Western Russia, in an area called Lososna, close to the town of Grodno. Manya's father was wealthy, deeply religious, and unlike many of his contemporaries, interested in technology. His land oil tile banks of the Neiman River included a grain mill that employed scores of peasants. Manya's mother was not interested in religion. She had received a secular education and fought her husband's plan to have their sons educated as rabbis. Manya was the eighth child of this conflicted marriage. None of her older brothers and sisters was to remain on the estate in roles intended by either parent. Instead, each pursued an ideological path ranging from joining the terrorist Social Revolutionaries, becoming a Tolstoyan peasant, emigrating as a farmer to Palestine with the Hibbat Zion, to obtaining a superior technical education and becoming an engineer in Palestine. Several eventually committed suicide when their feminist, romantic, or social ideals disappointed them.

Manya's family mirrored the contradictions of Jewish life in late nineteenth century Russia. At the same time as restrictions on Jewish occupation, education, and travel were lifted, allowing for a certain amount of assimilation into both the educated and revolutionary Gentile groups, Jews also experienced a backlash of antisemitism which provoked religious retrenchment, emigration, Zionism, and socialism. In her childhood, Manya was first profoundly religious and then equally committed to Russian peasants. At the age of fifteen she ran away to the city of Minsk to become an industrial laborer. There in her brother Gedaliahu's factory, she organized a strike of the five hundred workers against him, protesting the excessively long work day. This was to become the first of her numerous efforts to improve the working conditions of industrial and agricultural laborers. In Minsk where many young Jews, like Manya, had converged, first-hand confrontation with class exploitation and political oppression led them to form diverse political groups. Among the most important was the Bund, founded in 1897, whose purpose it was to pursue a revolutionary solution to the oppression of Jewish workers, in conjunction with the Russian socialist revolutionary movement vis-à-vis both the Czar and the bourgeoisie. Competing with the Bund was the Poalei Zion, or socialist Zionists, who advocated gradual emigration to Palestine while also trying to improve the economic condition of Jews still in Russia. A third set of groups was the terrorist Social Democrats and Socialist Revolutionaries who attempted to overthrow the Czar. Finally, the Hibbat Zion groups believed in immediate settlement in Palestine, but did not have a socialist orientation.

Manya befriended people in all of these groups and absorbed aspects of each ideology. The action she chose to get involved in, however, was the establishment of clandestine evening study clubs, where workers were taught basic literacy, history, economics, and socialism. She also joined a relief effort in the Tartar region, bringing economic and medical aid to peasants suffering from the drought and cholera. One consequence of the latter experience was her encounter with the *mir*, or Russian communal system, which she believed represented a form of social and economic justice. As a newly committed socialist, she set up an urban collective upon her return to Minsk. Collective, she believed, provide "the proletariat with the means of its struggle" (Shohat 1932, 22).

Manya's political activism inevitably led to her imprisonment and intensive interrogation at the hands of the Russian secret police. Through a curious relationship in prison, she became engaged in a cooperative effort with Sergei Zubatov, the head of the Moscow secret police, to establish a political party which would protect Jews from harassment as long as they limited themselves to labor issues and did not pursue a revolutionary strategy. Manya Wilbushewitz and Sergei Zubatov were successful in establishing the Jewish Independent Labor Party (JILP) in June 1901 and quickly achieved many of its goals. But growing unemployment soon weakened the position of the JILP among Jews, and disenchantment by von Plehve, Minister of the Interior, with Zubatov his underling, brought a swift end to the party. Zubatov was sent into exile and von Plehve agitated the Russian masses against the Jews, culminating in the traumatic Kishinev pogroms of 1903. At this point Manya, too, began to contemplate violence and joined a terrorist cell.

For the first time in her life Manya left Russia, her purpose being to gather funds in Berlin for her terrorist group. Recognizing the danger his sister was courting, her brother Nahum intervened and through a ruse brought her to Palestine on January 2, 1904, at the age of twenty-four. With her arrival she became one of the first members of the Second Aliyah, composed mostly of radicalized young Russians who came to Palestine between 1904 and 1914. Shortly thereafter, Manya learned that her terrorist group had been infiltrated in Russia and its members executed. With this tragedy she no longer felt capable of effective political action in Russia and instead directed her attention to labor issues in Palestine.

Palestine presented Manya with a new set of circumstance. In the three months since her brother Nahum had been in the country, he had befriended Olga (a midwife) and Joshua Hankin, who for the previous three years had been involved in attempting to purchase large tracts of land for the Jewish Settlement Association (or ICA). Nahum had been sent by their brother Gedaliahu, an engineer like himself, to conduct a survey of Palestine's geography and natural resources in order to lay the foundation for the development of industry. This information was to be used to plan capital investment and create durable circumstances for Jewish immigration. Manya accepted Nahum's invitation to join him on a six-week horseback study tour with four other individuals. The first was Joshua Hankin's brother, Mendel, who served as their Arabic-speaking guide. The second was Sophia Zevnegorodska, a young woman who had recently arrived from Russia accompanying a large group of children from the Belkind School orphaned by the Kishinev pogroms. She brought these children to a school at Shefiya near Haifa where Manya's future husband, Yisrael Shohat, lived temporarily. Two Arabs were hired to assist the group. Participation in this trip transformed Manya into a Zionist, although seeds for this transformation had already been planted by her earlier family life. Manya felt an attachment to the landscape, especially to a section called the Hauran, where she believed many Russian Jews could find refuge if an appropriate economic base was developed. The following is one of her many descriptions of the experience:

> We rode on horseback every day for ten hours. We would change horses. We passed all the Arab places in the country, from Dan to Beer-Sheva, and in Trans-Jordan. The trip lasted six weeks. I became tied to the land with a deep love, an unusual love, which filled my entire soul, mind and emotions. This love has remained with me always, and it burns in me now. It was as if a tic had been renewed between us that was 2000 years old. The beauty of the country and its natural environment had a strong influence on me. (Shohat 1904, 5)

This ideology of resettlement, new to Manya, reflected the basic Zionist position that Jews should return to Palestine. However, Manya's Zionism, unlike that of most Zionists of the time, had four special attributes: activism, large scale dimensions, self-labor, and collectivism. Whereas the World Zionist Organization at the time favored negotiations with world powers for a charter permitting mass settlement, Manya favored immediate "infiltration" of Jewish settlers. Since the number of Jewish settlers at the time was small, Manya's plan for hundreds in the Hauran was grandiose. Moreover, her idea that settlers should work the land themselves rather than be landowners, and her promotion of self-sufficient collectives, were viewed as extreme socialism. The settlers already in Palestine did not rely on their own labor, nor did they live collectively. Rather, they depended on Jewish philanthropy and Arab labor.

Self-labor and collectivism reflected Manya's conception of Zionism not as a transplanting of Jewish life from Russia to Palestine but as a transformation of the Jewish community so as to become ideal. Manya's efforts are noteworthy in the sense that she conceived of her plans before implementing them. Her ideas were rooted in her experience with Russian collectives combined with the socialist ideology she had adopted there concerning urban and rural class exploitation. At the end of her trip, Joshua Hankin introduced her to ICA officials to whom she presented her ideas about settling the Hauran, which they promptly rejected.

Not easily dissuaded, Manya next accepted Joshua Hankin's suggestion that she undertake a survey of the First Aliyah settlements so she could better address the criticisms of the ICA officials. At the same time, she hoped to supply him with information he needed to convince the ICA to purchase land in the Jezreel Valley (Wilbush 1974, 10). In the tradition of Russian youth and American and British reformers who collected statistical data on local working conditions, Manya set out to study the twenty-three Jewish rural settlements of Palestine then subsidized by the Paris-based Baron Edmund de Rothschild.

> I decided to clarify for myself, what does this new land really mean to me? I saw only agriculture. And where was the proletariat? My plan was to travel throughout the settlements and do a statistical survey in which I had expertise. I prepared statistical tables and I filled them out. (Later, these papers were taken from me). I was absorbed in this statistical study for a year.　　　　　　　　　　　　　　　　(Shohat 1904, 5)

Although Manya's economic study focused on the cause of the communities' perpetual annual deficits, it also included questions about the relations between employers and employees and between Jews and Arabs. One farmer described how Manya went about her study: "She attacked me with questions about the expenses and income of my farm, about Jewish labor and Arab labor, about the relations of the two groups in the country, and she even wanted to know if Arab men and

Jewish women fell in love with one another, and if this could bring the two peoples closer together." (Smilansky 1947, 696). From her survey Manya concluded that the economic arrangements of both the First and Second Aliyah groups were senseless and discouraging. Her observations about the settlements were as follows:

> After I thoroughly studied the economic situation of the Baron's ICA villages, I reached, in 1905, the firm conclusion that the system of agricultural settlement, which the officials of the Baron devised, was bankrupt in every sense of the word. As early as 1881–1882, a pioneering, wonderful, idealistic type of person came to Palestine, capable of minimal independent work. And now, after they spent twenty-five years in the country, we found them completely reliant on the ICA officials, lacking any faith in their enterprise, and employing Arab workers. They were all bitter and hopeless. They all believed in the Uganda option. Their sons did not continue in the farms and left the country because they could not stand the work regime that was established by the officials.   (Shohat 1961, 8)

One might question the objectivity of her findings—after all, she was already a committed socialist looking for the proletariat. Yet, Henrietta Szold, certainly not a socialist, came to the same conclusion after her first visit to Palestine in 1909, as described by biographer Joan Dash:

> Disillusion lurked in Zikhron Yaakov, which was ugly and planless, where everything seemed sad and neglected and some unhappy instinct had produced the look of a Russian village, squat and narrow and turned in on itself. The hired overseers of the Rothschild colonies, she learned, were dishonest and took no real interest in the settlements; the man who managed Zikhron lived in Haifa. It was common gossip the overseers seduced the young school teachers and married them off later on, when they were tired of them. Miss Szold had noticed many Arabs living in the villages. They were workmen, she was told, Jewish workmen were too expensive. So the Jews of the Rothschild colonies, who were pensioners of the Baron, living on his bounty, paid Arabs to do their work and complained about the Baron's administration.
> (Dash 1979, 5)

In the rural settlements of the First Aliyah, Jewish men and women carried out traditional family roles. The women remained at home and employed Arab women to help care for the children, while the men managed the farm and employed Arab laborers to work it. Because of this arrangement and political antipathy on the part of the First Aliyah, the new immigrants of the Second Aliyah had difficulty finding work. Unemployment was related to the underdevelopment of the economy and the preference among the First Aliyah employers for Arabs who demanded lower wages than Jews. Arabs were able to accept lower pay because their families had food-bearing land and had extensive experience in a low-income standard of living. Second Aliyah immigrants, on the other hand, were landless, without family support, and had no farming experience. Despite these work arrangements, the farmers of the First Aliyah were always in debt. And Jewish town dwellers in Jerusalem, Hebron, Safed, Jaffa, Haifa, and Tiberias did not fare much better. They survived on minor trade and foreign charity which Manya felt could not lead to economic development.

Having hypothesized that new collectivized agricultural settlements could be self-supporting, and that the towns and First Aliyah settlements offered no viable alternative, Manya presented her ideas to Yisrael Shohat and his brother Eliezer, two very young, penniless Poalei Zion members from her hometown of Grodno. The Shohat bothers had arrived in Palestine only two months after she did, but they came as committed Zionists with their ideology already in place. In response to near starvation, Yisrael, Eliezer and a few friends formed a workers' commune in Petah Tikva. When Manya visited them, the commune was very contentious. (Later, Yisrael and Eliezer Shohat were to become leaders of two competing workers' Zionist parties—Poalei Zion and Hapoel Hatzair). In addition, its members were striving to defy civilization and live at the lowest possible standard of living. Whereas Manya felt a higher standard of living and culture were desirable, they wanted to reduce their standard of living to what they perceived to be the level of the Arabs. She rejected their idea as utopian and unattractive, while Yisrael rejected her collectivist idea on the political grounds that in order to become part of the proletariat, they must avoid exclusivity. Cooperatives, he contended, foster group pride and dull class consciousness. Eliezer, in turn, opposed her idea on the grounds that the new immigrants were not yet, ready for collectivism and failure would doom the idea forever (see Shohat 1930, 6; Shohat 1961, 8). In addition, Yisrael was engaged in a different project altogether, namely one to develop an organization which Jews could use to protect themselves and their settlements from physical danger. He believed a mobile group of workers should be created which would both defend Jews and work the soil. Such a system was the only means, he believed, by which Jews could actually take possession of the land, since it was the principle on which Arab claims were based even after the land was purchased by Jews. From Manya's perspective, she was left no allies both the ICA and her fellow socialist Zionists opposed her. As it turned out, by 1907 Manya was able to bring both groups together.

A true believer in collectives, Manya's first step was to form a carpenters' cooperative in Yaffa based on her Russian experience in both carpentry and urban collectives. She "raised a loan for them and worked out its rules on tile basis of tile Russian Artel Movement which had a communal foundation. The cooperative lasted only three months, because when [she] left . . . internal dissension broke out and the cooperative fell to pieces" (Shohat 1932, 22). This experience may also have taught Manya the importance of developing skills to foster good group relations and settle labor disputes, skills she was to use repeatedly later on. For example, in early 1905, when Joshua Hankin involved Manya in his work of purchasing land in the Jezreel Valley, a conflict arose between the Hadera farmers and Hankin concerning 1,500 dunams which the farmers claimed Hankin had promised them. Manya was chosen to settle the dispute. Although she decided against Hankin, he accepted her decision and immediately implemented it.

Intent on moving forward with her idea of agricultural collectives, Manya decided to travel to the ICA offices in Paris in the summer of 1905 after one and a half years in Palestine. Supported by her statistical evidence, she hoped to convince the Baron and the ICA to buy the Jezreel Valley. She also wanted to broach the idea of agricultural collectives in the Hauran with Meyerson, the head of ICA. As an intellectual with several books of philosophy to his credit, she thought he might grasp the significance of collectives. Decidedly unenthusiastic about her socialist plans, the Baron gave her permission to attempt settlement in the Hauran, but he gave her no financial backing. While in Paris, she also turned to the internationally known Zionist, prolific writer, and physician, Max Nordau, but his reaction was worse. He listened to her detailed lecture for one and a half hours, filled with numbers and calculations, and when she was done, he remained silent. When she inquired why he was silent, he answered by saying that he was weighing whether or not to suggest she see a physician (Smilansky 1947, 696). To Manya the idea of an agricultural collective was vital but admittedly vague. To remedy this problem, she took advantage of her stay in Paris to study the concept, drawing on the resources of a relative, Ivan Wilbushewitz, who was employed as the head of a journal that published studies about the French colonies. With his help, she also obtained governmental material concerned with Algeria and Tunisia. However, she soon learned that information on agricultural management in these underdeveloped areas was oriented toward exploiting and exporting natural resources. More relevant to the Jews who sought to develop Palestine was the history of religious communes and utopian experiments. At the end of her studies, she concluded that there were no models for the settlements she envisioned, and that related models had all failed. Although her conviction about the value of collectives did not falter, her research yielded no economic blueprints for collective societies.

Manya then traveled from Paris to Basel in July 1905 to attend the Seventh Zionist Congress which resolved to obtain Jewish settlement rights in Palestine but to keep actual settlement limited. When she returned to Paris from Basel, she was approached by Meir Kagan, a friend from the former JILP, who asked her to abandon temporarily her Palestine project and turn her attention to the Jews still in Russia. Specifically, he asked her to try to raise funds in Paris and America to purchase arms that could be smuggled into Russia for Jewish self-defense. Manya turned again to the Baron, who gave her fifty thousand francs, on condition that his name not be mentioned. She also obtained ten thousand rubles from the twenty-eight-year old Reform rabbi and honorary secretary of the Federation of American Zionists, Dr. Judah Magnes, whom she had met in Basel. Altogether she raised 200,000 rubles from wealthy individuals and at mass meetings of Russian socialists and immigrants in Paris. With this money she went to Liège, Belgium, to purchase revolvers which she hid in her clothing and brought to Russia surreptitiously. Manya distributed these guns and ammunition to Jewish defense groups. On one trip she was cornered by a member of the secret police, and to avoid being killed, she killed him. To dispose of the evidence, she shipped his body in a trunk to a fictitious address. Manya remained in Russia and participated in self-defense efforts during the pogroms of 1906, but felt she had to do more. For three months she was a member of a terrorist group "to exact vengeance on the leaders of Russian antisemitism" (Shohat 1932, 23). In the spring of 1906, the group was infiltrated and its members arrested. Manya avoided detection, escaped from Russia, and returned to Palestine via Constantinople in late 1906.

Since she had failed in obtaining settlement funds from the Baron or convinced Palestine settlers to join, Manya decided to take another route. In early 1907 she traveled to the United States to seek funds and settlers, to continue her study of collectives, and to persist in her fund-raising efforts for Jewish defense in Russia. At that time Socialist Zionism was very young in America, the first group having been formed in New York only in March 1903 under the name National Radikal Verein Poalei Zion. Only in December 1905, after the Kishinev pogrom, did they hold their first national convention. In its program, the Socialist Zionists declared that normal social, political, and economic development of Jews could not take place without a land of their own, and that land should be Palestine. However, they demanded that any Jewish state should be based on socialist principles, with the workers owning land and the means of production (Urofsky 1975, 103). American Zionists were very small in number at the time, and even those who joined one of the many splinter organizations believed that Zionist aspirations would be fulfilled only in the distant future. Those drawn to Poalei Zion were immigrants living in urban ghettos where they struggled with their own poverty or tried to move out into American society. Thus it is not surprising that even "In America, [Manya's] mission was only half successful" (Smilansky 1947, 647). Smilansky also points out that Dr. J. L. Magnes introduced her to wealthy American Jews. These people were willing to contribute money for self-defense in Russia but rejected the idea of the collective.

During her half year in the United States, Manya was able to convince Magnes to visit Palestine, and after he later immigrated, the two of them worked extensively to promote peace between Arabs and Jews. While in the United States Manya also met Henrietta Szold, twenty years her senior, who described

Manya as an extraordinary woman, "a warm, palpitating and yet Tolstoian personality" (Dash 1979, 82). Despite the good impression Manya made, her idea of
collective settlements was seen as so fantastic that she was unable to find investors
or joiners. For a while she lived in a New York commune, but much of her time
was spent visiting communal settlements, such as the Dukhoborian who had
emigrated from Russia to Canada. These groups inspired her: "I saw that it was
possible to create and advance communistic colonization, although in place of religious idealism, we would have socialist idealism" (Shohat 1937, 56).

Manya returned to Palestine via Paris in August 1907 without having raised
funds for a collective and without any specific blueprint to meet the needs of the
Hauran. On her return, she traveled part of the way by ship with Chaim Weizmann
who was making his first trip to Palestine. Together they stopped in Alexandria
where she addressed Zionist groups, from there they went on to Beirut where they
were quarantined. Like most others who met her, Weizmann was struck by her charismatic personality, and Manya was to find in Weizmann an approachable political leader for years to come (Weizmann 1949, 124).

Throughout, her journeys, Manya sought principles on which to base her agricultural collective. She concluded that to avoid the creation of a class society, the
collective should be based on the abolition of private property. "We, the first socialist Hebrew workers in the country, who brought with us radical opposition to any
private property, couldn't even imagine that from private property a national society would develop for the Jewish people that wished to free itself in Palestine. And
it was obvious that the settlements of Rehovot and Hadera did not satisfy our soul
or capture our hearts" (Shohat 1961, 8). Second, to avoid competition between
Arabs and Jews, the collective should not attempt to take over existing Arab employment. "Before me the decisive question stood very sharply: either we came to Palestine in order to remain forever in the status of proletariat, begging at the doors
of the farmers who under no circumstances wanted us or our labor; or we came
here to create for ourselves a different form of settlement, sympathetic to our values" (Shohat 1961, 8). Third, to avoid exploitation within the collective, the members should be free to leave, unlike in the Russian mir where there was a supervisory
class of elders. Fourth, to assure a high cultural level, there should be limited work
hours and evening study groups. Finally, as an alternative to landowning or working for landowners, the collective should lease public lands. At that time the Keren
Hakayemet (Jewish National Fund) was starting to purchase lands, starting from
the assumption that the Land of Israel should be the property of the entire people,
and not of individuals. "And thus, I seized upon the idea of integrating the Keren
Hakayemet ideas with the principle of tenant farming, as it was practiced among
the Arabs" (Shohat 1961, 8).

This leasing plan derived from a particular form of Arab labor she had seen.
Similar to tenant farming (Shohat 1937, 55), this arrangement was also a varia-

tion of the system developed in Russia after the freeing of the serfs. This plan allows the farmer some independence even without owning the means of production. Specifically, the tenant farmer receives as a loan from the property owner, tools, land, seeds, animals, and living expenses. When the harvest is in, the tenant farmer pays back to the owner four-fifths of what has been earned. This covers the loan, gives the owner a profit, and leaves the farmer with a profit for his own purposes. These terms are even more beneficial to tenants if they are organized as a voluntary collective. Thus, a socially and financially successful system could be established without much initial investment.

At first Manya considered the idea of an integrated collective consisting of Arab and Jewish members, but she then determined that this would be impossible (Shohat 1929, 619). Unfortunately, Manya did not explain why she wanted to form an integrated collective in 1906, nor why she felt it was impossible to do so. The story of the relations between Arabs and Jews in Palestine before the First World War is complex (see Mandel 1976). Jewish ideology was not hostile to Arabs, nor did Jews come to Palestine with the intention of displacing Arabs. Arab nationalism had not yet emerged and Arabs were benefiting from Jewish settlements both in terms of employment and markets for their goods. Thus there were "generally close and good . . . day to day relations between peasants and settlers" (Mandel 1976, 31). At the same time, however, there were land disputes between the new Jewish colonies and Arab farmers who had lived on the sold property. These disputes led to Arab marauding and violence against persons and property. Manya's desire for Arab-Jewish cooperation was unusual in the context of the Arab-Jewish relations of the period, but not unusual in light of her commitment in Russia to Gentile peasants despite their hostility to Jews. In later years, Manya went on to become actively involved in creating organizations to promote Arab-Jewish friendship and cooperation. Most of these efforts were unsuccessful and unpopular.

Upon her return to Palestine in August 1907, Manya contacted Dr. Hillel Yaffe asking him to convince the Zionist groups or the ICA officials of her idea of agricultural collectives. According to her report, Dr. Yaffe answered, "There is no hope whatsoever for your plan. You will not find people who believe in such a thing. The Keren Hakayemet has no money for this type of experiment, nor would they understand it; and the Baron will under no circumstance agree to your idea. There is only one place, Sejera, which has the objective conditions for this type of experiment, but Krause will not dare to try it even if he is convinced of its value, because he'll lose his job if it becomes known in Paris" (Sohat 1961, 8). She then turned to Joshua Hankin, who, to her surprise, became convinced of the value of the idea. He in turn, persuaded Manya of the value of trying out her plan in Sejera rather than in the Hauran. He also agreed to present her case to the young agronomist, Eliahu Krause, the manager of the Sejera farm, who was also his brother-in-law. After much hesitation Krause agreed to try to implement Manya's idea on his responsibility, even though it endangered his own position (Smilansky 1997, 696). With this agreement in her pocket, Manya turned again to the two workers' parties—Poalei Zion and Hapoel Hatzair—to get volunteers for her collective in Sejera.

In Jaffa at a meeting of Poalei Zion on September 29, 1907, Yitzhak Ben-Zvi and Yisrael Shohat set up a secret group called Bar Giora, building on the idea that Yeheskel Hankin and Michael Halperin had suggested already in Russia, and that Alexander Zaid was dreaming of in Palestine. This idea was that the Jews of Palestine would create an organization to defend themselves. Those present at the meeting—Yisrael Shohat, Yitzhak Ben-Zvi, Yisrael Giladi, Yeheskel Nissinov, Yeheskel Hankin, Zvi Becker, Alexander Zaid, Moshe Givoni, and Komrov—discussed the need to set up a group of shepherds and a group of guards. At this point, Manya contacted Yisrael Shohat. He realized he could use her proposed settlement as a site on which to train a cadre of Jewish guards. He agreed to contribute his men, but did not tell her of his larger scheme (Shohat 1961, 8). As can be seen in the events to date, Manya was a pragmatist. Her socialist zeal did not deter her from seeking funds from capitalist philanthropists, nor did her commitment to particular principles prevent her from seizing the opportunity to implement something similar. All of the elements of such an opportunity had just presented themselves. She had a site, a plan, and a group of volunteers.

Sejera

Sejera was a community in the hills of the Lower Galilee, consisting of two parts: one section, founded by the ICA in 1889, was a short street with closely set small private homes on each side, and garden plots in front, inhabited by Jewish families from Kurdistan and Jewish converts from Russia. The other section, on slightly higher ground, consisted of a walled yard in which there were single rooms and was inhabited by individuals who came to work under Eliahu Krause's direction. The purpose of the farm at Sejera was to train Jewish farmers in self-sufficiency. Its manager, Eliahu Krause, was a progressive Russian Jew only two years older than Manya (see Michaeli 1973). Some people who trained on the farm—for example, David Ben Gurion—went on to live with and work for the families in the other part of the settlement. The students and farmers grew wheat and barley, and raised poultry and cattle. Those in training had to be accepted personally by Eliahu Krause and approved by the Paris office. While in training, they received a monthly wage.

Joshua Hankin and Manya Wilbushewitz arrived at Sejera just as Krause was assessing the farm's financial situation and discerning that the year would end in a deficit as had the previous years. In response to her request and Hankin's recommendation, Krause signed Manya on as a worker at Sejera. She was to work half-days in the dairy section and half-days as a bookkeeper. Sometimes she also participated in the plowing, walking in the furrows behind a horse (Smilansky 1947, 696). In addition, she helped Krause in his dealings with other workers. For example, Yitzhak Nadav remembered the following year when he came to Sejera and wanted to work as a builder, "I turned to Manya Shohat, who was the [central organizer] of the place, in the employ of ICA, with the suggestion that I get the work on the same conditions received by Arabs, or even worse conditions. Manya turned to Krause, and was able to get his agreement, on the condition that he give us only small jobs on an experimental basis" (Nadav 1986, 14).

When she first arrived, Manya obtained from Krause the right to form a collective from among some of the trainees already on hand and additional ones who would come. The workers in the collective would pool their expenses, would make joint decisions about how their work was to be done, and would not hire others to work for them. In all three ways, the collective would be different from the work arrangements both of the other trainees and of the settlers in the other section of Sejera. The collective members would also pool their wages in order to establish a fund to provide shelter, clothing, and food for new workers who would go where work was needed for a period of two years. In this way the collective would begin to participate in the task of settling the land. As it turned out, the collective also enabled people to work who could not engage in physical labor. Thus, Yisrael Shohat, suffering from chronic asthma, functioned as the treasurer of the grain mill of the farm (Paz 1947, 363). Twenty years after the collective was disbanded, Manya wrote a memoir about the way it functioned:

> According to the contract we drew up with Krause, we got to work
> in the fields and the dairy shed on the conditions of an Arab tenant
> farmer. We could use both the livestock and dry goods and seeds, and
> we were supposed to give him a fifth of the harvest. We got a place
> to sleep, but it was an awful place, and also an advance. We worked
> independently, on our own complete responsibility. We were
> responsible for organizing our own work. Krause used to sit with us
> once a week and advise us, as an expert, how to plan our week's work,
> in order to determine what our situation was and to help prevent
> mistakes. We asked him to give us lectures in agronomy. The workers
> there before us did not have a kitchen. The collective arranged a
> communal kitchen which some of these other workers also used. The
> relationship between these other workers and ourselves was very good.
> Despite that fact, they didn't believe that we would complete our year
> without a deficit, and they did not join us.   (Shohat 1929, 620)

Manya's idea was that in addition to their learning farming, these young Russian Jews could also learn how to organize a farm; they could acquire the skills to set up their own settlements and become independent of foreign philanthropy. She was able to entice the apprentices with the guarantee of a full year's employment and a remote place in which to engage in their efforts to set up a self-defense group. In October 1907 the experimental collective was established. Krause had agreed to a collective composed of eighteen people who would take responsibility for the fieldwork. This number was soon reached by drawing on people already on the farm, the Bar Giora group, other members of Poalei Zion, and newcomers. Some of the members were Poalei Zion people who had functioned as a collective of day laborers in Rishon Letzion and then for four months in the Jerusalem stonecutters commune. When that collective broke up, one member, Kayla Becker (Giladi), received a letter to join her friends in Sejera, which she did. A bit later she was joined by her sister, Zipporah, and her friend Alexander Zaid (see Giladi 1937, 135; Nadav 1986). Thus, those already in Sejera experienced the formation of the collective as a gathering of friends, relatives, and political allies. Strangers were immediately identifiable as "not one of us."

> In one of the meetings in Sejera of Bar Giora, there was talk of our members in Jerusalem and of the need to bring everyone together here. With great excitement we waited for them. And one day, while I was resting next to the wagon in the fields, Mendel Portugali came up to me and told me that they had come: Alexander Zaid, Yeheskel Hankin, and Gabriel, a person I had not yet heard of. We were surprised that Zipporah Zaid had not come. And only after a few days did I discover that "Gabriel" was none other than Zipporah, who had dressed in men's clothing, so that Arabs would not he able to recognize her on the road since they went on foot from Jerusalem along the length of the Jordan. We too wore black trousers at work in order to prevent the Arabs from understanding that we participated in the night watch.
>
> (Becker 1947, 511)

It is important to note several points about the members of the collective that contributed to its success: most already had experience in collectives; many were related to one another; and all were of the same political persuasion, some having known each other already in Russia. Many of the members were to fall in love with each other during the year—for example, Esther and Zvi Becker—or culminate their previous romances and marry as did Zipporah and Alexander Zaid. The lack of children at this stage made life somewhat easier for the collective. And although there were numerous violent conflicts with neighboring Arabs, these were on a small scale compared to the military problems that would later arise.

When negotiating with Krause for the establishment of a collective, Manya was adamant that it include women. She finally was able to convince Krause to accept women as full members even though in the rest of Palestine women were not given the same employment opportunities as were men (see Maimon 1960;

Bernstein 1987; Shilo 1981; Izraeli 1981). Manya believed that in addition to being unjust to women to deny them the right to do physical labor, it was also unfair to the Jewish community because working women could contribute to a "healthy Jewish future" (Schama 1978, 172). Under Manya's influence, Krause developed the reputation of being fair to and supportive of, women. Krause was even willing to take on women workers when there was a waiting list of men. Thus when Shifra Shturman arrived in Yaffa at the age of twenty-two, she was met by people who told her:

> There is only one little place, Sejera is its name, under the management
> of the agronomist Krause, in which there is hope for a young woman to
> obtain work [in the Galilee]. I went there and afterwards my sisters
> Ester and Sara came, and my brother Haim. One has to say to the
> credit of Mr. Krause that he accepted female workers despite the
> inclinations of the administration of the ICA and when it came to
> writing down the names of workers would substitute a male name for
> the female worker so no one would know. . . . Sejera was the first place
> open to women's work and there the idea of the movement of women
> workers started to blossom.   (Betzer 1947, 504–506)

Shifra was the first woman at Sejera. She later was joined not only by her sisters and Manya and the other women of the collective, but also by Lea Meron, Sara Hankin, Bilha Horowitz, Hanna Meisel, and others. These women, while not members of the collective, worked in close contact with them. Kayla Giladi shared Shifra's feelings of relief to be able to work at Sejera:

> In those days there was no possibility for girls of our type to find any
> kind of work. Not even as a servant in a private home. Krause was
> the first and only one who helped us learn to become competent in
> agricultural branches. He had a clear vision that agricultural settlement
> was not possible unless the wife (or woman) was also involved in it. In
> practice, we were equal in all the work with the boys. . . . Krause used
> to be proud of us, and when official visitors would come, he would bring
> them to the fields to show them the unforgettable picture of Jewish
> girls, wearing pants, ploughing behind the oxen.   (Giladi 1981, 62)

Many social movements involve a change in dress. The collective in Sejera was no exception. The women wore pants and other articles of men's clothing. Alexander Zaid wrote that the practice started after Zipporah came to Sejera dressed this way, and that Zvi Becker sewed the outfits for the women (Zaid 1947, 171). The women also carried arms (Zaid 1947, 172). Every morning before breakfast, they cleaned their oxen and prepared for their work in the fields. The women were also responsible for the kitchen (Giladi 1937, 136). In the evenings the men and women of the collective gathered to prepare the next day's work and to study. Krause taught them about modern agriculture; Manya lectured on socialism; Yisrael Shohat discussed the affairs of the day; David Ben Gurion (not a member of the collective but also on the farm) gave Hebrew lessons, and a local Arab taught them Arabic (Shva 1969). The collective established committees with specific functions, such as setting up the work assignments, and created ad hoc groups to settle disputes among members or with Krause.

The social relations among members and between them and Krause seem to have been excellent. The men and women of the collective admired Manya, Yisrael, and Krause, who in turn admired each other and the members of the collective. Kayla wrote about Manya and Yisrael: "Yisrael Shohat seemed to me to be a kind of Sheikh among his friends, and they were all under his personal influence and listened to him, even though they were all close to one another. . . . I became a good friend of Manya Wilbushewitz, who was very strong, and her idea was that all women should be strong and could thus take part in all the difficult and dangerous work which men do" (Giladi 1937, 136).

Shifra wrote about Manya: "Manya brought with her enthusiasm, and lively social and cultural life" (Better 1947, 505). Manya had the same influence on Ester Becker: "Manya was unlike the other women, both in her appearance and in her personality. She captivated me. Manya had enormous power of persuasion. She was the center of the life of the place. She approached everyone as a sister, as a mother. She was courageous in her nightly guard duty and in riding on a wild horse. She had enormous initiative; she had a feel for new ideas and actualized them in her life" (Becker 1947, 510).

Despite the success of the collective, its contract was not renewed after its year had expired. Most of the men had other preferences, and the ICA refused to continue with the experiment. Thus they developed the Jewish guard organization, Hashomer. Some of the members stayed on, while most moved elsewhere. Five of the women stayed behind to train the newcomers and to take on other jobs (Giladi 1937, 139). Zipporah Zaid, for example, cooked meals for Alexander Zaid and Yitzhak Nadav because when the collective left, the communal kitchen was shut down. At the time, Yitzhak, Zipporah, and Alexander lived together in a cave near the village, which Alexander felt was necessary so that they would achieve pure simplicity (Nadav 1986, 15). Yisrael Shohat was opposed to the women becoming guards, although he was persuaded to accept two (Zaid 1947, 174). Krause continued to give the women complete autonomy in managing the work and responsibility for training the newcomers, a situation which aggravated the newly arriving men.

It must be acknowledged that because Yisrael Shohat had brought his Bar Giora men to Sejera, he was as much the collective's leader as was Manya. During the experimental year, he convinced Manya that the idea of Jews assuming guard duty responsibility in place of Arabs was more important than continuing the collective agricultural experiment. Thus they established the Jewish guard organization, Hashomer. At the end of the contract period, Yisrael argued that the group was so small that it could not go on to Hauran to establish its own settlement, nor could it stay at Sejera which was a training farm. Moreover, Krause's superiors in Paris informed him that Manya could not stay at Sejera since she was a socialist. Thus, despite Manya's success, the group did not renew its agreement for another year with Krause. Manya and Yisrael became lovers at Sejera and in mid-May 1908, they married. Manya believed that only monogamous marriage complied with "the laws of nature." Rejecting free love, Manya was known for advocating freedom within marriage (Ben-Yocheved 1937, 389). Many couples followed Manya's and Yisrael's path and married. In subsequent years, most of these couples had children. Manya became instrumental in developing forms of collective childrearing although she was not successful in convincing the men of Hashomer to give women the same roles as men in guard duty.

Just as Manya had predicted, on the basis of her studies, the Sejera collective fulfilled the conditions of their contract with Krause, repaid what it owed, and made a small profit. Her experiment vindicated her belief that a collective agricultural economy was a viable means of Jewish settlement in Palestine given the conditions that existed in Sejera. In addition, the collective model demonstrated that workers did not have to live in degrading conditions and could sustain a cultural life. The group's simultaneous success in establishing Hashomer, the guard organization, would become a focal point for the lives of most of the members for decades to come. Finally, the collective supported her conviction that women were as capable of agricultural work as were men. For Manya, at the age of twenty-seven, the completion of the contract ended her search to identify the ideal socio-economic conditions. It is not surprising that when looking back on that year, she wrote: "That was the happiest year of my life. For all of us, those were beautiful days. . . . We sensed that in the future our experiment would be used as a landmark for many of the workers who would go to the land of the Jewish National Fund to work on their own responsibility; we felt that we were creating a basis for collective work for the future, for ourselves, and our children after us."

The positive experiment in Sejera produced several important results according to Manya:

> [1] we overcame doubts about living, producing, and working as a
> collective in Palestine and we forged a path for collective settlement.;
> [2] in the course of the year the collective life and the common goals
> of the members in Sejera tied the members to one another deeply
> and permanently; [3] the collective framework made it possible for
> the members of Bar Giora to realize, to strengthen, and further
> develop their self-confidence to establish Hashomer as a legal defense

organization that would train the population to defend whatever it had created, and to defend the whole nation. Only the Hauran plan we were not successful in realizing.

(quoted in Ben-Zvi 1976, 66; for a discussion of the group's relation to Hauran, see Zaid 1947, 173)

Interestingly, in her list of achievements at Sejera, Manya did not mention the other victory—the demonstration of women's ability. This omission is remarkable because after Sejera, when the group was transformed into Hashomer and some women went on to Um-Juni (later Degania), the women became very dissatisfied with their roles. In the next agricultural collectives (i.e., early kvutzot and kibbutzim) women were excluded or confined to kitchen and laundry work (see Betzer 1947; Izraeli 1981). Because of these problems, Hanna Meizel established a separate training farm for women at Kinneret in 1911 (Shilo 1981) and women workers organized by holding national meetings starting in Merhavia in 1914. Thus, Sejera has a unique place in the history of Jewish women in Palestine and in the history of socialist experiments. The ridicule of women by men was largely suppressed at Sejera during the collective period because of Manya's personal charisma, Krause's values, and the sheer number of women, which made them a substantial portion of the group. In the next collectives (kvutzot) established by groups at Degania and Kinneret, these factors were missing (see Betzer1947).

The evolution of Manya Wilbushewitz's thought and action up to 1907 thus took many different paths, which was characteristic of young Russian Jews of her time. Her supportive siblings, personal courage, close relations with a wide variety of people, her perseverance and charismatic personality may have made her even more open than others to the currents of contemporary thought. Although she went on to accomplish many similarly creative goals, her creation of the first Jewish agricultural collective in Palestine became a key factor in the creation of a strong socialist component of Israeli society. The role of a woman in laying the foundation for the subsequent development of kibbutzim, and the special role of women in Sejera are two of the many overlooked aspects of this period.

References

Becker, Ester. 1947. "From the Life of a Shomer Family: My Entry into the Guarding of Sejera." In *The Book of the Second Aliyah*, edited by Bracha Habas. Tel Aviv: Am Oved (Hebrew), 509–520.

Ben-Yocheved. 1937. "Dvorah Dreckler." In *The Hashomer Anthology*. Tel Aviv: Archive and Museum of the Labor Movement (Hebrew), 386–393.

Ben-Zvi, Yanait, Rahel. 1976. *Manya Shohat*. Jerusalem: Yad Yitzhak Ben-Zvi (Hebrew).

Bernstein, Deborah. 1987. *The Struggle for Equality: Urban Women Workers in Prestate Israeli Society*. New York: Praeger.

Betzer, Shifra. 1947. "With the First Ones in Um-Juni and Merchavia." In *The Book of the Second Aliyah*, 504–506.

Chizick, Hanna. 1947. "Haim Shturman." In *The Book of the Second Aliyah*, 720.

Dash, Joan. 1979. *Summoned to Jerusalem: The Life of Henrietta Szold*. New York: Harper & Row.

Frankel, Rafael. 1981. "Ideological Variations in the Forms of Collectives in the Days of the Second Aliyah." *Katedra*, 18:112–117 (Hebrew).

Giladi, Kayla. 1981. "Jewish Girls Plough with Oxen." In *The Beginning of the Kibbutz*, edited by Muki Tzur, Yair Zevulun and Hanina Porat. Tel Aviv: Sifriat Poalim (Hebrew), 62.

————. 1937. "From Sejera to Kfar Giladi," In *The Hashomer Anthology*, 135–146.

Givoni, Moshe. 1937. "The First Days." In *The Hashomer Anthology*, 528–531.

lzraeli, N. Dafna. 1981. "The Zionist Women's Movement in Palestine, 1911–1927." *Signs* 7:87, 114.

Krigser, Sarah. 1947. "The Start of Our Agricultural Training." In *The Book of the Second Aliyah*, 506–509.

Maimon, Ada. 1960. *Women Build a Land*. New York: Herzl Press.

Mandel, Neville. 1976. *The Arabs and Zionism before World War I*. Berkeley, Calif.: University of California Press.

Michaeli, Ben Zion. 1973. *Sejera, Its History and Personalities*. Tel Aviv: Am Oved (Hebrew).

Nadav, Isaac. 1986. *Memoirs of a "Hashomer" Member*. Israel: Ministry of Defense Publishing House (Hebrew).

Near, Henry. 1983. "To Each His Degania." *Katedra*, 29:63–78 (Hebrew).

Paz, Saadia. 1947. "The Collective in Sejera." In *The Book of the Second Aliyah*, 363–364.

————. 1937. "Conquests." In *The Hashomer Anthology*, 516–525.

Schama, Simon. 1978. *Two Rothschilds and the Land of Israel*. New York: Simon and Schuster.

Shapiro, Joseph. 1961. *Work and Land*. Tel Aviv: Am Oved (Hebrew).

Shilo, Margalit. 1981. "The Women's Farm at Kinneret, 1911–1917: A Solution of the Problem of the Working Woman in the Second Aliyah." *The Jerusalem Cathedra*, 1:246–283.

Shohat, Manya. 1904. "Chapters from the Beginning. A. Seeking a way." Mimeograph. Yad Ben-Zvi Archives, Jerusalem (Hebrew).

————. 1930. "The Collective." In *Women Workers Speak*, edited by Rachel Katznelson Shazar. Tel Aviv: Moetzet Hapoalot (Hebrew), 3–7.

————. 1932. "In the Beginning: the Collective." In *The Plough Woman: Records of the Pioneer Women of Palestine*, edited by Rachel Katznelson-Shazar. New York: Nicholas L. Brown, Inc., 19–26.

————. 1937. "Guard Duty in the Land."In *The Hashomer Anthology*, 51–56.

————. 1961. "The Roots of the Kibbutz Family." *Al Hamishmar*, 4, 9,61:8 (Hebrew).

Shva, Shlomo. 1969. *The Daring Tribe*. Merhavia: Sifriat Poalim (Hebrew).

Smilansky, Moshe. 1947. "First Meetings." In *The Book of the Second Aliyah*, 691–697.

Urofsky, Melvin. 1975. *American Zionism from Herzl to the Holocaust*. New York: Garden City, Anchor Press.

Weizmann, Chaim. 1949. *Trial and Error*. New York: Schocken Books.

Wilbush, Nahum. 1963. *Expedition to Uganda*. Jerusalem: Zionist Library (Hebrew).

————. 1974. "The Routes of My Life: Autobiography of Nahum Wilbush." In *Anthology of the History of Industry in Israel*, edited by Shmuel Avitzur. Tel Aviv: Melo, Ltd. (Hebrew), 9–18.

Zaid, Alexander. 1947. "The First Days." In *The Book of the Second Aliyah*, 165–178.

Daughters of the Nation

Between the Public and Private
Spheres in Pre-State Israel

"WE WANT EQUALITY and emancipation for women, which will enable us to fulfill our roles both as mothers and as effective individuals in society." Thus spoke the early pioneer Yael Gordon in 1914 to young women workers assembled for their first convention. Weaving together the public and the private, Gordon envisioned a reality in which the collective and the personal not only supplemented and complemented each other, but formed a single fabric:

> This must be our aim, especially in this young society being formed
> in Palestine out of the desire of the (Jewish) people to preserve its
> character and its "self" through work and creation. The young Jewish
> women who come here want not only to fulfill their national roles as
> daughters of our nation, but also to find themselves, the "self" of the
> woman-person, who has no more fitting place in the world in which to
> find the roots of her soul and to give it expression than in the workers'
> sector of our land.[1]

Gordon's vision of totality was directed at young women who had emigrated from Eastern Europe to Palestine. They had experienced severe difficulties, hardship, and disillusion, but they still maintained a dream of self-realization as wives and mothers and as shapers of the new society they planned to build. But this totality was never to come about, nor was it included in the dominant goals of their new Jewish society, which gave predominant position to the public and the collective, while pushing the personal and the private to the margins.

Yael Gordon and the women who congregated around her were part of the early waves of Zionist immigration. Towards the end of the nineteenth century and into the twentieth, large numbers of Jews began immigrating to Palestine. They came as settlers, under the auspices of the Zionist movement, aiming to establish a new Jewish community. It was to be a self-contained society, separate from its immediate Arab surroundings, which would develop its own institutions, culture, identity, and lifestyle. It aspired to establish (or reestablish) Palestine-Eretz Israel as the core of Jewish existence, to which many Jews would come, creating a Jewish majority. This community, known as the Yishuv (literally the settlement), was eventually conceived as a Jewish National Home, and as it grew and consolidated, it became the basis of a sovereign, independent state. The initial pioneering immigrations of the early twentieth century were composed of far more men than women, but the later, and much larger immigrations of families in the mid-1920s, the 1930s, and 1940s redressed the numerical imbalance.[2] Nevertheless, immigration to Palestine was hardly a gender-blind phenomenon. Quite to the contrary, the immigration policy toward women and men, as well as their roles in family life and in labor-force participation, were clearly and often explicitly, gender determined. The unequal and marginal position of women in the labor market, and their sole responsibility for family care, created a distinctly different life pattern for women than for men. The prime importance attributed to the public sphere, where women's participation was intermittent and often marginal, and the invisibility of the private sphere, women's main arena, reinforced the exclusion of women from foci of power and influence. Thus, while women shared in some of the processes of transformation resulting from Jewish immigration to Palestine, the consequences of their gender restricted the full impact of change.

To discuss the experience of women in the prestate Jewish society, the Yishuv, is to focus on the inexorable and contradictory pull and tension between the private and the public spheres. Women were there, they immigrated with the men, they settled with them in rural and urban settlements, and they were committed to the common goals of national redemption. They were members of political parties and of the Histadrut, the large and powerful General Federation of Jewish Labor; they voted for the elected institutions of the Jewish Yishuv and served in paramilitary organizations. Women also formed their own associations, working-class women establishing the Women Workers' Movement (WWM), affiliated with the Histadrut, and middle-class women founding separate organizations aimed at obtaining civic equality for women and advancing the welfare of the community. Nevertheless, their varied forms of participation could not conceal the essentially gendered nature of the new Jewish society and women's relative marginality within it.[3]

The Yishuv—A Society of Immigrants

Before to the end of the nineteenth century, small Jewish communities of Middle Eastern and North African and European (Ashkenazi) origin coexisted in

Palestine, then an outpost of Turkey's Ottoman Empire. By the end of the nine-teenth century, this small Jewish population, itself composed partially of immi-grants, witnessed the arrival of the early waves of Zionist immigration. After the First World War, with the beginning of British rule under a League of Nations mandate and the expression of British commitment to the establishment of a Jewish National Home, these waves of immigration increased and became the major source of the extremely rapid growth of the Jewish community.[4] The immi-gration policy of the British mandatory government was governed by two con-cerns, one economic and the other socio-demographic. The first emphasized the need to avoid the unemployment likely to occur due to excessive immigration. Thus, Jewish immigration was restricted to the number and types of people who could be expected to find employment in Jewish-owned economic enterprises. The second major consideration took into account the social needs of a self-contained community, that is, the creation of family life and natural growth, and thus encouraged the immigration of men and women in approximately equal numbers. As women found it far more difficult to find employment than men, they immigrated to Palestine primarily as the dependents of male immigrants, who were expected to find employment more easily and thus provide for their womenfolk.

This gendered pattern of immigration was shaped by the three categories of immigrants defined by the British authorities. First were immigrants who could be expected to provide their own income from independent means or a profes-sion which they could practice. Second were immigrants who had no means of their own and would have to find places of employment as wage earners. These immigrants were granted labor immigrant permits. The third group of immi-grants were defined as dependents, relying either on permit-holding immigrants or on residents of Palestine who would be responsible for providing their upkeep.[5] Men and women were distributed very differently among these three broad cat-egories. As women were far more vulnerable to unemployment, they were removed, to a major extent, from those classes of immigrants who were expected to make their own living on arrival in Palestine. Women were allowed to come as depend-ents, wives, and as elderly mothers, but only to a very limited extent as prospec-tive workers. Women were not entitled to the immigration permits granted to the owners of private means, even if they possessed such means, or shared them with their husbands. Nor could they be considered heads of families who would bring their dependent husband and children with them. Thus, married women only immi-grated to Palestine as the dependents of their husbands. Single women, who had no one to be dependent on, could obtain a labor immigration permit, but these were limited. As a result, although men and women immigrated to Palestine in similar numbers, two thirds to 90 percent of all women came as dependents, as compared to 10 to 20 percent of all men. Labor permits, on the other hand, were allocated to over 50 percent of all men and only to 10 percent of the immigrant women.[6]

It should be noted that women who immigrated to Palestine as dependents could later seek work, since there was no formal way of blocking such a possibility. Nevertheless, the categories of dependents were intended to ensure that those included in them had someone who would maintain them and thus avoid the need of their seeking employment. Furthermore, such a provider had to be, by definition, a man. A woman could not be recognized as the provider for her immigrant husband, even if she was capable of doing so. Nor could a woman resident in Palestine apply for the immigration of her parents, even if she was able to provide for them. Only her husband could formally undertake such a responsibility. Thus, already before their arrival in Palestine, women were considered hardly able to earn their own living, and certainly unable to have others dependent on them. This, most probably, reflects women's actual difficulties in Palestine's labor market, but it also reinforced the dominant perception of women as dependents rather than as self-sufficient entities capable of supporting others.

The occupational experience of women immigrants, prior to their immigration, tended to have a negative impact on their future prospects. Only a very small proportion of all adult women immigrants, between 10 and 20 percent, specified some previous occupational experience. A closer look will show how limited that experience actually was. The largest group among these women had been students, who had no practical experience in wage labor. Another group had been in agricultural training farms established by the various Labor Zionist youth movements. The training they received might have been useful for those joining collective agricultural settlements, but provided little benefit for the vast majority who ended up in urban centers. An additional group of women had worked in the manufacture of clothing, a common industry among the Jews of Eastern Europe, while another group claimed to have had previous experience in domestic service. Finally, only a small percentage of the respondents could attest to a skilled, white-collar, semi-professional occupation such as accountants, nurses, or teachers.[7] Certainly, the vast majority of the adult Jewish women who immigrated to Palestine had little relevant occupational experience to enable them to become active, equal partners, let alone self-sufficient members, of their new community.

FAMILY LIFE

The Yishuv was a society composed of families. Despite the emphasis on collective and cooperative associations, in practice no alternative was created for the family unit or for the functions it served, either in the urban centers or in the agricultural settlements—the moshavot and the moshavim—which together accounted for over 90 percent of the Jewish population.[8] Among the pre-Zionist communities of the Ashkenazi Orthodoxy and the Jews of Middle Eastern countries there was a strong commitment to the establishment of families, and women these communities tended to marry at a relatively early age. Among the more recent immigrants, soon to become the majority of the Jewish population, many arrived already married, and most others married as well, although at somewhat older ages than women in these longer established, tradition-oriented communities. According to two community studies conducted in Jerusalem and Haifa in the late 1930s, just over half of all women aged twenty to twenty-four were married. The rest, all but 5 percent, were married by thirty-five to forty.[9] There is little evidence of alternative lifestyles adopted by women who chose to remain single. Furthermore, the majority of women bore children, and there is little evidence of families who remained childless.[10] The number of children varied according to the ethnicity of the family and its socioeconomic status. On average, families of European (Ashkenazi) origin, who were predominantly of the recent Zionist immigration, had one to two children per family, while the Oriental and Sephardi families had five to six children. In the latter case, families of higher status and income tended to have fewer children, while the poorer families had far more.[11]

The Yishuv was family oriented ideologically as well as demographically. The varied Zionist utopian visions of the new Jewish society to be built in Palestine, which differed and even conflicted among themselves in many respects, shared a basically traditional view of the family and of woman's status within it, despite apparent rhetorical differences. Thus, socialist-radical Zionists advocated a reconstructed society which would liberate women from their traditional roles within the family, while in traditional religious Zionist circles such reform was strongly opposed. In fact, however, according to Rachel Elboim-Dror, in both extremes the traditional gendered division of labor and patterns of authority were well preserved with no serious pursuit of any alternative order of relations.[12]

The type of family which developed in the Yishuv did, indeed, embody traditional patterns. The family unit continued to fulfill the same functions it always had. As before, the women, and the women only, were responsible for the social roles to be carried out by and within the family-childrearing, socialization, and daily sustenance.[13] As before, this was done under the implicit or explicit authority of the men. In some cases, as in the Labor Movement, this was somewhat concealed by equality-conveying rhetoric, in which, for example, husband and wife were called "the two heads of family," and the right of married women to be economically independent of their husbands was fully acknowledged.[14] Nevertheless, such rhetoric had little impact on the working class, while true egalitarian practice within the family was never seriously contemplated by either leadership or rank and file.

The family, despite the important role it played in the vision of the society of the future, was hardly acknowledged in the present. It was all but invisible to those who determined what should be considered the major concerns of the

Yishuv. The male political, labor, and cultural elite established an implicit dividing line between the public and the private, the collective and the individual, the masculine and the feminine. And yet, precisely because of the many functions carried out within the family, orchestrated primarily by women, the latter could not be totally disregarded. Thus, fulfillment of their family roles was publicly valued not only as women's calling and obligation, but also as their contribution to the collective goal of nation-building.

To the extent that women carried out their expected roles, little note was taken of it. To the extent that they did not, they were held to be at fault. Thus, in 1943, the demographer Roberto Baki noted the low birthrate among newly arrived Jewish families, which fell well below the rate necessary for ensuring "the demographic future of the Jewish people." While he referred to families as the unit of reproduction, rather than specifically to women, he condemned the "massive use made by married women, of means of abortion."[15] Aba Houshi, the powerful workers' leader in the town of Haifa, criticized women far more directly and sharply. In a public address he claimed that women were responsible for the privatization of the family and its isolation from public concerns. Furthermore, he claimed that women endangered the future of the Labor Movement by their petit bourgeois lifestyles, which could threaten the solidarity of the movement and the socialization of the second generation.[16] Thus, the private actions of women within the family took on collective significance, but only by default, with none of the positive recognition which was awarded public action.

Within the Women Workers' Movement (WWM), which organized all women who were members of the Histadrut, the conception of the family and of women's role in it was different, although only to a limited extent. The WWM fully accepted that a woman's primary, although not necessarily exclusive, role was to care for her family. The bearing of children, motherhood, socializing and educating the younger generation, and the creation of a home, were women's vocation. They were women's duties, but also, claimed Rachel Katznelson, one of the leading figures of the WWM, their source of power, which neither the Movement, nor women individually, had yet learned how to use. But this was only half the story. According to the WWM, women, all women, and most especially married women, should not be restricted to their home and family, but should be active participants in the labor market. It was precisely this combination of "love and labor," so unique and so difficult, which was women's real vocation. Katznelson, addressing an assembly of young women workers, declared that while "work and family life are fierce enemies in the life of the female worker," this was not the case for the working man, who was able to combine his occupation, his public activity, and his family life without conflict. She called upon the WWM to recognize this immense problem, which differentiates between the status of men and women:

And yet, there are mothers among us . . . and if we ask ourselves: What
is it to be a mother, a worker's wife, and a mother? We must answer that
a family must have more than one child. And if we remember that the
worker's wife should educate the children, care for the house and its
upkeep, be in touch with doctors and educators, we may say once again:
enough, there is strength for no more. . . . This is the problem which
faces the WWM, which faces every woman worker. . . . We often forget
that work and motherhood are the sources of life. It is well known that
the sources of life cause difficulties. That does not indicate that women
are discriminated against, that an evil hand is abusing women. We must
educate the young women to understand that this [combination of work
and family] is also a source of happiness, of a rich and full life. . . . We
must turn to the young woman and say you have a great destination
before you; you must find the harmony between your two roles: being a
mother and being a worker.[17]

The male leadership of the Histadrut, the General Federation of Jewish Labor, one
of the most important elites of the Jewish community, did not refute this position.
They did not claim that a woman's place is in her home and her home alone. They
even paid rhetorical homage to women's equal right to be employed at all times,
whether single or married, in times of prosperity and in times of depression.[18] Yet
they did absolutely nothing to promote that right, to help women learn a trade,
or to provide services which would enable mothers more easily to leave their homes
for a full day of work. The WWM itself, which was established under Histadrut
t auspices at the urging of women activists to deal with women's acute difficulties,
was not able to do much better, since it had neither the power nor the resources
to make a substantial difference.

IN THE LABOR MARKET

The Palestine economy was not very hospitable to women. Frequent unemployment, competition from cheap Arab labor, and the predominance of infrastructure-
oriented industries were not conducive to the employment of women. The service
industry was also predominantly male for lack of other opportunities for men, leaving room for only a small proportion of qualified women. Thus, while male workers vacillated between periods of full employment and severe unemployment; women
at all times faced difficulties in finding work and retaining it.[19] Women's labor force
participation in Palestine increased over the years for which we have adequate information. In 1922, approximately 16 percent of all women over the age of fifteen
were employed. This rate of employment wavered somewhat but on the whole
increased steadily so that it reached 23 percent of women over fifteen by the end
of the 1920s, and close to 30 percent by the mid-1930s through the mid-1940s,
when employed women composed a small, but increasing, share of the total labor
force.[20]

The women who were employed were predominantly young and single and were dropping out of employment, to a major extent, on marriage. As such, the pattern of Jewish female employment in Palestine was similar to that in many other countries. Only approximately one quarter of the women who were employed had passed, the age of thirty.[21] Similarly, approximately three-quarters of all working women were single and only one quarter of them were married women. Both of these related factors changed somewhat during the years of the Second World War so that more women above the age of thirty were employed, and a larger proportion of them were married women. This might well be due to two factors: many young women had enlisted in the army, making room for somewhat older women, and as many men were enlisted, their wives then sought employment.

Women of Sephardi and Oriental communities exhibited somewhat different employment tendencies in the labor market. Gurevitz's 1943 study of the Jewish community in Jerusalem, with its half Ashkenazi and half Oriental population, demonstrates the lower level of labor force participation among Oriental women. While approximately 25 percent of Ashkenazi women of all ages were employed, only 15 percent of the Near Eastern women were. Or, from a somewhat different angle, while Ashkenazi women accounted for approximately one-third of all Ashkenazi wage earners, Near Eastern women accounted for approximately 23 to 24 percent of the wage earners of their communities.[22] The wage-earning women of these communities also differed somewhat in their age distribution. A proportionately larger share of working women among the Oriental communities were both very young and quite old. Three-quarters of the Ashkenazi working women were between the ages of twenty and fifty. Only about 10 percent were in their late teens (with very few younger), and 12 percent were above the age of fifty. Among the Near Eastern women, 10 percent of the female wage earners were girls aged ten to fourteen, while older women of fifty years and upwards were also more likely, relatively speaking, to be employed.[23] In general, married women were employed under two conditions: either when they were skilled, professional women or under conditions of extreme hardship.

The occupational distribution of Jewish women in Palestine was, on the whole, similar to that of women in other industrializing and already industrialized countries. Their gender was the major factor in explaining their occupational location, rather than the specificities of the Jewish Zionist settlement in Palestine. Only women's participation in agriculture, and the particular conditions under which this took place, was specific to the new Jewish experience. The other major female occupations—domestic service, the textile and clothing industry, the food industry, small commerce, clerical work, and liberal professions—were no different from those of women elsewhere.

Domestic service attracted the largest proportion of women prior to the large Zionist immigrations. According to an early survey of the Jewish community in

Jaffa, in 1905, 43 percent of employed women worked in domestic service, including cleaning, cooking, laundry work, and ironing.[24] Among Oriental communities, such as the community of Jerusalem, the proportion was still higher. According to Gurevitz, about 60 percent of employed Oriental women worked in domestic service,[25] a proportion that went up to 70 and 80 percent among Yemenite and Kurdish women.[26] But a high rate of employment in domestic service was characteristic of the Jewish Zionist immigrants from Europe as well, despite their higher level of education, their dislike for domestic service already established in their countries of origin, and their aspiration for creative labor, related to the construction of a new society. Domestic service, cleaning the homes of those who could afford to pay, although at low rates, was hardly a source of satisfaction. And yet, due to the absence of sufficient alternative employment opportunities, many women, between 30 and 40 percent of working women and possibly more, crowded into domestic service. Only during the Second World War, as other opportunities opened to women with no training or skills, did many leave domestic service. Here, too, the-trend in Palestine was very similar to that in many European countries.

The conditions of work were difficult. According to surveys carried out by the WWM in 1928 and 1929, women worked eight hours a day and more, and often as many as seven days a week.[27] The women complained of the degradation they felt from the condescending and authoritarian attitude of the lady of the house. This was expressed primarily by the Ashkenazi women, many of whom were young women who had to leave their agricultural communal settlements, and opt for the only work available in the towns for women with no special skills. It should be remembered that the Oriental women met with far greater exploitation and degradation, but left few accounts of their feelings. Frequent among the Near Eastern domestic servants were women fifty years and older and young girls, ten to twelve, who worked long hours cleaning, cooking, and shopping to help support their large families and to enable their brothers to attend school.[28] The rhetoric of collective solidarity, a favorite theme among the Yishuv's male elite, seemed more applicable to the public sphere than the private one of the mistress and the maid.

The other large concentration of women was in the garment and textile industry. This, too, was already a common situation in Europe by 1905, and needle skills remained one of the few types of industrial proficiency which women brought with them when immigrating to Palestine. At first women worked mainly in their homes. Soon factories were established by entrepreneurs who had been in the garment and textile trades prior to their immigration. These attracted many young women, some of whom had previous experience in the garment industry, while others learned the necessary skills on the job. The concentration of Jewish women in the clothing trades was also characteristic of the Jewish immigrants to the United States, especially in the large urban centers where much of the garment industry was in Jewish hands.[29] The wages paid to female industrial workers in Palestine were very low, far lower than those paid to the men, even for similar work.[30]

Lack of employment opportunities and lack of skills led other women to commerce and trade. These were mainly small family shops, which many of the families had run prior to their immigration, or at least had been familiar with, and for which there were plenty of customers from among the new settlers. Here, too, the pattern of employment was very similar to that of Jewish women who immigrated to the United States, despite the different ideological and political contexts of the immigrations.

The more advantageous occupations which women could obtain were clerical work and the liberal professions. The increase in women's schooling in many industrializing countries made them suitable candidates both for clerical work, and for further training in education and the medical professions. The Jewish women who immigrated from Eastern Europe were no less well educated than were women in Western Europe and North America, probably more so. Indeed, some women did obtain clerical work, while others were engaged in education, nursing, and to a much smaller extent, in medicine. At this time, all of these occupations were dominated by men. Clerical work was called for mainly in public and government institutions, where men were preferred, except in the highly routine work of stenography, typing, and telephone operation. Kindergarten teaching was done by women, as was much of primary education, but high school teaching was still predominantly male. Most of the doctors were men, although some women, who had received their medical training in Europe prior to their immigration, continued to practice medicine in Palestine.

So far, all of these trends were characteristic of the entrance of women into the labor market in Europe and North America in general, and among Jewish women in those locations in particular. The one significant difference in Palestine lay in the field of agriculture. In most industrializing and industrialized countries, the trend was for people to move from the rural to the urban sector. The Jewish immigration to Palestine entailed at least some movement in the opposite direction. Approximately a quarter of the Jewish population in Palestine lived in agricultural settlements, a situation which had not existed in Eastern and Central Europe prior to their immigration, and the other 75 percent lived in towns and urban centers. Women in the rural sector were employed largely in wage labor in the seasonal work of picking and packaging, mainly in privately owned citrus groves. Some were also members of cooperatives (moshavot), in which women had the heaviest load in that they had full responsibility for home and family as well as for much of the work of the farm. Others were members of the communal agricultural settlements (kibbutzim), where some of the women were responsible for the communal services of cooking, laundering, and child care, while others worked in agriculture, primarily the cultivation of vegetables and the care of livestock. The traditional nuclear family underwent far-reaching changes in the kibbutz, but, as Fogiel-Bijaoui and others argue, this did not change women's basic responsibility for motherhood, or eradicate tradition al male/female spheres in the allocation of work.[31] Working in agriculture was the one major change in the experience of Jewish women in Palestine, as compared to either the young women who remained in Europe or who immigrated to the United States. Much of the work in agriculture was typical of women agricultural workers and of women peasants elsewhere in the world,, though the social and political context of the Yishuv was very different from that of traditional, rural societies.

Relatively few middle-class women, who devoted most of their time and energy to their home and family, were employed. Yet, they too, sought ways to move beyond the limits of their private sphere and participate in the communal and national endeavor.

Through the Eyes of Middle-Class Women

Middle-class women enjoyed a significantly higher standard of living and were not vulnerable to the economic fluctuations which were so detrimental to working class families. Those few who were employed were primarily professional women who continued to pursue their careers after marriage. Many of the women devoted their full attention to the care of their families. Yet others perceived their caretaking role as extending beyond the limits of their private sphere and into the realm of the community. Their particular qualities as women, they claimed, would enable them to make a unique contribution to the evolving society, by tending to the welfare and hygiene of the needy: the poor, the sick, and the disoriented. For this purpose they established a variety of organizations, similar to organizations of middle-class, educated, liberal women in Europe and North America. Among these was the Federation Hebrew Women, which worked in close affiliation with Hadassah, an American Jewish women's Zionist organization, and WIZO, the Women's International Zionist Organization.[32] Their main concern was with poverty and nutritional and hygienic deficiencies which they encountered mainly in the ultra-Orthodox and the Oriental communities. They also were concerned with immediate problems of new immigrant families who met with severe difficulties in their new environment.[33] Through these activities they elevated their private commitment to the care of their families to a communal vocation and a national goal. Men were far too busy supporting their families and providing political leadership to society and state. It was up to the women to cater to society's social needs.[34]

The middle-class women activists were ambivalent in their attitude towards the pioneering women of the Labor Movement. On the one hand they had great respect for them. The *poalot*, women workers, epitomized the new Jewish woman who fully participated in the national movement and the building of the land. The liberal, middle-class women accepted, albeit ambivalently, the image of femininity cultivated by the young pioneering women. Although they argued at times that the pioneering women were adopting a "masculine stance," rejecting their beauty and denying their femininity, in most cases they accepted "simplicity" and "a natural look" as a legitimate form of feminine beauty: "None is more beautiful than the pioneer woman [the *halutzah*], wearing a light plain dress and a simple cloth hat adorned by curls, as she ascends the mountain path in the bright sun of Eretz Israel towards the huts of her commune, or as she does her work in the greenhouse." "Our young girl" continued the writer, "who imitates the ways of her boyfriend, who strides along with him wearing wide male sandals, does not want to eradicate beauty. But rather, her notions of beauty are different from those of the spoiled women who engage mainly in mental rather than in physical work. And indeed a number of young women have been able to attain a new form of beauty."[35]

Despite this acceptance, even glorification, of pioneering women, there was also strong ambivalence and reservation regarding them which centered on the aspiration of the working women, as perceived by their bourgeois observers, to emulate men. They attributed to the pioneering women the desire to eradicate every difference between men and women, to be as men are, to act as men act, walk as men walk, work as men work. They further argued that the women of the Labor Movement had indeed achieved full and absolute equality:

> Within the labor movement in Eretz Israel, women's equality has been achieved to the most extreme degree. All forms of work, from the cutting of stone to the managing of important enterprises, are done by the woman together with the man. . . . In her private life, as well, she is given the complete right of independent action.
>
> Furthermore, due to the serious intention of helping women attain equality, men share in the work of the kitchen and the farm, doing what is considered "women's work," so as to clear the way for women to enter "men's work."[36]

This perspective and course of action, it was argued, was wrong and harmful. The denial of any difference between women and men caused, the former to take on hard physical labor which was damaging to their present and future health, and might damage the "health and the harmonious order of the nation."[37] Their denial of the special role of women in the construction of society, it was further claimed, diverted them from any alliance with others of their sex for the advancement of women's social work among those in need. Thus, the controversy over the definition of femininity and over the relations between the masculine and the feminine, was perceived as having a broad national significance.

It can be said with all fairness that the women of the working class, the majority of whom were directly affiliated with the Labor Movement, enjoyed much less equality than middle-class women imagined. As noted above, they, too, were seen primarily as dependent on their husbands. Most of them, once married, were no longer employed, and most of the employed women were not married. Nevertheless, their view of the relation between women and men, and between the private and the public spheres, was indeed different from that of middle-class liberal women. The activists of the WWM aspired to harmonize between the private sphere, which they also saw as women's particular domain, and the public sphere, which they sought to share with men. They did not see their role in the public sphere as an extension of their domestic lives: the WWM insisted that in this realm there was no uniquely feminine role or vocation and that here, if only potentially, women were equal members of the same movement.

The ambivalence of the middle-class activists towards the women of the Labor Movement was not extended to the women of the Oriental communities, with whom they came in contact almost solely as providers of aid and guidance. Their reference to the Oriental family, and the women within it, was almost always in terms of the hardship and deprivation experienced by these women, often burdened with the care of small children, who were either married to husbands unable to make a living, or were widowed.[38] Begging was rampant in this community where children, especially young girls, whose educations were extremely limited, were often sent to work. Girls of twelve and thirteen were married off, either to young boys only three or four years older, who were little able to provide for a new family, or to much older men, widowers in most cases. Child mortality was very high. According to one survey carried out by the Federation of Hebrew Women, eight to nine children had died in each of the families of the poor neighborhood of Shimon Hatzadik Jerusalem, populated by 120 families who immigrated from "countries of the east."[39] The women were weighed down by poverty, deprivation, and exploitation. A member of the Federation of Hebrew Women from Tiberias wrote, "These women live a life of sorrow. Poverty, want, and illness, beatings by a husband angered by lack of income, these are her daily lot. If the woman bears no children she is beaten by her husband, as she is if she bears no sons. And to whom can the miserable woman turn, who will protect her?"[40] This mixture of censure and compassion has little to say about any other aspect of these women's lives, nor were any attempts made to present the ways they perceived themselves, their relations with others, their hardships, or their aspirations.

Overwhelming difficulties affected many women, Orientals and others. Day-to-day difficulties were most severe for women who had to fend for both themselves and their families. They were not expected to fulfill that role, they usually did not have the skills to do so, and little help was extended by the institutions of the Yishuv.

Women on Their Own:
The Hardship of Everyday Life

Despite the predominance of the nuclear family and its internal, gender-based division of labor, many women did not fit neatly within this model. Although the basic social design and immigration policy conceived of women as "dependents" who could not take on the responsibility of supporting themselves or others, such situations did occur. Some women were self-sufficient, while others also supported their children, and frequently other family members such as older parents and younger siblings. Single women who arrived alone in Palestine had to live on their own earnings. Although 50 percent of all women were married by the age of twenty-five, another 50 percent remained single for some years more. Many such single women initially became members of agricultural collectives. As time went by, however, financial demands from family back home frequently forced them to leave the collective and move into town, where they expected to earn some money. The triple pressure of having to find scarce work, to earn enough to make ends meet, and to have some money left over to send to their needy families caused severe hardship for many young women.

There were also women who arrived in Palestine as dependents, but due to changed circumstances had to fend for themselves. Some came as dependents of residents of Palestine, for example, a young girl brought over by her brother, or an older woman who joined her son or daughter.[41] Often, the economic condition of the local residents had changed, due to recurring unemployment, and the dependent newcomer had to join those searching for work. Married women who had depended on their husbands' income found themselves the sole source of their family's support, despite a lack of skills and experience and heavy demands at home, when the hard depression which hit the economy of Palestine after 1936 created large-scale unemployment.

There were still other women who had been supported by their husbands or by their partners who found themselves unexpectedly on their own. This could come about in numerous ways. Among the young men and women of the pioneering movements an intimate and romantic attachment did not necessarily lead to marriage. Couples often lived together for some time, especially in the communal settlements, before formalizing their relationship. It sometimes happened that such couples parted, possibly after a child was born, and young women found themselves on their own, totally unable to meet the daily needs of shelter, nourishment, and child care while the mother was off looking for work. *Dvar HaPoelet*, the journal of the WWM, told the story of one such young woman who had immigrated to Palestine with the man she loved, with whom she had had a free and informal commitment. On arrival in Palestine, the young man left her and joined a group which settled in a kibbutz while she remained in town, a worker. There she waited for her child: "She dreaded the reality surrounding her. Once she sought to abort the child, but the doctors could not do so and he stubbornly continued his existence, until, in due course, he emerged into the world. . . . She looked at him and wondered to herself how she would manage with the child, where would they find bread to eat, a shelter over their heads?"[42] After months of hardship and despair, she had to take the child to the kibbutz where his father lived and, heartbroken, leave him there.

Yemenite women were vulnerable in yet another way. Taking a second wife was an accepted custom in their community, and older women, mothers of five, six, and seven children, found themselves solely responsible for their upkeep, if their husband chose to prefer a second, much younger, wife.[43] Finally, there were the widows, women who probably were not employed previously, but having lost their husband, the primary provider of the family, had to fend for themselves. The rate of widowhood among women seems to have been surprisingly high. Among women over the age of fifty, according to Gurevitz's study, approximately 50 percent were widows, just under 50 percent in the case of Ashkenazi women, and slightly over 50 percent among the women of the Oriental communities.[44] Among the widows were women who had young children still dependent on them, which further exacerbated the difficulty of obtaining a sufficient income.[45]

These varied circumstances caused grave difficulties for many women. We first hear of acute hardship among women during the First World War, a time of great distress for the Jewish communities of Palestine as a whole. In later years, with the increased immigration of the mid-1920s and the ensuing depression, many young women were in urgent need once again. Helvig Gelner, responsible for the affairs of women workers in the Labor Department of the Zionist Executive, wrote of the poor health of many of the single women who could not afford proper food or proper medical care:

> Most of the young single women in Tel Aviv and in Haifa are not members of Kupat Holim [the Histadrut Sick Fund]. When they enter the country the Immigration Department [of the Jewish Agency] pays one month's dues on their behalf. But, due to the severe economic condition of the women workers today, most of the women don't continue to pay their dues, and are not eligible for care and medical help in time of illness. The lack of sufficient work, and the strenuous tasks in which women are employed, are an added cause for various illnesses. It is precisely those women workers who live under the most difficult conditions, and are thus most vulnerable to illness, who are unable to pay their dues, and are therefore denied treatment, and even a place to lie in times of sickness.[46]

Their condition, she adds, continues to deteriorate until they become severely, irreparably ill.

In the 1930s the WWM established a labor exchange to attend to women's special needs and difficulties in finding employment. And yet, there was little they could offer. Work was scarce, and much of it was outside of the towns, where most women, especially mothers, did not want to go. All that the women's labor exchange could offer was domestic service or cleaning work in public institutions. Even these positions were scarce, and the competition for them was strong. Two letters written in April of 1938, by women who had been turned down by the women's labor exchange, tell their own stories and those of many Gila Bloch, a single woman who arrived in Palestine in 1925, described the difficulties she had faced during the years since her arrival:

> Thirteen years ago I arrived in the country. Since then I have been a member of the Histadrut. When I came, in 1925, I joined a women workers' training farm where I worked for two and a half years. From there I moved to Degania A [a kibbutz] where I worked until 1930. For personal reasons I left the collective. From that time I began my struggle for existence as a single woman worker. For a long time I worked in domestic service. At times I suffered from unemployment. During all the years after I left Degania A I supported my elderly parents living in Russia and sent them every penny I could. In 1934 I was sent by the women's labor exchange to work in the boarding school of the Reali high school and I worked there for less than two years. Because of cuts I was fired in August 1936. In December of that year I was called back for three more months, and from March 1937, to this day I have not been working. For a year and a half I have been unemployed. During this time I was allocated only two days of work by the labor exchange.[47]

Esther Dantziger was also a single woman who had to support members of her family. She too had arrived over ten years earlier, but found herself unable to provide for her own needs or for those dependent on her:

> For the past two years I have borne the burden of a large family. . . . [This has been] well beyond my ability. I have not been working for five months. I had to undergo an operation and I lost my place of work. Since then I hoped to obtain work in a babies' home taking care of babies. I was not given the job as I lacked formal training, even though I had the experience. I was promised work in the kitchen but I have now learned that there are difficulties there, as well, and my chance is not great. My elderly parents are dependent on me, and so is my brother who arrived in the country a few months ago, with wife and baby. In addition, I brought over my orphaned niece, who is also in need of my help. I myself came to the country in 1927, and I think that in every respect I deserve the vacant job in the babies' home.[48]

Some of the difficulties related in these letters were relieved during the years of the Second World War, as unemployment ceased and there was much demand for workers. Nevertheless, single women still faced severe difficulties and marginalization since wages were low, the cost of living spiralled, and accommodation was both scarce and overpriced.

Conclusion

Women of all classes, social movements, and communities in the Yishuv were primarily wives and mothers, with total responsibility for their family's domestic needs. Women were far less apparent in the public sphere, even though there were no formal regulations prohibiting women from public action and no ideological conceptions that portrayed women as belonging in their homes alone. Many women were employed, including married women, and there were women who were active in the different political parties, and others who established separate or autonomous women's organizations, such as the WWM and the Federation of Hebrew Women. Nevertheless, a clear line of demarcation did exist, explicitly and implicitly, between the private and the public spheres, and this dichotomy did not disappear as Yael Gordon had optimistically predicted in her 1914 speech. Nor did these separate and distinct spheres supplement or complement each other. The masculine and predominantly male public sphere was where the most valued actions-politics, institution building, economic development in short, all that was equated with nation building, took place. Women were active in. it, but only a few, to a limited extent, and not at the very center. The feminine and predominantly female private domain was where the backstage action took place, where families were nurtured, and children were socialized, but this private sphere was never valued in itself. The contribution of "the daughters of the nation" within their homes was measured, if at all, only by the direct and indirect impact of their actions on the public arena. It was only there that contributions were acknowledged, and thus women's efforts and experiences, trials and tribulations, remained largely unnoticed.

Notes

1. Yael Gordon, cited in Deborah S. Bernstein, *The Struggle for Equality: Urban Women Workers in Prestate Israeli Society* (New York: Praeger,1987), 6.
2. Jewish immigration to the United States at the turn of the century was also one of families for the most part. See Paula E. Hyman, "Gender and the Immigrant Jewish Experience in the United States." In *Jewish Women in Historical Perspective*, edited by Judith R. Baskin (Detroit, Mich.: Wayne State University Press, 1998), 312–336.
3. The historiography of this period has, until recently, had little to say about women's experience or the gendered nature of the Jewish society of the Yishuv. For a discussion of the reasons for this, see Deborah S. Bernstein, "Introduction." In *Pioneers and Homemakers: Jewish Women in Pre-State Israel*, edited by Deborah S. Bernstein (Albany: State University of New York Press, 1992), and other relevant articles in this anthol-

ogy. Valuable primary documents are preserved in *The Plough Woman: Memoirs of the Pioneer Women of Palestine*, edited by Rachel Katznelson Shazar, trans. Maurice Samuel (New York: Herzl Press, 1975 [1932]).

4. A. Gertz, *Statistical Handbook of Palestine—1947* (Jerusalem, 1947), 46–47.

5. For a detailed discussion of immigration policy, as well as its gender implications, see Aviva Halamish, "Immigration and Absorption Policy of the Zionist Organization, 1931–1937." (Ph.D. diss., Tel Aviv University, 1995), esp. 248–253.

6. Halamish, "Immigration and Absorption Policy," 394–413; *Report on the Administration of Palestine* [Hebrew]; and see "Palestine," Department of Migration, *The Statistics of Migration and Naturalization* (Jerusalem, 1944), 351.

7. Report on the Administration of Palestine, for the years 1933, 44; 1934, 74; 1937, 64; 1938, 72; 1940, 39; Department of Migration, Statistics, 1942, 18; 1943, 18.

8. The kibbutz was the one place that did provide alternatives for many family functions by making them the responsibility of the commune. Nevertheless, despite important improvements, women remained responsible for most of the parenting and for carrying out the various communal services traditionally associated with the domestic realm such as laundry, kitchen, and child care responsibilities.

9. David Gurevitz, *The Jews of Jerusalem* (Jerusalem, 1940), 52.

10. Roberto Baki, "The Custom of Marriage and Birth among Different Segments of the Yishuv and Its Influence on Our Future." In *Immigration, Settlement and Natural Mobility among the Population of Palestine* [Hebrew], edited by Roberto Baki (Jerusalem, 1945), 105–248.

11. The families of the Ashkenazi Orthodox communities were similar in this respect to the Oriental communities, and also in their large number of children.

12. Rachel Elboim-Dror, "Gender in Utopianism: The Zionist Case." *History Workshop* 37 (1994):99–117.

13. Deborah S. Bernstein, "Human Being or Housewife: The Status of Women in the Jewish Working Class Family in Palestine of the 1920s and 1930s."In *Pioneers and Homemakers*, 235–259.

14. Deborah S. Bernstein, "On Rhetoric and Commitment: The Employment of Married Women during the Depression of 1936–1939." *Women's Studies International Forum* 20, 5–6 (1997):593–604.

15. Roberto Baki, *Natural Growth in Palestine and the Future of the Yishuv* [Hebrew] (Jerusalem, 1943), 13, 15.

16. Aba Houshi, quoted in Bernstein, *Struggle for Equality*, 192–194.

17. From a lecture of Rachel Katznelson in a seminar of women workers, Tel Aviv, 1937. Yad Tabenkin Archive, Efal. Collection of Lilia Basevitz, Unit 15.

18. Bernstein, "Rhetoric and Commitment."

19. The most comprehensive study of women's role in the labor market is that of Hanna Zacks Bar-Yishay, "Female Labor Force Participation in a Developing Economy, Pre-State Israel as a Case Study," 2 vols. (Ph.D. dissertation, University of Minnesota, 1991). See also Bernstein, *Struggle for Equality*.

20. Bar-Yishay, "Female Labor Force Participation," 128.

21. Ibid., 134–138.

22. Gurevitz, *Jews of Jerusalem*, Tbs. 10, 23.

23. Ibid., tbs. 27, 28, 10.

24. Bar-Yishay, "Female Labor Force Participation," 140.

25. Gurevitz, *Jews of Jerusalem*, Tb. 29.

26. Ibid., tb. 25.

27. Bernstein, *Struggle for Equality*, 74–84.

28. A number of articles describing the domestic service of young girls appeared in the journal of the WWM, for example, "The Two Girls" [Hebrew], *Dvar Ha-Poelet* 3 (1936):174; "In the Grocery," [Hebrew], *Dvar HaPoelet* 5, 2–3 (1938):64.

29. See Susan A. Glenn, *Daughters of the Shtetl* (Ithaca: Cornell University Press, 1990), 90–131.
30. Bernstein, *Struggle for Equality*, 129–130.
31. See Sylvie Fogiel-Bijaoui, "From Revolution to Motherhood" in *Pioneers and Home-makers*.
32. Middle-class liberal women also played a leading role in the campaign for women's suffrage and established the Association of Hebrew Women for Equal Rights in Eretz Israel.
33. Herzog, "The Fringes of the Margin," 290.
34. The Federation of Hebrew Women published a journal called *Ha-Isha* (The Woman), during the years 1926–1928. It is a good source from which to learn both about the activities of these women and about the way they perceived themselves and others.
35. "Reviews," *Ha-Isha* 6 (1928):11.
36. *Ha-Isha* 2 (1926):6.
37. Ibid., 7.
38. All examples are taken from write-ups in Ha-Isha. The WWM expressed a very similar approach to Oriental women in its journal, Dvar Ha-Poelet.
39. "Social statistics of the Neighborhood Shimon Hatzadik in Jerusalem" [Hebrew], Ha-Isha 4-5 (1926): 32.
40. Tova Gurevitz, "Life of the Hebrew Woman in Tiberias." [Hebrew] *Ha-Isha* 4–5 (1926):38.
41. Despite the formal policy that women were not able to bring over family members as their dependents, we do hear of cases in which this was done.
42. "The Mother." [Hebrew] *Dvar Ha-Poelet* 3, 4–5 (1936):80–81.
43. For example, "Family Troubles among the Yemenites." [Hebrew] *Dvar HaPoelet* 8 (1938):268–269.
44. Gurevitz, *Jews of Jerusalem*, Tb. 10.
45. One reason for the high proportion of widows in Oriental communities was the tendency to marry older men to very young women. Thus, when a man died he might well leave behind a much younger widow, still tending to the needs of small children.
46. Helvig Gelner in a report to Joseph Shprintzak, 16 June 1926, Central Zionist Archives, S9/1807.
47. Gila Bloch to Appeals Committee of the Haifa Labor Council, April 1938. Archive of Haifa Labor Council, Haifa, 40–57–119.
48. Esther Dantziger to Appeals Committee of the Haifa Labor Council, April 1938. Archive of Haifa Labor Council, Haifa, 40–57–119.

TAMAR MAYER

From Zero to Hero

Masculinity in Jewish Nationalism

In late 1994, a year after the signing of the Oslo Accords, one of Israel's major newspapers, *Yediot Achronot* carried a lead story entitled "We used to be men, now we are zero" (November 11, 1994). This story concerned members of an elite military unit who had deserted their post because they were so disappointed by the turn that their military service had taken, once Israel began training soldiers for peacekeeping missions after pulling out of the Gaza Strip and beginning its withdrawal from the West Bank. No longer were these young men able to perform the tasks which had motivated them to join this elite unit, during the days of the *Intifada* and for which they had trained to be, in their own words, "killers" who enforced Israeli military rule among Palestinians (Shachor 1994, 6).[1] Now, as a result of the Oslo Accords, the soldiers said, they were instead assigned to guard daycare centers in Jewish settlements. "What started as an attempt to be a man, turned into an addiction for action," (Shachor 1994, 6), said one of the deserting soldiers in an attempt to justify his unit's act. These soldiers rail from duty, as they said in the article, because in peace missions there is no action, no glory, no rush.

In short, several of them said in their testimony, they had wanted to join the elite unit because they believed that in the Israeli Defense Forces (IDF) they would get a chance to become "real men," they would be transformed "from nerds, from zero" into units of a "mighty machine" that would enable them to give everything, even their blood, "for the country, for their flag" (ibid.). In 1994, just as peace seemed a real possibility, those young men actually claimed to feel cheated by the military: instead of becoming real men, they now felt they were zero.

While this story of desertion may be uncommon among Israeli soldiers, it provides, nevertheless, a rare inside look at the way many young Israeli men have

come to feel about volunteer service in elite military units. The strong relationship
between masculinity, militarism, and Jewish nationalism articulated by these men
has its origins in the early days of Zionism when Jews, first in Europe and later
in Palestine, felt forced to defend themselves against the Other—first European
nationalists whose anti-Semitism was already well established by the early days
of Zionism, and then the indigenous Arab population of Palestine who resented
attempts by Zionist immigrants for take over and "Judaize" Arab lands.[2] Over
the course of the twentieth century the constant threat, real or imagined, of annihilation has made Israeli Jews rely heavily on military and physical strength; in
turn, militarism has become intimately connected to the construction of both
Jewish nationalism and Israeli Jewish masculinity. Although both Jewish men
and women in Israel are conscripted into the Israeli Defense Forces, it is men
who "do the real defense work" (Izraeli 1994). They are the ones who actually
serve in combat and eventually risk their lives for Israel's survival. Especially in
the most decorated units, as a result, a cult of heroism has developed among young
Jewish men. And the continuous sense of threat from the Arab world to Israel's
existence has further sanctified the IDF as a major institution in Israeli society—
justifying, reinforcing and even sharpening the image of the Jewish warrior, whose
masculine identity has become intertwined with Israel's security. For many Israeli
Jewish men, in fact, the military has become the only rite of passage into
manhood. As long as Israelis believe that they have enemies who remain committed to Israel's annihilation, the priority of defense will continue to shape
Jewish nationalism in Israel, and the military will continue to prevail as one
of the major institutions in the lives of Israeli Jews and an important arena of
masculinity.

   In this essay I shall examine the close relationship between nationalism and
masculinity in Zionism during the first decades of the twentieth century. I focus
here on the foreign, specifically German, influence on the construction of the masculine New Jew, and on the subsequent development of the Jewish warrior ideal
in Palestine. The central role that Zionist youth movements, the new Hebrew education and paramilitary activities played in this construction are also discussed here,
because they too have been instrumental in the construction of the New Jew, the
mythological symbol of Jewish nationalism.

   Although it is well established by now that gender identities are generally constructed in opposition to one another and that we cannot understand the construction of the masculine without understanding the construction of the feminine,
in Israel and in other societies that have perceived themselves to be under siege,
militarism continues to be instrumental in the construction of gender identities.
I focus here, therefore, on the interrelationship in Israel between militarism and
masculinity, and leave a thorough analysis of masculinity in opposition to femininity to others.[3] The relationship between masculinity and militarism has had

a profound effect on the kind of nationalism that was born with Zionism and which later has been refined in Jewish Israel. The almost intimate relationship between masculinity and Jewish nationalism is, I believe, a product of the initial Zionist project, which assigned men and women different positions in society, and an outcome of modern Jewish history's survivalist orientation, which has led to a prioritizing of national security needs that has constructed men as superior to women. This notion of male superiority is further anchored in Jewish religious tradition, especially as there is no constitutional separation in modern-day Israel between what might be called "church and state."

Jewish Nationalism and Masculinity

Almost from its inception, Jewish nationalism has been closely intertwined with masculinity. The transformation of "the political status, the socioeconomic profile, and the psychological self-image of the Jews" in Europe (Shimoni 1995, 3) —central to Zionism—was based, in large part, on the construction of the New Jew, the Muscle Jew. Most of the gender references to the Muscle Jew are to men, illuminating the connection between masculinity and Zionism and the invisibility of women in Zionism.

Although Zionist writings appear as early as the mid-nineteenth century, Zionism became an organized movement only in the late 1890s, as Theodor Herzl, the father of modern Zionism, organized the first Zionist Conference in Basel in 1897. At a time when many people in Europe perceived the nation as the legitimate foundation of the state, Herzl appreciated Bismarck's success in mobilizing the German masses around the nationalist banner and dreamed of a similar future for the Jewish nation.[4] He dreamed that nationalism would free the Jews from problems caused by two thousand years of living in exile. Significantly, as also in the German case, Herzl's quest for freedom was associated with a complete transformation of the national as well as the individual character—both of which, in his view, involved notions of manliness. Herzl's explicitly gendered contempt for European Jewry is captured well in his diary when on June 8, 1895, after visiting with some well-to-do and educated friends, he wrote, "They are Ghetto creatures, quiet decent timorous. Most of our people are like that. Will they understand the call to freedom and manliness?" (Herzl 1956, 39). Clearly for Herzl manliness and freedom were closely tied together, and both directly connected to militarism and patriotism. Herzl planned to call up historical events of mythical proportions, such as the legendary Maccabee fighters (almost all men), as a way to set the stage for and to mobilize the nation and the actors of Zionism. On June 7, 1895 he wrote: "I must train the youth to be soldiers. But only a professional army. Strength: one tenth of the male population; less would not suffice internally. However, I educate one and all to be free and strong men ready to serve as volunteers if necessary.

Education by means of patriotic songs, the Maccabean tradition, religion, heroic stage-plays, honor" (Herzl 1956, 37).

For Herzl the most important idea of Zionism was to teach Jewish men—the principal figures of Zionism—to be free and to reclaim the masculine past of the nation. This was necessary, he believed, because years of life in the Diaspora had given Jews many feminine characteristics and made them, as a result, easy targets for anti-Semitism. As Zionism would free the Jews of Europe from their constant battles with anti-Semitism, create a Jewish national culture, normalize Jewish national life and offer Jews the tools with which to negotiate with both modernity and anti-Semitism, Herzl hoped it would also free them from their "feminine" nature.

Although women, too, were ghetto dwellers and were integral to the makeover of the Jewish people that Herzl hoped for, women were clearly not essential to Herzl's program for national change. In Herzl's vision women did not need to be transformed in the way men did because there was no real dissonance between their behavior and their gender identity. As a result, women were not as central to Zionism as men as a diary entry (June 11, 1895) makes clear: "No women or children shall work in our factories. We want a vigorous race. The state takes care of needy women and children. Old maids will be employed in kindergartens and in mothering the orphans of the working class. I will organize these spinsters into a corps of governesses for the poor" (Herzl 1956, 41). As Herzl saw Zionism, women's importance seems limited to their role in reproducing and sustaining the Jewish nation. Women did not feel in the early days of Jewish nationalism that they occupied secondary roles. They rather believed that Zionism offered them a new kind of equality: the right to vote and to be elected to office. But once they actually emigrated to Palestine to create the new society, women came to realize that their dream of equality between the sexes was not likely to be achieved; that in fact their position in the new society and in the new land of Israel was not much different from what it had been in Europe (Bernstein 1987).

Zionism and the New Jew

Thus the national project of Zionism was to transform Jewish life in the Diaspora, which was possible, many believed, only by creating a new person, the New Jew, the New Hebrew. The New Jew was to be the antithesis of the ghetto Jew whom Herzl and other Zionist thinkers saw as helpless, passive, and feminine and thus in need of major transformation: Ironically, the early Zionists' notion of the Jews' passivity and femininity was actually in many ways an internalized version of the prevailing anti-Semitic view of the time. The impulse to feminize the Other was not new in the late nineteenth century; it had enabled modern society to build cohesiveness (Mosse 1996) and influenced much of the anti-Semitic rhetoric of the time.[5] The Jewish man's passivity was often caricatured and ridiculed on the streets of Europe and in European newspapers.[6] Even more, the Jewish man's body was seen as "aged, weak, or effeminate," calling up yet another countertype to modern masculinity: homosexuality (Mosse 1996, 70). The Jewish male's stereotyped body was "given specific bodily features and measurements to demonstrate [his] difference from the norm" (ibid.). Like the homosexual, the Jewish man was seen as limp and slim, and both the Jewish man and the homosexual were condemned as transgressors of a masculine standard of beauty.

Given a prevailing anti-Semitic discourse in Germany during the late 1890s, it is no surprise that the fathers of Zionism dreamed that national liberation would bring "freedom and manliness" to the Jews of Europe. And because most of the Zionist writings in the late nineteenth and early twentieth centuries focus on the Jewish man's body, the Jewish woman and her body remained invisible. "In the collapse of Jewish masculinity into an abject femininity, the Jewish female seems to disappear" (Pellegrini 1997, 109). Therefore, even as Jewish women escaped the anti-Semitic ridicule to which Jewish men were subjected, they also were left out of the body and character reform advocated by Zionist thinkers such as Herzl and his close associate and second in command Dr. Max Nordau.

A major element of the Zionist reform agenda involved social engineering that intended to create a dignified, masculine "Muscle Jew." Nordau called on the Jews to reconnect with their Jewish past and with ancient Jewish heroes like Bar Kochba, "to again become deep-chested, strong-limbed, and fierce-looking men" (Nordau 1900,10). The New Jew's characteristics were to mimic those of the gentiles: tall, virile, close to nature, and physically productive. The New Jew was to become in some sense an *Übermensch*, a superhuman, whose fit body would help his Jewish mind to excel and who would thus be able to stand up to anti-Semites.[7]

The transformation of the Jewish man's body would best he accomplished, Dr. Nordau believed, through involvement in gymnastics. As a psychiatrist, Nordau believed that he saw many physical and mental similarities between Jews and "degenerates," who in his view were "not just criminals prostitutes, anarchists, and pronounced lunatics [but also] authors, and artists" (Nordau 1895, vii).[8] Because of physical and mental similarities that the two groups exhibited—physical frailty and a tendency toward nervousness—Nordau prescribed gymnastics as a healing regimen for both Jews and "degenerates." Gymnastics, Nordau believed, would be the most effective way for Jews to develop their bodies. "Solid stomachs and hard muscles will allow Jews to overcome their stereotype . . . to compete in the world . . . and to recapture [their] dignity" (quotes from Nordau's essays in Mosse 1993, 164) and to calm what he observed as nervousness in both groups. Specifically, a physically fit body, according to Nordau, would lead to creating a masculine identity (Mosse 1993, 165) and to what later would be referred to as the "muscle Jew."[9]

Given the historical events of the twentieth century, it seems ironic as well that much of the Zionist ideology of nation and masculinity was derived from the German experience. Nordau's and Herzl's commitment to gymnastics as a way to achieving the desired transformed body was in fact greatly influenced by the German philosophy and practice of the day. Gymnastics had been essential both to the construction of masculinity and to national ideology throughout Europe but most specifically in Germany since the early nineteenth century (Kruger 1996; Mosse 1996, 1993, 1985; Hoberman 1984). In Germany, gymnasts became the "national stereotype in the making" (Mosse 1985, 50) and gymnastics festivals became such an important way to organize the crowds and mobilize the masses that they became "a part of the national liturgy" (Mosse 1975, 132). For gymnastics was uniquely suited for enabling the individual to develop his own body and, at the same time, building the group solidarity which nationalism requires.

The nineteenth-century gymnastics society in Germany, better known as the German Turner Movement, became crucial to the development of the German nation-state, the *Deutsche Reich*.[10] Practiced in schools, clubs, and in the army, and as an expression of order and discipline (Kruger 1996), *Turnen* (gymnastics) became "a system of rationalized and formalized exercises" (Kruger 1996: 413) which helped develop a specific culture of the male body connected to a specific *deutsche Kultur* (German culture). The development of gymnastics in clubs and of regional and national gymnastics festivals which used flags, ribbons, uniforms and songs helped to create and sustain the us/them distinction so essential to nationalism (Kruger 1996). Over the years, as they drew more and more people, these festivals became a way of pioneering the ideals of German national self-representation (Mosse 1975), by demonstrating the benefits of controlling mind and body as well as loyalty to the Reich (Kruger 1996). Significantly, the Turner Movement of Germany was exclusively male and thus helped to build a connection between the development of male culture and bonding and the development of German nationalism (Reulecke 1990).

Herzl, Nordau, and other Zionist leaders, who were influenced by German culture and impressed by German nation-building achievements, advocated similar programs for Jewish nation-building.[11] Nordau called on the delegates to the second Zionist Congress of 1898 to establish and join gymnastics clubs. The establishment of new Jewish gymnastics clubs and their spread throughout Western and Central Europe testifies to the importance of Nordau's plan for what he called *Muskeljudentum* (Muscle Jewry).

Although some of these clubs predated Nordau, their numbers were small and no national ideology was associated with them. After Nordau, almost all of the pre-existing Jewish sports clubs joined the Zionist movement, and many of the newly established ones were given the names of ancient Jewish male heroes like Bar Kochba and the Maccabees. The New Jew, the Muscle Jew, was to take as role models Jewish heroes of the past, especially those whose battles with the Romans and the Greeks dramatized their willingness to fight for the land and to sacrifice their lives, if necessary, for their belief in the national cause (Shapira 1992). Nineteenth-century Jewish athletes—exclusively men—trained in the explicit spirit of nation-building: mimicking the German gymnastic model of order and discipline; performing as a group with banners and ribbons; using Hebrew in their drill exercises and singing Hebrew songs (Berkowitz 1993:108). The motto of these Jewish athletes reflected the us-them requirement of nationalism, the fighting spirit, and the idealized masculinity of the gymnastic clubs: "We fight for Judah's honor/ Full strength in youth/So when we reach manhood/Still fighting ten times better" (quoted in Berkowitz 1993, 109).[12]

Jewish youth movements, especially the ones that developed in Germany and in Central Europe, also borrowed their format —and their emphasis on masculinity— from their German counterparts. Like the Turner Movement, nineteenth-century German fraternities and youth movements advocated a return to pre-industrial nature through hiking—enabling them at once to spread their ideology throughout Germany and, at the same time, to connect the German landscape with the spirit of the nation (Mosse 1975)—and through songs, dances, and plays, which helped reinforce the love of both physical movement and the nation.[13] As in the German case, Jewish youth movements rejected family traditions, revolted against bourgeois values, and emphasized a return to nature, simplicity, and male comradeship (Reinharz 1996, 279). Emerging Zionist youth movements were influenced as well by Lord Baden-Powell's Scouting movement in Britain; some of the Slavic youth movements also emphasized a return to nature and a rejection of the values associated with modern industrialism (Naor 1989).[14] As Zionist youth movements, first in Europe and later in Palestine, adopted the rhetoric and structure of these other youth movements, they also added their own unique pioneering mission. Because Jewish nationalism could truly develop only through a return to the historical homeland of Eretz Yisrael, the goal of all Zionist youth movements ultimately became emigration to Palestine.[15] It was only there, according to Zionism, that Jews could become rooted, control their own economics and politics, create a Jewish majority, revive the Hebrew language, and thus achieve national liberation (Berkowitz 1993; Luz 1988; Vital 1982, 1975).

Youth Movements, Education and Nationalism in Palestine

The Zionist youth movements which were formed in the early twentieth century in Europe— initially the Maccabees and, later, Hechalutz (pioneer) the Scouts, Hashomer Hatzair, Hanoar Hatzioni Beitar, and Gordonia—had a profound impact on the construction of Jewish nationalism and masculinity, as both developed together in Jewish Palestine.[16] Although these movements were ideologically different from each other, they all shared the Zionist commitment to a national revival in Palestine (Lamm 1991). As they spread throughout Europe and in Palestine between the two world wars, all of them trained Jewish youths for life on the farm and instilled in both boys and girls the commitment to personal fulfillment of the national goal, including the sacrifice of the material comforts of home for the sake of rebuilding the homeland, and the Zionist ideals of heroism, love of the land and physical labor (Almog 1984).

The ideal New Jew—the youth movement graduate turned pioneer settler (*chalutz*), colonizer, and defender—became the emblem of Zionism. Although women were *chalutzot* [feminine plural form of chalutz] too, and their contributions were crucial to the success of the Zionist project, they did not come to symbolize Zionism's achievements. While both men and women opened up the frontier, built kibbutzim, and created a new Hebrew culture in Palestine, it was mostly men who were involved in fighting the indigenous population of Palestine who took the more publicly visible agricultural jobs, which called for greater physical endurance. In his memoirs about life in Sejera, one of the first Jewish colonies in Palestine, David Ben Gurion, who later became Israel's first prime minister,wrote in 1907 about gender differences: "All members of the *moshava* [colony] work. The men plow and plant their land. The women work in their garden and milk the cows. The children herd the geese on the farm and ride horses towards their fathers in the fields" (Ben Gurion 1971, 35). It appears that despite the Zionist ideal of gender equity, which some of the women had hoped for before they came to Palestine, men and women were assigned different tasks in the Jewish colonies which reproduced an all too familiar set of inequities.

Members of the youth movements identified so wholly with the revolutionary message of Zionism that we can say they were "the soldiers of the Zionist revolution" (Guri 1989). In turn, and in tandem, as the message of Zionism spread throughout the many Jewish communities of Europe and the number of young emigrants to Palestine increased, the Yishuv (Jewish community in Palestine) found that it had to design an educational plan that would accommodate and reinforce the message of Zionism. As in other national movements, like the German and the Slavic ones, both formal and informal education were crucial to the spread of Jewish nationalism, and teachers and youth movement leaders became the agents of such change. Education in the Yishuv, especially after the late 1890s, was in Hebrew (a language that most new immigrants did not know), and emphasized the tie to the historical homeland and to the Jewish heroic past as well as physical activities and the development of a close tie with nature. Furthermore, in the spirit of Zionism, students in the Yishuv, during the 1930s, 1940s, and after statehood, studied agriculture as a topic in school, and several agricultural boarding schools were established so that students could learn how to be productive farmers. In addition, students received training in self-defense and paramilitary activity, so that they would be able to defend themselves.

Just as it had in Zionist youth movements, Hebrew education in the Yishuv had an anti-intellectual orientation which emphasized applied subjects and activities that developed physical fitness and strength rather than the life of the mind. At the center of these curricula were activities that developed physical, endurance, bravery, and heroism among youths (Reichel 1997; Alboim-Dror 1996) and trained young settlers, especially men, for their future defense duties. Long, exhausting hikes in the rugged terrain of Palestine became an important tool for merging the Zionist message of love of the land and the building of physical strength. These hikes were the climactic events of each school year and in the youth movement, increasing in difficulty as each youth moved up the movement hierarchy. Eventually they would also become an important rite of passage in the Israeli Defense Forces.

Thus the Zionist culture that emerged in Jewish Palestine idealized the New Muscle Jew, the antithesis of the stereotyped intellectual European Jew. But while both boys and girls participated in Zionist education in the Yishuv and both men and women built and developed their homeland together, Zionist culture was unmistakably gendered; for it was largely men who claimed the additional mission of national defense.

Paramilitarism and the Cult of Toughness

Schools and youth movements also redesigned ceremonies and the celebration of Jewish holidays to fit the Zionist message of bravery, redemption, and national liberation. These nationalistic celebrations emphasized nature and homeland, and the revival of old Jewish heroes, in particular the Maccabees and Hasmonites. Because all these heroes were men, the new focus of these holidays contributed greatly to the cult of masculinity that became integral to the emerging Jewish culture in Palestine. Many of the celebrations during the Yishuv involved shooting, horseback riding, and gymnastics competitions (Alboim-Dror 1986), virtually none of which included women participants. Furthermore, as it had in German youth movements, singing played a crucial role in building attachment to the nation and the homeland and strengthening the commitment to defend both. Ultimately, Israeli songs which recalled warriors' experiences on the battlefield and memories of fallen friends and which told stories about military culture were adopted as if they were youth movement songs, and even became a dominant force in the music repertoire that later developed in Israeli popular culture. Thus that largely male warrior culture came to shape youth culture in modern Israel (Shakham 1995).

Even in the early years of Jewish Palestine, the emerging priority of security contributed in crucial ways to the masculine image of the Zionist success story.

Once they began arriving in Palestine in large numbers and transforming the land which they saw as unclaimed, Jewish settlers were, inevitably, met with growing resistance by the indigenous Arab population of Palestine. As Arab attacks on Jewish settlements and farms became more violent and more regular, the Jews of the Yishuv in the pre-state years resorted to defending themselves, establishing several organizations whose sole focus was protection of the new Jewish communities. These organizations were aided by youths who had been trained in Zionist schools and youth movements for their security mission. But, as Uri Ben Eliezer (1995) argues in *The Emergence of Israeli Militarism 1936–1956*, much of the military activity of both attack and defense was wholly unorganized. Militarism developed in different locations and by different people without much plan and with little coordination (Ben Eliezer 1995, 35).

Among the most important of the Jewish guarding and fighting organizations that were created in the first two or three decades of the century were *Hashomer* (the guard) established in 1909, and *Hagana* (the defense) and *Palmach* (strike force), both established in the 1940s. Hashomer, in particular, helped to create the warrior associated with Zionism and, hence, contributed to the masculinization of Jewish nationalism. In the words of its own publication: "Hashomer created a new type of Jew, a brave Jew who is not afraid of danger and who is ready to fight face to face, a Jew who knows the way of life and the manners of the Arabs and tile Bedouins and is better than they are in fighting, riding a horse . . . and . . . in his brave spirit" (*The Hagana* 1968, 16)

Hashomer was a selective group of men who, like the members of the Palmach, the Hagana and many other military units that came on their heels, were sworn to secrecy and therefore appeared to be elitist (O. Almog 1997, 168), and indeed they were.[17] Hashomer was the first significant Jewish defense force whose members recognized that the mission of security was intimately connected to settlement activity, and that settling on the land in strategically distributed communities had an important security value.[18] The *shomrim* (guards) became mythologized in the folklore that developed in the Yishuv and in the period before statehood. Alexander Zaid, the armed *shomer* on horseback, riding in defense of his people and land, became the epitome of this image of Jewish masculinity, the New Jew.

In the late 1930s and early 1940s, as a result of both the ideological program for a strong New Jew and increasing Arab attacks on Jewish settlements, paramilitary training became an integral part of the curriculum of both high schools and youth movements in Jewish Palestine. This training of school-age Jewish youths for their military service taught them how to use guns, trained them in survival techniques and instilled in them a sense of responsibility to the community. Students learned Jewish military history, with an emphasis on the battle experiences of contemporary and historical heroes, and developed extensive knowledge of their physical environment. Teenage members of the youth regiments who came out of these programs—mostly but not exclusively males—joined the Palmach and the Hagana for their secret missions against both the British and the Arabs, and at times also against other underground Jewish organizations.

In turn, the youths who became leaders, counselors in the youth movements and who joined elite units became role models in their movement, school, and neighborhood. The impact of these men on succeeding generations was demonstrated by the desire of the younger ones to follow in their footsteps. In a letter published in *Siach Shakulim* (1988 [1981]) (Conversations of Mourners), Yitzchak Kadmon writes about the inspiring effect on him of his counselor in the Scout movement Dani Mass, who died in January 1948 during Israel's war of independence:

> Mass is for me a substitute for God's toughness—Israel's God. He is
> an object of my admiration. A counselor in the Scouts who observes
> us, kids, from above. . . . Kids gather around him for an activity, all
> listening: "We can see the revival on the horizon," Dani says quietly.
> "We will have to sacrifice ourselves, to give all that we have and all
> that there is within us, so to ensure for us and for those who will come
> after us . . . a home here on our forefathers' land. I say goodbye to you.
> I cannot tell yon where I am going. It is a glorious place. One day I will
> call for you to come to me."
>
> I saw him strong, . . . wide eyed, and with a smile of an angel. We
> were scared little kids in the dark, boys and girls; we got closer to him
> and we touched him. Dani was the figure with whom I wanted to
> associate. I wanted to imitate him, to hear and see him. Such charisma
> . . . and in those days I did not yet know what charisma even was.[19]

Dani Mass was a representative of a whole generation: tall, strong, brave young men who were willing to die for their Zionist ideals. They influenced many younger men who came after them and who themselves would become heroes for the generations that came after them, earning places in the pantheon of national heroes, which I shall discuss shortly.

From the early days of Zionism several of the new Jewish military and paramilitary units operated underground, and made membership by invitation only (older members recruited new ones). Because of their selectivity and their reputed bravery, because of the hallowed culture of male bonding that was associated with them, these units became legendary in the emerging Jewish Israeli culture and, increasingly, the most desired units for which young men wanted to volunteer. This canonization of the elite military unit continues to date, and further marks the intense connection between militarism, masculinity, heroism, and the Jewish nation.

Many of the men who joined the elite units of the Hagana and the Palmach and, after statehood, the Israeli Defense Forces, were graduates of youth movements and of agricultural farming boarding schools, especially Kaduri, Ben Shemen, and

Mikve Yisrael, which all prepared the youths to be kibbutz farmers as well as fighters.[20] The hierarchy in elite units, and the culture of hazing, the intense military training, and the male bonding associated with these units, mimicked the male-culture of Hashomer and of the agricultural schools. The routine abuse and cruelty that young men had to endure as a rite of passage in these schools and in the paramilitary units of the Hagana and the Palmach marked their manliness. These codes of behavior, the rite-of-passage ceremonies and the cult of toughness associated with them further mythologized the male warriors of Israel.

Special units, particularly the tiny, short-lived Unit 101 of the early 1950s and, later, the paratroopers, made specific contributions to the image of the tough man whose daredevil courage enables him to do anything for his nation. Such units set the standards for acts of extreme courage in the battlefield which became virtually normative for the elite units of the IDF. Until the early 1950s the IDF was not involved in attacks on individual communities across the border. But members of Unit 101 and the paratroopers entered enemy territory regularly as they searched for suspected terrorists in retaliation for attacks on Jewish communities. These small units' strategies of rounding up and often separating the men, to make them pay collectively for disturbing the life of Jewish communities in Israel, along with infiltration and the disparate attacks across the border in the middle of the night, were new at the time and later became normative military operation for IDF missions. Furthermore, infiltration of enemy territory by a handful of Israeli soldiers, blowing up homes and killing suspects (and sometimes their families), round ups and nighttime face-to-face confrontations with the enemy (Morris 1995; Milshtein 1968), became as a result the ultimate tests of bravery. Since then the bar of bravery of the IDF soldier has constantly been pushed up, as members of each generation surpass those of the previous one in what they are willing to endure in the name of nation-building and national survival. And as the bar of bravery has been going up, so has the bar of masculinity which mirrors it.

The Pantheon of Heroes: Myth in the Making

Men who proved their courage on the battlefield and who were willing to give their life for national survival became cultural legends in Jewish Israel—for example, Meir Har-Zion, a "cold-blooded fighting Jew with an armor-plated conscience" (Elon 1971, 232), veteran of many of these infiltration missions and battles about whom Moshe Dayan wrote: "His fighting instincts and courage set an example for the entire Israeli Defense Forces" (quoted in Lion 1971, 232). Har-Zion and his fellow fighters are remembered in modern Israel in a way that echoes the Hellenistic standard of masculine beauty: tall, wide shouldered, beautiful, and brave heroes. The process of memorializing these men and retelling stories about their bravery and vision, commitment to the community and willingness to volunteer has mythologized and canonized them collectively, further reinforcing the strong connection between masculinity and Jewish nationalism. The process of canonizing soldiers as heroes has acquired an almost timeless status in Israel's short history, as, regardless of the war, the mythologizing narrative is exactly the same.[21]

Over the years more than twenty thousand Israeli soldiers have died in defense of their country. Their death has been remembered as the price, the sacrifice, the Jewish nation has had to pay for its independence and freedom (Witztum and Malkinson 1993). Because the price of freedom has been so high, all fallen soldiers are eulogized as heroes.[22] I offer here two representative examples of the kind of narrative that Israeli parents employ to talk about their fallen dead sons, and the kind of heroic memory employed in Israel, both published in *Siach Shakulim* (Conversations of Mourners; the translation of both pieces is mine). One mother wrote:

> Ask me why did he go?
> Went with no return
> I answered: he went with all the heroes.

And a father wrote:

> Our son Yisrael died in the battlefield with the last injured man on his
> back, while taking care of the wounded soldiers under fire. In his actions
> he set an example. . . . The stories of his heroism are told in the books
> that appeared after the Six Day War. He can serve as a role model . . .
> especially for the youths who are about to conscript to the IDF.

In the deepest sense, the choice of who gets remembered and what gets memorialized is in every culture, inevitably, ideological, and is crucial to the nationalism that gets constructed. And because remembrance "shapes our links to the past and the ways we remember define us in the present . . . and nurture [our] vision of' the future" (Huyssen 1993, 249), memory has been central to the collective consciousness of every nation. National memories are perpetually reconstructed as narrative as they are selectively recollected, reinterpreted, and retold. Changing over time to fit particular national needs, they rarely reflect real events with a high degree of accuracy. Frequently, instead, as many scholars have argued, these narratives—especially the narratives about historical events that shaped the nation—take the form of myth, one of the most essential ingredients of nationalism (Gellner 1996, 1983; Connor 1994; Hobsbawm 1990; Smith 1986). And which stories or events of the past are used in the present depends greatly on the present needs of the nation, since these myths anchor the present in the past and link the past to the present, reviving for the present the glories of the past and marking the uniqueness of the nation.

In Zionism, too, as in other nationalisms, myth and memory have been crucial to the construction of the nation. These myths have emphasized the Jewish struggle for survival both in the Diaspora and in Palestine, as well as the miraculous status of victory won repeatedly in defiance of the Jews' numerical inferiority.[23] This notion of miracle has been built up in virtually all the myths of Jewish nationalism, further grounding and dramatizing, in national mythology the modern Jewish military hero. Significantly, historical military figures like Bar Kochba and Judah Maccabee rather than important rabbis—for example, the Ramban and Rambam, Rashi or the Gaon of Vilna—have served as the heroic exemplars of which Zionism and the Zionist New Jew have been constructed. These historical heroes became the first members of the pantheon of Zionist heroes; in turn, members of Hashomer and others who died after them miraculously defending the Jewish colonies have also been inducted into this pantheon.

The most influential member of the Zionist pantheon of heroes to date has been Joseph Trumpeldor, whose heroism and dying words have influenced generations upon generations of Jewish children in Palestine and, later, in Israel. A highly decorated Russian Jewish officer who lost an arm in the Russo-Japanese war, Trumpeldor came to Palestine as a Zionist in 1907,

fought against the Ottomans in World War I, and in 1919 became the commander for Northern Galilee. According to legend, Trumpeldor was fatally wounded in the battle of Tel Hai but refused to desert his post and be evacuated. When he finally received medical care he is supposed to have said to the physician who treated him: "No matter, it is worthwhile to die for our land" (ein davar, kedai lamont b'ad artsenu) (Ben Gurion 1971, 135).[24] Despite the fact that no one but Trumpeldor's doctor (a recent immigrant with limited Hebrew competence) heard them, an improved version of Trumpeldor's words—"it is good to die for our country"—became what is arguably the most influential motto in modern Zionism, recited annually by Jewish school children from the 1920s to the present (Zertal 1994). To die for one's land became the ultimate modern Jewish sacrifice; it gave meaning to the death battle and, as Mosse (1990) argued, it enabled fallen soldiers to continue to have a significant impact on the living.

Rivka Gover, who lost her two sons in the 1948 war, demonstrates this point eloquently: "After all, our sons did not just give us their life, they gave something more important than that. They returned to us our national and human dignity" (1948; printed in *Siach Shakulim* 1988 [1981]; my translation). And it was Trumpeldor who came to epitomize that heroic sacrifice, because he stood alone, outnumbered, in defense of his land (Azaryahu 1995). Significantly, a father whose son died in the 1948 war used Trumpeldor's motto to make highly nationalized sense of the loss of his son: "When we received the message that our son Ilan had fallen—it was for us, of course, a terrible hit but nevertheless we were ready for it. After all, we did not raise our son on almonds and raisins alone, we reared him also on *it is good to die for our country*[25] (*Siach Shakulim* 1988 [1981], original emphasis, my translation).

Many of the young men who died in Israel's wars, though certainly not all of them, have been memorialized in remembrance albums, at times published by their families and friends, at others by their military unit; and in the case of *Gvilei Esh* (Parchments of Fire) by the newly established government of Israel.[26] In addition to making available to their family and friends the writings of the fallen, their poetry, art, or sections of their diaries, these albums often provide biographical data which stress the status of the dead as heroes who died for the sake of the nation. Even the subtitle of *Gvilei Esh* reads (in English translation): "Comprising the literary and artistic works of the fallen heroes of the war of liberation in Israel," thus cementing the connections among death, the masculine hero, and the Israeli Jewish nation.

Finally, it seems clear that in all arenas of national mythology, the hero is always a male, and that the act of heroism is always associated with military might and masculinity. In Hebrew, as in Arabic and in many ancient Semitic languages, both the word "man" (gever) and the word "hero" (gibor) come from exactly the same three letter root (G-V-R). So do the phrases for "to overcome" (lehitgaber), "to strengthen" (lehagbir), "masculinity" or "manliness" (gavriyut) and "heroism" (gvurah) (Hirschfield 1994, 100) as well as one version of the name for God (gevurah) (Gal 1984:190). In a culture like the one that has developed in Israel —as a result of its struggles to survive—national strength and heroism have become deeply coupled with masculinity. Moreover, because all these words are derived from the same root, the hero (gibor) and his act of heroism (gvurah) become God-like (gevurah). Ultimately it may even be the case that, because Jewish nationalism has revived the connection of the Jewish people to its biblical homeland and religion, it has felt important to justify this connection that men become God-like in their military endeavors.

Conclusion

As early as 1899, one of the most famous Hebrew poets of the time, Shaul Tchernichovsky, made an explicit connection to Greek masculine ideals when he wrote about the New Jew in his poem "Facing the Statue Apollo":

Youth-God, sublime and free, the acme of beauty:
I am a Jew—Your eternal adversary,
I am the first of my race to return to you!
My people is old—its God has aged with it . . .
The God of light, the god of light calls to every sinew in me:
Life! Life! . . . To every bone, to every vein . . .
I have come to you, I bow before your image

Your image—the symbol of the light of life,
I bow, I kneel to the good and the sublime,
To what is worshipped in the fullness of life
To that which is splendid in all creation.
I bow to life and courage and beauty.
                              (translated by D. Kuselewitz, 1978)

Apollo was, according to Tchernichovsky, the standard of courage and beauty for
the New Jew: brave, standing tall, always ready to defend his community with pride;
the antithesis of the stereotype of the Diaspora Jew, the success story of Zionism.
These images of the tall and proud New Hebrew, tiller and defender of tilled land,
appear frequently in Hebrew writings from the late 1890s onward (see Berlowitz
1983). They were also captured and reinforced in posters that were created in Palestine by Jewish artists, in the 1930s and the early 1940s as well as after statehood.
These images became the blueprint for the construction of Israeli young men before
and after statehood: the masculinist New Jew, who was always ready to help his
people, defend the land and build it.

When national survival is attributed almost exclusively to the heroism of warriors, nationalism and masculinity become inseparable. And when a nation cul-
tivates its own myths of survival recalls the struggles of its past, and celebrates its
heroes, it perpetuates the intimate tie between nation and male and continually
constructs the image of both its desired nationalism and its desired soil. This son,
in whose image the younger generation is socialized, is most dear to the nation
when he takes up arms and willingly risks his life for the survival of the nation and
when he wins military battles on the nation's behalf. The communal goal of military victory connects masculinity and nationalism in a militarized society like
modern Israel.

Nationalism and masculinity, then, actively participate in one another's
construction. They are both, in addition, constructed in opposition to an Other.
In the Jewish case, in fact, both nationalism and masculinity have been constructed
in opposition: first, to the Ghetto Jew and, later, to the indigenous Arab population of Palestine. To mobilize the Jewish people, Zionist leaders called up mythologized stories from the past about the Jews' struggles to survive and their unrelenting
fears of annihilation—"the whole world is against us"—continually emphasizing
the miracle of Jewish survival in the face of numerical inferiority—"the few
against the many." These inevitably masculinist myths—built around victories made
possible by the military courage of Jewish men—have shaped the construction of
Jewish nationalism so that when we examine it from virtually any angle we find
survival and male bravery as twin narratives.

Because the Jewish nation has remained in constant (real or imagined) fear
of annihilation —in a state of what Baruch Kimmerling (1993) calls "a cultural
militarism"—and has seen itself as engaged in continuous fighting, it has had to

rely heavily on military prowess and on its sons, and to construct its sons as its defenders, Israeli Jewish men have socialized into their gender roles by the reality of the first sixty years of Zionism in Palestine and by the messages that they have received in the youth movements, the educational system, paramilitary training and, ultimately, in the modern IDF itself.

Zionism and masculinity have become inseparable; not only have they constructed one another but also they continue to be one another's lifeline. Zionism provided the blueprint for the New Jew's gender identity as well as the arena for perfecting the details of his manliness; and masculinity, bravery, and heroism became in turn what the poet Natan Alterman (1973) has called the "silver platter" on which the Jewish state was given. Because both nation and gender are culturally constructed, and because cultures inevitably change through time, we can expect that Jewish Israeli nationalism and gender identity will change as well. Now when the Israeli military no longer needs men as elite fighters, their masculine identity is threatened. They feel that they are zero—that they must either be real men or they are nothing. But just as the myths on which Zionism is based have been increasingly questioned and the motivation, on the part of young Israeli men to die for the nation is on the decline, we may well find in the future major changes in both Zionism and masculinity. These changes, I believe, will indicate the maturity of the Zionist project.

Notes

1. The word "killers" appears several times in the newspaper article. While the article is written in Hebrew it uses the English word "killers," but adds the suffix to denote the plural masculine—*killerim*.
2. I distinguish between a nation and a state and, therefore, between nationalism and patriotism. While the nation is a glorified ethnic group whose members have an attachment to a specific territory, the state is a political unit. Therefore, I see loyalty to the nation as nationalism and loyalty to the state as patriotism. In the case of Israel, two distinct nationalisms exist in the land:. Jewish nationalism and Palestinian nationalism. For Jews in Israel, nationalism and patriotism overlap and are often interchangeable.
3. See for example Sharoni (1994).
4. Herzl's fondness for Bismarck is evident in several different entries in his diaries: on June 15, 1895 he wrote: "Napoleon was the sick superman, Bismarck was the healthy one" (Herzl 1956, 52).
5. For a more detailed discussion of the marginalized man as "feminized" see for example McClintock (1995) and Enloe (1989).
6. For an excellent discussion of the construction of the "feminized" Jewish man see Boyarin (1997). Boyarin argues that much of the feminized identity of Jewish men over the years, from as early as the Talmudic period, was internalized "and that Jewish men identified themselves as feminized" (1997, 12). But the problem with Boyarin's assertion is that the activities in which Jewish men engaged and which may have branded them "feminine" in the eyes of the non-Jews were clearly not open to Jewish women at the time and thus could not have contributed to a feminine self-identity. This is a clear example, I believe, of how culture-specific gender construction is.

7. The description of the male ideal is taken from Nietzsche's moral system as described in his *Also sprach Zarathustra* and critiqued by Nordau in *Degeneration* (1895). The *Übermensch* possesses traits such as "severity, cruelty, pride, courage, contempt of danger, joy in risk, extreme unscrupulousness" (Nordau 1895, 422), traits that Nordau believed could lead to tyranny. While the New Jew should not possess all these specific traits, he should nonetheless be brave, virile and ready to fight.

8. This quote is taken from an open letter by Nordau to Professor Caesar Lombroso to whom he dedicated his famous book *Degenerates*. According to Sander Gilman (1986), Lombroso, a Jew himself, had initially developed the notion of "degeneration" mostly for prostitutes and criminals, and only later accepted the anti-Semitic notion that Jews were more prone to specific forms of mental illness.

9. In his 1902 essay "Was bedeutet das Turnen für uns Juden?" which appeared in *Jüdische Turnzeitung*, Nordau explained to his Jewish audience that gymnastics would give them the self-confidence which they were lacking. Further, he asserted that Jews would make excellent gymnasts because they were smart; it was not enough to be physically fit, he believed, but essential as well to be daring, in complete control of one's muscles and fast and precise—all of which come from the brain.

10. The father of the German gymnastics movement was Friedrich Ludwig Jahn whose *turnen* activities began as early as 1811 in Berlin and were to instill "the love of the fatherland through gymnastics" (Mosse 1975, 128).

11. Internalizing antisemitic characteristics of the Jews as feminine and the Zionists' attempts to reverse them brought major criticism upon Herzl and Nordau from Eastern European Jews and from writers such as Karl Kraus (founder of the Viennese literary journal *Die Fackel*) and others, who "equated the attitudes of Zionism, represented by Herzl, with that of the anti-Semites" (Gilman 1986, 235).

12. Judah refers to Judah Maccabee.

13. The German Youth Movement began among schoolboys in Berlin in 1801 and focused initially on allowing boys to roam the countryside without adult supervision. Soon, however, the movement became politicized and the participants (all males) were asked to be part of the German national consciousness (Mosse 1985, 45).

14. Baden-Powell's Boy Scout movement was intended for white boys in whose hands the future of the empire lay. By participating in the movement white boys would learn, Baden-Powell believed, self-control and become "tall, muscular, eyes straight ahead, body at attention" (Enloe 1989).

15. Members of the Zionist movement were split over a territorial solution and not all agreed on historic Eretz Yisrael as the location for the Jewish homeland. Through the early Zionist congresses several territorial proposals were discussed, including locations such as Uganda, Birobidzan, and Argentina.

16. According to Lamm (1991), in the first quarter of the twentieth century twenty-five different Zionist youth movements were established in Europe and they differed from one another on the basis of their political ideology.

17. There were also a few women members in Hashomer but they did not participate actively in security missions. Rather, they learned how to use guns and defend themselves, ride horses, and participate in the hard life of the colonies.

18. The first Jewish defense force in Palestine was actually Bar Giora, which was formed in 1907 as a secret organization that assumed the guarding and protection of the Jewish colonies from Arabs and Bedouin. This was the first organization whose goal was to train Jews to use guns for self-defense. It is from this organization that Hashomer was born in 1909.

19. *Siach Shakulim* is published by the *Yad Labanim* organization dedicated to memorializing the fallen sons. Established after the 1948 war by a mother whose son had died in battle, *Yad Labanim* has become an official institution in Israel.

20. A large number of the most decorated and highest ranking officers in the Palmach and later in the IDF were graduates of these schools, especially *Kaduri*.
21. The pantheon of Jewish heroes is comprised almost exclusively of men. Although some women did die defending the land, their numbers have remained small, and although they contributed to the cult of heroism, they have not been made central to it. Two of the more famous women who have been marked as heroes are Hanna Senesh and Chaviva Reich, two paratroopers who joined the British army during World War II.
22. George Mosse (1990) suggests that with the development of the "cult of the fallen soldier," at least in public, the national gain from the soldiers' death outweighed the personal loss.
23. For a thorough discussion of myths in Zionism see Wistrich and Ohana (1997), Gertz (1995), Zertal (1994), and Zerubavel (1995).
24. The Hebrew word *artzenu* could be translated as either "our land" or "our country." In 1919, when Trumpeldor died, the likelihood of an Israeli state was nothing more than a dream, and therefore the more fitting translation in this context is "our land." But since children have recited this verse in the late 1940s and thereafter, the meaning has most likely become "our country."
25. "Almonds and raisins" refer here to the Yiddish song "rozinkes mit mandlen." In this specific context, the father emphasizes that he raised his son not only on Yiddishist, Diaspora culture but also on the new Jewish culture of Palestine. *Shlilat Hagola* (the negation of the Diaspora) was an important theme in Zionist ideology—only by rejecting the Diaspora, many believed, could the New Jew be born.
26. The first of these commemoration books was the *Yizkor Book* of 1911, which was a way to memorialize Hashomer members who had died. For an excellent analysis of the debates surrounding this book see Frankel (1996). The first *Yizkor Book* set the standard for memorializing the fallen soldiers in the wars to come, as well as the memorial books for the many Jewish communities in Europe that vanished at the hands of the Nazis.

References

Alboim-Dror, R. (1986) *Hebrew Education in Eretz Yisrael 1884–1914*. Jerusalem: Yad Ben Zvi Institute.

———. (1996) "He goes and comes back, from within us comes the first Hebrew' on the youth culture of the first aliyot." Alpayim (12):104–135 (in Hebrew).

Almog, O. (1997) *The Sabra—A Profile*. Tel Aviv: Am Oved (in Hebrew).

Almog, S. (1984) "From 'muscular Jewry' to the 'religion of labor'." *Zionism* (9):137–146 (in Hebrew).

Alterman, N. (1973) *HaTur HaShlishi*, vol. l, 1943–1952. Tel Aviv: HaKibbutz Hameuchad, 54.

Azaryahu M. (1995) *State Cults: Celebrating Independence and Commemorating the Fallen in Israel, 1948–1956*. Beer Sheva: Ben Gurion University of the Negev (in Hebrew).

Ben Eliezer U. (1995) *The Emergence of Israeli Militarism: 1936–1956*. Tel Aviv: Dvir Publishing House.

Ben Gurion, D. (1971) *Memoirs*, vol. 1. Tel Aviv: Am Oved.

Berkowitz M. (1993) *Zionist Culture and West European Jewry before the First World War*. Cambridge, U.K.: Cambridge University Press.

Berlowitz Y. (1983) "The Model of the New Jew in the Literature of the First Aliya." In *Alei Siach* (Literary Conversations), 17–18; 54–70.

Bernstein, D. (1987) *The Struggle for Equality: Urban Women Workers in Prestate Israeli Society*, New York: Praeger.

Boyarin, D. (1997) *Unheroic Conduct: The Rise of Heterosexuality and the Invention of the Jewish Man*. Berkeley: University of California Press.

Connor, W. (1994) "When is a nation?" In *Ethnonationalism: The Quest for Understanding*. Princeton, N.J.: Princeton University Press, 210–266.

Elon, A. (1971) *The Israelis: Founders and Sons*, New York: Penguin.

Enloe C. (1989) *Bananas, Beaches and Bases: Making Feminist Sense of International Politics*. Berkeley: University of California Press.

Frankel, J. (1996) "The Yizkor Book of 1911—A Note on National Myths in the Second Aliya." In J. Reinharz and A. Shapira, eds., *Essential Papers in Zionism*. New York: New York University Press, 422–453.

Gal, R. (1984) *A Portrait of the Israeli Soldier*, New York: Greenwood Press.

Gellner, E. (1983) *Nations and Nationalism*. Ithaca, N.Y.: Cornell University Press.

————. (1996) "The coming of nationalism and its interpretation: the myths of nation and class." In G. Balakrishnan, ed., *Mapping the Nation*. London: Verso, 98–145.

Gertz, N. (1995) *Captives of a Dream: National Myths in Israeli Culture*. Tel Aviv: Am Oved (in Hebrew).

Gilman, S. (1986) *Jewish Self-Hatred: Anti-Semitism and the Hidden Language of the Jews*. Baltimore, Md.: The Johns Hopkins University Press.

Guri, C. (1989) "Youth movements as a serving elite." In M. Naor, ed., *Youth Movements, 1920–1960*. Jerusalem: Yad Ben Zvi, 221–226.

————. (1968) *The Hagana*. Tel Aviv: Museum of the Hagana (in Hebrew).

Herzl, T. (1956) *Diaries*, edited by M. Lowenthal New York: Dial Press.

Hirschfield, A. (1994) "Men of men: the hero, the man, and heroism." *Mishkafaim* (22):9–15.

Hoberman, J. (1984) *Sport and Political Ideology*. Austin: University of Texas Press.

Hobsbawm, E. (1990) *Nations before Nationalism: Programme, Myth, Reality*. Cambridge, U.K.: Cambridge University Press.

Huyssen, A. (1993) "Monument and memory in a postmodern age." *Yale Journal of Criticism* 6 (2):249–261.

Izraeli D. (1994) "On the Status of the Woman in Israel: Women in the Military." *International Problems: Society and State* (33):21–26.

Kimmerling, B. (1993) "Is Israel a militarized society?" *Teoria U'vikoret* (4):123–140 (in Hebrew).

Kruger M. (1996) "Body culture and nation-building: the history of gymnastics in Germany in the period of its foundation as a nation-state." *International Journal of the History of Sport* 13 (3): 409–417.

Lamm, Z. (1991) *The Zionist Youth Movements in Retrospect*. Tel Aviv: Sifriat Ha-Poalim (in Hebrew).

Luz, E. (1988) *Parallels Meet Religion and Nationalism in the Early Zionist Movement (1882–1904)*, Philadelphia, Penn.: Jewish Publication Society.

McClintock, A. (1995) *Imperial Leather: Race, Gender, and Sexuality in the Colonial Contest*. London: Routledge.

Milshtein U. (1968) *The Wars of the Paratroopers*. Tel Aviv: Ramdor (in Hebrew).

Morris, B. (1995) *Israel's Border Wars, 1949–1956: Arab Infiltration Israeli Retaliation and the Countdown to the Suez War*. Tel Aviv: Am Oved (in Hebrew).

Mosse, G. (1975) *The Nationalization of the Masses: Political Symbolism and Mass Movement in Germany from the Napoleonic Wars through the Third Reich*. New York: Howard Fertig.

————. (1985) *Nationalism and Sexuality Middle Class Morality and Sexual Norms in Modern Europe*. Madison: University of Wisconsin Press.

————. (1990) *Fallen Soldiers: Reshaping Memory of the World Wars*. Oxford, U.K.: Oxford University Press.

————. (1993) *Confronting the Nation: Jewish and Western Nationalism*. Hanover, N.H.:

Brandeis University Press.

——. (1996) *The Image of Man: The Creation of Modern Masculinity*. New York and Oxford, U.K.: Oxford University Press.

Naor, M., ed. (1989) *Youth Movements, 1920–1960*. Jerusalem. Yad Ben Zvi.

Nordau, M. (1895) *Degeneration*. London: William Heinemann.

——. (1900) "Muskeljudentum." *Jüdische Turnzeitung* (June): 10–11.

——. (1902) "Was bedeutet das Turnen für uns Juden?" *Jüdische Turnzeitung* (July):109–113.

Pellegrini, A. (1997) "Whiteface performance: race, gender and Jewish bodies." In J. Boyarin and U. Boyarin, eds., *Jews and Other Differences: The New Jewish Cultural Studies*. Minneapolis: University of Minnesota Press, 108–149.

Reichel N. (1997) "Roots or horizons: the image of the ultimate pupil in Eretz Israel 1889–1933." *Katedra* (83):55–96 (in Hebrew).

Reinharz, J. (1996) "Ideology and structure in German Zionism, 1880–1930." In J. Reinharz and A. Shapira, eds., *Essential Papers in Zionism*. New York: New York University Press, 268–297.

Reulecke, J. (1990) "Das Jahr 1902 und die Ursprünge der Männerbund-Ideologie in Deutschland." In G. Völger and K. v. Welck, eds., *Männer Bande Männer Bunde: Zur Rolle des Mannes im Kulturvergleich*. Cologne: Rautenstrauch-Jocs-Museum Köln, 3–10.

Shachor, S. (1994) "We used to be men, now we are zero." *Yediot Achronot*, November 11 (in Hebrew).

Shakham, A. (1995) "Song of the young, songs of the future." In *Shorashim: Studies on the Kibbutz and the Jewish Labor Movement* (9):175–192 (in Hebrew).

Shapira, A. (1992) *Land and Power: The Zionist Resort to Force, 1881–1948*, London: Oxford University Press.

Sharoni, S. (1994) "Homefront as battlefield: gender, military occupation, and violence against women." In T. Mayer, ed., *Women and the Israeli Occupation: The Politics of Change*. London: Routledge.

Shimoni, G. (1995) *The Zionist Ideology*. Hanover, N.H., and London: Brandeis University Press.

Siach Shakulim [Conversations of Mourners] (1988 [1981]). Tel Aviv: Merkaz Yad Labanim.

Smith, A. (1986) *The Ethnic Origins of Nations*. Oxford, U.K.: Basil Blackwell.

Tchernichovsky, S. (1978 [1899]) "Facing the statue of Apollo." Translated by D. Kusclewitz. Tel Aviv: Eked.

Vital, D. (1975) *The Origins of Zionism*. Oxford, U.K.: Clarendon Press.

——. (1982) *Zionism: The Formative Years*. Oxford, U.K.: Clarendon Press.

Wistrich, R. and Ohana (1997) *Myth Memory and Trauma: Transfiguration of Israeli Consciousness*. Jerusalem: Van Leer Jerusalem Institute (in Hebrew).

Witztum, E. and R. Malkinson (1993) "Bereavement and commemoration in Israel: the dual face of national myth." In E. Witztum and R. Malkinson, eds., *Loss and Bereavement in Jewish Society in Israel*. Jerusalem: Ministry of Defense Publishing House, 231–255.

Zertal, I. (1994) "The sacrificed and sanctified: the construction of a national martyrology." *Zemanim* (48):26–45 (in Hebrew)

Zerubavel, Y. (1995) *Recovered Roots: Collective Memory and the Making of Israeli National Tradition*. Chicago and London: University of Chicago Press.

Law and Religion

NIRA YUVAL-DAVIS

Bearers of the Collective

Women and Religious Legislation in Israel

IN RECENT YEARS there has been a growing interest in looking at law and legislation not only as instruments carrying out a specific social policy but also as carrying out specific social ideologies by the assumptions they make about society. Among the areas that are beginning to be examined from this point of view is that of the different assumptions that various laws make concerning the nature and role of women in the society.[1]

Most of the discussion has been about how women are socially constituted as wives and mothers by law. This article discusses another legally constituted role of women, which, while being closely related to the roles of women as wives and mothers, can and should nevertheless be considered separately. This role is that of women as reproducers, not only of the labor force and/or of the future subjects of the state, but also as the reproducers, biologically and ideologically of the national collective and its boundaries.

It is important to make it clear that when I talk about the national collective I am talking about a different entity from that of the civil society. The latter includes all residents of a country, including members of national minorities and other outsiders, and does not include members of the national collective who live outside the borders and might never have lived there (as in the case of contemporary American Irish and Jews). Marx and other Marxists have analyzed the relationship between the civil class society and the state. But very little work has been done on the relationship between the national and/or patriarchal collective and the state. This essay, it is hoped, will advance the discussion in that direction, by examining the legal mechanisms, especially the religious legislation, by which women are legally constituted as bearers of the collective. It will also begin to explore the implications this has for the definition of the national/patriarchal collective itself. My empirical focus will be the legal position of women in Israel, a specific situation which is unique in some ways. At the same time it has enough in common with situations in many other countries to allow some generalizations.

This essay does not attempt a systematic examination of all aspects of women's position in Israel. There have been some attempts at this elsewhere.[2] What interests us here is the extent to which Israeli law formally rejects the application of universalistic principles of equality to its female citizens, in spite of the fact that the Israeli Declaration of Independence in 1948 rejected any discrimination on sexual grounds. This need not surprise us. The Declaration also rejected other forms of discrimination-racial and religious, which have not been adhered to.

Before turning to examine the legal situation, I should like to emphasize that legal equality does not mean social equality, as British women have come to realize since the passing of the Sex Discrimination Act. In Israel it is even easier to evade such an act, since Hebrew is a sexed language, and every occupation has by definition to be either female or male, so that the demand for equal pay for equal work can be got round simply by establishing two separate occupational categories. In Israel, in any case, the legal situation is far from admitting women's equality even formally. This may best be demonstrated by the failure of a proposal in 1975 for a Foundation Law in the Israeli Knesset concerning equal rights for women. Israel has no constitution; instead it passes Foundation Laws from time to time which have legal status comparable with that of constitutional laws. Then-prime minister, Yitzkhak Rabin of the Labor Party promised publicly in July 1975 to the Minister of Religious Affairs, Yitzkhak Raphael, that such a law shall never be allowed to pass.

In 1951 a law called "the law of equal rights for women" was indeed passed in the Israeli Knesset. It was, however, not a Foundation Law. Article Five of this so called revolutionary radical law stated explicitly that in questions of the permission and prohibition of marriage and divorce, the principle of equal rights would not be upheld.[3] The woman MP who had proposed the law refused to vote for it once this amendment had been put in. In the Law of Jurisdiction of the Rabbinical Courts, it is established that questions of marriage and divorce of Jews who are citizens of, or resident in, Israel will come under the exclusive jurisdiction of the Rabbinical Courts and that the marriage and divorce of Jews in Israel will be conducted according to the Jewish Orthodox Halakhic Law. As Rabbi Saul Berman (1977) wrote: "Womanhood, within Jewish Law, constitutes an independent juristic status, shaping to varying degrees every legal relationship." The extent to which this independent juristic status is a euphemism for plain discrimination can be glimpsed when we look at the Rabbinical Courts which have exclusive jurisdiction on family laws.

Since the judges in these courts are civil servants appointed by the president according to the recommendations of an appointments committee whose composition and authority are anchored in secular law, one might suppose that women could be appointed to these posts, since Article One of the law of equal rights for women states that women should have equal access to professions regulated by law. Not so. One of the qualifications for appointment to judge of the Rabbinical Court is rabbinical ordination, for which, by religious law, any woman, no matter how knowledgeable she may be, is unfit precisely because she is a woman. The religious law prohibits women from even appearing as witnesses in Rabbinical Courts. Women are also prevented from participating in elections of chief rabbis or municipal rabbis, from sitting on religious councils, and from participating in elections to those councils, despite the fact that these bodies are state-financed and that these prohibitions have no authority in the secular law.

These are the men and these are the institutions which determine nearly every aspect of Jewish family life and the nature of Jewish marriage, affecting the relations between parents and children, affecting pensions, national insurance, and a host of other practical aspects of daily life. They are backed by the only authoritative law in Israel in this domain: Halakha. The guiding principle of this law, which dates from the end of the second century CE, with remnants of even earlier dates, states that a woman becomes her husband's property in marriage. This can occur in one of three ways: by payment of money, by the giving of a promissory note, or by coition.[4] From then on the woman is forbidden to all except her husband and cannot sever the tie until he dies or divorces her. Although she may ask for it, she can only be the passive recipient of the divorce (the term in Hebrew is "banishment").

We can only mention briefly some examples of the consequences of this state of affairs (but see Aloni 1976 and Lahar 1977 for more details). When, for instance, a man disappears, as many did in the aftermath of the 1973 war, and there is no clear evidence that he has died, his wife is prohibited from remarrying because she is still his property. If evidence of his death becomes available and his widow subsequently remarries, after which her first husband reappears, then, although she has acted in all innocence, she is banished (divorced) from both men and the children of the second marriage are declared bastards. She would have no financial claim in law against either husband. No such fate descends on a man in a parallel case.

The principle that a woman is her husband's property does not extend only to the husband. If a man dies leaving his wife childless, she cannot remarry until her husband's brother has had an opportunity to claim her, the aim originally being to have a baby born and called after the dead husband. In modern Israel this is seldom carried to its logical conclusion, especially as there is a prohibition of polygamy. Instead, use is made of an ancient custom, *halitza* (taking off a shoe), whereby the brother and the widow exchange prescribed phrases and (literally) spit (on the floor) for a shoe (which the kneeling woman has to take off the man's foot), and thus the brother is released from his obligation. In 1967 a case occurred in which both the brother and the widow were deaf mutes. The exchange of ceremonial formulas was therefore impossible, and the couple were required instead to perform *yibum* (levirate marriage). However, the brother was married already, so in order to avoid intercourse that was mere fornication, the Rabbinical Court, armed with permission from both Chief Rabbis as a protection against bigamy, sanctified a marriage for a night. A hotel room was hired by the court, intercourse took place in front of witnesses, and divorce was given the following morning, leaving the woman free to marry whom she pleased—unless, of course, she would have liked to marry a Cohen, who is not allowed to marry a divorced woman (Aloni 1976:9, 47). This case is extreme, but others equally obscene are a common occurrence; blackmail being the most frequent. Vulnerability to blackmail can occur in any number of cases which are the result of the application of the *Halakha* (Jewish law) to the Israeli family law.

In the first place, a variety of marriages are prohibited, including marriage to a non-Jew. Within the Jewish community there are more subtle obstacles. Anyone named Cohen, Katz, Adler, Kaplan, or bearing any other name which purports to imply that he is descended from the ancient priesthood may not marry a female divorcee. If such a marriage does take place, it is valid, and of course binding on the wife. But if it is exposed then the husband must divorce his wife, and retains all their joint property, owing her nothing. Such marriages often occur, in ignorance of the consequences, in other countries, or surreptitiously in Cyprus. The offspring are condemned to be labelled as "bastards" (*mamzerim*) to the tenth generation. This label in turn carries with it marital restrictions.

Bastardy is also the fate of children of Jewish mothers who married and divorced their first husband by civil ceremonies in other countries. The marriage holds (by coition) but the divorce does not, and the children are considered to be children of a married woman not from her husband, and therefore bastards according to the Jewish Halakha, forbidden to marry legitimate Jews for ten generations, and even the way of religious conversion is blocked for them. The same applies, of course, in the case of a woman who is separated from her husband and who lives with another man. If the fact is known to the Rabbinate, the woman would not be allowed to marry her lover, even when divorced, and any child born to the couple will be declared as a bastard.

A vast network of self-appointed informers ensures that the rabbinical authorities have up-to-date lists of culprits and potential culprits. In its private life, the non-religious majority tries to regard the religious aspects of the law as an extension of the bureaucracy, everyone hoping that his own case is routine, not one of the horror-story exceptions. In recent years, the increasing immigration of Russian Jews of "suspicious" marital circumstances, and the increasing numbers of war widows, have made the exceptions more and more common, and one can observe a growing discontent among the nonreligious sections of the population which is embodied in various movements and platforms calling for liberalization of the law. This discontent, however, is limited in scope and specific in its intentions, the acceptance of the system as a whole being too well entrenched in the public mind.

Religion and the State in Israel

It is important to remember that the above situation exists in a state in which most citizens are not religious. Only 22 percent declare themselves as committed religiously. Although their number has tended to rise somewhat in the last few years since *tshuva* (repentance) has become a popular fashion in Israel—parallel to the general rise of the Right—they are still clearly in the minority among the Jewish population. The percentage of religiously committed people is higher among the non-Jewish inhabitants (less than 10 percent in Israel proper) who are ruled by their own religious authorities.

In order to understand how and why the non-religious majority of the population tolerates the situation I have described (which affects men also, although it primarily discriminates against and controls women), we have to understand the relationship between religion and the state in Israel as a Zionist state. The founding document of the *Knesset* (parliament) states: "The state of Israel is a state of the law and not a state of religious theory." And indeed, most of Israeli civil and criminal law originated in secular traditions, the main one being Anglo-Saxon law which operated in Palestine under the British mandate. However, there are several legislative areas in which the non-separation of religion and state comes into force. In part, it was the continuation of the legal system operated in Palestine since the time of the Ottoman Empire, in which legal affairs were handled by the religious denominations. But although many other things changed, this state of affairs continued to exist in Israel—as indeed in most of the other countries that were once part of the Ottoman Empire, since it proved congenial to their national/religious ideology. The situation in Israel was summed up by Dr. Zerah Verhaftig, the Israeli minister of religion, in the following way (Verhaftig 1964):

> I had a discussion with a journalist of a non-Jewish paper abroad. He asked me which basic laws am I prepared to define as characterizing the Jewish state. I said that contemporarily there are two and a half such laws. These are: the Law of Return, which characterizes the state of Israel as a Jewish state, as it guarantees to every Jew in the whole world, if he so wishes, to come to the country as his homeland. . . . The second law is the law of marriage and divorce. This law guarantees the physical wholeness of the nation, the stability of the Jewish family. . . . Another half a law is the section in the Order for Rules and Judgment

arrangements in Israel which recognizes Saturday (the Sabbath) as the
rest day in Israel . . . (although) if the spiritual character of this day is
not guaranteed it is not yet a Jewish Sabbath.

Of these two and a half laws, the first two deal with questions relating directly to
the definition of boundaries of the national collective and its reproduction. The
first one, which guarantees automatic citizenship to any Jew who migrates to Israel,
relates to the relationship between the dispersed Jewish communities and the Israeli
state situated in the Promised Land as the state of the Jews, wherever they are,
are potentially its citizens and therefore it can legitimately represent the Jewish
people—as in the case of receiving compensations from West Germany for the Second World War Holocaust—and can ask for financial and political help from all
the Jewish communities in the world. The Jewish Diaspora, then, is situated by
the Law of Return in two positions. On the one hand, it is situated within the boundaries of a passive national collective; on the other hand, it acts as a major supplier
of Jews as active citizens of Israel, and thus as reproducers of the Israeli nation.

The other suppliers of human reproduction for the national collective are the
Israeli Jewish families, which are regulated by the second law Dr. Verhaftig men-
tions. As one writer puts it (Yekhezkeli 1964):

Have you ever thought seriously, what is the right interpretation to that
solid concept "the House of Israel"? This concept has a double meaning
which are interdependent: each family in Israel is called "the House
of Israel" and also the people of Israel in its entirety is called "the
House of Israel." This means that one depends on the other, and one is
conditioned by the other; the guarding of the family is the guarding of
the nation, and the efficient way to guarantee the existence and virility
of the nation is by the strengthening of the Israeli familial cell.

This view of the Jewish family as the pre-eminently efficient way to guarantee the
existence of the nation becomes even more crucial when one remembers that the
sole criterion of Orthodox Jewish law—which operates in Israel as a state law in
the matter of defining whether or not a person is a Jew—is whether or not that
person has been born to a Jewish mother (see the Israeli Nationality Law, amended
in 1970). Except for religious conversion for those who were born to non-Jewish
mothers, there is no other way to become a Jew, circumcision notwithstanding.
No personal commitment is required (like Baptism or Confirmation) although
it is desired for Jewish males—"Israel, even when it sins is still Israel," states the
Talmud (Shavu'oth 39).

The non-separation of membership in the religious collective and in the
ethnic-national collective relates directly to the history of the Jews as a people
class/caste.[5] Moreover, the specification that membership in the collective is
defined according to the origin of the mother rather than the father relates to the

history of the Jews as a persecuted minority—in many cases, especially after riots and pogroms it was difficult to determine the origin of the father of the child.

What is most significant, however, from the point of view of this paper, is not the traditional orthodox Jewish legislation, but the fact, and the implications of the fact, that this religious law defining who is a Jew was incorporated into the Israeli legislation. Zionism as an ideology, and Labor Zionism in particular, tended to present itself as an alternative to the Jewish religion as the centre of the New Jewish mode of existence. However, as we have seen, there was never a total separation of the two in Israel.[6] Those who fight against the unholy alliance of the state and religion, and who are Zionists, tend to explain this phenomenon as a result of the historical tactical alliance that Ben-Gurion established with the religious-Zionist parties as convenient government coalition partners in the early fifties.

Ben-Gurion and the religious parties' leadership agreed in principle on the religious status quo, in which basically certain areas of legislation and policy, especially in the areas of the family and food production, will take place according to Jewish Halakha. In return, the Labor party got their way in matters relating to the military and foreign affairs, which they considered crucial and on which the religious parties were neutral until after the 1967 war when they enthusiastically began to settle in the occupied territories, and eventually became the allies of the Likud, the right-wing party.

But non-separation of religion and state within Zionism continued to exist and continued to enjoy the support of the majority of the Labor Zionist movement even when they no longer had the religious parties as coalition partners. The non-separation relates to more basic issues within Zionism—the basic Zionist claim over Palestine has a religious origin and therefore needs a religious legitimation for it to hold. Nor could the Zionist movement claim a monopoly over world Jewry were it to detach itself totally from the religious tradition which constitutes the essence of Jewish culture.

The laws concerning marriage and divorce are especially crucial in that respect. Whenever anyone has proposed, as did the League against Religious Coercion in the late fifties, establishing civil marriage and divorce in Israel, the religious, and many of the secular Zionist parties, vehemently objected, fearing what they called "a national split." With all the problematics of bastardy laws, the religious parties threatened that such legislation would create a situation in which religious Jews would not be able to marry children of non-religious families, for fear of bastardy (bastards, as I have mentioned, are not allowed to marry a kosher Jew for ten generations). Even liberal-minded Zionists like Shulamith Aloni, who published a book titled *Women as Humans* (1976), does not recommend the abolition of the religious domination over personal laws in Israel, but only to create secular alternatives for cases, like marriage between a divorced woman and a Cohen, which are not religiously legitimate. And even with such a moderate suggestion she brought upon herself the wrath of many. Controlling women and their familial status, therefore, is of crucial importance to the Zionist movement which gives the utmost importance to reproducing the national boundaries of the Jewish people, in and outside Israel.

This situation, however, produces its own contradictions, as more and more Jews outside Israel do not use Orthodox legislation in order to marry and divorce, and who feel that the monopoly of Orthodox legislation over the control of personal status will indeed eventually create the split in the national collective of which Orthodox Jewry, and the Zionist movement, are so afraid. Growing contradictory pressures are produced by Conservative and Reform American Jews who are Zionist but not Orthodox. But, of course, abandoning the non-separation between religion and the state will be impossible in Israel, as we have shown, as long as it continues to be a Zionist state, and not a state of its citizens.

Religion and Family Laws in the Middle East

The explanation we have embarked upon so far has been specific to Israel as a Zionist state. However, some aspects of the situation are not unique to Israel and are to be found in most of the other countries formerly part of the Ottoman Empire and where a special relationship between the state and religion exists. Unlike Judaism, which historically crystallized among stateless minorities, Islam has been historically associated from the outset with political statehood, first the Arab and then the Ottoman Empire. Some of the religious critiques of the state-religion relationship in Israel have claimed that part of the trouble there originates in the fact that Judaism is not equipped with suitable legislation necessary for political independence.[7] This can hardly be said about Islam, although it did evolve in primarily pre-capitalist economies. In some Islamic states the Islamic criminal and civil laws still persist to some extent and there are, in the last few years various attempts, the latest and most significant of which is Iran, to even revitalize them. What is most significant, however, is the fact, that even where those laws were abandoned in favour of secular laws modelled after the West, all of them—with the exception of Tunisia— incorporated the religious laws in the area of family law, especially in what pertains to laws of marriage and divorce.[8] The exact manner in which this incorporation has taken place varies from one country to another, and we cannot enter here into a specific examination of each country. The usual case is that matters of marriage and divorce are decided upon in special family courts in which the judges can be religious, professionals, or civil administrators, but the laws applied are religious and blatantly discriminate against women, including the fact that no judge can be female and the weight of women's evidence counts as half of that of men's (still an improvement in comparison to the Jewish courts).

Polygamy is still allowed in many Muslim countries and wives are still bought by the husbands from the fathers (although in the more progressive Arab countries the bride-price is officially controlled to safeguard against inflation which would prevent marriages). The Muslim marriage contract is not between the bridegroom and the bride but between the bridegroom and the bride's father.

In Islam, unlike in Judaism, membership in the collective is defined via the father and not the mother, but the need to control the women is no less, or even greater—there is a need for strict regulations to ensure the chastity of the women and the legitimacy of the claim that their children are indeed the descendants of the male members of the collective. The Muslims have a historical context of conquests, not of pogroms, in which their religious tradition crystallized. They are so indifferent to the origins of the mothers that women who marry Muslim men do not even have to convert. In case of divorce, however, their children are taken away to the father's family. On the other hand, if Muslim women marry non-Muslims, they can lose their legal status and, unless they convert to another religion, become legally "present absentees." These are the ways in which in Islamic states, as in the Jewish one—and I hasten to say, most probably also in other states in their specific forms—women are used, via the religious laws and otherwise, to delineate the legitimate boundaries of the collective as well as to reproduce it. And for that purpose they are strictly controlled.

The Collective and the Control of Women

We have seen that control of women carries crucial importance for national/religious collectives, for their reproduction as such, and not only in terms of the reproduction of the labour force. We followed in greater detail the raison d'être for the reproduction of the collective in Zionist Israel, for its own purposes, but we have seen that by no means is it a unique feature of Israel, and that at least the Islamic countries operate in a similar manner.

The control of women as bearers of the collective does hot always have to be carried out by means of religious legislation. In a sense all the struggle for and against birth control should be examined in this light. The ideology of the reproduction of the collective can introduce itself in a wide variety of contexts.

The famous Beveridge Report (1942, 154) states: "With its present rate of reproduction, the British race cannot continue; means of reversing the recent course of birth rate must be found." And in the Soviet Union, mothers of ten children or more get the title of "heroine mother" (*The Guardian*, March 1979). Offering the title of "heroine mother" to mothers of ten children has been a practice also in Israel, established by David Ben-Gurion in the first days of the Jewish State. However, unlike in the Soviet Union, in Israel this title can be borne virtually only by Jewish mothers. The financial rewards given by the Institute for National

Insurance to mothers of many children are limited only to those women who have, or used to have a family relative who served in the Israeli army (in which Arabs do not usually serve). The reason for this discrimination is that, as was discussed above, unlike the Soviet Union and most other States, Israel is not a state of its citizens, not even of its Jewish citizens but, as a Zionist state, it is a state of Jewish people wherever they are, and as such, various means are taken by the state to ensure the reproduction of the Jewish national collective.

Religion, then, does not always have the same relevance to the collective as it does in others. Traditionally in the social sciences, religion used to be seen as a remnant from an earlier epoch which, with modernization will "wither away." However, religion, like the state, concerning which similar hopes were cherished by many, did not comply. In many third world countries, and elsewhere, religion persists and in many even shows signs of growing importance. Israel is one case, but the phenomenon is widespread and growing all over the Muslim world as well. Libya has had a fundamentalist Islamic regime years before Khumeini took over in Iran, and in a country like Egypt movements like the Muslim Brotherhood are gathering renewed strength after being supposedly crushed in the mid-sixties, and attack the state for concessions to the equality of women which ironically seem insufficient and minor to us.

At a recent conference on underdevelopment and Greece, at the London School of Economics (March 1978), Gunder Frank quoted Henry Kissinger as admitting that, with the recent revolution in Iran, modernization theories must be thrown into the waste paper basket. Frank remarked that the same revolution might bring the theories of the sociology of development to that same sad end, unless they can successfully theorize these developments.

In the West, the reign of the Church has been associated with feudal times, and secular law with the rise of the modern nation-state after the French Revolution. As Althusser puts it (1969, 224): "Feudalism is freedom, but in the 'non-rational' form of privilege; the modern state is freedom, but in the rational form of a universal right . . . in the state, the state of law and right."

But, secularization of the state seems to be a specific historical development in the Christian West, and is by no means universal. Modern states of law and right found it possible to incorporate within their legal systems—which are supposed to be based on the rational form of a universal right—sections that retain the religious non-rational elements.

Conclusion

It is beyond the scope of this essay even to attempt to theorize about the relationship between religion and nationality in the third world. My concluding remarks are just a tentative attempt to amplify the implications of this relationship on the position of women within the collective in Israel. We have seen that the most fundamental religious legislation, which tends to be incorporated into the secular legal system, even if no other areas of the religious law apply, is the personal law. This latter tends to exercise rigid control over women, the reproducers, so as to enable the collective to continue its reproduction within its traditionally defined boundaries. Women make possible the social cohesion of the collective, not so much by being exchanged, in the sense utilized by Claude Lévi-Strauss, the French anthropologist—as we have seen in the Muslim case, it is irrelevant whether or not the women belonged to the collective before marrying into it—but by reproducing it in the legitimate manner and thus reproducing its specific character. Whether or not the exchanged women are used and controlled by the collective, and as such are excluded from full membership in it, to a greater or lesser extent. This is the case, as we have seen in Judaism, even when the mother, and not the father determines membership of the collective. This is the dimension of women's oppression which is the least affected by the class membership of any individual woman.

The incorporation of religious laws into the secular legal systems adds to the former normative power, the coercive power of the state, and thus strengthens its monopoly. In this way, the traditional patriarchal power relations of the collective are transformed and subsumed into the modern nation-state. This process is in no way unique. More often than not, the establishment of nation-states in the third world incorporated the pre-existing power and the class relations in the society into the political system, and strengthened it further by putting at its service the additional repressive and ideological apparatuses of the state.[9]

However, as in every social situation, these processes produce their own contradictions. Incorporating the patriarchal relations into the nation-state's legal system adds to its power, but it also heightens and eventually brings into question (as protest demonstrations by women in Iran have shown) its own particularism. The hope for the future might be that the collective controllers will come to realize that, as Althusser put it: "Just as a people that exploits another cannot be free, so a class that uses an ideology is its captive too." (Althusser 1979:235) But, as we know from other social conflicts, of class struggle and national liberation, the hope that the oppressors will realize their own limitations becomes a realistic hope only when the oppressed launch their own struggle against their own oppression.

Notes

1. For a discussion of how women are constituted by law as mothers see Wilson (1977); for how women are constituted as wives see Land (1978).
2. In Hebrew the best available book is Hazleton (1978).
3. Files of the Israeli Supreme Court, Zilberg 202/57.

4. This is the reason why children of unmarried Jewish women are not considered, according to Halakha, to be bastards—their mothers "married" their fathers via coition.

5. For historical analysis of the Jews as a people-class, see for example A. Leon (1976) and N. Weinstock's introduction.

6. Labor Zionism was the dominant political trend within the Zionist movement for about fifty years until its defeat by the right-wing Likud party in the last elections. Labor Zionism, unlike right-wing Zionism, used socialist or social-democratic slogans in addition to the nationalist ones, although the former were always used basically as tools to further the latter and their validity within Zionism has always been severely restricted to Jews only.

7. The main one among them is Professor J. Leibovitz (1958) who claims: "The lack of realistic statist function to the people of Israel has been the necessary condition and the basic assumption of the crystallization of the Halakha as we know it."

8. Tables which systematically compare the situation in different Islamic countries in this respect can be found in Raset (1969).

9. What we have seen in Iran, especially in the initial stages of the political transformation, is a popular anti-imperialist revolution, which, thanks to the space created in the Third World as a result of the relative weakening of the influence of both superpowers with the growing impact of OPEC, could afford to go back to its own tradition and not recruit Western counter-ideologies to imperialism like socialism. But that same "victory of the people" has been a victory for the patriarchal collective of the national majority, and the series of mass demonstrations by Iranian women, before they were repressed as well as the struggle of the Kurdish minority, reflect awareness of this.

References

Aloni, Shulamith (1976). *Women as Humans*. Tel-Aviv: Mabat Publications (Hebrew).

Althusser, Louis (1969). *For Marx*. London: Allen Lane.

Berman, Rabbi Saul (1977). "The Status of Women in Halikhic Judaism." In *Koltun*.

Beveridge, Sir William (1942). *Report on Social Insurance and Allied Services*. London: Hmso.

Chetwynd, Jane and Oonagh Hartnett, eds. (1978). *The Sex Role System*. London: Routledge and Kegan Paul.

Hazleton, Lesley (1978). *Israeli Women: The Reality Beyond the Myth*. Jerusalem: Idanim Publications (Hebrew).

Hecht, Dina and Yuval-Davis, Nira (1978). "Ideology without Revolution: Jewish Women in Israel." *Khamsin* (6):87–118.

Koltun, E., ed. (1977). *The Jewish Woman*. New York: Schocken Books.

Land, Hilary (1978). "Sex Role Stereotyping in the Social Security and Income Tax System." In Chetwynd and Hartnett (1978).

Leibowitz, J. (1958). "Biblical Law as Legal System in the State of Israel?" *Sura* 3 (Hebrew).

Leon, A. (1970). *The Jewish People: A Marxist Interpretation*. New York: Pathfinder Press.

Raset, Fadela M. (1969). *La Femme Algerienne*. Paris: Maspero (French).

Rotenberg, M., ed. (1964). *Religion and the State*. Tel Aviv: The National Religious Party Public Relations (Hebrew).

Verhaftig, Zerah (1964). "The State of Israel as a Jewish State." In Rotenberg (Hebrew).

Wilson, Elizabeth (1977). *Women and the Welfare State*. London: Tavistock Publications.

Yehezkeli, M. (1964). "Three Questions in the Name of Justice: A Letter to Those Who Call for the Right of Secular Law." *Beit-Jacob* 64 (Hebrew).

Yuval-Davis, Nira. "Marxism and Jewish Nationalism." Paper presented at the 1979 meeting of the Conference of Socialist Economists.

Paradoxes and Social Boundaries

Ultra-Orthodox Jewish Women and their World

Lɪᴛᴇʀᴀᴄʏ, ᴡᴏᴍᴇɴ, ᴀɴᴅ ᴛʜᴇ *ʜᴀʀᴇᴅɪ* (ultra-Orthodox) community in Israel are the three sides of this study's theoretical triangle. The connection between literacy and women stands at the center, with the haredi community connecting them. The linkage between literacy and women in haredi society is a paradoxical one: women are educated to maintain their ignorance. The sociological significance of this paradox in the community and among its women lies in the tension between the rich, varied, multifarious social reality of non-haredi Israeli culture of the 1980s and a community that is trying to remain homogeneous. The purpose of educating haredi women is to give them bodies of knowledge that will help them discern a single voice in the cacophony of modern society. As we have seen, however, the very act of gathering for study, even under these conditions, enables them to listen to a whole range of voices—even if they themselves continue to hum the desired tune. The haredim have constructed an educational system for women because there is no need to teach women, and the women have learned to be educated in ignorance in order to survive as educated women.

The educational process is supposed to grade a bumpy, potholed reality, making it smooth and easy to navigate. This exemplifies the way the haredi community deals with a whole range of paradoxes it faces: it strips them down into their individual components and compresses them into a single dimension. In the case of women's literacy, however, the way out of one paradox throws the community into another. The issue of women's literacy throws light on the social, conceptual, and value context of the haredi community as a whole and thus reveals other internal contradictions.

This model of behavior is not unique to the field of scholarship; it envelops the haredi community on all sides. This is because the haredi community, as a part of modern society, is open to outside stimuli that continually challenge it and force it into a constant reexamination of the content of its world. During the course of this reexamination, paradoxes emerge that create incongruity between values and behavior that cannot be left unresolved.

Men and Women

The haredi community sees gender categorization as manifest, ongoing, and explicitly significant for the course of life. Compared to Western secular society, where unceasing attempts are made to gain a new understanding of the differences between men and women, and to reshape relations between them accordingly, haredi society seems to be "an island of conservatism and stability." This island image is applied by outsiders to the haredim, and by the haredim to themselves. Yet, as we have seen, actual social action goes beyond the island and shows that the community is actually an integral part of Israeli society. This means that the haredim are constantly reexamining, in thought and action, the set of categories they use to decode their social reality, including the categorization of men and women. The social category called "gender" is here part of a cultural structure. Within the discourse of deconstructionism but without a theoretical discussion, the research (ethnography and its interpretation) aims to unveil some mechanisms of that gender structuring.[1]

The structure of "the natural order of things," within which the division of the sexes was presented, was largely researched by the first wave of feminist study.[2] The first order of business was to negate the "factual" disciplines, among them biology, ecology, and economics, and to promote a sociopolitical interpretation of "the natural order of things."[3] The road was then prepared for the study of the sociology of ideologies. Feminist studies conducted in Western societies have shown that these societies seem to have a democratic, egalitarian ideology regarding economics, education, law, art, the family, and so on. Yet alongside this apparent ideology there are invisible ideologies that undermine this declared equality.[4]

The opposite situation is true in the haredi community. The declared ideology speaks of inequality between men and women, defined as "differentiation." Under the force of this ideology, all things—including power roles, authority, control of resources, dress, education—are assigned. Haredi women accept this ideology a priori. Yet, in their daily experiences, in the society in which they function, within their relevant time and space, they carry out social activity that oversteps the declared ideology and infuses it with themes and behaviors that stem from their existence. This activity is parallel to the hidden ideological level in Western society, but its contents are, of course, different.

I would argue that women have a significant role in the non-automatic process of being placed within categories. This role, which Australian sociologist S. Burton adds to gender studies, stresses the active side of the women within the daily reality of their lives. Part of this study focuses on the question of how, in practical terms, subordination and dependency between women and men are created. What are the local reasons for this subordination in each context; and how does each group of women, in every culture, live with it, interpret it, give it meaning and validity, and perhaps try to change it?[5] It is therefore not enough to expose the gap between the sexes and its policy ideology, while presenting society as male. The social sciences must also study the entire input of women into each society.

With the aid of Burton's argument, we may show the transition from ethnography to methodology, and from there to the theoretical contribution. Instead of an all-inclusive theory about categorization and its cultural endurance, Burton breaks the argument down from ideology to praxis, to the "how." The study of the praxis illuminates the institutionalization of ideology, which then closes the circle. Anthropology can enrich this method because of its unmediated observation of those social processes.[6]

Observations of haredi women demonstrate the dynamic that creates the categorization, the meaning of the categorization in daily life, and its effects on the behavioral level—the construction of boundaries. My observations revealed two sources of dissonance, at foci of intensive social activity surrounding the status of women: the issue of luxury and the issue of education. Examination of them will aid in understanding the dynamic of the categorization of men and women and its implications for haredi women's lives. The problem of women's education and its social solution have been treated separately, while the subject of luxury will be presented as a part of the enterprise of erecting social boundaries in the haredi community.

The Flour and Torah Paradox

The public discourse in which the haredi community engages, and which may be seen as a "social arena," treats economic prosperity as a misfortune.[7] Research by Friedman (1986a, b) and by Shilhav and Friedman (1985) provides a good explanation of this public apprehension about wealth, and gives examples of this public attitude toward luxury.

In the post-industrial age, the haredi community exists in a state of permanent and ongoing repudiation of the secular-modern values of the society surrounding it. Yet its existence is possible only within such a society. Relative prosperity, government appropriations, and the deferral of military service allow haredi men to extend their period of study and to avoid working for a living. Their families become dependent on government stipends or the money brought in by working women. They live in economic hardship, which is particularly problematic because the families realize that they could improve their lot considerably if the father stopped his studies and went to work. Thus, economic prosperity allows men to learn because the government has the funds to support them. Yet these same studies create privation. Therefore, public discourse defending the scholars condemns prosperity as a value and the use of resources for needs other than study.

The condemnation of prosperity is evident in the following selections from *Marveh Latsameh*:

> We live in a period of material abundance. People have never had so much money, food, so much entertainment and amusement equipment. . . . We live in a period in which spiritual void has brought mankind to a state in which the purpose of life is enjoyment. Crime has increased in proportion to material abundance. . . .This leads us to the problem of luxury, a problem that grows by the day, which is reaching the dimensions of a matter of life-or-death, bankruptcies, heart attacks, nervous disorders, divorce, bad relations between husband and wife that undermines education in good values, *Hoshen Mishpat* [the section of the Shulkhan Arukh dealing with the laws of commerce and property], and laws of monetary dealings. . . . Once and for all we must lance this boil, this inflated colored balloon that sows devastation and destruction in the Torah, in the whole and the pure, values and morals, and the bitter fruits that grow from this we must eat in both worlds, this and the next. . . . The concept of "being original" is very popular today, everyone wants to be original and innovative, but let us be honest with ourselves and take a look at the small matters of dress, food, or what is called "the culture of consumption"—has the banner of originality not become one big social fraud.[8]

Or as Nava (one of the haredi women interviewees) said during one of her lessons on worms and insects: "What they say today is that every generation has its trial. There was the emancipation, the Holocaust, Zionism, and now it's luxury. That's what a lot of people say, that our generation is being tested with luxuries. And even if that seems much less than the previous trials, it is very dangerous. First, every generation is less strong, and also because it doesn't seem like a trial. People think it has no meaning, but it is a very great trial."

Abundance, luxury, and the culture of consumption are practical and valuable components of capitalist society. In the above quotations, however, they are portrayed as a real threat to the existence of the haredi community. Sometimes they are described as a general threat to the Torah, to purity, to values, and so on. (It is necessary to take into account the pathos that is an inseparable part of both spoken and written haredi public discourse.) Sometimes they are broken down into specific dangers, such as divorce, heart attacks, and nervous breakdowns. Either way, there is a contradiction between the condemnation of abundance and reliance on it, between the possibilities it opens for the haredi community and the fear of what it is liable to do, between the desire to foster the community's uniqueness and the integration that economic prosperity creates between the haredi community and the other groups that participate in the market.

Most haredi homes have electrical appliances, such as large refrigerators, washing machines, sewing machines, food processors, and modern ovens; some even have air conditioners, dishwashers, dryers, and other appliances that make life easier for large families. Many babies are dressed in disposable diapers and fed instant cereals. There are, of course, variations among different economic strata, between the families of working men and those of men who study at a *kolel* (full-time college for men), between the various hasidic groups, and between various places of residence. But in general the economic well-being of the haredi community is rising along with that of the rest of Israel's population.

The great attention lavished on the subject of luxury and its implications demands explanation. The tension between "flour and Torah," that is, between the needs for material and for spiritual sustenance, is not new, of course, but a paradox has now formed around these two elements. The sages said: "If there is no flour, there is no Torah." The contemporary discourse states: "If there is no flour, there is no Torah, and if there is flour, there is no Torah either." Haredi society seeks to be freed of this paradox, as of others.

Haredi society lives in anticipation of the time in the not-too-distant future when today's generation of avrechim (yeshiva and kolel students) must start marrying off its children. Unlike the previous generation, which had some resources from which to provide financial assistance to its children, the current generation has nothing. It also has a larger number of children than its parents' generation did, and the standard of living is higher.[9] In preparation for this approaching crisis, the public discourse has been enlisted in the condemnation of prosperity and the glorification of living simply. Haredi society's unique organization as a learning society, made possible by prosperity, may be destroyed by the very thing that created it. The haredi community thus chooses to equip its "religious package" with strict, demanding, particularistic, sexist, and puritanical values. These values contradict what is occurring around (and even within) the haredi community, and create the "counterculture" that is supposed to separate the haredi community from its surroundings and protect it. In order to protect itself from other similar communities, the public discourse is charged with values of *humra*, strictness.[10] It is in this that the counterculture acquires its specific traits. Everything secular society takes as a value is revised, and in every area in which other religious groups advocate leniency, the haredim advocate severity. Every community presents itself to its potential members as a club into which it is hard to be accepted.

In this way, Friedman argues, communities try to make themselves unique and elitist in comparison with their competitors (Friedman 1986).

Resolution of the paradox of luxury seems to be assigned largely to the women. The general discourse that describes luxury as this generation's trial leads into specific accusations directed at women. The generation's trial is thus turned into women's most important trial. The haredi community considers itself to be a collection of individuals aspiring to a modest lifestyle, with minimal needs, but this aspiration encounters a barrier on its way to realization—the covetousness of females. This is the reduction of the flour-and-Torah paradox, and it is stated in such a way that it vanishes, leaving the field clear of men. The women are left alone, and they must cope with this "terrible trial" on their own.

In each of the quotations presented above there is a transition from sounding a general alarm to pointing an accusatory finger at women and girls:

> A mother must accustom her children from the earliest age and tell the children that what they have is sweeter than honey. . . . My daughter, do not envy your friend or your neighbor. . . . The dress Mommy bought you is the prettiest. . . . What joy is it for a mother that from dawn until dark she has nothing to do but to cook, knit, and sew for her children, grandchildren, and great-grandchildren.
>
> They present themselves with an ultimatum, what do you mean that everyone around me has and I don't. This ultimatum leads to discord and fights that disturb the home's well-being in a way that the girls grow up in such an atmosphere so that they, too, will present their husbands with ultimatums, like their mothers, and the husbands that are not able or not interested in holding up under the pressure of the demands are liable to send their wives back to their parents' house, sometimes along with the children.
>
> We must feel that we are not missing a thing. If we feel that we do not have to wear the latest fashionable coat then our daughters will also feel comfortable in clothes a little bit different from her peers, and will maybe even take pride in her originality.

> Hannah: I also heard from my husband about the generation's trial. People talk about it a lot. What I don't understand is how you connect that subject with what we're discussing.
>
> Nava: It begins when someone says that you can go to Levinsky Street and buy fresh by weight, everyone jumps on her. Who wants to take the trouble to go into town to buy at a bargain when you can buy in the supermarket. This is where it begins, when women do not want to cut back, the most important thing is convenience.

An article in Marveh Latsameh takes a romantic and accusatory attitude to the present generation of women:

But there is no need to go so far afield. One can simply ask how did my mother manage with three babies without a washing machine? . . . She had to prepare Sabbaths and holidays for a large family. . . . And how did my mother lug blocks of ice for her icebox and carry those heavy blocks up to the third floor. . . . And today . . . families buy sewing machines and freezers and even dryers and dishwashers. . . . But still it is obvious that we have no time to visit a sick aunt or to help a friend who needs it because we are very busy people and we have to invent a machine that will visit the aunt for us.[11]

Rabbis, educators, teachers, and important women charge public discourse with diatribes against the "phenomenon of luxuries." They have much to say about the "generation's trial," about the "threat of luxuries," and about the "filth in money." Despite this, the haredi community, just like other communities in Israel and the West, partially measures a family's or community's success by its economic attainments. Within the universe of values itself, and in conjunction with the social reality, this creates unresolvable and unsolvable paradoxes. After having brought the issue of luxury into the public discourse as part of constructing its counterculture, haredi society must free itself from the vicious circle that this choice causes practically. It would seem that breaking free of the paradox of luxury, which is, as noted, a typical and prominent example of the entire process of circularity, is largely imposed on females and is linked to the more fundamental value of modesty.

DIAPERS AND DIAMONDS

In the twenty-fifth anniversary book of the Sharansky Beit Ya'akov college in Tel Aviv, David Zaritzky writes as follows: "Place the woman once more on the throne prepared at the time of creation for the Jewish mother, and she will be happier with diapers than an ostentatious woman is with a diamond-encrusted necklace, and a night up with her child will be more enjoyable to her than a night of dancing in a café. Beit Ya'akov took modesty, which had been pushed into a corner, and dressed its students, took the light that had not yet been outshone and which was tossing under the feet of the rock-and-rollers and crowned the heads of our mothers with it."[12]

Transferring the generation's trial onto women's shoulders made an additional reworking necessary. It was no longer sufficient to say that women should be more modest in their demands. The request must have a reason and must be accompanied by a threat. The reason added to the demand to refrain from pursuing luxuries was more particularly directed at women than the other reasons we have seen; it is part of observing the rules of modesty.[13]

No one in the haredi community will come out against modesty. As a vague and comprehensive value, everyone in each haredi group accepts modesty submissively. As a result, it becomes an efficient and important tool. Everyone wants to be modest, and everyone may be accused of having violated its rules. So by declaring that a woman must eschew luxury in order to preserve her modesty, one links the demand to a threat to a woman's reputation. This threat exposes women, as a public, to a multitude of reproofs and rebukes.

The observational evidence shows that every time women gather for any purpose—study, celebration, charity, and so on—they were admonish about modesty. The admonishments may be categorized in accordance with four dimensions each of which require separate discussion, but will be presented at only the most basic level:

1. Extent—the proportion of the event devoted to the admonishments.
2. Location—where the admonishment occurs, that is, at home, in the neighborhood, or outside the Development.
3. Source—who admonishes—man or woman, an external figure invited for that purpose, or a local figure on his or her own initiative.
4. Message—the content of the admonishment and what it is linked to.

Two of many admonishments I observed are described below.

SELF-CHASTISEMENT

After about six months in which there was no activity at all, the women met at the Beit Ya'akov School that serves the Sephardi haredi children in the adjacent neighborhood. At 8:45 P.M. some thirty women, most from Gur, were present in one of the classrooms. Two Sephardi women with kerchiefs on their heads sat in a corner, apart. Some of the young women were new in the Development—young newlyweds who had taken the place of women whose period of "exile" had ended, enabling them to return to Bene Brak or Jerusalem. The room was animated. The women collected in groups; most knew each other from their studies at the Beit Ya'akov College from which they had recently graduated. They were dressed well, in colorful and fashionable knits, and wore modern wigs, some of which reached the shoulder. About a third of the women present were pregnant. Nava stood at the front of the classroom by the teacher's desk. At twenty-three, she had been married for more than two years, but still had no children. She began to speak, but the noise did not die down. She persisted, and slowly silence fell over the room, the girls shushing one another.

"I apologize for the delay," she said. "The teacher refused to come in a cab for reasons of modesty, so she will arrive on the nine o'clock bus."

At the set hour Mrs. Frieda Hertig, a teacher at the Beit Ya'akov College in Bene Brak, arrived. The girls made a gesture of rising (lifting their behinds slightly). Frieda, thirty-three years old, dressed in a plaid wool dress, had a slender figure and wore a short wig of the reasonable type (not modern but not the simplest, most inexpensive type, either). She did not greet us with a "good evening" or "hello"; instead she immediately began: "There was a flute in the Temple. A pipe flute. Thin, smooth, and simple. The flute had an incomparably pleasant and beautiful sound. The king so loved the flute that he ordered that it be plated in gold. They took it to the best craftsmen and plated it with the finest gold. The flute lost its sound. When they took the gold off, it once again played with a wondrous sound. This is the way Jewish women are our beauty lies in our simplicity."

Her voice was dramatic. She reads from notes with all her accents correctly placed, her grammar impeccable. The teacher then explained the metaphor, nearly word by word. She did not leave a single symbol unexplained.

Afterwards she recalled that women from the Development had asked her to speak about modesty. There were giggles from the audience, and the speaker herself smiled. Yes, simply that, whoever expected something else can still leave.

> The fact that you live in this Development is a result of you all being connected to the same righteous man. This is the rebbe's commandment. Even if it is technical, such a community, such a public, has much power. Not as it would be if we lived scattered around. You are together, the society has a voice. So in just such a place there is a problem of modesty. It is true that our generation is being tested with a great trial in the matter of consumption and modesty and we all need great changes, but to what point? A woman will wear a slit in her skirt? Where does that boldness come from? Lord of the Universe, to be first? The one that comes after her will need much less courage, but the first one, where does she get the strength from, from where? A woman who goes out of her house and everything is exactly in place, every hair, the clothes, that doesn't come naturally, right? You have to devote time to that, so she leaves the house with a sign on herself—this is what interests me. She didn't notice? She doesn't know that that's what people see on her? So let me judge her leniently—she's simply a fool.
>
> A while ago there was a conference on modesty at the Modi'in Hall and rabbis spoke there. What have we come to that we have to talk about this subject in public, that rabbis come before women to talk to them about this? So our generation is bringing the rabbis down as well.
>
> Everyone wants to be different. I cut some advertisements out of *Hamodia*, nothing special, just advertisements for furniture, clothing, such things. Every second word is exclusive, special, unique. People devote so much time to not being like their neighbor. A woman runs to every store there is to buy a special dress. With my own ears I heard a very respectable woman who was, mazel tov, about to marry off her daughter, and don't get me wrong I haven't married off a daughter and haven't had to face the test. She said that she had combed the United States of America in order to find her a special wedding gown. Who are we doing that for? Do our avrechim deserve that kind of treatment?

Ahhhh . . . It's not for our husbands? So then we really shouldn't have to think about it. We're a link in a chain that goes back to Sarah, and we give to our daughters, what will we give them? They say of Abraham our father that he reached Egypt with Sarah and they stood on the edge of the Nile. He saw her reflection in the water and told her "Now I know that you are a beautiful woman." What did he see in her? The sages say that all the women of the generation of Egypt knew that their behavior would cause Israel's redemption. That's our beauty, not outward beauty.

The teacher went on, her tone changing from one appropriate for a friendly conversation to one of serious preaching. From time to time she would throw in a midrash or biblical verse (about the Shulamit from the Song of Songs, for instance). The women sat quietly, most of them staring at the floor.

At the end of the lesson her former students and current colleagues gathered around her, chatting with her happily. Tsipi told her: "Good for you, we've been waiting for this talk for a long time, let's hope that something gets moving." The other women left in twos or threes. Hannah and I exited, leaving a room in which there was a palpable sense of relief.

We stood and talked in the cold of a February night by the fence around Hannah's building. Slowly the women emerged from the school and passed by us. Devorah was carrying a tape recorder, on which she had recorded the lecture. She came up to us.

"That's it, I've done my part."

Devorah, very active in the Development, had invited Frieda Hertig to speak. She had been a resident for seven years. Recently, her husband had been appointed manager of a well-known hotel in Bene Brak, and they were about to move there. His father had a hotel in Lugano, Switzerland, so he knew the work.

Devorah worked at home, styling wigs. She was always dressed with particular elegance, sporting a variety of wigs-long ones, adorned with colored pins and loud pink lipstick. She and her sister were always together and formed the nucleus of the group of "Tel Avivians" in the Development. As she was standing with us, a young girl approached her and said:

"So, when will you have time for me, I've got to have my second wig, the long one, styled for the wedding. You know that it's urgent for me, I've got to have it styled, it looks horrible."

Hannah smiled at me, lowering her head. What a fitting conclusion for both the lecture and the woman who arranged it.

Devorah also smiled, turned her back, and began to stride toward the stairwell, blurting:

"Leave me alone now, call me on the phone."

INVITATION TO A REPRIMAND

At the wedding hall on Hamasger Street in Tel Aviv a fundraising night was held for the dining hall of the yeshiva in the Gur Development in Hatzor Hagelilit. The walls were covered with decorated wallpaper with velvet maroon-colored flowers. At the entrance were huge mirrors, and on the floor wall-to-wall carpeting. The hall was packed. Some four hundred women were socializing, dressed in their best clothes. It was Saturday night, and the glow of the Sabbath still remained in the women's faces. The noise in the hall was deafening. The women tried to get places around those tables with the best views of the stage in the front of the hall. In a few minutes there would be speeches by the head of the yeshiva, its patron, and by a respected woman, a teacher from London. Afterwards the girls from the Gur College in Bene Brak were to present a musical entertainment—or, as the program stated, "A Musical with Many Morals."

After the talks by the head of the yeshiva and the fundraiser, Mrs. Yaffa Mendel of London mounted the stage. She was wearing a simple dark dress and a short wig.

> We are the daughters of Eve. Why? We give life. We have a role with regard to others. To be a helpmeet. Helpmeet? Not at the expense of the husband and children. Not to run off in the evenings to fundraisers. To be public activists. A helpmeet to minimize demands. Yes, you can take a pencil and paper and add it up. How much clothing do you need, how many wigs? What difference does it make where the buttons are and how the collar lies? It will make your husband happy. Maybe it won't make the neighbors happy, but God yes, that's how you can collect money for charity, not at parties. Your husband will study with his mind at rest, the children will be cared for and the woman will be at home with her small demands.

The women slowly reached out for the coffee pots and the chocolate filled cakes on the tables. Each of them had paid 20 shekels for the evening, and here an important woman from London was telling them that they shouldn't have come, that this was not the proper way to raise money. They knew that the speech would be over in a few minutes, however; it would be possible to look up from the floor and enjoy the show, even if it was called "A Musical with Many Morals."

Modesty is the basic, broadest, and most inclusive standard of a woman's behavior. It can measure an entire range of her activities—her dress, her speech, her education, the way she educates her children, her work at home and outside it, and more. The standard of modesty is enlisted whenever there is a need to oversee what any woman is doing. "Luxuries" are described as a negative phenomenon embracing all of society, powered mainly by women. The standard of modesty becomes a preventative and threatening factor, in order to persuade women that (1) luxury is indeed the curse of this generation; (2) women are the motivating and determining force in the world of consumption; and (3) women have the central responsibility for the success or failure of this generation's trial. The logical parallels among these three statements are not left to a woman's own comprehension. Every private or public opportunity is used to explain them to her.

The use of the standard of modesty turns each individual woman into a target of evaluation and judgment, and exposes her to the danger of slander. Modesty can also be a standard by which a community is judged, as we saw in Frieda Hertig's talk. This teacher had charges to make against "the women of the Development." She conveyed her message that life in a homogeneous and constricted community obligated them to a higher standard than that applied to other women. The lecturer had been invited by several local women who felt that the situation was deteriorating. As I recall, nothing in particular had occurred in the Development to arouse the women. In the daily routine a talk about modesty is always appropriate. The women, for their part, accept such lectures as part of the obligations of the community, and take great comfort in them. This was made clear to me during one of my conversations with Hannah.

> Hannah: So, did you enjoy Mrs. Hertig's talk?
> I: Not particularly. I felt a little like a first-grader getting chewed out.
> Hannah: I know, you like really high talk, about Maimonides and about faith in the Book of Psalms.
> I: That's true, but I couldn't help noticing how all the women sat like good little girls while she gave them a piece of her mind.
> Hannah: For you it doesn't make a difference, what do you understand, but they, when they go to Bene Brak to buy a dress, talk about Maimonides doesn't help them. Maimonides doesn't help you put the money back in your wallet. You need something that makes you strong, that gives you the strength, that gives you the strength.

Teacher Frieda Hertig had been invited to come especially from Bene Brak in order to give the women strength. Some of the women understood her the way Hannah did; others listened, but were not inclined to carry out her instructions on a practical level (like the woman who needed her wig styled for a wedding). There were even those who told me that, in their opinion, the women in the Development were very modest and that they did not understand why they were being reprimanded. Nevertheless, the women accepted the admonishments about modesty as a valid form of discourse. They knew that it could surprise them at a party or a play, in their homes at the Sabbath table, or among friends in the Development while the children played. It was plain to them that this was the price they had to pay so that the show, in both senses of the word, could go on.

Yaffa Mendel, who spoke before a gathering of charity volunteers at a benefit evening, went even further. She told them explicitly: It's good you came, because this is the place to tell you that you shouldn't have come. In other words, those who came to hear the lecture heard the lecturer tell them that the proper place for women was not at a charity evening but at home. (Note the parallel to Rabbi Wolf's exhortation: Go to school in order not to learn.) Mrs. Mendel proposed that women save for charity out of their personal budget: one less wig meant more for charity. Like many others, she linked modesty in a women's material demands with her husband's and sons' success in their studies and with God's will. These linkages are so consequential for haredi women that the only possible response is what I observed in the hall—to lower one's head and nibble some chocolate cake.

Understanding Haredi Women

The concept of "modesty" is, then, the central axis for understanding the social and personal existence of the haredi woman. Anthropologist Rhonda Berger-Sofer, who studied the women of Ha'eda Haharedit in the Mea She'arim neighborhood of Jerusalem, tried to show that women serve as the haredi community's shock absorbers.[14] This is why women are drawn toward nature while men are pushed toward culture. Since they are in contact with the mundane, the profane, and the material, women can maintain contact with the outside, that is, with the secular environment. Modesty is enlisted in this case to defend women from the outside. The importance of a woman's reputation is an insurance policy that ensures that the woman will not take her contacts with the outside too far.

Vimla Jayanti, an anthropologist who worked in the same community, argues that modesty is for the most part an educational tool. She found that the ethic of modesty may be found everywhere a female is educated. In her opinion, the use of modesty does not have a particular direction, and in her study she argues that the standard of *balebeitishkeit*, of homemaking, is more relevant to oversight and critique of women. This standard, which is of great significance in other haredi communities (including Gur) as well, is especially strong among Ha'eda Haharedit. The families of this community live in constricted economic circumstances and lack any thorough education for women, and the difficulty of finding work for women outside the home and the neighborhood makes the virtues of the housewife more significant than any others.[15]

In a society where people sometimes have trouble obtaining food, clothing, and shelter, "abundance" in the normal sense of the word presents no threat. Austerity and getting by with little form part of this dimension of homemaking, which becomes the major criterion according to which women are evaluated and supervised.

Yet in the haredi community outside the walls of Mea She'arim, it is the women who are the agents of breaking free of the paradox of luxury. This generation's success or failure in its trial depends, as we have seen, on the women. But here, as in all else, any possible outcome will be to their detriment. If the generation fails its test, it will be "because of the demanding women"; if the generation passes the test, it will be because the men knew how to oppose women's demands, how not to give in.

Among the many possibilities available to the religious community, it chooses and nurtures the ideological option of modesty. This choice is consistent with encouraging married men to continue their studies and with fostering the image of an "ascetic community," and is even a consequence of it. Puritanism (which itself may well contradict previous Jewish values and be something of a borrowing from Christianity) aids women in their daily lives. It turns their plight into worship, their relative poverty into a social virtue, and their private troubles into partial comfort.

The counterculture constructed in opposition to secular society is mainly directed at the middle-class members of the community. Wealth is not an undesirable state. The existence of a moneyed class as a small part of Jewish society does not constitute a threat to the "ascetic community." On the contrary, this class supports religious and charitable institutions and provides mates for poor scholars. The problem of consumption and luxury termed "this generation's trial" is a problem of the middle classes. Life in a Western society with a competitive market enables everyone to experience consumerism and welfare.[16] The sense of unlimited possibilities is an incentive for economic activity. For a very narrow segment of society these expectations are realized, but among much larger segments they remain a dream difficult to achieve, and this causes great pressure in daily life. In traditional Jewish society there were rich and poor, and the division of labor between them, between flour and Torah, was understood by all. In Israel today, the haredi community has chosen to artificially constrain the certain ability that exists to blur the distinction between these traditional classes. As men are induced to extend their years of study, consumption becomes a delaying and pressuring factor, and the battle to restrict consumption is organized socially as a campaign of and against women.

The boundaries drawn by the haredi community for itself within Jewish society exist as a result of a paradoxical situation. The haredim live in a pluralist society that allows them to undermine its foundations. They charge their cultural choice with values that run contrary to the capitalist society of abundance, and present consumption as "this generation's disaster" and austerity as "this generation's trial." In this same way they wish to protect the learning society, which urges men to abstain from entering the labor market; this is the way they present the economic strain that this society creates. Yet only a society of relative prosperity can bear the burden of this choice. Any attempt to resolve and connect the components of this paradox immediately gives rise to new paradoxes, while any attempt to break it down into its components—state and religion, for instance—is still far away.

The subject of women's education and status, which stands at the center of this book, constitutes a classic example of this circuitous process. At the first stage, the orthodox community was provoked into establishing formal education for women, in order to counter the process of secularization and general education that was experienced by most European Jews. Orthodox schools for women were established in order to prevent the girls from being sent to non-Jewish or Zionist schools. In an attempt to circumvent the process of education, orthodoxy had no choice but to become part of it. Haredi women began to study.

During the second stage, with the move to Israel, the educational discourse was charged with anti-Zionist and anti-nationalist values. The community was part of the Zionist-nationalist state, economically dependent on its resources and mindful of events on the socio-cultural level. This attentiveness to what was happening in the secular arena guided the construction of the community's cultural essence. This society, which some assume wishes to close itself off within its own walls, makes a great effort to know what is going on "out there." It turns these findings upside-down and presents them as a behavioral standard to its members.

The haredi educational system for women offers a feminine ideal type. It is the opposite of the set of feminine traits common in the surrounding society, and it is appropriate to the learning men's society. No wonder, then, that women's education has been defined by the haredim as an attempt to recreate a generation of simple and ignorant women like those mothers and grandmothers who never studied at all. This contradictory attempt to educate for ignorance has been presented here in all its facets. We have seen that there is methodical direction of the presentation of the pragmatic aspects of knowledge before women. There is a tendency to divide knowledge into "masculine" and "feminine" fields—or what the women call the "substantial" and the "practical." The women's educational system opens certain doors for them and takes care to keep others locked. Yet from the moment women become literate, they themselves conduct negotiations over the essence of the boundaries between different fields of knowledge. Women still do not study the Gemara, which is the main part of male knowledge and the source of literate and social power in the haredi world. Yet they can cite laws from the *Shulkhan Arukh* (book of laws) quote homilies from the ethical literature, and recite a midrash to illustrate their point. They overhear their husbands studying the Gemara with their study partners at home, and they go over Talmudic disputations with their sons. Most important, they know how to navigate between the different fields of knowledge and to test one field with the help of another. When they are presented with practical study, they attack it with abstract questions; when they are offered abstract knowledge, they bring it down to earth.

If one speaks with them on Maimonides' view of the barriers between man and his creator, they find a way of interpreting the issue with the aid of their shopping list. If one preaches "thou shalts" and "thou shalt nots" about slander or modesty, they suggest speaking of Torah instead of gossiping, they make abstract comparisons with the male world, they describe the preaching as "spiritual strengthening," or they let the preaching fly over their heads.

This is how they make their way through their world, a world whose social order they accept a priori. On the one hand, they know how to experience this world as ignorant and simple women and accept the rule of the male world; but on the other hand, they are sufficiently literate to be aware of the situation they are in and to find meaning in it.

Haredi men have constructed an educational system for women because "there is no need for women to study." Haredi women have learned to be educated, and to educate, in ignorance, in order to survive as educated women.

Notes

1. Nicholson 1990.
2. Kristeva 1981.
3. Strathern 1988.
4. Bem and Bem 1971.
5. Burton 1985.
6. Strathern 1988.
7. On discourse as a social field of events, see Foucault (1970, 1980).
8. From *Marveh Latsameh*, in order of appearance: Yisrael Pollak, 35, 5746 (1986):15–19; Elhanan Hertzman, 50, 5746 (1986):22; N. Shapira, 50, 5746 (1986): 42.
9. While I was writing this book, after my observations were completed, I continued to maintain contact with the Gur women, as well as with other acquaintances in the haredi community. I presented several of my conclusions to them. With regard to the coming economic crisis, a man with a key position in the haredi community noted to me that every (middle-class) couple that has married has cost each side of the family about $60,000. This money was raised from personal holdings and from loans from haredi community funds (gamahim). The gamahim are now on the verge of collapse, and private capital has shrunk. There have been attempts to engineer a general restitution of debts involving the entire deficiency of funds on the part of several rich overseas haredim, but these have not brought results so far. In his estimation, the "learning society" may well suffer a severe blow in the near future. Couples getting married will be forced to live in rented apartments, and the stipends provided by the *yeshivot* (religious colleges) to their students will not be sufficient to pay for rent and living expenses. Some of those studying today will have to find work. This may well be the most weighty reason for the haredi community's increasing involvement in the government and public spheres. Such involvement guarantees a steady flow of government funds to sustain the learning society, or at least a large part of it.
10. The distinction between humra (strictness) and kula (leniency) is made on two levels. One distinguishes between the greater and lesser religious observances ("Run to perform a kula observance just as to a humra observance" [Avot 4:2, 2:11]). The second distinguishes between different ways of carrying out an observance whether on a certain question of observance the rule should be lenient or severe (Eruvin 4:1; Pesahim 4:1; Orla 2:6).

It is in this context that what is called "religious extremism" should be understood. The extremism is not motivated by devotion to God; it is a social solution to cultural competition. The groups freed of public responsibility for all of Israel charge their identity with severe demands in order to set themselves apart from the secular masses and from their religious competitors as part of their cultural marketing strategy.

11. "Muvan Me'elav," 34, 5747 (1987):25–26.
12. Zaritzsky, 5769 (1969):94.
13. The significance of modesty in the lives of Jewish women has received much attention, both in internal (orthodox) literature and in the research literature: Halevy-Steinberg 5743 (1983); Ki-Tov 5723 (1963), 5733 (1973); Fuchs 5744 (1984); Naftali 5745 (1985); Rotenberg 5742 (1982); Schenirer 5715 (1955).
14. Berger-Sofer 1979.
15. Jayanti 1982.
16. Lasch 1978.

References

Bem, S. and D. Bem. 1971. "Trainining the Woman to Know Her Place: The Power of a Non-Conscious Ideology." In M. Hoffnung Garskof, ed., *Roles Women Play*. Pacific Grove, Calif.: Brooks/Cole.

Berger-Sofer, R. 1979. *Pious Women*. Ann Arbor: Mich.: University Microfilms.

Burton, C. 1985. *Subordination*. Sydney: George Allen and Unwin.

Friedman, Menachem. "Life Tradition and Book Tradition in the Development of Ultra-Orthodox Judaism." In H.E. Goldberg, ed., *Judaism Viewed from Within and from Without*. Albany: New York: State University of New York Press.

Fuchs, Y. 5744 (1984). *Laws of the Daughter of Israel*. Jerusalem: n.p.

Jayanti, B. 1982. "Women in Me'a Shearim." Master's Thesis, Department of Sociology and Anthropology, Hebrew University, Jerusalem.

Ki-Tov, A. 5724 (1963). *The Book of Our Heritage* Jerusalem: Beit Hotsa'at Sefarim.

Kristeva, J. 1981. "Women's Time," translated by A. Jardine and H. Blake. *Signs: A Journal of Women and Society* 7:13–35.

Lasch, C. 1978. *The Culture of Narcissism*. New York: W.W. Norton.

Naftali, G. 5745 (1985). *Guide/Epistle for the Bride*. Bene Brak: Tefutsa.

Nicholson, Linda. 1990. *Feminism/Postmodernism*. New York: Routledge.

Rotenberg, Y. 5742 (1982). *The Jewish Home, the Jewish Family*. Bene Brak: Netsah.

Schenirer, S. 5715 (1955). *A Mother in Israel*. Tel Aviv: Netsah.

Shilhav, Y. and M. 5745 (1985). "Spreading Within Isolation—The Haredi Community in Jerusalem." Jerusalem: The Jerusalem Institute for Israel Studies, 15.

Strathern, M. (1988). *The Gender of the Gift*. Berkeley and Los Angeles: University of California Press.

Zaritszky, D. 5729 (1969). *Anniversary Book*. Tel Aviv: Hotsa'at Beit Ya'akov.

The Ritualized Body

Brides, Purity, and the Mikveh

For discourse is not only an instrument of persuasion, operating along
rational (or pseudo-rational) and moral (or pseudo-moral) lines, but it is
also an instrument of sentiment evocation. Moreover, it is through these
paired instrumentalities—ideological persuasion and sentiment evocation—
that discourse holds the capacity to shape and reshape society itself.
> —BRUCE LINCOLN, *Discourse*
> *and the Construction of Society*

For three sins women die in the hour of giving birth: For carelessness in
keeping niddah *[laws of menstrual purity],* challah *[removing a portion*
of dough as tithe to the priesthood], and [Shabbat] candle-lighting.
> —MISHNAH SHABBAT 2:6

THE MIKVEH IS A PURIFICATORY RITUAL bath primarily used by women in conjunction with menstrual and childbirth bleeding. Popular discourses regarding *niddah* (menstrual impurity, which is resolved through immersion in the mikveh) and ceremonial prenuptial immersion in the mikveh demonstrate how rituals work on sensory and corporeal levels to create effects that seem "really real" (Geertz 1973). By engaging in the intimate corporeal drills of the niddah–mikveh ritual sequence, Jewish Israeli women reenact or re-embody events, values, stories, and symbols of cultural significance, thus drawing themselves into, or being drawn into, collective narratives of gender and purity.

Attention to ritual is of crucial importance because, as Bruce Lincoln has shown so well, hierarchies, including gender hierarchies, are established and defended "through those discourses that legitimate or mystify their structures, premises, and workings" (1989, 173). Symbolic discourses such as ritual, myth, spectacle, gesture, costume, and icon obviate the need for the direct use of coercive force, which anyway remains "a stopgap measure: effective in the short run, unworkable over the long haul," and transform simple power into legitimate authority (4–5).[1] Hierarchies certainly make use of physical coercion and rational persuasion, but more than that hierarchies are created and sustained by authority—by "a posited, perceived, or institutionally ascribed asymmetry"—that permits certain people to command the confidence, respect, and trust of others, or "an important proviso to make [others] act as if this were so" (Lincoln 1994, 4). Ritual contexts, with their suspension of rational questioning and their aura of divine directive, authenticity, and tradition, are especially potent frameworks for forging relationships of authority and subordination.

In Israeli society, as in much of the world, control of women's bodies is enacted as much through symbolic discourses and ritual performances as through direct expressions of power. The advantage of symbolic control is that it has the capacity to evoke feelings of allegiance and loyalty among those who might seem (to outsiders) to have a great deal to lose from cooperating with authoritarian institutions. The "problem" with symbolic control is that it tends not to be absolute or complete; it continuously needs to be reenacted, inspected, scrutinized, checked, and double-checked. This pattern of surveillance, epitomized in the Jewish-Israeli niddah and mikveh ritual complex, has some very serious corporeal consequences for women. By encouraging women and men to pay excessive attention to women's bodies, women come to be seen as "more bodily" than men. This collective perception feeds into a gendered conceptual schema in which men are construed as associated with projects of culture, while women are construed as mired in their own corporeality (Ortner 1996). Because culture is by definition "above" nature—the process of making culture is the process of conquering nature—this conceptualization further legitimates social programs of controlling (socializing or enculturing) women's bodies.

In many cultures, including Israel, men and women believe that women's bodies in their normal state are too natural. In the particular Jewish-Israeli version, the hyper-naturalness of women's bodies tends to be interpreted as illness, weakness, vulnerability, or niddah, and tends to be treated through the expert care of physicians, politicians, and rabbis who sometimes collude and sometimes compete for the power to define and control women's reproductive and sexual resources.

Niddah and Mikveh in Contemporary Israeli Culture

When a woman has a discharge of blood which is her regular discharge from her body, she shall be in her impurity for seven days.

Leviticus 15:19

Israeli women are acquainted with a variety of beliefs regarding menstruation. The modern notion that menstruation is a normal, healthy, unmysterious physiological process is taught in family and sex education programs in Israeli schools. Contemporary folk culture has embraced such medicalized menstrual syn-dromes as PMS. Gynecologists are likely to treat menstruation as pathological if the menstrual cycle deviates from absolute regularity of timing or flow. Media advertisements for feminine hygiene products commodify menstruation. And tra-ditional Jewish conceptualizations of menstrual purity and impurity continue to carry a great deal of weight for many women, even when juxtaposed to these other views.

Purity in Jewish culture is a multilayered, dense concept. Before the destruc-tion of the Temple in Jerusalem in the year 70 CE, the laws of niddah and mikveh were part of a sizable complex of laws dealing primarily with the Temple cult. With the destruction of the Temple most of these laws—with the exception of those concerning menstruation and childbirth—became irrelevant to Jewish life. As post–Temple Judaism developed, women's bodies became in a sense a symbol of the Temple, and some of the ritual and legal attention that had formerly been focused upon the Temple began to become focused upon women's bodies (see Meacham 1989). Over the centuries, preoccupation with women's purity became an expres-sion of Jewish religiosity and identity (see Wasserfall 1992).

Jewish texts such as the Talmud and the Shulkhan Aruch contain detailed exegeses of the biblical law cited in the epigraph at the beginning of this section. Very briefly, couples are expected to refrain from sexual relations during the days of the woman's menstrual flow and for seven clean days afterward, following which the woman meticulously washes herself and then fully immerses three or more times in a ritual bath (mikveh) of "living water" (directly channeled rain water or spring water) in the presence of a mikveh attendant who has previously checked her to make sure that her body is truly clean. The couple is then allowed to resume sexual relations.[2]

For Jewish women, *halakhic* (legal) treatment of menstruation is embedded within ideological conceptualizations that explicate and embellish the laws. For example, some Israeli women say that menstruation is a punishment given to women because of Eve's weakness or transgression. Linking menstruation (and its attendant cramps and "mess") with Eve draws the bodies of individual women into a mythic narrative, thereby imparting symbolic weight to women's physio-logical processes. By rooting menstruation in Eve's sin—her vulnerability to the snake which led her to endanger Adam—these women understand that they them-selves suffer because of some essential female weakness. Part of the attraction of niddah and mikveh rituals is the opportunity to mitigate some of the consequences of Eve's punishment. Logically enough, some women perceive a connection between menstruation, which removes blood from women in order make them pure, and the ritual salting that removes blood from meat in order to make it kosher (Cicurel 1998).

While only a minority of Israeli women (approximately one quarter) attend the mikveh regularly, almost all Jewish Israeli women receive a crash course in mikveh ideology and practice when, as brides, they are obligated to immerse in the mikveh by the Orthodox rabbis who hold a monopoly on weddings and divorce in Israel.[3] Outside of a few discrete populations of dedicated secularists, most Israeli women are likely to have at least some contact with a friend, neighbor, relative, or co-worker who uses the mikveh and who extols its virtues.[4] Mikveh committees, active throughout the country, distribute literature on the mikveh and send out volunteers to teach women about the benefits of keeping the laws of ritual immersion. And at least among Israel's large North African and Asian ethnic populations, regular use of the mikveh never disappeared from the cultural map. Today's young women almost certainly have mothers or grandmothers who observed the laws of mikveh immersion. For these reasons, I see the conceptualizations and ritual routines of niddah and mikveh as constituting a corporeal landscape salient, or at least familiar, to the majority of Israeli women.

Mikvehs are located in almost every Israeli town and settlement, and in many neighborhoods in the larger cities. The Israeli mikveh establishment is quite institutionalized. Almost all mikvehs are administered by municipal religious councils; mikveh attendants are trained in courses run by state-sponsored rabbis; pamphlets and brochures available at the mikvehs are published by various governmental and nongovernmental agencies and organizations; and in some cities, such as Beer Sheva (see Cicurel 1998), the rabbinate employs women counselors who go door to door trying to convince women to use the mikveh and who organize meetings at which they teach about the benefits and laws of niddah. In the following discussion my own observations carried out over the past decade at mikvehs in Jerusalem are augmented by field work conducted by Inbal Cicurel in Beer Sheva and Ayelet Kaveh in Ramat Gan and Kfar Saba.

Israeli women frequent the mikveh for a number of reasons. For Orthodox and ultra-Orthodox Ashkenazi women, the mikveh is one aspect of a total lifestyle structured around observance of Jewish law. Most of the conversations I held with ultra-Orthodox and Orthodox Ashkenazi women at the mikveh centered upon fine points of Halakha (Jewish law) regarding timing of immersion—keeping track of the menstrual cycle and checking oneself internally twice each day during the week following menstruation to make sure that bleeding has ceased, worrying about having made a mistake of some sort regarding observance of the law (perhaps a bit of glue from an adhesive bandage had not been sufficiently removed from the skin, thus constituting a barrier between one's body and the water of the mikveh), fretting that the children at home have not yet been put to bed or that unexpected guests are wondering why the hostess has disappeared, or boasting about having managed to make it to the mikveh in difficult circumstances (as, for example, during a trip to Turkey, or when the extended family is visiting for a bar mitzvah, or despite having late meetings at work every night that week, and so on). These women were generally less than interested in long discussions (with me) about niddah and mikveh, and unless specifically asked rarely volunteered reasons for using the mikveh or feelings about keeping the laws of niddah.[5]

The other large category of mikveh attendees (in the 1990s) is comprised of second- and third-generation Israeli women whose parents or grandparents came from Asia or North Africa.[6] Most of these women consider themselves to be secular or traditional; a smaller number are Orthodox, or ultra-Orthodox. The dress of the women in this group displays their fairly wide range of religious observance: some wear skirts to below their knees while others come to the mikveh wearing sleeveless tops and shorts. Many do not observe other features of traditional Jewish law yet feel strongly about the importance of niddah and mikveh. The repertoire of reasons they offer for choosing to use the mikveh incorporates a range of personal, natural, and supernatural considerations. Some talk about the good feeling they have after immersing in the mikveh, a feeling of calm, spiritual uplifting, serenity, and total cleanliness of a magnitude that cannot be attained just from one's regular bathing and hygiene routine. Ayelet Kaveh's informants described "a feeling of dirt that has to come out [so you can feel clean], and clean from within" (26). Others speak about how you "feel brilliant, your face is radiant, shining." A number of women came to Kaveh after they immersed to show her the radiance of their faces. Especially interesting to me in these sorts of comments is the linkage of "spiritual" and "physical" dimensions. Women describe spiritual uplifting that occurs through bodily practices and bodily transformations that occur pursuant to spiritual rituals. What women are in fact portraying is a very particular construction of the female body—one in which women's physical state rather easily changes (for better or for worse) in response to their spiritual state. And conversely, spiritual rewards, and punishments, are meted out to women through their bodies.

Medical Basis of the Niddah System

The Israeli mikveh establishment has developed rhetoric and techniques designed to draw women into mikveh observance. Although parts of the discourse generated by the mikveh establishment feel irrelevant to the secular and traditional Asian and North African women with whom I have spoken—for example, the rules concerning internal checking to make sure that bleeding has stopped—other aspects of this discourse resonate deeply and powerfully for many women, and have quickly become absorbed into the folk repertoire of beliefs about women's bodies.

One of the more popular mikveh booklets currently distributed to brides and made available at Israeli mikvehs is entitled *Nisu'in shel Osher—Happy Marriage*

(Neriya 1989). Like other booklets of the same genre, it interweaves "expert" medical advice with Jewish law. The booklet "proves" the medical basis of the niddah system, opening with, "Dr. Shik Moyna, the researcher who became famous for discovering a test for diphtheria, who was the first to lecture in approximately 1920 on the topic of 'menstruants' poison—hemanotoxin."[7] Afterwards other "important professors" confirmed his findings, determining that menstrual blood contains a kind of poison that seems to damage men and fetuses, a fact "already known" to the medieval Jewish sage Maimonides. Weaving modern science and ancient misogynist taboos, the booklet continues: "It is customary to believe that this poison has a negative influence on materials that need to ferment, like yeast, dough, wine, and so on" (16). In addition, "Most science recognizes another danger that threatens men who have contact with women during the niddah period. The menstrual discharge contains elements of blood, bits of the uterine wall, mucus, and various kinds of bacteria. When there is an open wound the bacteria can cause an infection [of the urethra]" (16). Women not only endanger men, but are even dangerous to themselves. "Medical science also recognizes the possibility that intimate relations during the menstrual period can damage the woman . . . There is a larger danger of infection in the pelvic area. . . . It is accepted among specialists in gynecology that cervical cancer, a disease found among civilized and noncivilized nations, is rare among Jewish women who observe the laws of menstrual purity" (16). These scientific proclamations are interspersed with names of European physicians and esoteric bibliographic references, building an aura of incontrovertibly "expert" scientific proof. The psychological aspects of menstruation are also addressed:

> It has recently been found that in women's bodies there is a temperature curve. From the day that menstruation starts until the middle of the cycle the temperature stays the same—low. Afterwards, it goes up and stays high until the day the next period starts. This cyclical movement marks all of the most important life processes for women—heart function, blood pressure, muscle strength, metabolism, etc. This movement also affects the woman psychologically. She has hours and days of uplifted spirits and loads of energy, which are switched by hours and days of the opposite. . . . Often, the woman's mood in the down days is low. In that period many women suffer from certain depression and from hypersensitivity. The feeling of discomfort leads to a desire to close oneself in and be alone. (18)

The booklet emphasizes that women are weak during the days of their period. Jewish law prohibits intimate relations for the seven days following menstruation, "the time in which the womb regains its strength. This also gives the woman a time for emotional calmness, and allows her to recover before resuming intimate relations." In Israeli mikveh discourse women's bodies are presented as so frail as to require a great deal of rest in order to carry out the tiring labor of sexual relations. In another booklet entitled *L'Bat Yisrael Likrat Nisu'eha* (To the Daughter of Israel Approaching Marriage; Neriya 1983), which is handed out to brides in a number of towns around the country, the young woman is advised to organize her month so as to do her heavy housework during the days in which she is forbidden to her husband, and in that way she can be more rested during the time when they can have sexual relations. On the day of her immersion, she should sleep so she will be rested for the evening. "Sleep calms down the nerves and relaxes the muscles so that all of the organs are able to fill their task successfully."

Health and illness are central components of contemporary mikveh discourse in Israel.[8] Women are told—and tell each other—that sexual relations at the "wrong" time of month can cause cervical cancer. Mikveh booklets and counselors offer statistics showing that Jewish women have lower rates of cervical cancer, and quote doctors explaining that the uterus is more prone to infections which "may" cause cancer when it is "open" during menstruation and the week following menstruation. Inbal Cicurel has noted that in Beer Sheva the mikveh counselors explain to women that after menstruation a membrane starts to build up around the womb in order to protect a possible pregnancy. In the area of the vagina there is an acid that protects the womb from germs. The bleeding is alkaline and neutralizes that acid, and intercourse further jeopardizes the vulnerable womb. This folk medical model presents menstruation as a wound that takes seven days to heal, during which time the womb is vulnerable to germs. Over the course of the time in which she carried out her field work in Beer Sheva, Cicurel witnessed an increase in women offering medical explanations for keeping niddah and mikveh. As did Kaveh and I, Cicurel found that the source for these ideas is the mikveh establishment: books, mikveh attendants, counselors, and especially lectures by Orthodox gynecologists.

While it may be tempting to shrug off the idea of "You will get cancer if you don't dip" as an obvious rhetorical device used to convince women to observe the laws, it is important to understand that this rhetoric also constructs a certain kind of female body, a body that is naturally disease ridden and requires "expert" guidance to avert disaster. According to Cicurel, the Beer Sheva counselors teach women that twice daily internal vaginal checks during the week following menstruation (to make sure that there is no further bleeding) is preventative medicine that may lead to early discovery of illness (cancer) and so save women's lives and especially their fertility. One wonders how women who indeed check themselves twice daily for at least one week each month (per rabbis' orders) are affected by holding the prospect of "discovering" malignancies so actively in their consciousness—whether they come to think of their bodies as always on the verge of being sick.

I make particular note here of the borrowing of a discourse propagated by the cancer establishment (oncologists, cancer associations, and so on). In current medical jargon early detection has been renamed "secondary prevention," implying that submitting one's body to frequent expert examination can actually prevent cancer rather than merely reveal it at an earlier stage. While the borrowing from preventative medicine and early detection discourse seems to suggest a certain degree of cooperation between the medical and religious establishments, in this case the cooperation is more rhetorical than concrete. Despite the preventative medicine rhetoric, the rabbis who have authority over the mikvehs (at least in Jerusalem) have refused to allow women's health organizations to distribute or display material on breast self-examination at the mikvehs even though the timing of immersion after menstruation and the privacy afforded women during their extended bathing and other preparations for immersion make it a good opportunity for breast self-exam.[9] The rabbis claim that it will distract women from the true purpose of the mikveh.

Rabbis, mikveh attendants, and booklets, such as *Nisu'in shel Osher*, acknowledge the problems that can transpire if a woman's cycle is less than twenty-five days long, in which case ovulation occurs before immersion and the resumption of sexual relations therefore hinders or even precludes conception. If this happens, according to *Nisu'in shel Osher*, the woman should go to a doctor who will give her hormones to regulate her menstrual cycle. In addition, she should take her temperature every morning to see when she ovulates. Acknowledging that ritual observances may exacerbate certain problems in women with short menstrual cycles, this advice construes ritually induced infertility as an illness appropriately treated by doctors. The suggested solution is for women to focus obsessive attention on their ovulation (in addition to the attention already focused on bleeding), to consult with a physician, and to take hormones, which may make them feel unwell or gain weight—a corporeal taboo of the highest degree for modern Israeli women. That many Israeli physicians collude in this practice, giving hormones to perfectly healthy women made "sick" by cultural codes, says a great deal about the cross-cutting ways in which various institutions work to construct female corporeality.

Mothers and Miracles at the Mikveh

Mikveh attendants hold a pivotal position in propagating mikveh ideology and in spreading miracle stories about the benefits of niddah and mikveh observance. While miraculous urban legends do take on a life of their own and circulate from mikveh to mikveh, the role of mikveh attendants in spreading the stories is crucial. The head attendant in a Ramat Gan mikveh is particularly fond of tales of infertile women who conceived after dipping in the mikveh. She, like other mikveh attendants, tells these stories replete with details and with individual twists: the problems faced by the particular infertile woman, previous attempts to conceive, the words the doctor used when he told her the good news that her pregnancy test had come back positive, and so on (Kaveh 1998).

The theme of fertility is central to mikveh discourse. Women's responsibility to bear children constitutes a meta-discourse in Israeli society. What we hear from mikveh attendants is a sub-discourse tying women's maternal duty to purity and obedience to Jewish law. A favorite story of the Ramat Gan mikveh attendant tells of a woman whose doctors discovered a large growth in her head. Before the operation to remove the growth, she came to the mikveh to dip and request God to take the cancerous grow from her head and put a live growth (a baby) in her stomach. Shortly afterward she discovered she was pregnant and went to the doctor to check the growth in her head. Miraculously, it was gone. This story, a fairly well-known Israeli urban legend, combines a number of motifs crucial to the cultural construction of women's bodies. First, the use of the same word, *gidul* (growth), for both cancer and fertility suggests that cancer and fertility are reversals of one another—analogous to other key dichotomies such as sickness and health, evil and good, and impurity and purity. Just as the transition from impurity to purity is mediated by ritual immersion in the mikveh, so is the transition from cancer to fertility. Pushing this symbolic construct a step further, I would suggest that the geographic transformation of the location of the growth from the head to the stomach further aligns purity and the national mission of motherhood with the body rather than with the mind or spirit. The good woman is one who embraces her corporeality and lets her stomach grow; the bad woman is one whose head grows. A second motif intimates that in women purity and impurity—observance and non-observance of Jewish law—are manifested in corporeality. Finally, this story revolves around the theme of authority over women's bodies. The heroine in the story submits to the authority of both God and the doctors. Religion and medicine are presented as simultaneously collaborating and competing for control of the woman's body; the doctor wants to operate but God cures her before the doctor has a chance to use his knife. In the end, the doctor is forced to admit his defeat when he tells the woman that the cancer has totally disappeared.

If sexual relations at the wrong time of the month are injurious, dipping in the mikveh and keeping the laws of niddah are said to be healthy. Stories are told of women who suffered from a variety of diseases that were cured by dipping in the mikveh. The mikveh is also said to contribute to mental health and to happy marriages, and especially to fertility. Many stories circulate in Israel of relatives and friends who were blessed with children after they began to properly observe the laws of mikveh and niddah. Dipping in the mikveh in the ninth month of pregnancy is a well-known charm for an easy birth; dipping after a bride just emerged from the mikveh is a charm for conceiving.

Cicurel found the wish to protect husband and children to be the most frequently expressed explanation for keeping the laws of niddah separation. The women with whom she spoke translate *karet* (being cut off from the Jewish people—the biblical punishment for sexual relations during menstruation) as any kind of accident to husband or children—from bike accidents to death. The Ramat Gan mikveh attendant, for example, tells of a little girl saved from falling from a high building because her mother dipped. I have often heard women say that observance of niddah and mikveh brings the woman's family one form or another of good fortune. Stories circulate about children or other family members who were saved from death or illness because the mother immersed in the mikveh. More generally, observance of menstrual rituals is said by women to have a positive influence on the family and household: to bring *sh'lom bayit* (conjugal harmony) and "make order in life." Women who began observing the laws of menstrual purity later on in their marriages often talk about the difference between "children of purity" and "children of niddah." Kaveh found that children born in purity were described as calm, serene, and responsible; the earlier children as more difficult to raise, stubborn, wild, and needing more parental supervision.

Perhaps the most poignant maternal mikveh stories have to do with a soldier who was saved because his mother dipped. Among the variants of this story are soldiers whose units were blown up but one soldier alone was saved, and soldiers who at the last minute were not assigned to units that were attacked by the enemy, both because the mothers dipped in the mikveh. Cicurel cites the story of a mother who inexplicably was urged by the mikveh attendant to pray for her family, beginning with her soldier son rather than with her seriously ill son. It turned out that the next day her soldier son was traveling with a group of fellow soldiers and their car fell off the side of a cliff into an abyss; her son was the only one to survive the accident.

The flip side of these stories, of course, is the understanding that mothers who do not dip endanger their soldier sons, a belief that fits well with the wider Israeli Jewish conceptualization of women as endangering the collective through the vulnerability of their demanding female bodies. These stories seem to suggest that women protect and aid the state through corporeal rituals; that women's purity, together with men's fighting skills, defend Israel (see Yanay and Rapoport 1997). But whereas men perform specific actions to defend Israel, women's burden of defense rests inside their very bodies—a heavy load to carry, and one from which there is never weekend leave.[10]

Mikveh and Marriage

Contemporary mikveh discourse also emphasizes the effects of women's menstrual observances upon their marriages. I, like Cicurel and Kaveh, have heard repeatedly that mikveh observance will lessen the chances that your husband will cheat on you, get sick of you, or leave you. Among the advantages of niddah observance

cited most frequently by women throughout Israel is that it improves sexual relations with the husband. The enforced separation each month keeps one like "a
bride all the time," it "preserves the excitement in marriage," and makes it "so the
husband and wife won't get sick of each other" and will "continue to desire one
another." Many women told me stories about straying men who came back to wives
who began keeping niddah, or marriages on the verge of divorce that were saved
when the wife's friend told her, "What do you have to lose, just try to go to the
mikveh and it may help."

Cicurel interprets these sorts of marital anecdotes in terms of women's economic vulnerability and dependence upon men. Israeli society is highly con-
sumer-oriented, yet women's salaries, significantly lower than men's, are rarely
sufficient for attaining the standards of consumer achievement that women are
encouraged to see as optimal. In the predominantly working-class Beer Sheva neighborhoods in which Cicurel carried out her field work, some women seem to view
their immersion in the mikveh as a contribution that compensates for their lower
contribution to family income. Cicurel, as did I, heard stories in which the observance of niddah protected a husband's job. A popular tale cited by Cicurel tells
of a wife who started to observe niddah after a few years of marriage, and a few
months later her husband told her of his new prosperity at work and asked her to
keep on helping his business by continuing to immerse each month (n.d., 19). In
a dramatically double-barreled variant on the theme of women's vulnerability, Cicurel
has heard Beer Sheva mikveh counselors teach women that not observing the laws
of niddah and mikveh may lead to cancer of the uterus, which leads to suffering
and loss of fertility. But more than that, they also "tell the women that their husbands would not be able to carry the burden of a wife with cancer and thus by not
keeping niddah, they may lose them as well" (10).

While contemporary mikveh discourse places a great deal of responsibility upon
women and women's bodies—responsibility for the health, safety, and prosperity
of husband, children, and state—it is clear to women that authority in the matter of niddah and mikveh lies with men. Women are urged to consult with rabbis, or to ask their husbands to consult on their behalf, regarding a range of
matters, including, for example, ambiguously colored vaginal secretions. Rahel
Wasserfall itemizes the ways in which a husband can exercise control over his wife's
mikveh observances: he can force her to have sexual relations before going to the
mikveh, he can insist that she immerse before the completion of the seven
"clean" days, and he can forget or refuse to send his wife to the mikveh (1990).

Brides and Menstrual Rituals

We turn now to a most particular type of female body, one that embodies and symbolizes not only the purity of the collective but also its very survival and conti-

nuity—the body of the bride. Negotiations between Orthodox and secular political parties in contemporary Israel have bolstered a legal framework laid down by the Ottomans: The mainly secular state grants religious authorities exclusive jurisdiction over matters of marriage and divorce. This arrangement creates social inconsistencies that are problematic for women. In most spheres of public life, women are, by law if not always in practice, accorded the same rights as men. Women, like men, have the right to vote and to hold political office; women, like men, benefit from Israel's universal education and health care systems. Israeli law prohibits economic discrimination on the basis of gender. Israeli girls and women are told, in many arenas and in many ways, that they are full citizens of a democratic state and that they can expect equal treatment from the state and its institutions. Yet when women become engaged to marry—as most women do in Israel's pro-family and pro-natality culture—they encounter an entirely different understanding of gender and an entirely different set of social rules. In the framework of traditional Jewish practices and rituals of marriage and divorce, women and men are not equal. This state-sponsored bifurcation echoes traditional rabbinic gender patterns. Talmudic scholar Judith Romney Wegner (1988) has argued that in the Mishnah and Talmud, Jewish women like Jewish men are considered to be people possessing both entitlements and obligations, and gender equality characterizes many spheres of life.[11] In the private domain of sexual and reproductive status, however, most women, including wives, minor daughters, and levirate widows, are considered legal chattel, who as property lacking rights and duties do not have jurisdiction over their own biological functions. Following Wegner's reading of the Mishnah and Talmud, it seems to me that the apparently inconsistent Israeli status quo—women can file complaints in labor court because of wage discrimination but must submit to an all-male rabbinic court in order to receive a *get* (bill of divorcement) that by Jewish law can be granted only by a husband and never by a wife—reiterates a very ancient and fundamental gender pattern already evident in the writings of the Sages.

As a consequence of the Israeli law requiring all weddings to be conducted by religious officials authorized by the state, Jews who marry in Israel are obliged to go along with a variety of ritual practices which, while often meaningless or even offensive to the bride and groom, are seen as religious commandments by the state-supported Orthodox religious establishment.[12] Perhaps the most intrusive practice is that requiring Jewish brides to immerse in the mikveh before the wedding, and to bring a note attesting to their ritual purity from the mikveh attendant to the rabbi who conducts the wedding. The obligatory prenuptial mikveh encounter—coming at a time of transition in personal and social identity in the lives of young women—exposes all Israeli women, not just Orthodox women, to a persuasively presented, Jewishly authentic, corporeal culture. Before I turn to a more detailed discussion of ritual immersion of brides, I wish to make clear that the intense corporeal scrutiny during the mikveh ritual is but one part of a much broader con-struction of the body of the bride—the ultimate female body—as an object of legit-imate public surveillance. Much of the traditional Jewish wedding sequence directs public attention to the bride's appearance. Perhaps the best example is the traditional Yemenite bride—in contemporary Israel a kind of iconic, folkloristic, collective bride—whose gown and head covering weigh so much that she can hardly move. Unable to run, barely able to walk a few steps, her clothing makes her into a passive, visual platform for others to explore. Her dress and headgear are cov-ered with myriad symbolic designs and objects embroidered and sewn onto the fab-ric. Yemenite folklorist Zipporah Greenfield spent twenty years studying a traditional Yemenite bridal dress; she told me it has taken her that long to read all of the symbols inscribed onto the body of the bride.

One of the still popular highlights of traditional Ashkenazi weddings is the *bedeken* (covering) ritual in which the groom walks up to the bride who is sitting passively and quietly on a queen's throne; he looks at her face for a moment, and then places her veil over her face. The collective, mythic meaning of the ritual is made explicit when the biblical verses invoked for Rebecca before she was sent off to meet Isaac, her future husband, are pronounced: "O sister! May you grow into thousands of myriads. May your offspring seize the gates of their foes" (Gen-esis 24:60). The bedeken ritual dramatically assimilates the body of the bride to a mythic, national body. At some weddings the veil is opaque, literally blinding the bride; thus the bride indicates that "she is totally committed to her husband and has unquestioning trust in him" (Chill 1989, 280).[13] The palpable sexual charge of the bedeken ceremony—the bride and groom supposedly have not seen each other for some time before the wedding—hitches individual passion to legitimate sexuality to the future of the collectivity. The veiled bride bears on her body the textual legacy of Rebecca and the burden of sightlessly reproducing that legacy. Only the groom can uncover the face of the modest and pure bride; ownership is manifested as the right to reveal what is hidden from others.

In addition to these gendered corporeal constructions drawn from tradi-tional Jewish scripts, the Israeli fashion industry—as is the case throughout the West—pitches beautiful and expensive gowns, hairstyling, and cosmetic applications for brides, items that accurately assume the bride's beauty to be an essential part of the marriage transaction and wedding ritual. Special salons for brides offer full-day treatments that include manicures, pedicures, depilation and waxing, facials, professional makeup, and hairstyling. This is typically followed by a round of photog-raphy shoots in front of culturally potent backdrops—famous buildings, shrines, gardens, and so on, visually associating the bride's body with national "treasures."

In a pioneering study of how women's bodies are manipulated cross-culturally, Mary Daly (1978) has argued that rituals such as Indian suttee, Chinese foot bind-ing, African genital mutilation, and certain aspects of Western gynecology dismantle the individual integrity of women; they function to prevent women from comprehending their own agency, from holding onto a sense of their own selves. By inscribing women's bodies with potent symbols, these sorts of ritual practices serve to transmute real women into cultural icons and distance women from ownership of their own bodies. The wedding complex, and particularly the required mikveh immersion, seem to me to suit the model suggested by Daly. Scrutiny of the young woman's body by a duly appointed representative of Jewish law and the Israeli state, and detailed instructions that prepare her to scrutinize her own body in preparation for subsequent monthly immersions, can be seen as techniques for teaching the bride, in a classic state of liminality, to view herself as a symbolic object rather than an autonomous subject. At the successful completion of the prenuptial immersion ritual, the mikveh attendant pronounces the bride a "pure daughter of Israel."[14] Several mikveh attendants told me how eager they are to use the opportunity of the compulsory prenuptial immersion to draw women into mikveh observance: the nicest room at the mikveh is always saved for brides, and attendants pride themselves on the time they spend talking to brides, a conversation that follows earlier lessons by a mikveh counselor or rabbi's wife employed by the Ministry of Religion or municipal religious council.

Mikveh attendants, and the rabbis who direct their work, recognize that the prenuptial immersion presents a unique window of opportunity for drawing women into the niddah and mikveh system. Like officiants at rites of passage in other cultures, they understand that at times of transition the self is especially vulnerable and pliable. What surprises me is how quietly the non-Orthodox majority in Israel goes along with a ritual practice that involves repudiation of the bodily freedom and privacy of young women. While some brides find ways to trick or escape the mikveh system, few openly confront it. As far as I can ascertain, the compulsory immersion of brides has never been debated on the Knesset floor. One cannot but wonder whether the absence of public outcry reflects a certain acquiescence to a culture of gendered corporeal surveillance which, although not usually expressed through mikveh rituals by most secular Israelis, is in fact widely accepted as good and true. As we saw, much of the typical secular wedding sequence directs communal attention to women's passive bodies as well. Diverse streams in Israeli society, not only the Orthodox establishment, see women's bodies as potential sites of improper, impure, or dangerous behavior. The secular state, and not only the rabbis, institutionalizes through law its claim to a moral stake in women's bodies. Physicians and politicians join the religious establishment in justifying scrutiny of women's bodies and behavior through appeal to higher principles of the public good. And indeed, we have seen throughout this book that various institutions, not only the religious establishment, attribute heavy collective responsibility to women's bodies, while according women little authority or autonomy. Even the most secular Israeli brides, having recently completed their service in the IDF, are quite accustomed to "legitimate" institutional expressions of corporeal control.

Still, secular young women, raised on Western books, television, cinema, and educational curricula which, at least purportedly, teach independent thinking, are inclined to find the mikveh requirement burdensome. Brides may be made especially uncomfortable by the mikveh attendant who supervises the immersion, asking numerous questions regarding the date of the last menstrual period, whether during the seven days from the end of menstruation to the date of the ritual immersion the bride had twice each day inserted a cloth inside her vagina to check that the bleeding had stopped, and whether she had thoroughly cleaned her eyes, ears, nose, teeth, navel, hair, and so on prior to immersion. Here is how one secular woman described her prenuptial mikveh encounter some years earlier: "It was the most humiliating experience of my life. I felt like a baboon when the mikveh attendant picked hair off my back [hair stuck on the body constitutes *hatsitsa*, a barrier between one's body and the water]. I felt like I was in a concentration camp. I felt like a baboon in a concentration camp."

This informant, I believe, did not use the words "concentration camp" lightly (these words are never used lightly in Israeli discourse); she used them to express her sense of the mikveh ritual as coercive and abusive. Still, as I said earlier, it is rare for brides to object openly to the mikveh requirement. The anger of Israeli women is often directed at the mikveh attendant, who is felt to be intrusive by many brides, or who is perceived as holding the gates of the mikveh closed, for instance, to unmarried women who wish to use the mikveh. In fact, however, the entire system of niddah and mikveh is explicated by, arbitrated by, and controlled by male rabbinical authorities. The mikveh attendant is repeatedly told to make no decisions on her own, and a telephone for her to use to call the rabbi is one of the most essential pieces of mikveh equipment. Mikveh attendants hold heavy responsibility for the kosher (valid) purification of Jewish women. An error on their part could lead families into sin and have spiritual repercussions for the next generation. Yet they are told again and again by the rabbis who oversee the mikvehs that they must never make any halakhic decision on their own, that they must call a rabbi even if the case at hand is identical to a case they saw the evening before (for example, a case in which a scab on a woman's body might constitute *hatsitsa* between her skin and the mikveh water, thus invalidating the immersion).

In addition to the mikveh immersion required by rabbis who officiate at wedding ceremonies, some Jewish ethnic groups in Israel continue to carry out traditional prenuptial mikveh ceremonies in which the family of the groom, represented by the groom's mother, plays a central role. The elderly Kurdish Jewish women among whom I have conducted field work in Jerusalem told me that it was a matter of principle for the bride's mother not to teach her about sexuality or niddah and mikveh, so that the bride would learn only the customs of her husband's family and not her own (Sered 1992). It is not uncommon nowadays to find that the mother-in-law competes with the mikveh attendant for the right to inspect, supervise, and control the bride's body.

The role of the mother-in-law is especially prominent at bridal mikveh parties. Parties at the mikveh were and still are celebrated the night before the wedding, particularly among North African Jews. At this occasion, women friends and relatives accompany the bride to the mikveh, where she disrobes and immerses in the ritual bath in the presence of her future mother-in-law and a small number of female relatives. While these parties do provide opportunities for groups of women to gather together away from the gaze of male authorities, and the singing and dancing that follow the bride's immersion are joyous and sometimes poke fun at men, the chief purpose of the parties is to provide the family of the groom with an opportunity to inspect the body of the young woman who will be entrusted to bear, birth, and raise their male descendants.

The groom's family has several interests that can be protected by the mother-in-law at the mikveh. First, they want to know that the bride is healthy and equipped with a normal female body; in other words, that she is a likely candidate for bearing healthy sons. Second, they want to know that the bride is not pregnant; in other words, that she will not pass off a child of another man into her husband's family. And third, the mother-in-law herself may want to test the waters and see that the bride is compliant; in other words, that she will accept the control of her mother-in-law and not behave as either a free agent or as a member of her natal family. The mother-in-law is delegated to organize relatives and guests, prepare food and music, and use the party to make a public statement that this bride is from now on part of her husband's family. Thus the mother-in-law, like the mikveh attendant, is a representative or a gatekeeper of a patriarchal institution in which she, as a woman, lacks full-fledged membership. Indeed, she herself was subjected to the same scrutiny when she was a bride. An elderly Moroccan rabbi living in a Jerusalem neighborhood in which I have carried out field work (see Sered 1999b) talked to me about the meaning of traditional prenuptial mikveh rituals, opening with a discussion of henna (red dye spread on the hands of women throughout the Middle East, North Africa, and India at weddings and other ceremonies). Note his interpretation of the ritual as one in which symbols are literally stamped onto the body of the bride: "HeNnA stands for Challa [bread tithe], Niddah [laws of menstrual purity], Hadlaka [lighting Sabbath candles].[15] These are the three commandments that are necessary for the bride. I heard this from an official source. They teach the bride. They put the color on her hand so that she will look beautiful for the groom. They put it on her hand as a stamp (hotemet) that she has entered the correct Jewish life. It means that you have entered the burden of keeping the commandments.

Our conversation then turned to the issue of the presence of the mother-in-law when the bride immerses. Note here his explicit pronouncement regarding the ontological status of the bride: She is merchandise that is legitimately scrutinized and evaluated by potential purchasers and therefore she should not express agency, she should not "get angry."

> It is written in the Mishnah (K'tubot 7:8) that they bring the relatives of the groom to check the bride, that she doesn't have any *moom* (defect). It isn't her fault. Some kind of scar. Sometimes. They want to know and check the merchandise (s'*hora*). We are not simple. Sometimes there is an argument. But if people understand the halakha (law), they take it in the correct spirit (that the law says the bride should be checked and rejected if she is sick or deformed). This is an open eye. To see what is going on with the bride's body. The bride shouldn't get angry, it is written in the Mishnah to check the bride. The groom will see only her face before the wedding (not her entire body, so he can't know if she is normal and healthy).

The mikveh attendant's scrutiny of brides is an expression of the interest of the religious establishment (and of the state) in the bodies of women; the role of the mother-in-law is an expression of the interest of the extended family in the bodies of its women. These two sets of interests do not always sit well with one another and arguments are not uncommon when these two parties confront one another. Both sets of interests may also come into conflict with the perceived self-interest of the bride, shaped as it is by the Western entertainment industry with its marketing of romance and beauty and by the consumer economy with its emphasis on female beauty, rather than on purity, modesty, or fecundity. That brides tend to be more outspoken in protesting the intrusiveness of the mother-in-law than the intrusiveness of the mikveh attendant says a great deal about the relative powers of the state and of the family over women's bodies in Israel today. But more to the point, the conflict between the mother-in-law and the mikveh attendant rests on the shared assumption that women's bodies are legitimately controlled, that rituals enacted on women's bodies have implications for the collective, and that without the performance of corporeal rituals, women's bodies will be, in one way or another, impure, imperfect, and unhealthy.

Notes

1. Given the intimate emotional and geographic relationships between men and women in most cultures, symbolic rather than overtly violent means are usually the preferred means for structuring heterosexual society.
2. During the time in which the Temple was the focus of Jewish life, menstruation precluded involvement in Temple worship. At the end of the seven-day period of impurity, women were required to bring a sacrifice to the Temple, before resuming participation in Temple ritual.

3. Levi, Levinsohn, and Katz (1993) report that 24 percent of Jewish Israeli women go to the mikveh (16 percent regularly and 8 percent occasionally).
4. Levi, Levinsohn, and Katz (1993) number this group, depending on the measure, at between 7 percent and 20 percent of the Jewish population.
5. I suspect this differs from Ashkenazi women in the United States.
6. Their mothers and grandmothers were more religiously observant, but most are now postmenopausal and so rarely have reason to come to the mikveh.
7. I suspect they are referring to Bela Schick, who developed a test for diphtheria antibodies.
8. I have made an informal study of mikveh booklets in the United States. While there is some overlap, my sense is that booklets emphasizing miraculous healing are more popular in Israeli than in the United States.
9. In mikvehs in the United States it is not uncommon to find breast self-examination guides hung up in each room for the convenience of mikveh patrons. The pattern I am describing represents the particularly Israeli playing out of Jewish themes, which is not the only way these themes can be or are played out.
10. In Jewish cultures, women's bodies often are understood to be sources of pollution, while men's bodies are seen as sources of blessing (rabbis hold up their hands in blessing as do priests, and some put their hands on heads of people to bless them; physical contact with tombs of saints is believed to spread blessings, and almost all holy tombs are of male saints).
11. In public life, gender differences were significant: women were excluded from the world of learning and from roles of community leadership (see Wegner 1988, 75ff).
12. I suspect that members of the Knesset have little knowledge or concern for what goes on in the mikvehs. The coercive nature of the prenuptial mikveh rituals is a minor byproduct of the law that gives religious authorities (Jewish, Christian, and Muslim) a monopoly over marriage and divorce in Israel.
13. I thank my student Marilyn Froggatt (Hebrew University, 1998) for pointing out to me some of the more interesting aspects of the *bedeken* ceremony.
14. The ethnography on which this section is based was collected during systematic observations of brides' visits to the mikveh over a period of four months at one mikveh in Jerusalem, and twenty years of less systematic observations.
15. These three commandments often are grouped together as the paradigmatic women's commandments. It is written in the Mishnah that women die in childbirth as a result of neglecting these commandments.

References

Chill, Abraham. 1989. *The Minhagim* (The Customs). New York: Sepher-Hermon Press.

Cicurel, Inbal Esther. n.d. "The Rabbinate Versus Jewish Women: The Mikvah as a Contested Domain." Unpublished manuscript.

———. 1998. "The Mikvah—Why Do They Use It? Female Views and Uses of the Jewish Ritual Bath." Master's thesis, Ben Gurion University, Department of Sociology and Anthropology.

Daly, Mary. 1978. *Gyn/Ecology*. Boston: Beacon Press.

Kaveh, Ayelet. 1998. "Keeping the Purity Laws: A Form of Healing." Seminar paper. Bar Ilan University, Department of Sociology and Anthropology.

Lincoln, Bruce. 1989. *Discourse and the Construction of Society: Comparative Studies of Myth, Ritual, and Classification*. New York and Oxford: Oxford University Press.

———. 1994. *Authority: Construction and Corrosion*. Chicago: Chicago University Press.

Levy, Shlomit, Hanna Levinsohn, and Eliahu Katz. 1993. *Beliefs, Observances and Social Interaction among Israeli Jews*. Jerusalem: Louis Guttman Israel Institute of Applied Social Research.

Menahem, Tirzah. 1989. "Critical Edition of Mishnah Masechet Niddah with Commentaries upon Nusach and Chapters on the Development of the Halacha and on Realia." Ph.D. diss., Hebrew University, Jerusalem.

Neriya, Rachel. 1983. *To the Daughter of Israel Approaching Marriage*. Kfar HaRoeh: n.p.

————. 1989. *Happy Marriage*. Jerusalem: The National Center for Family Purity in Israel.

Ortner, Sherry. 1996. *Making Gender: The Politics and Erotics of Culture*. Boston: Beacon Press.

Sered, Susan. 1992. *Women as Ritual Experts: The Religious Lives of Elderly Jewish Women in Jerusalem*. New York: Oxford University Press.

————. 1999b. "Talking about Mikveh Parties, or, The Discourse of Status, Hierarchy, and Social Control." In *Women and Water*, edited by Rachel Wasserfall. Hanover, N.H.: University Press of New England.

Wasserfall, Rahel. 1992. "Menstruation and Identity: The Meaning of Niddah for Moroccan Women Immigrants to Israel." In *People of the Body*, edited by Howard Eilberg-Schwartz. Albany: State University of New York Press, 309–327.

Wegner, Judith Romney. 1988. *Chattel or Person: The Status of Women in the Mishnah*. New York: Oxford University Press.

Yanay, Niza, and Tamar Rapoport. 1997. "Ritual Impurity and Religious Discourse on Women and Nationalism." *Women's Studies International Forum* 20 (5/6):651–663.

Society and Politics

JUDITH BUBER AGASSI

The Status of Women
in Kibbutz Society

IN ALL SOCIETIES, any situation is considered to be a social problem, if it conflicts with current moral values. In modern society, the existing status of women used to conflict with the following current values: equality before the law and equal political rights for all citizens. This conflict was deemed problematic in the period of the classical women's movement and was resolved by legal reforms and by admitting women to the vote. Yet, the modern value of equality of opportunity still stands in clear contrast to the inferior economic and political status of women.

The same development can be seen in the cases of racial and ethnic inequality. As soon as the ideal of equality of opportunity was accepted, the recognition followed suit that the social segregation of the previously underprivileged group constitutes covert discrimination. A well-known example was the case of Afro-Americans, the public rejection of the old maxim of separate-but-equal and the acknowledgment that inevitably segregation causes inequality. In the case of racial and ethnic minorities, the focus of debate was education. In the case of women, the focus of debate is the segregated labor market, that is, sex-typing of jobs. The next step in this development of values, then, is the refusal to recognize any stereotyping, which prescribes for the underprivileged group a group ideal diverging from the general human ideal and assigning to them a limited stereotypical social role. In Western industrial societies, the problem of women is understood by many to imply removal of the remnants of overt and covert discrimination. The modern women's movement has taken an additional theoretical step and considers the problem to constitute sexism as such, that is, the view that being male or female is a decisive characteristic of a human being.

In general, as has also become obvious in the course of the symposium, the ideologues of the kibbutz movement view the problem of women in modern society as much less weighty than the liberal progressive thinkers of Western in-dustrialized countries. The sociologists of the kibbutz movement view the focus of the women's problem in the kibbutz merely as that of the greater dissatisfac-tion women show than men with their social and particularly their occupational roles.

Traditional socialist explanations for the inferior status of women are class soci-ety and the bourgeois family. The first explanation claims that as long as the exploita-tion of man by man persists, women will remain doubly exploited. The second explanation views the financial dependence of women in bourgeois societies as the cause of their inferiority. A variant of this is the view that as long as large num-bers of women are not active in production, they will lack both economic and politi-cal power. A more modern explanation is that of the double role or the double burden: modern women, who are employed in addition to their household duties, have lower aspirations or less energy and therefore also lower occupational achievements, because they suffer from the demands of their double roles or from the weight of their double burden.

The modern explanation for the diffusion and persistence of the problem of unequal status of women is the claim that during the entire history of mankind sexism was the prevailing position; only due to the recent development of pro-duction technology, which has devalued male superior muscle-power, and due to the recent development of medical control of human fertility, which has permit-ted women to control their life-plans, has the abolition of sexism at all become feasible.

Many kibbutz social scientists view the present situation in the kibbutz as an ideal state, because there is no financial dependence of women on men, and because women's status is not determined by that of their husbands. In addition, women are obliged just as much as men to work full-time outside the private fam-ily household. Despite the fact that many kibbutz social scientists consider the sit-uation to be quite satisfactory, some of them seem to find minor imperfections and thus space for change.

Many participants who are not kibbutz members seem to think that property relations in modern society are to blame for a large portion of the social problems within it; therefore, one may assume that they expect a radical change in prop-erty relations would also result in a radical solution to the women's problem. No one has openly expressed the view that the problem of women is solved in social-ist society, neither in its Moscow nor in its Peking model. Moreover, the major-ity would view the problem as solved only in a society that truly offers women equal opportunity, that is, truly equal access to rewards, satisfaction, and power. That would be the Scandinavian ideal, let's say, which, admittedly, has not yet been real-ized in any modern Western industrial society. The women's movement identifies with this ideal, yet it views even more explicitly as the ideal state that of the androgynous society, that is, the society in which sexism has been removed not only by far-reaching legal, economic, and social reforms, but also through a far-reaching psychological-educational revolution.

Corresponding to the mentioned views and opinions concerning the causes of the problem of women, we also find various opinions concerning the necessary ways and means to its solution. Thus, for instance, those who hail from various socialist traditions propose the following solutions: abolition of private property; liberation of women from household work; abolition of the family; formation of cooperative or collective social units; obligation for all women to participate in productive labor. Concerning the problem of dual role and double burden, kibbutz ideologues do not demand the abolition of the family; indeed, contrary to assumptions among American sociologists, they never did so even in legendary revolutionary pioneering days. They believe they have succeeded in their attempt to solve the problem by abolition of private familial consumption and childcare. Outside the socialist tradition, there are those who follow the American legalist tradition and see the means in organizing women in order to achieve both equality of formal rights and implementation. Both the progressive camp, which demands equal opportunity, and the more radical feminist camp consider the removal of the additional burden for women as possible only through a radical equal sharing of domestic service activities and childcare, inclusive of baby care, by both parents and/or adults of both sexes.

On the basis of the experiences of the last decade, both groups have come to the conclusion that the struggle against occupational segregation is central to the struggle against covert discrimination. Linked to this is the wider fight against sex-typing and stereotyping as well as against the ossified images of masculinity and femininity held by both males and females.

The Status of Women in Kibbutz Society

The empirical evidence for such an evaluation of the status of women in the kibbutz is the following: first, we have data about occupation according to sex in two of the four kibbutz federations; second, there are demographic data of these federations which permit the calculation of the rate of leaving the kibbutz by men and women, born or raised in the kibbutz; third, we have rather comprehensive attitude studies especially about men and women of the second generation by kibbutz social scientists. Before discussing the interpretation of these data, I want to mention shortly the components of the situation of women, which is specific to the kibbutz, on which, so it seems, all agree:

1. Private domestic and childcare work of women is lighter than the average burden of married women and mothers outside, yet heavier

than that of married men and fathers inside the kibbutz. Baby care during the first months of life is considered almost exclusively the task of the mother, who receives assistance from the nurse (*metapelet*).

2. Women are not dependent financially on the income of their men. Yet, the kibbutz family fulfills nowadays considerable functions as a consumption unit.

3. Women are more affected by the occupational prestige and non-financial rewards of their husbands than men are by those of their wives.

4. Higher education and vocational training of women, although improving constantly, in quality still lag considerably behind that of men.

5. The achievements of girls in high school decline considerably compared to those of boys and to their own earlier ones.

INTERPRETATIONS OF THE DATA

Most sociologists and educators in and outside the kibbutz agree on these five points, yet concerning the proper interpretation and significance of statistical data and attitude studies there exist considerable differences. The fact which appears to me as a key factor for understanding the problems of women in the kibbutz is the sharp polarization of occupational activities of the sexes, with which I will deal in the next paragraph. To me lesser political activity of women and far larger rate of second-generation women who have left the kibbutz appear directly correlated with their occupational situation, while a majority of kibbutz sociologists deny such a correlation. Concerning lower achievements of girls in kibbutz high schools, kibbutz educators like Dar (1974) and Alon (1975) noticed the connection with the limited and unattractive occupational perspective of women in the kibbutz. Michal Palgi (1976) interprets the attitude studies as evidence for her claim that general satisfaction of women with life in the kibbutz as with their work are as high as that of men. Therefore, she claims, the problem of women in the kibbutz either does not exist at all or is minimal. Obviously, I differ from her both in my interpretation of the studies and in my conclusion.

The data in Menachem Rosner's well-known study (1967) about attitudes of the second generation include replies to a question about the desire to change one's present workplace; double the percentage of women as that of men in the age group of twenty to thirty wanted to change. Yet, only a small percentage of these women could point to an alternative desirable workplace in the kibbutz. Also, 57 percent of the young men in this age group answered, they had found relevance and achievement in their work, as against only 45 percent of the young women. Yet, Palgi does not evaluate this as evidence for a more pronounced dissatisfaction among women with their occupational role. She dismisses this evidence on the ground that these two questions were included in a more complex set of questions concerning attitude to work, which set, she claims, has enough internal consistency to justify the comparison of men and women only regarding the overall replies to the whole set, not to individual questions.

Sociologists and psychologists of work are well aware that the conventional direct question about satisfaction with work, or, more accurately, with the current job, tends to obtain very inaccurate and therefore hardly informative results. This is due to the absence of differentiation, but also to the prevalent tendency among interviewees to view any question concerning satisfaction with any of their main life spheres as ego-involving and, thus, near-automatically to respond in the affirmative. It is, therefore, advisable to add to the direct question other questions meant to elicit from the interviewee expressions of satisfaction or its absence with different aspects of the job, as well as different kinds of satisfaction or its absence. In my comparative study (1979) concerning attitudes of women toward their jobs, I have suggested an additional classification of satisfaction into superficial and consistent. Superficial satisfaction with work appears to me an important attitude to work, in that it tends to accompany the instrumental attitude toward work. I see superficial satisfaction as the combination of the affirmative answer to the direct question regarding satisfaction with one's job, with the negative answer to the question, whether one would recommend one's job to a good friend or offspring of the same sex. There are important attitudes toward work expressed in apparently inconsistent answers. Not only is the inconsistency apparent; regular patterns are easily discernible. Therefore, I reject the method deployed by Palgi (1976) which claims that wherever a majority of interviewees answers consistently any set of questions, only the sum of all their answers is valid for comparing the attitudes of two subgroups of interviewees, and that the noticeable difference in the answers of these two subgroups—men and women in our case—to two very specific questions is to be considered a priori irrelevant. I find this rule both superficial and misleading, at the very least in the present case. For me the data signify that the interviewed young kibbutz women are less satisfied with their occupational activities than young kibbutz men. This assumption is based not only on the answers to the two questions mentioned above, but also on the generally known fact that in the service branches, where most women and hardly any men work, the turnover of workers is much higher than in other kibbutz branches. Thus, it frequently becomes extremely difficult to staff those female jobs. As mentioned, these were the facts, which, though not recorded statistically, constituted the background to numerous discussions about the work situation of women. Had the problem of de facto dissatisfaction of women with their jobs not existed at all, the outdrawn discussion about the service branches and their image, which predated any discussion about polarization in labor division between the sexes, would not have come about at all.

OCCUPATIONAL POLARIZATION AND ITS SIGNIFICANCE

Tiger and Shepher (1976) claim that the pronounced occupational polarization of sexes, which they were the first to document statistically for two of the four kibbutz federations, constitutes proof for their thesis that women in the kibbutz—just as women everywhere else—due to their natural tendency to domestic and child-care activities (as the learning of these skills is easier for women than others) will always end up performing these activities, whatever the ideology and socialization of their society. Kibbutz society, thus, serves as evidence for their thesis that occupational polarization and segregation among the sexes is permanent and unavoidable. Therefore, the goal of modern feminism to overcome the differentiation of social roles of the sexes has no chance of being realized.

I do not know any other social scientist from the kibbutzim who agrees fully with this extreme antifeminist interpretation of the situation. Yet, I also do not know any kibbutz sociologist or educator who shares my analysis of occupational segregation as the mainspring of de facto inferiority of opportunities of women in the kibbutz, and who also considers a far-reaching change of this situation necessary and feasible. Within the kibbutz movement, discussion hardly ever concern the abolition of the present polarized division of labor or a radical improvement of content, task characteristics, work roles in the service branches, but only an improvement of their bad image. The usual arguments are: (a) for kibbutz society, satisfaction of the consumption needs, and especially the care and education of children, are as important as economic production; (b) therefore, the customary labeling of service branches as not productive or not profitable is taken from a system of values alien to the kibbutz; (c) everybody must realize that efficient management of the services is economically of utmost importance for the kibbutz—as soon as a careful bookkeeping has been introduced in these branches.

This last mentioned reform has since been carried out extensively. Similarly, it has been recognized that—due to the erroneous concept of non-profitability of the services—the technical development of these branches had been neglected, and that work in kitchen and dining hall, for example, had remained unnecessarily heavy and time-consuming. As a result, during the last decade the service branches underwent considerable technical modernization. Yet, no socio-technical reorganization, aimed at fitting these workplaces to the psychological and intellectual needs of the women working there, was attempted. It was tacitly assumed that the motive of women's dissatisfaction was lack of prestige: whereas more and more men are supposed to need extensive vocational training or even higher technical or academic education for their work, most women's work remains unskilled or semi-skilled and a minority's lower semi-professional.

Therefore, it was decided to upgrade the prestige of women's jobs by upgrading their training in the following ways: vocational training for workers in childcare, food and clothing services was extended and specialized; women were sent to courses for beauticians, hairdressers, and physiotherapists; a two-year course for social workers was instituted; the graduates of the kibbutz seminars for kindergarten and grade schoolteachers were granted a bachelor's degree. Earlier, Gerson had advocated one-year seminar training, and recently even two-year academic training for all Kibbutz Artzi infant care workers (metaplot). Thus, it is claimed that two inequalities have been abolished: the educational level of women as well as the prestige of women's jobs had been equalized to that of men. I contend that neither is true. Whereas the total time spent by kibbutz women on any kind of further education or training may now be equal to that of men, the quality of this training and its usefulness to the trainee are on the average considerably lower for women than for men. Sending women to courses has indeed become a kind of compensatory reward for working for long years in jobs they disliked. A large number of these trainees do not expect to have a chance to use the newly acquired knowledge and skills in daily work in the kibbutz, or at least not in the near future. Very few women receive training that would be marketable outside the kibbutz, be that technical, semi-professional, or professional training. In particular, until recently at least, such training was offered within the kibbutz movement and did not lead to a generally recognized diploma or degree.

No amount of training will raise the prestige of a job in the long run if its intrinsic quality is not improved. I want to state, that up to now jobs that are considered in the kibbutz as unsuitable for normal healthy men, yet suitable for normal healthy women, that is, nearly all consumer service jobs, childcare and education (excluding high-school teaching), and routine industrial and clerical jobs, have a level of task characteristics lower than those that are considered typical men's jobs. In kibbutz work that is sex-typed as women's work a genuinely progressive occupational career is much rarer than in that occupied by men. To refute the claim that the occupational polarization discriminates de facto against women, it is customary in kibbutz circles to contend that this is a voluntary segregation: women are free to work in any branch, it is said. Yet, they prefer the convenient physical conditions of the service branches to agricultural work in the open air "because they don't want to ruin their complexion." In reality, many kibbutz women have tried to become skilled or technical workers in agriculture or industry. Nowadays, nobody can force any member to work in a specific job. Yet, several widespread norms and organizational arrangements exercise enormous social pressure on women, either not to choose masculine occupations or to give up such careers in their early stages.

Here the most important double norm is to consider women, as a group, solely responsible for smooth functioning of all services and to consider all service jobs and especially childcare unsuitable as regular employment for men. As a result, not only men, as a group, exercise social pressure on women who do not want to work in the service branches, but women, as a group, unconsciously do the same. Kibbutz ideologues take pride in their society as a "conscious" society, planned according to the needs of its members. Without a radical and conscious fight against this double norm, there exists no chance to overcome occupational segregation and with it de facto discrimination against women. Rosner (1967) has shown that among kibbutz men prejudice is widespread against placing women in skilled manual technical engineering and managerial occupations. Apparently, even this finding is not taken seriously. Recently, cases of open discrimination against women in kibbutz industry have also been documented: six young women who, in spite of prevailing prejudice, had chosen technical occupations and trained for them, were excluded from promotion into any higher qualified or managerial positions, these positions being exclusively occupied by young men with less training and experience. Summing up, this occupational segregation and polarization is not considered a serious problem by any kibbutz sociologist. Palgi (1976) even claims explicitly, that here we have a situation of difference, yet equality. Spiro (1979) speaks of equivalence having replaced equality as an ideal.

The Familism Debate

Familism, or the symptoms of its apparent growth, is frequently mentioned in discussions about the status of women in the kibbutz, usually as endangering this status. What are supposed to be the symptoms? Social scientists of the Kibbutz Artzi federation consider the demand of parents to let children sleep in their family's apartment instead of in the children's house, as the central and most dangerous symptom of familism. Whereas the Kibbutz Artzi is opposed on principle to such a change, it has been introduced in recent years by majority vote in a growing number of kibbutzim of the other federations. Recent studies claim to have found a clear correlation between familial sleeping arrangements for children and a general rise in the activities of the family as a consumption unit, the latter trend, however, being common to the entire movement.

It is claimed, that the rise of familism weakens the impact and advantages of collective education of the peer group, and, perhaps in the long run, lowers the readiness of the kibbutz population to engage in wider public issues, as Gerson (1979), for example, contends. I cannot here enter the discussion. But, I want to challenge the claim that this kind of familism is the main and inevitable danger to women's status in the kibbutz. Having the children sleep at home or eating more meals at home only affects the situation of women negatively, if the burden of looking after the children at night, getting them up in the morning, fetching food from the store or kitchen, falls on the shoulders of mothers more than of fathers. Unfortunately, this is very likely, but certainly not inevitable. And without any further familist changes, it is already a well-established pattern, that women are expected to carry the larger share of private childcare and household chores.

Yet another innovation was introduced widely in the Kibbutz Artzi, the "hour of love," that is, freeing mothers to spend one hour during the workday with their infants. This innovation has limited the chances of women to advance in work outside the immediate confines of the kibbutz. Indeed, mothers who were negatively affected by this innovation have complained about it. Nevertheless, kibbutz social scientists disregard its effect on the occupational status of women. Naturally, Shepher sees in it just another expression of women's natural tendency to revert to their traditional activities.

Outside kibbutz circles, the concept of familism is used differently. What is usually meant here are values and norms that prescribe early marriage for all adults and several children for all married couples. This is a view of the family, including also the extended family, as the centre of all positive human relations. This kind of familism and natalism has existed in kibbutz-society for decades and is there even stronger than in contemporary Israeli Jewish non-Orthodox society in general, where familism is currently much stronger than in Western societies. Familism/natalism tends to emphasize the differences between the sexes, especially the specific reproductive functions of women, and to favor sex-specific traditional social roles. These prevalent values seriously inhibit the process of psychological and intellectual emancipation of kibbutz women. Gerson (1968) seems to have some qualms about the upsurge of familism, chiefly because of its encroachment on the concerns and functions of the collective, but also because of its anti-feminist connotations. Yet, even he is still so much preoccupied with rebutting the antiquated and erroneous claims about the supposed instability and marginality of the family in the kibbutz that he, just like the great number of kibbutz social scientists and ideologues, hardly notices the elements of sexism, anti-feminism, and illiberality encouraged by this well-established kibbutz familism.

Why should this be so? Apparently, what is at work here, is a combination of those interests that buttress familism and sexism in the wider society as well, especially the protection of the short-range interests of male privilege and convenience and the "national interest" in a high birth rate, with the specific interest of producing enough offspring to maintain a stable kibbutz population. It is high time, kibbutz people realize that those shortsighted interests conflict with their declared goal of full equality of opportunity for women.

Conclusion

The kibbutz in its present form cannot serve as a model for the solution of the problem of women in society, neither for those aiming at full equality nor certainly for those aiming farther at the abolition of sexism. It is in the long-term interest of the kibbutz to widen the horizons and the chances for development and self-realization of its women and daughters, to attract young women, and men, for whom full equality of rights and chances and full equality of evaluation of the sexes constitutes a basic value. In order to achieve these goals, it is essential, that kibbutz society decides against the conventional occupational polarization and against traditional familism. Both tasks appear to me feasible as well as essential for the further existence of the kibbutz as an attractive and exemplary way of life.

References

Alon, M. 1975. *Youth in the Kibbutz*. Tel Aviv (Hebrew).

Dar, Y. 1974. Sex Differences in Educational Achievements of High School Students in the Kibbutzim. Tel Aviv: Research Center for the Ichud Movement (Hebrew).

Blumberg, Rae Lesser. 1976. "The Erosion of Sexual Equality in the Kibbutz: Structural Factors Affecting the Status of Women." In *Beyond Intellectual Sexism: A New Woman a New Reality*, edited by Joan Roberts. New York, 320–329.

Buber Agassi, J. 1979. "Kibbutz and Sex Roles," *Crossroads* 4, 145–175.

————. 1979. *Women on the Job*. Lexington, Mass.

Gerson, M. 1968. *Education and Family in Kibbutz Reality*. Tel Aviv (Hebrew).

————. 1979. *Family, Women and Socialization in the Kibbutz*. Lexington, Mass.

Mednick, S.M. 1975. "Social Change and Sex Role Inertia: The Case of the Kibbutz." In *Women and Achievement*, edited by S.M. Mednick et al. New York, 85–102.

Padan- Eisenstark, D. and H. Hacker 1975. "Women in the Moshav Shitufi in an Ideological Trap." *Megamot* 21(4): 423–439.

Palgi, M. and M. Rosner 1974. *A Survey of Mobility of the Women to Productive Branches and Central Offices during the Yom Kippur War and afterwards*. Givat Haviva: Center for Social Research on the Kibbutz (Hebrew).

Palgi, M. 1976. *Sex Differences in Commitment to the Kibbutz and Its Causes*. Givat Haviva: Center for Social Research on the Kibbutz (Hebrew).

Rosner, M. 1967. "Women in the Kibbutz: Changing Status and Concepts." *Asian and African Studies* (3): 35–68.

Spiro, M. 1979. *Gender and Culture: Kibbutz Women Revisited*. Durham, N.C.

Talmon-Garber, Y. 1972. *Family and Community in the Kibbutz*. Cambridge, Mass.

Tiger, L. and J. Shepher 1975. *Women in the Kibbutz*. New York.

MANAR HASSAN
Translated by Sharon Ne'eman

Growing Up Female
and Palestinian in Israel

Even before she first sees the light of day, the female Palestinian infant is enveloped in a dense network of webs, whose purpose is to reproduce the patriarchal social system. This network will be woven and expanded into a tangle of bonds and chains that will condition and shape her spirit, supervise her education and rearing, and transform her into one of the mainstays of the patriarchy.

Each birth is anxiously awaited by the parents. The women in the family pray for the birth of a male offspring. The mother-to-be receives best wishes for the birth of a son, wishes which contain an implicit condemnation of the other, unwanted possibility, the birth of a daughter. The father's "sensitivity" increases as the date of birth draws near. Will his wife bless him with a son, thus improving his status and even changing his name to reflect his paternity; or will she disappoint him with a daughter, detracting from his worth as a man and leaving him with his childhood name?

During the *Jahilah*, or pre-Islamic period, there were tribes that buried their newborn daughters alive. While Islam forbade this custom, it did not, however, change the basic value of women. It did not proscribe the physical or mental castration of women, nor did it modify their status as inferior beings who, under certain circumstances, could even be murdered in defense of that monster known as "family honor." From the moment of her birth, the patriarchal society, through the agent of the nuclear and extended family, operates a system of conditioning designed to transform the child into the epitome of possible female development: a wife, that is, a handmaid and receptacle for male lust and desire, and a mother.

The success of a Palestinian girl is determined by her ability to measure up to the social expectations transmitted to her through the family. The faster she succeeds in renouncing her own needs as a child, detaching herself from them, and internalizing as many stereotypical female characteristics as possible, the more favorably she will be looked upon by her environment, including the deity, her father. Strive as she may, however, she will never receive the appreciation displayed toward a son. Even after reaching physical maturity, she will forever remain a second-class human being; any man, even her retarded younger brother, is superior to her by virtue of his masculinity alone. The Arabic term which best defines the status of the Palestinian woman is *qasar*, meaning "handicapped" or "minor," that is, irresponsible, undeveloped, immature, irrespective of her age, education, or social status.

From childhood, I remember a girl who was always held up to us as an example of a "good" girl. She was a relative who, from the age of three, utterly renounced her own needs as a child and assumed the role of a highly valued assistant servant within the female ranks of her family. The family spoke admiringly of her enthusiastic participation in women's housework: hanging laundry, washing dishes, and performing spontaneous services for male relatives. The greatest token of their appreciation was a gift presented her at the age of three: a wooden bench placed beside the kitchen sink, to make it easier for the devoted little girl to wash the dishes. In our village, this girl served as a positive role model to which every other girl of roughly the same age was compared. The purpose was to instill a feeling of constant guilt in those girls who did not, could not, or would not attain such a high standard of proper behavior. Many of the scoldings, punishments, beatings, and humiliations I received as a child were accompanied by unfavorable comparisons to the shining example of that girl.

However, service to men, performance of female tasks, and formal acceptance of female values are not enough. The girl must provide her family with a guarantee of her intentions, a loyalty oath, as it were, which promises good behavior and provides continuous proof of proper conduct, including not only what she actually does, but also what she feels about her actions. She must fulfill her obligations while completely internalizing the expectations of society, and must feel within herself that these are indeed the rules of suitable behavior. In other words, it is not enough for her to be a handmaid; she must view this role as if it was her greatest wish and desire. She must love these functions in the I-love-my-Master manner of a lowly slave, who considers her slavery the epitome of human existence. Failure to comply with these leans leads to severe punishment, not only for actions but also for incomplete acceptance or latent criticism. Incomplete internalization of female traits is viewed as incipient rebellion, as a threat to the very foundations of the patriarchal family. Such phenomena are duly punished, with Islamic religion and tradition—which justify the natural inferiority of the woman and her possibility of becoming no more than a successful servant to a man—providing criteria for compliance with expectations and constituting a constant, omnipresent system of evaluation. This reality is in stark contradiction to all humanistic principles of individual freedom, and the right of a human being to develop her own talents and capabilities.

The division of characteristics into masculine and feminine, observed in many societies, is even stronger and more rigid among Palestinian society. While curiosity is admired in boys, in girls it is considered in bad taste and evidence of preoccupation with trivialities. Initiative, a welcome trait in boys, is viewed as shameless boldness in girls and punished accordingly. The desire to leave home in order to study is rewarded in boys with sympathy, admiration, and even financial support; in girls, on the other hand, it is seen as laziness, shirking of responsibility, and parasitism. Girls who try to imitate boys, even at a very early age, are punished and censured in a thousand ways as brash, foolish, lazy, and even dishonorable creatures whose low morals bring shame to their families.

These contradictions become even more pronounced in adolescence. Teenage Palestinian women receive no sex education whatsoever—not from the family, the community, nor from the school system. An adolescent trained to the role of wife and mother awaits her womanhood eagerly, assuming that her maturity will finally satisfy her patriarchal environment and compensate her for her oppressed childhood. She is swept into the emotional whirlpool characteristic of adolescence, but the joy she feels in the physical changes in her body and in the intensification of her emotions, is shocking to her family. Condemning glances become even sterner. Every bodily change imbues her with feelings of guilt and sin much stronger than those that accompanied her childhood. The adolescent soon realizes that she is constantly on trial, that the judges are not only her family but the whole society, and that she is doomed to the solitary confinement of her feelings. Thus, along with the loss of her lights as a child (games, fun, and even laughter), she is branded as a criminal, a danger to family and society: a walking explosive charge whose every movement is observed and criticized or even condemned. In order to survive in this suffocating environment, the adolescent begins to censor herself: not only her feelings, but her movements, her bearing, and her outward glance; she becomes a marionette, hanging from the strings of censure and oppression.

The attitude toward menstruation illustrates this process. Palestinian girls receive no sex education due to flip belief that ignorance and innocence are synonymous. Thus, the menarche appears as a bolt from the sky or as a mysterious illness. When the women of her family discover her state, the feeling of illness is exacerbated by a sense of guilt and sin. The subject is discussed in whispers, far from the ears of men. The teenager is given no scientific explanation of the physiological phenomenon; yet the menses themselves become a monthly proof of her sinful state.

The instructions received by the young woman are practical and explicit, but do not include any comprehensive explanation capable of reassuring her or increasing her understanding. On the contrary, these instructions carry additional concealed messages. The menstrual flow is to be absorbed with cotton wool, which, of course, must be hidden before use and burnt clandestinely afterwards. Even used toilet paper, which may be thrown into the bathroom wastebasket, as is the practice in many Palestinian households, has a lower negative impact. Thus a completely normal physical process becomes a focus of guilt and conveys a feeling of perpetual pollution.

As stated above, the instruction of the adolescent female takes place in whispers and in secret. This, at first glance, might create the impression that the women of the family constitute a protective and supportive phalanx within the mechanism of patriarchal oppression. However this is not the case. The mother, as a trained agent of the patriarchal system, must report to the father that his daughter has become a walking time bomb, liable to sully the so-called family honor. Thus, while exerting pressure on her daughter to conceal any fact related to her development, she herself, of course, reports to the Supreme Commander. This becomes immediately apparent: supervision is increased, and the father's disapproving and fearful glances make it clear that the terrible sin is known to him. The feeling of guilt becomes a permanent element in the life of the adolescent female.

The most important training the Palestinian woman undergoes during adolescence is preparation for her intended role as merchandise to be sold on the marriage market. She prepares her dowry, perfects her knowledge of handiwork in embroidery, sewing, and knitting circles which abound in nearly all Arab towns and villages. The patriarchal family views its females as goods which must be preserved so that they can be offered for sale in the best possible state; accordingly, there is no need for serious investment in their education. In high school, the number of young women enrolled is far smaller than that of young men; the disproportion increases in institutions of higher learning. One-third of Palestinian college students (within the Green Line) are females, and only one-fifth of Palestinian college graduates are females. If one considers schooling in terms of the investment required from family resources, one finds that, as the need for investment increases, the number of Palestinian women students declines. Thus, for example, the number of Palestinian women doctors educated within the state of Israel can be counted on the fingers of one hand, due to the large investment required. It should also be noted that the higher a woman's level of education and personal independence, the lower her value on the marriage market. Even educated Arab men prefer to marry wives whose level of education is less than, not equal to, their own. The main reason for reluctance to invest in daughters' education is rooted in the tradition according to which sons bring their wives into the family, whereas daughters abandon their family for another; in other words, any investment in a daughter will benefit not the investor, but the family of his son-in-law.

The status of Palestinian women within the state of Israel is basically no different from that of Arab women in other countries. Despite the avowedly democratic nature of Israel, Israeli Palestinian women rarely marry out of free choice. Even rarer is intermarriage between members of different Arabic-speaking communities, Druze, Christians, and Moslems, despite their belonging to a single nation. This does not derive solely from the divide-and-conquer policy of the Israeli authorities, but also from the structure of the Palestinian family. The privileges accorded to Israeli Jewish women are not granted to Palestinians. First of all, the family of the Palestinian woman decides whom she will marry. For example, it is common to find exchange marriages, in which a family gives its daughter in marriage to the son of another family, so that the son of the first family may marry the bride he has chosen, or in order to rid itself of the burden of an older, unmarried daughter. Second, marriage and divorce are entirely in the hands of the *qadi*, or religious judge and registrar of marriages; the Israeli Palestinian women cannot appeal to the district court, as can her Jewish sister.

One of the claims frequently made concerning the status of Palestinian women within the Green Line is that it is much higher than that of her sisters in the Arab countries, due to the fact of her residence in a democratic country. This claim has no basis in reality. The special status of the Palestinian population within the Green Line, that is, its subjection to national, political, social, and cultural oppression, led to the development of defense mechanisms based on a return to patriarchal tradition and the zealous preservation of the values implied by that tradition. Enlightenment and its attendant humanistic values are forced to recede before the threshold of the patriarchy. The *hamula* (extended family) and its values become sacrosanct as a distorted response to the cultural oppression of the Israeli regime. The primary victim is the Palestinian woman, the last remaining property of the dispossessed Palestinian male. It is a common error to view the national and cultural repression on the part of the Israeli government as a foreign or alien force exerting equal pressure on all components of Palestinian society. Not all classes and sectors of oppressed people suffer equally, nor do they share an equal interest in liberation. The traditional leadership and the upwardly mobile have some interest in freeing themselves from discrimination and oppression. But the lower classes of laborers and peasants suffer far more, as they are also exploited within the Palestinian social framework itself. At the bottom are the women, especially the women of the lower classes, since some of their oppression is a result of the patriarchal framework itself. This means that for women, national and social liberation are closely interrelated.

The hamula and its values are viewed favorably and encouraged by the Israeli authorities. Covert cooperation obtains between the traditional Palestinian leadership and the state of Israel, which may be seen in the attitude toward such phenomena as the murder of women in defense of family honor, on one hand, and the attitude toward Palestinian women political prisoners from the occupied territories, on the other.

The Palestinian tradition of family honor means that the honor of the Palestinian man resides within the body of his wife, daughter, or sister. Wherever the woman goes, the man's honor goes with her; if anything happens to her, it is deemed not to have affected her personally, as she is no more than a receptacle for the honor of her family. This is especially striking in cases of rape. In every rape of a Palestinian woman, the responsibility devolves on her. By "responsibility," I mean that it is she who will eventually suffer all the consequences of the dreadful crime committed on her person. I became personally acquainted with the cast, as it were, of one such drama which took place in an Arab village in the Galilee. A respectable married man raped a young woman in her twenties from a family considered less respectable than his own. The woman's family tried to pressure the man into marrying her. He refused, but, fearing revenge, approached an official of the Israeli administration and confessed to him, promising that, if no charges were pressed against him, he would serve as a collaborator for Israeli authorities. The man was given a gun, which he carried openly and proudly; the entire village was aware that he was under the protection of the government. The young woman was fortunately not murdered, as a seventy-five-year-old man from a remote village agreed to marry her; a short time later, she became a widow. This incident illustrates the relationship between the Israeli authorities, the Palestinian notables, and the traditional leadership in general, and the deals concluded among those parties at the expense of the Palestinian woman.

In a symposium on family honor murders held in Beer Sheba in 1983, the Israel government advisor for Arab affairs, Nissim Kazaz, proposed that a rape victim be married to the rapist. None of the participants appeared shocked, and no negative reactions were expressed. This phenomenon is familiar in Palestinian society; it often happens that the rape survivor's father begs the rapist to marry his daughter; otherwise, the father will be forced to kill her. Middle Eastern studies expert Gideon Karsel, who investigated the phenomenon of murder "in defense of family honor," stated that between twenty and forty corpses of women are discovered each year, of which only a small fraction are reported as those of murder victims.

The cooperation between the government and the patriarchal leadership is strikingly reflected in the behavior of the police toward young Palestinian women who run away from home. The police generally return them to their families or villages, in exchange for an empty promise by the father or other notable that the young woman will be "looked after," yet all the parties involved are aware that blood may be spilled. Indeed, in many such cases, before twenty-four hours have elapsed, the young woman's body is found in a well or distant field. The police classify these murders as suicides or accidents despite the fact that they have evidence that the deceased was in real danger in her own home. Murderers in defense of family honor have developed a wide range of methods for ensuring an alibi, and the police are content to simply accept these and close the case. Journalist Matti Regev stated, "I know of several cases in which the police delivered the victim into the hands of the murderers" (Monitin 1988). The courts are also considerate toward these murderers, exhibiting a patronizing sort of understanding. The prison system shows them an especially lenient attitude; some are pardoned or have their sentences reduced.

The return of a persecuted young woman to her family via a qadi, sheikh, or other notable not only reflects the cynicism of the law-enforcement apparatus which uses the victim as a commodity in order to improve its own relations with the notables and the traditional leadership. Essentially, it amounts to recognition on the part of the Israeli authorities of the right of patriarchal tradition to determine the punishment to be meted to rebellious daughters. In other words, the state, which is responsible for the security and welfare of all its citizens, is prepared to renounce its sovereignty in this sector in order to reinforce the traditional leadership, at a very low cost: the body of one more Palestinian female.

Family-honor killings are generally viewed by the Israel public and press in a folkloristic manner, which actually belies a deep-rooted racism. This approach enables Israelis to look down on Palestinian society as primitive, and to draw implications for Palestinian national ambitions and the struggle against oppression. Even the leftist parties are not beyond reproach in this respect. The Progressive Peace List, for example, expunged all reference to women's liberation from its Arabic language platform. Uzi Borenstein spokesman of the New Communist list, explicitly referred to the phenomenon of murder for family honor as folklore, comparing it to the kidnapping of wives by Georgian Jews. Most members of the Israeli Left hesitate to deal with the subject. On one hand, they are part of a racist Israeli society, on the other, they are afraid they will be accused of racism.

The Palestinian uprising, which began in December 1987, swept many Palestinian women in the occupied territories into its wake. Many have since been arrested and have been subjected to sexual abuse during their detainment. Analysis of the situation of Palestinian women political prisoners and of the attitudes toward them exposes the social mechanisms blocking the Palestinian woman's way, as well as the crude and cynical exploitation of the values of traditional patriarchal society by the Israeli administration. The Jerusalem group Women for Women Political Prisoners has assembled dozens of testimonies regarding the extraction of confessions from female prisoners by means of sexual abuse and threats of rape. Additional testimony indicates the attitude shown toward the women by their own families, both in prison and after their release. In a number of cases, parents prevented their daughters from returning to school after their release. In one case, a young woman was beaten by her father for having been exposed to sexual abuse by Israel Security

Services investigators. And in Gaza, a young woman was murdered by her family because of a rumor that she had been raped while detained by the military administration. On 14 March 1989, the Palestinian newspaper *al-Nahar* published a full-page interview with Israeli Jewish members of "Women for Women Political Prisoners." Although the interviewees were quoted with meticulous accuracy, the entire passage dealing with sexual abuse was omitted from the interview. These incidents reflect the fact that a woman exposed to bodily harm or sexual abuse is held responsible for her own abuse.

In Palestinian society, nationalist ideologies often limit the struggle of women to the area of national liberation. These ideologies are propagated by persons who consider themselves radicals and even Marxists. An obvious example is Gazi al-Khalili, a self-styled revolutionary who published a book entitled *The Palestinian Woman and the Revolution* (1981). This book includes many passages that reveal a profound masculine anxiety regarding any possibility of a real Palestinian feminist struggle and warns against separate, independent organization on the part of women (al-Khalili 1981, 57). For example, in a passage comparing the Palestinian woman to the soil of Palestine, that is, using the word "rape" to reflect the conquest of the land by Zionism, he claims that the Palestinian woman has no choice but to renounce some of her own demands in order to preserve national unity. This claim, made under the guise of "understanding" the situation of doubly oppressed Palestinian women, projects the message that the Palestinian woman should renounce her own specific demands (al-Khalili 1981, 112). Further in the book, the author states that there is a "dialectic connection" and tension between the term "women's liberation" and the national question, and proposes slogans advocating woman's role as mother, sister, and helpmate in the Palestinian rearguard, not as leader, but as agitator, spurring the men to combat (al-Khalili 1981, 113). Yet the main thrust of his argument is revealed when, dividing the struggle into stages, he claims that in the stage of national liberation, women must actually renounce their aspiration for gender liberation and concentrate on national liberation. According to al-Khalili, the national struggle has no room for women's liberation, which belongs to the later stage of socialism (al-Khalili 1981, 140). This is a classical reformist approach, which defers missions of immediate urgency into the rosy future, in order to avoid them in the present.

Al-Khalili refuses to consider women's liberation as a vital democratic mission. His hysterical hatred of the women's movement leads him to claim that the entire enterprise is bourgeois and reactionary (al-Khalili 1981:45). He pretends to understand the educated woman, forced to suffer the limitations imposed on her by society, and he blames the woman herself. He argues that the educated woman must understand the society in which she lives; she has no right to an individual perspective which could lead to revolt against her society's values. He accuses the "rebellious" woman of displaying bourgeois values and a lack of national responsibility (al-Khalili 1981, 56, 57, 123). Al-Khalili's hypocritical howls against Palestinian women "infected" by the women's liberation movement, as well as his opposition to all-female organizations, indicate his affinity with the petty bourgeois radical faction, which desires national liberation, but no real social change; defending a social order characterized, among other things, by the low status of women. His arguments also indicate a profound masculine anxiety, which uses ideology to perpetuate the oppression of woman. Despite their radical camouflage, al-Khalili and his likes are, in reality, frightened creatures who spread a poison more virulent than the chains of the patriarchal family structure itself.

References

al-Khalili, Gazi (1981). *The Palestinian Women and the Revolution*. Acre: al-Aswar Press (Arabic).
Regev, Matti (1988). "The Sacrifice of Fatma." *Monitin* (January; in Hebrew).

Between the Flag and the Banner

Dilemmas in the Political Life of Israeli Women

THE POLITICAL LIVES OF WOMEN IN ISRAEL have been shaped by an acute dilemma: a choice between their desire to foster national progress and their quest for feminist self-fulfillment. Women who wanted to play an equal part in building the new homeland rejected sex as a basis for political mobilization and interest aggregation; but those subject to gender discrimination found themselves shut out of the national effort. The perplexing choice for women was between participation in collective efforts at the expense of their particular interests, and adopting a feminist position that would guarantee their rights as women. The first option implied subscribing to overarching collective goals and acting from *within*; the second involved adherence to feminism and mobilizing from *without*. This account is of women's politics in one particular country, but it may be valid for other societies too. The dilemma women in Israel face may well be that of women in emerging nations, especially during periods of social and political upheaval. At such times participants are subject to heavy demands, and the call for loyalty to the common goal is great. Identification with a national movement may impose constraints on the development of partial mobilization centering on issues such as the cause of women.

The underlying argument is that carrying the double burden of predominating common values as well as submission to particular and partial interests obstructs both effective mobilization and influence. Vacillation between two contrasting loyalties weakens the effectiveness of action and hinders social change. The dilemma is real in that giving up collective values may exact its price in social rewards; conceding particular interests may take its toll in personal integrity.

When a choice is made, however, either because collective (national) demands ease off, or because the group under question is willing to pay the price entailed in breaching established norms, change is more likely to occur. The origins and nature of the quandary of Israeli women and its consequences for political power and influence are discussed in what follows.

Israel as a Case Study of Women and Politics

As we approach the mid-1990s, the literature on the place of women in political life abounds with case studies of various countries. Although these studies ask similar questions—How do women fare in the power game? What are their beliefs? To what extent are they represented in decision-making bodies? Is their political behavior different from that of men? How intense is their mobilization to political life? What shape has this mobilization taken?—and use similar conceptual frameworks—theories of mobilization, theories of patriarchy—the countries where the studies were done may be differentiated by two parameters, which need not be mutually exclusive: rate of political development and type of political regime.

The majority of case studies on women and politics have been conducted, to date, in Western industrialized countries. These cover the United States (Kirpatrick 1974), Canada (Bashevkin 1985), Europe (Lovenduski 1986), New Zealand (Catt and McLeay 1993), and the Nordic states (Haavio-Mannila et al. 1985). Studies have focused on the partisan arena (Lovenduski and Norris 1993), and on women's movements (Mansbridge 1986; Costain 1992). The subject attracting the foremost attention from scholars of women and politics is the female share in the political elite, and the processes enabling them to enter decision-making institutions, that is, national and local elections (Epstein and Coser 1981). Public policy regarding women has also been subject to academic treatment (Gelb and Palley 1987; Gelb 1989; Boneparth and Stoper 1989). With the expansion of feminism, however, instructive case studies have been published on the political life of women in developing countries in Asia and Africa. Good examples are Egypt (Sullivan 1986), Turkey (Arat 1989), India (Panda 1990), Pakistan (Mumtaz and Shanheed 1987), and Malayzia (Danez 1987).

The studies on women and politics in these two types of country have generally reached diverse conclusions. Scholars in the developed industrialized world usually lamented women's minor share in the country's political resources and their disproportionately small contribution in shaping their national life. Even where women have secured impressive political gains, such as in the Scandinavian countries, they were still perceived as being subject to patriarchal norms and structures (Haavio-Mannila and Skard 1985). By contrast, writers focusing on the role of women in developing countries that have failed to attain the economic standards of the West, generally claim that women have contributed their share in national development, albeit in their own unique way. In Egypt, for example, women were found to play legitimate and important roles in public life. They were described as "agents of change, helping to transform social customs as well as laws and, through work, contributing to increasing production." This was done by concentration in such fields as health, education, and welfare, which are associated with women's traditional interests (Sullivan 1986, 164). In Taiwan, owing to the mandatory reserved-seat system, "women have made significant strides in their political participation and representation over the last several decades that rival the progress that took nearly a century in the United States and Western Europe" (Bih-er, Clark, and Clark 1990, 193).

The second category of country dealt with in these case studies may be distinguished by the characteristics of the political regime. Most studies have focused on women in democratic societies, which also happen to be economically developed. In conditions of democracy, women's rights are enshrined in constitutional guarantees. Although their participation in political life may be hindered by informal and undeclared male discrimination, they nevertheless enjoy freedom of association and civil liberties. These circumstances have fostered the emergence of a gender consciousness, deemed a necessary condition for promoting gender equality (Rinehart 1992). Students of women's politics in democratic countries generally agree that feminism is on the rise, that an increasing number of women is participating in politics, and that the gender gap in political life is gradually closing.

Studies of women, however, are no longer confined to the democratic, developed world but have been extended to states governed by authoritarian elites, or those that are undergoing processes of democratization. Prominent among the first type is the former Soviet Union (Lapidus 1978; Browning 1987), where women's inequality stood in sharp contrast to the professed egalitarian principles of the communist regime. According to Soviet theorists, women's interests were adequately represented in the political institutions by male politicians. Feminists, however, attributed women's vulnerability to the glaring absence of women's consciousness. The predominance of class struggle over other forms of social activity had attenuated women's awareness of gender interests. Their omission from positions of power seriously affected their ability to challenge their subordination in all its forms.

Among the non-democratic regimes are former colonies, where struggles for national liberation had taken place. In the past many studies of nationality ignored sex as a significant issue (Gellner 1983; Smith 1986). The forces that spawn nationalism appeared so sweeping and all-encompassing as to dwarf problems associated with gender. Women's equality tends to remain a non-issue as long as national redemption has not been attained. Diminution of gender as a basis for women's mobilization is particularly evident when nationalism cannot readily assert itself but requires the investment of major human resources. Under these circumstances gender problems are simply ignored. In recent years more attention has been devoted to the issue (Walby 1991). The possible clash between national objectives and feminist interests, however, has not received much attention. In Israel this clash has played a decisive role in the shaping of women's politics.

Serious scholarly attention has been given to women's roles in countries undergoing processes of democratization, particularly in Latin America (Molyneaux 1985; Alvarez 1990). It has been argued that Latin America's democratic transitions, by all accounts the region's salient political trend in the 1980s, cannot be properly understood without consideration of the role played by women and by feminists; conversely, the changing role of women cannot be assessed outside the context of transition politics. The transition from military authoritarian rule to democracy happened to coincide with the reemergence of feminist movements and the rapid growth of organizations among poor urban women throughout Latin America. As noted by Alvarez (1989, 18), Brazilians witnessed the emergence and development of perhaps the largest, most varied, most radical, and most successful women's movement in contemporary Latin America.

The countries covered by the two sets of case studies—democracies and authoritarian or democratizing nations—leave a lacuna which is filled by Israel. On the one hand, Israel is a vigorous democracy where a variety of interests compete and clash; yet it differs greatly from the Western world in its strong national vision. It is a democracy sustained by the rule of law and the guarantee of civil justice, but it is a mobilized democracy where the elite exerts tremendous power over the people. Israel has been placed by the World Bank in the category of high-income economies (World Development Report 1991). With a per capita GNP of nearly $13,000 in 1992, it can hardly be considered a developing society. Yet the composition of its population, a substantial proportion of which originated in traditional societies in Asia and Africa, and its ongoing war with its Arab neighbors have blurred its image as an affluent country. Furthermore, Israel is a young-ancient nation. It was established in 1948, in the huge post–World War II wave of struggles for independence that swept many countries in Asia and Africa. At the same time, the state was founded on an ancient biblical heritage. It is mostly a secular society, with less than 30 percent observing religious tenets, but the great majority of the population subscribes to basic principles of the Jewish faith. Finally, Israel is a sovereign state, a member in numerous international organizations. At the same time, it constantly nurtures its relations with the Jewish communities in other countries. Recently a proposal was raised to extend Israeli citizenship to Jews living outside the country (Karmon 1994).

All of these paradoxes place Israel in a unique situation, passed over by scholars of women's politics in other corners of the world. Being both a democracy and a mobilized state, an affluent society with marked attributes of development, the case merits special attention. How do women fit into this myriad and compounded environment? Why do they have to choose between adherence to the (national) flag and the (feminist) banner?

Making Choices: Between the Flag and the Banner

The title of this essay intimates that the national flag and the feminist banner are incompatible, if not mutually exclusive. A short review of the discrepancies between the two is in order to demonstrate the reasons for this incongruence.

Democracies can be placed on a continuum extending from a service state to a visionary state. In the first, government is content to provide services and reconcile conflicting interests among different groups and individuals. This pattern prevails in most industrialized nations, where the authorities may be concerned with the affluence and welfare of their citizens but they are not guided by, or committed to, a transcendent mission. In the classical description of the Western state, these authorities respond to the public mood and assuage grassroots pressures in order to stay in power. By contrast, in a visionary state, there is more emphasis on mobilization and socialization (Apter 1965, 25). Here "the government has a predetermined vision or goal, and its primary function is to educate and mobilize on its behalf" (Liebman and Don-Yehiya 1987). Where vision prevails, a highly articulated system of symbols and myths defining the community socializes the population and mobilizes it for the realization of national goals. In a visionary democracy there is constant tension between the collective imperatives of society and particularistic needs of subgroups within it, including women.

Vision is likely to develop in democracies facing intransigent opposition from without and/or rapid social change within. In such circumstances the vision centers on a strong national identity, defined in terms of allegiance to one's nation-state (Gellner 1983, 3). The purpose of national identity is to deepen individual commitment and loyalty to the regime, to increase solidarity among society's members, and to provide them with a sense of a community (Seton-Watson 1977). A community in this regard does not consist only of "common institutions and a single code of rights and duties for all the members" (Smith 1991, 9) but also of a strong sense of belonging. Where allegiance to the vision pervades, sustained by a comprehensive socialization structure, particularistic groups, including women, may be reluctant to carry their own banner. The sweeping force of national goals obstructs the crystallization of their own needs.

In Israel the two pillars that both necessitate and sustain the national vision are the state's precarious security and its mission of ingathering the exiles. Pursuing goals associated with feminism might conceivably have hindered the realization of these goals.

Women and Security

Surrounded as it is by hostile neighbors, Israel has had to cope with external threats and incessant belligerency. These factors have had decisive effects on the country's polity, economy, and value system. The problem of national security has dominated the political agenda, displacing almost any other item. Despite the inception of the peace process, media headlines, government discussion, and public attention still reflect the primacy of security in Israeli life. That questions of survival rank first is evident also from the structure of the national budget. Israel expends far more on its security than other Western nations. Annual military expenditures have usually exceeded 20 percent of the GNP. The country's well-known defense burden has contributed to a dominance of the economy by the government to a degree hardly known in other democracies. It has been noted that "Israeli policymakers have economic responsibilities that resemble those of Eastern Europe, in the context of aggressive political parties, labor organizations, and other features of the democratic West" (Sharkansky 1988, 5). The impact of security on public life has been accentuated by the lengthy service of Israelis in the armed forces. Compulsory service in the military for young men is at least three years. Many serve for five years and continue to do so in reserve units about one month a year, until they are in their fifties.

Living in a state of siege has not been easy for Israeli women, because the host of norms, values, and attitudes that sustain military might have excluded women and driven them to the margins of society. The halo sparkling around the military generated a positive attitude toward the use of force. The image of the Sabra (native-born Israeli) is of a youngster characterized by strength, courage, and action. A general unease with emotion is masked by an ethos of heroism. Emotionalism, a typical feminine characteristic, has been rejected as a form of weakness that is both incompatible with the norm of the pioneer-warrior and ineffective in times of danger. Only recently, a heated public debate took place when a senior army commander condemned the display of soldiers weeping over a dead comrade, killed in battle, disapproving such an outlet of emotion.

To this may be added women's lesser contribution to the country's security. Although women recruits march in parades after basic training, and are often shown on television screens abroad, rifles on their shoulders, for the array they are wearing "paper khaki" (Hazleton 1977, 138). In 1949 the Defense Service Law was enacted. After heated discussion in the Knesset, fueled by religious opposition to recruitment of women, it was decided to conscript women for a shorter period than men and to exempt two categories of women: married and/or religiously observant. It was also decided to establish a women's corps entirely separate from other units in the Israel Defense Forces (IDF). As women have always been considered a burden by military authorities, exemption from duty is easily obtained. A woman merely has to declare herself religious to be excused from army service. Over the years the Defense Service Law has been amended several times but the principles underlying military service by women have remained intact. A Commission on the Status of Women pointed out: "When the IDF was first established, the state recognized the right of women to serve in all jobs on a voluntary basis. As time elapsed equality has disappeared. The only considerations are army efficiency and economic ones. Jobs are opened and closed to women on this basis. As a result, the IDF lags behind other armies which are more resourceful in absorbing women" (1978; quoted by Bloom 1991, 135).

At present women serve only twenty-two months in the military; they are not allowed to join combat units. Some progress has been made regarding the status of women in the armed forces as increasingly more enter occupations previously closed to them. By and large, however, women soldiers are still the secretaries, the clerks, the telephone operators, the nurses, the teachers, and the social workers of the IDF. There are no women pilots, tank crews, or paratroopers. Women do not serve in artillery units nor are they found on battleships. One woman, the commander of the Women's Corps (Chen), takes part in the meetings of the IDF's General Staff, but her rank is lower than that of her male colleagues. Thus, despite the many myths concerning the role of women as soldiers (Yuval-Davis 1985), they serve mostly in subordinate and supportive roles, unless in welfare occupations traditionally held by women. The woman soldier's life, concludes Bloom (1991, 137), "remains sufficiently circumscribed to allow her both to do national service and to return to society understanding her role as a woman." The seeds of duality are sown in the preeminent institution of Israeli society, the armed forces.

The exclusion of women from active service has confined them to nurturing roles and has hindered their entrance to the power arena. Women were expected to contribute to the national effort by sticking to their traditional female roles. The male-dominated society could be benevolent to women as long as they conformed, in their attitudes and activities, to established patterns of female behavior. As they could not demonstrate bravery in the battlefield, women had to excel in the kitchen to prove their patriotism. Waintrater (1991, 118) describes how women channeled their anxiety during the October War (1973) into the things they do best: baking cakes. Their massive engagement in this endeavor resulted in a flour shortage. The women were baking too many cakes, and continued to do so even when the shortage became publicly known. Women were expected to make life easier for the men at the home front, to nurture, to care, and to love. Scores of women volunteers have always swamped the country whenever war has broken out, ministering to wounded soldiers and providing them with goodies to lift their spirits. The normative constraints on women's equality generated by the siege mentality have been summed up by a woman legislator as follows: "The Israeli

woman is an organic part of the family of the Jewish people and the female constitutes a practical symbol of that. But she is a wife and a mother in Israel, and therefore it is of her nature to be a soldier, a wife of a soldier, a sister of a soldier, a
grandmother of a soldier" (quoted by Hazleton 1977, 141). When asked, "How
do you live in the military milieu, in a society based on the supremacy of men?"
the wife of the chief of staff described in a nutshell the impact of the defense requirement on women's status. She said: "It is obvious that we, the women, are 'helpmates' and the husbands, members of the armed forces, can function only owing
to the support given to them at home." Breaking the caring tradition would have
breached a fundamental norm: doing one's best for the country's survival. Hence
women had to choose between the national imperative, relegating themselves to
domestic commitments and responsibilities, and a feminist advocacy, which
would relieve them of this constriction.

Women and Immigration

Immigration has played a profound role in the process of nation-building. As stated,
ingathering of the exiles has been one of the major functions of the Jewish state.
Since its creation the state of Israel has absorbed over two million Jewish immigrants, four times the size of its population when it won independence. The Law
of Return, giving the right to all Jews to immigrate to Israel and to automatically
acquire citizenship on arrival, highlights the national commitment. Immigration
is widely discussed in the media and documented by official sources since its
scale is deemed a major indicator of the nation's strength and the fulfillment of
ultimate Zionist ideals. The immigrants are of varied backgrounds and from
numerous countries of origin. In the early days of statehood, most were either European Jews, Holocaust survivors, or Jews from Arabic-speaking countries in the Middle
East and North Africa. The most recent large-scale immigration (some half a million people) are from the countries of the former Soviet Union, which have
opened their gates to let Jews out after a long period of severe restrictions. From
another corner of the world have come black Ethiopian Jews.

In the country's formative period the hardships involved in immigrant absorption underlined the difficulties in Israel's process of modernization. The majority
of immigrants arriving after the establishment of the state came from countries
that were relatively deprived and underdeveloped socially and economically—
between 1948 and 1954 immigrants from Arabic-speaking countries constituted
51.7 percent. Most of them found it extremely hard to adjust to the advanced economy of the fledgling state, populated mainly by Jews from the developed world.
From the perspective of the Israeli authorities, however, there was no choice but
to "drag these 'backward' immigrants into the modern age, as they saw it, for the
(mostly economic) good of the State of Israel as well as the good of the immigrants

themselves" (Lehman-Wilzig 1990, 29). While the plight of these immigrants was particularly severe, Israel as a whole suffered its worst economic situation ever. Data reveal that from 1951 to 1953 the per capita national income plummeted by 14.3 percent, and real income fell by 10.6 percent in 1952 alone.

The grave constraints on resources militated against women's economic equality. During the first seven years of statehood, over 400,000 new immigrants came to Israel, swelling the population by approximately one-third. The economy could not absorb such a large number of newcomers into the labor force. Government employment policy was directed at creating jobs primarily for men, not women, who were left out of the labor market owing to the national imperative of immigrant absorption (Izraeli 1991, 166). With the expansion of the state's economy in subsequent years, increasingly more women joined the labor force. Men's employment needs, however, took precedence over women's. Consequently, unemployment rates have always been higher for women than for men. Furthermore, women were channeled into low-paying and/or feminine jobs that would not interfere with the work done by men and would not encroach on the successful absorption of the new immigrants.

Another byproduct of immigration causing women's economic inequality was a growing demand for volunteer service. Although the state guaranteed the basic needs for the immigrants' absorption, the burden of defense and the economic hardships weighed heavily on government agencies and left much to voluntary activity. Women were expected to contribute to the national effort of immigration absorption not through the power of their productive labor, but rather by enfolding the newcomers in their compassion. As we shall see, women's voluntarism was channeled through party institutions, and was not a product of community or grassroots activity. It therefore posed no threat to state authorities nor did it challenge widely endorsed values. Women conformed to these norms by rallying to the flag and dutifully pitching in. They were encouraged to undertake social work among immigrants, to settle them into their new surroundings, and to accustom them to their new environment. Their contribution to immigrant absorption has been vividly described by Pope (1991, 227):

> During the first years after independence, the Council of Women
> Workers served the interests of the state by focusing on the problem of
> immigrant absorption. Hundreds of female volunteers were encouraged
> to undertake social work among immigrants, who were temporarily
> housed in transit camps. In addition to food distribution and relief
> work, the Council held Hebrew language courses among women, which
> helped to foster their new Israeli identity. Together with the Histadrut's
> Agricultural Center, it encouraged auxiliary farming on small plots in
> immigrant housing developments, and initiated basic vocational
> training to enable women to join the workforce.

By channeling their efforts into volunteer activity, women accepted a secondary role in the country's economy. In Israel volunteer work has a well-established status as a legitimate form of participation in public affairs. Being outside the competitive systems of the labor market and party politics, it is considered, however, a marginal public activity, especially suitable for women (Bar-Yosef and Padan-Eisenstark 1993). Admittedly, women's movements took pains to prod women to enter the workforce, albeit on two conditions: that work and domestic commitments be in harmony and that the work contribute to the national effort. A woman choosing a feminist course, putting her own needs for fulfillment above the exigencies of the country, jeopardized a fundamental, highly imposing, national norm. To sum up, it was unusual for Israeli women to turn their backs to the security needs of the country and its mission of ingathering the exiles, even though adherence to these goals was incompatible with gender equality.

Conceptual Framework

The conceptual framework for this essay draws on a major theme in feminist literature: women's vacillation between operating outside or inside the political establishment; between mobilizing their own resources or those of the male-dominated political elite.

The first option—working from without—is predicated on women's mobilization capacities, their ability to recruit and activate members, to solicit financial resources, and to establish a stable and effective organizational structure. Most important, however, is the enhancement of prospective members' consciousness and identification with the group's cause. It has been widely acknowledged that movements are most readily mobilized around common interests. On the face of it, women do share interests as much as any other group that attempts to wield political influence. Confronted with widespread stereotyping and inequality in the workforce and in political life, they act to promote equality (Sears and Huddy 1990). A precondition for women's successful mobilization, however, is their awareness of their gender interests (Katzenstein 1987; Rhodes 1990). It has been assumed that when women's consciousness is raised a distinct pattern of feminine attitudes and behavior will follow, manifesting itself in a gender gap. Most research to date on the women's movement in the United States has adopted the mobilization perspective (Freeman 1975; Conover 1984; Mansbridge 1986; Gelb and Palley 1987).

Effective mobilization for the feminist cause involves organization as well as attitude. When women act from without, they usually adhere to values not shared by men. They are also inclined to be organizationally detached from mainstream political institutions, being either self-sufficient or relying on the women's constituency at large for human and financial resources. When leaning toward mobilization, women are expected to cut through the partisan arena and act in concert with other women. They are likely to coordinate their strategies and co-operate within the feminist arena in their efforts to influence policy. In short, when women embark on the course of mobilization, they opt out of mainstream poli-tics, and they tend to let the feminist voice ring out.

The other option noted above—acting from within—implies integration or association with existing centers of power, adherence to widely accepted norms, and concentration on conventional political processes (Klein 1984; Costain 1992). It has been suggested in the literature that links to political parties and elites are indispensable for political influence (Klandermans 1990, 127). Alliance with the establishment provides women with extensive communication and recruit-ment networks. Studies have shown that influence of nongovernmental actors on policy making depends not only on consciousness enhancement, but on the extent to which organizations can activate allies with substantial political resources. Ties with the party system and government institutions could thus increase group impact in political life (Costain and Costain 1987). The implications of the integration theory for women's consciousness and organizational behavior are self-evident: instead of joining women's associations, women make use of existing women's sections and subunits within the roof-organization of political parties and trade unions or any other established political organ, and work in cooperation with its predominantly male elite. Women's promotion of welfare legislation within social-democratic parties or trade unions in the Scandinavian countries is a good example of acting from within. The integration model thus presumes a low level of feminist identification, organizational links with male-dominated political groups, and alliance with establishment associations rather than with other women's groups.

To sum up, the mobilization theory concentrates on the uniqueness of female interests and the need to confront the male-dominated polity through orga-nizational and ideological means. It assumes that women are fundamentally dif-ferent from men, and that the difference should be acknowledged and utilized as a political resource. The integration theory, on the other hand, centers on co-operation and alliance with men, assuming that female interests are not exclusively feminine and may be shared by men as well. Each of these options has its pitfalls and hazards. Excessive reliance on mobilization may hinder effectiveness. This was the case of the women's movement in the United States struggling to ratify the Equal Rights Amendment, as related by Mansbridge (1986). Intemperate resort to integration may be hindered by patriarchy, by men's attempt to monopolize, cajole, and direct women's politics. This was the case in the Scandinavian countries, as we are told by Hernes (1989).

The two-pronged choice—mobilization or integration—has been linked to another major feminist dilemma: private or public. A large body of scholarship has accumulated demonstrating women's inequality in political life and their rarity in policymaking institutions. That women are still second-class citizens, at least in this respect, has become a truism. A major pretext for the gender bias in politics has been propounded in the distinction between private life where women predominate and public life where men are most evident (Elshtain 1981). Some scholars have emphasized the significance of the historical, gender-differentiated separation between the public and the private in the writings of the great political theorists of the past (Okin 1979, 1989; Pateman 1989). Researchers have also focused on more mundane lifestyles, in which responsibilities are not evenly divided between men and women. The sexual division of labor in the economy and in the home, so it has been asserted, operates to keep women at bay regarding political activity. How to defeat this inhibiting distinction is subject to controversy.

One school of thought argues that the solution lies in freeing women from "biological tyranny" and dismantling all social and cultural structures that are erected upon this tyranny, including the family. The most radical version of this solution calls for test-tube babies to replace biological reproduction (Firestone 1972). More moderate accounts, however, regard women as victims of male subordination, sustained by women's domestic chains. Women's private family roles in marriage, motherhood, and homemaking are the main culprits, impairing their full integration into political life (Sapiro 1983). Increasingly, demands have been pressed to establish women as sovereign rulers over the representation of their lives (Jones 1993, 193), rather than to mold them in norms forged by a male-dominated world.

According to another school, the isolation and debasement of women under the terms of male-dominated structures must be fought, but not the functions associated with private life. Instead of excluding the private life from the public scene, integration between the two should be sought. Instead of eradicating values associated with the private world, women should entertain their own morality of nurturing and caring and share it with men. They "must take care to preserve the sphere that makes such a morality of responsibility possible and extend its imperative to men as well" (Gilligan 1977; quoted by Elshtain 1981, 336). Instead of declaring war on men, the proponents of the private world have urged the expansion of the underlying principles governing its practices. Women's "different voice" in social interactions—a voice that stresses cooperation rather than conflict, maintaining relationships rather than achieving abstract justice—should be sounded in public. Titled against each other are, therefore, two feminist theories. The first propagates an intelligible, visible, and clear-cut separation between the female and the male world, arguing that this move is a precondition for the eradication of patriarchy and its associated gender inequality. The second postulates that the public and private arenas should be integrated in way beneficial to both. Turning the personal into the political is likely to eliminate women's disadvantage.

The two theories—mobilization/integration and private/public—could be linked together. Those favoring mobilization endorse self-sufficiency and a concomitant separation between men and women. The proponents of integration may accept the need for cooperation and the benefits attached to a joint activity. Needless to say, a clear choice between these two options—mobilization or integration— exists on paper only, as women more often than not opt for the two strategies at one and the same time. Yet the undeniable tension between autonomous activity and reliance on partisan resources has been seen to limit women's exercise of effective political power (Bashevkin 1985). In Israel this tension is more acute owing to the disparity between the national imperative and feminist interests. Mobilization would have meant women placing their unique needs at the fore, activating the women's constituency, and forging alliances within the women's arena, in short, rallying around the banner. Integration would have implied heavy reliance on establishment political parties and national institutions and adamant adherence to norms associated with these institutions. To track the choices women in Israel have made, three specific research questions should be considered:

1. What is the scope and the type of women's organization for political action? If mobilized for action outside the conventional political structure, women will concentrate on grassroots activity, removed from the partisan arena. If integration is the way chosen, the presence of women will be felt in stale agencies and nationally elected institutions.

2. What are the sources for the emergence of women's voice? In the mobilization model, women themselves are the source for political power. Enlisting wide constituencies of women to the feminist cause is a precondition for an effective activity outside the political establishment. Integration could be carried out on the elite level by women activists who derive their power from political parties, regardless of women's consciousness or willingness to take part in public life.

3. What are the outcomes of women's political activity? When acting in politics, women attempt to influence public policy. Discerning how much the government responds to outside pressure and how much to internally generated initiatives on women's issues is not an easy task. But when mobilization underlies women's politics, their influence on policy decisions is expected to be clear. Conversely, when integration is the dominant feature, women may gain from the achievements of other actors, not necessarily associated with the women's movement.

Landmarks on the Path to Equality

Historical developments have set the stage for women's politics in Israel. The most notable characteristic in this country is the sharp contrast between legislation on women's equality and reality, between formal regulation and daily life. By any account, Israel is numbered among the few in the world termed "first-wave countries" (Pharr 1981, 173). These are ranked by the rate of advancement of women's political rights as across the world in the last century. Suffrage was granted in pre-state Israel by the British mandate authorities in the early years of the century, some twenty years before the establishment of the state. Although the Jewish population in the country numbered just a few thousand people who were coping with enormous difficulties, the small community granted its women the right to vote at about the same time as the United States and Sweden. When judged by the "threshold of activism," Israel again is in good company, together with the Anglo-American and Scandinavian countries. Women have held high political office; women have organized for political activity; a gamut of legislation has upheld women's rights.

Equality between men and women in Israeli society was inscribed in the state's birth certificate, the Declaration of Independence. This document—one of the first of its kind to include sex as a group classification for the purpose of equal social and political rights—specified that "The State of Israel will maintain equal social and political rights for all citizens, irrespective of religion, race, or sex." Although the principles of equality spelled out in this document are not endowed with constitutional force, they have been applied as constitutional principles in court. Next, the major steps to make women equal to men were taken in four consecutive phases, corresponding to economic and political changes.

The first phase was in 1951, being the passing of the Women's Equal Rights Law entitling women to legal equality and equal rights to carry out legal transactions. Regulation of personal matters, however, was left untouched under the authority of religious jurisdiction. The law was adopted in one of Israel's most difficult times. The country was still licking its wounds from the devastating War of Independence; it was plagued by one of the severest economic crises ever, and it was preoccupied by the absorption of mass immigration. Added to this was governmental instability caused by a deep rift between the central governing party Mapai and the religious bloc on the one hand, and left-wing Mapam on the other. Technically, controversy with the orthodox parties centered on educational facilities for the new immigrants, but the real rivalry was over mobilization of the new constituencies. The government also came under severe criticism from the left for adopting a pro–U.S. stance when that power was engaged in the Korean War. With the approach of elections to the Second Knesset, which took place in 1951, two years before they were due, what the government needed most was legitimacy. The

Women's Equal Rights Law served as the perfect means for buttressing the governing party. It proved that the government did not yield to religious pressures while upholding religious control over matters of women's (and men's) personal status; it catered to the interests of women without violating those of men. Israeli women took pride in the new law, largely overlooking the paragraphs detrimental to women's status.

The second phase came in the wake of the International Year for Women (1975), when an ad hoc Commission on the Status of Women was appointed by Prime Minister Yitzhak Rabin. It is true that the creation of the commission was linked with Israel's international standing at the time. Still shocked by the exhausting effects of the Yom Kippur War of October 1973, what Israel needed most in the mid-1970s was international support. The government had to cope with external threats as well as with internal difficulties. In 1975 Israel was subject to a sweeping denunciation by the United Nations General Assembly, which adopted a resolution equating Zionism with racism. Israeli zealots of *Gush Emunim* (Bloc of the Faithful), the pro-territories movement, staged demonstrations in areas densely populated by Arabs. In short, the government was in dire need of proving that Israel was a legitimate member of the international community. Establishing a commission to further the women's cause served this end.

The commission's main function was to act as a fact-finding body. Its comprehensive recommendations, however, served as a blueprint for women's equality. The women's movement applauded the establishment of the commission, which was headed by one of its members. But it rejected any attempt to forge women's interests apart from national collective ones. Instead, it stressed that the commission should define local circumstances and adjust them to the special needs of the state and its women citizens. It further demanded that intensive dialogue between men and women should be maintained and partnership in rights and duties required by the Israeli reality should be emphasized. Women thereby evinced antagonism toward a feminist message. Still, the commission's work generated campaigns identified with the Western feminist movement. Assertiveness training groups for women were started nationwide and counseling centers for victims of domestic violence were opened.

The commission presented its report and recommendations in February 1978 and these led to the institutionalization of concern for women within the government system. Consequently, the third phase of women's equalization was characterized by large-scale bureaucratization. Israel witnessed a turnover in government when the perennial opposition—the Likud—replaced the long-time party in government, the Labor Party. The establishment of the National Unity Government revealed that the rifts sundering Israeli society were not as deep as perceived. The state appeared to have entered a new phase when power was gradually shifting from the political parties to the bureaucracy. Ideological contentions still permeated the Knesset and the public arena, but issues were settled mostly on the administrative level. Women's equality was quietly placed on the bureaucratic agenda as the commission's recommendations gradually penetrated state agencies. In 1984, a National Council for the Advancement of Women was established, whose members were nominated by the prime minister. Its function was to advise the prime minister on all issues pertaining to women. Various governmental units were set up whose sole function was to promote women's equality. Among these are the bureau of the Advisor to the Prime Minister on Women's Status, charged with taking the lead in promoting equality; the Department of Women's Employment in the Ministry of Labor and Social Affairs; and advisors on women's status in most government ministries.

The fourth and so far the final step toward gender equality was taken in the 1990s, when women's issues were relocated high on the legislative agenda. The introduction of primaries as

a means of selecting parliamentary candidates sharpened politicians' sensitivity to the public mood. Although, as will be shown, there is no gender gap evident in the Israeli electorate, and women's issues do not loom large in ballot choices, catering to women's interests, nevertheless, appears promising from the electoral perspective, at least as viewed by prospective candidates. Consequently, unprecedented Knesset activity on behalf of women has been taking place. In April 1994, a subcommittee on the status of women was established, whose chairmanship has rotated between Labor and Likud representatives. Legislative measures promoting women's status have already been initiated in the short time-span of the subcommittee's existence.

To sum up, when judged by institutional arrangements, Israel shows an egalitarian facade corresponding to its phases of development. Initially, the state wooed women in order to gain legitimacy; in the second phase promoting gender equality appears to have been a part of an adaptation process to winds blowing in other Western societies. In the third phase, women's rights were elaborated in the bureaucratic arena. In the current fourth phase, more legislative measures are again being undertaken. Now, however, it is not the party that seeks legitimacy but each legislator, adjusting to altered political circumstances. The foregoing discussion indicates that while women's equality has received adequate attention, this has been confined to the institutional level rather than converted into action.

References

Alvarez, S. 1990. *Engendering Democracy in Brazil: Women's Movements in Transition Politics*. Princeton, N. J.: Princeton University Press.
Apter, D. 1965. *The Politics of Modernization*. Chicago: University of Chicago Press.
Arat, Y. 1989. *The Patriarchal Paradox: Women Politicians in Turkey*. Rutherford, N. J.: Fairleigh Dickinson University Press.

Azmon, Y. and D. N. Izraeli, eds. 1993. *Women in Israel*. New Brunswick, N. J.: Transaction Publisher.

Bar-Yosef, R. and D. Padan-Eisenstark. 1993. "Role System under Stress: Sex Roles in War." In Azmon and Izraeli, 1993.

Bashevkin, S. B. 1985. *Toeing the Lines: Women and Party Politics in English Canada*. Toronto: Toronto University Press.

Bih-er, C., C. Clark, and J. Clark. 1990. *Women in Taiwan Politics: Overcoming Barriers to Women's Participation in Modernizing Society*. Boulder, Colo.: Lynne Rienner.

Bloom, A.R. 1991. "Women in the Defense Forces." In B. Swirski and Marilyn P. Safir, eds., *Calling the Equality Bluff: Women in Israel*. New York: Pergamon.

Boneparth, E. and E. Stoper. 1989. *Women, Power, and Policy: Toward the Year 2000*. New York: Pergamon.

Browning, G. K. 1987. *Women and Politics in the USSR: Consciousness Raising and Soviet Women's Groups*. New York: St. Martin's Press.

Catt, H. and E. McLeay, eds., 1993. *Women and Politics in New Zealand*. Wellington, New Zealand: Victoria University Press.

Costain, A. N. and W. D. Costain. 1992. *Inviting Women's Rebellion: A Political Process Interpretation of the Women's Movement*. Baltimore: The Johns Hopkins University Press.

Danez, V. H. *Women and Party Politics in Peninsular Malaysia*. Oxford, U. K.: Oxford University Press.

Elshtain, J. B. 1981. *Public Man Private Woman*. Princeton, N. J.: Princeton University Press.

Epstein, C. F. and R. Coser, eds., 1981. *Access to Power: Cross-National Studies of Women and Elites*. Boston: George Allen and Unwin.

Firestone, S.1972. *The Dialectic of Sex* . New York: Bantam Books.

Gelb, J. 1989. *Feminism and Politics: A Comparative Perspective*. Berkeley and Los Angeles: University of California Press.

Gelb J. and M. Palley 1987. *Women and Public Policies*. Princeton, N. J.: Princeton University Press.

Gellner, W. 1983. *Nations and Nationalism*. Oxford, U. K.: Blackwell.

Gilligan, C. 1977. "In a Different Voice: Women's Conceptions of Self and of Morality." *Harvard Educational Review* (47):481–517.

Haavio-Mannila, Elina et al., eds., 1985. *Unfinished Democracy: Women in Nordic Politics*. Translated by Christina Badcock. Oxford, U.K.: Pergamon Press.

Hazleton, L.1977. *Israeli Women: The Reality behind the Myths*. New York: Simon and Schuster.

Hernes, H.M. 1989. "Women and the Welfare State: The Transition from Private to Public Dependence." In A. S. Sassoon, ed., *Women and the State*. London: Unwin Hyman.

Izraeli, D. 1991. "Women and Work: From Collective to Career." In Swirski and Safir, 1991.

Karmon, A. 1994. *Jewish Sovereignty* (Hebrew). Tel Aviv: Hakibutz Hameuchad.

Katzenstein, M. F. and C. M. Mueller. 1987. *The Women's Movements of the United States and Europe*. Philadelphia: Temple University Press.

Kirkpatrick, J. 1974. *Political Woman*. New York: Basic Books.

Klandermands, Bert P. 1990. "Linking the Old and New: Movement Networks in the Netherlands." In R. J. Dalton and M. Keuchler, eds., *Challenging the Political Order: New Social and Political Movements in Western Democracies*. New York: Oxford University Press.

Klein, E. 1984. *Gender Politics*. Cambridge, Mass.: Harvard University Press.

Lapidus, Gail W. 1978. *Women in Soviet Society*. Berkeley: University of California Press.

Lehman-Wilzig, S. 1990. *Stiff-Necked People, Bottle-Necked System*. Bloomington: Indiana University Press.

Liebman, C. S. and E. Don-Yehiya. 1987. *Civil Religion in Israel: Traditional Religion and Political Culture in the Jewish State*. Berkeley: University of California Press.

Lovenduski, J. 1986. *Women and European Politics: Contemporary Feminism and Public Policy*. Brighton, Essex: Wheatsheaf Books.

Mansbridge, J. 1986. *Why We Lost the ERA?* Chicago: University of Chicago Press.

Molyneaux, M..1985. "Mobilization without Emancipation? Women's Interest, the State, and Revolution in Nicaragua." *Feminist Studies* (11):227–254.

Mumtaz K. and F. Shaheed, eds. 1987. *Women of Pakistan: Two Steps Forward, One Step Back?* London: Zed.

Okin, S. 1979. *Women in Western Political Thought.* Princeton, N. J.: Princeton University Press.

Pateman, Carole. 1989. *The Disorder of Women: Democracy, Feminism and Political Theory.* Stanford, Calif.: Stanford University Press.

Pharr, S. J. 1981. *Political Women in Japan.* Berkeley and Los Angeles: University of California Press.

Pope, Juliet. 1991. "Conflict of Interests: A Case Study of Na'amat." In Swirski and Safir, 1991.

Rinehart , S. T. 1992. *Gender Consciousness and Politics.* New York: Routledge.

Sapiro, V. 1983. *The Political Integration of Women.* Urbana: University of Illinois Press. 1983.

Sears, D. O. and L. Huddy. 1990. "On the Origins of Political Disunity among Women." In L. A. Tilly and P. Gurin, eds., *Women, Politics, and Change.* New York: Russell Sage.

Seton-Watson, Hugh. 1977. *Nations and States: An Inquiry into the Origins of Nations and the Politics of Nationalism.* Boulder, Colo: Westview.

Sharkansky, I. 1988. "Too Much of the Wrong Thing." *Jerusalem Quarterly* 45 (3):26.

Smith, A. D. 1986. *The Ethnic Origins of Nations.* Oxford, U.K.: Blackwell.

Sullivan, E. L. 1986. *Women in Egyptian Public Life.* Syracuse, N.Y.: Syracuse University Press.

Waintrater, R. "Living in a State of Siege." In Swirski and Safir, 1991.

Walby, S. 1991. "Women and Nation." *International Journal of Comparative Sociology* (33):81–100.

Yuval-Davis, N. 1985. "Front and Rear: The Sexual Division of Labor in the Israeli Army." *Feminist Studies* (11):649–676.

Homefront and Battlefront

The Status of Jewish and Palestinian Women in Israel

GENDER INEQUALITY IS MANIFESTED at all levels of life in Israel. While most Israeli literature describes the origins of the gender social gap, this essay analyzes the social mechanisms that continue to sustain gender inequality. These mechanisms exist despite the spread of ideology that espouses equality between the genders, despite new legislation to promote such equality, and despite the growing integration of women into the labor force and other public spheres. While many societies tend to blur the boundaries between private and public as a means to eradicate perception about gendered social division, this paper claims that, in Israel, the opposite occurs. Life in the shadow of a protracted Arab-Israeli conflict and constant threat has become a powerful mechanism that reproduces a gendered binary world. In military terms, the social dichotomy is characterized as "home front" and "battle front"; in sociological terms, the separation between the family and the military epitomizes the public/private split. In Israel, security, the army, and soldiering dominate the public sphere and are the bastions of male discourse. Family and familism are perceived as the pillars of Israeli communal and private lives and are the women's castle. These basic cultural frames serve as a major mechanism for reproducing the gendered division of labor, and, consequently, gender inequality. They not only locate women in traditional roles, but also dilute protest and temper the rise of a strong feminist movement. I argue that this process occurs in both Jewish Israeli and Palestinian, communities, though in reality it unfolds differently due to their basically different social locations vis-a-vis the Arab-Israeli conflict.[1]

Gendered Division of Labor as a Cultural Frame

Gender inequality in modern Western society is supported by the perceived cultural separation between the public and private spheres of life.[2] The hierarchical character of these realms accords the public domain greater prestige and superiority. The notion of two separate spheres of life is maintained by cultural assumptions that hold that each exists according to different principles of social order and having different social functions. Specifically, the public sphere is generally seen as meeting economic and political needs and rests on principles of association that are rational, substantive, competitive, and utilitarian. Social relations within this sphere are contractual and fundamentally formal. The private sphere, in contrast, is perceived as the intimate realm, in which life proceeds according to principles of mutuality, compromise, concern, and emotion. The distinction between them is seen as natural, hence the tendency to associate each domain with natural biological differences between the sexes.

Cumulative research shows that the public/private distinction is a cultural perception that emerged in the course of Western industrialization, urbanization, and bureaucratization.[3] The entrenchment of the dichotomy gave rise to concomitant institutions, legislation, and norms. Because the public sphere is identified with the modern, industrialized world, it is thought to possess greater force and prestige. The gender dichotomy parallels the dual-spheres distinction: the home is perceived to be the sphere of women's expertise, while public life is seen as the male preserve. Besides a gendered division of roles, these cultural assumptions generate an unequal ascription of power and social prestige. The dichotomy between men and women in different worlds is inherently injurious to the idea of universal equality, which, by definition is not gender-dependent.

The exclusion of women from an ostensibly universal arrangement is made possible by the place assigned to the family in nationalist societies, particularly if their security is under threat. There is a connection between women's role as reproducers and their subjugation. In many societies various religious precepts, traditional customs, and legislation stipulate the process by which families become part of the collective group (marriage, divorce, the children's legitimacy). Nevertheless, the institution of the family assumed a new role with the rise of nationalism at the end of the nineteenth century.[4] As the perpetuation of nationalism evolved into an end in itself, mechanisms for subordinating women to men and to the goals of the collective group were simultaneously reinforced. Women, as reproducers, are therefore perceived as representatives of the collectivity ("mother of the nation"). They are considered responsible for the nation's continuation by giving birth, ensuring the transition of the culture, and educating the new generation. They represent the nation's honor and symbolize its boundaries.[5] Laws that control childbirth or prevent such control, abortion laws, and so forth seek both to define the family and to control the women who produce it. In a cultural conception of this kind, women's place in the private sphere is not only strengthened, it is magnified. The powerful sense of belonging and of contributing meaningfully to the group, which accompanies women's role, blurs the discrimination and subjugation underlying the gendered division of roles.

These cultural distinctions persist in Israeli society. Women's entry into the Israeli public sphere causes them to be perceived by the society, and frequently by themselves, as intruders in a forbidden realm-hence they are not equipped with the requisite predisposition or resources. Women are currently active in economic and political realms, but they are still held responsible for running the household and raising the children. The dominant cultural assumption is that their first preference is for family roles and that if forced to choose between the private and the public sphere, they would opt for the former. Each gender's image is shaped in the spirit of these conceptions, which in large measure define their sexual identities as well. At the same time, these assumptions become intervening factors in women's prospects for work in the labor market.[6] These factors also affect their advancement in politics.[7]

As many scholars have indicated, the line between public and private is socially constructed and historically constituted; it varies from one society to another and from one historical period to another.[8] Western women's struggle for equality involves, inter alia, a challenge to the private/public distinction and a demand to re-examine the gendered division of social roles. In Israel this struggle is barred not only by Jewish and Arab traditional cultures, but by another cultural frame that is juxtaposed with the public/ private dichotomy: the security frame.

Security as a Cultural and Political Interpreting Frame

The most instructive lesson to be gleaned from reading the cumulative research on national security in Israel is that Israel has never had one, systematic, written and/or oral security doctrine. From the early days of the *Yishuv* (the pre–1948 Jewish community in Palestine) to the present, there has been disagreement on the scope of the danger facing Israel and on how best to achieve and ensure national security. Not only the general public, but political leaders and military experts are unable to reach a definitive conclusion on the subject. Scholars, too, are divided on how extensively the military-security doctrine pervades and influences civilian life or how damaging the process has been to Israeli democracy.[9]

Beneath the disputes among the Jewish public, which are so profound and painful that they have at times threatened to generate civil war, lies an unspoken consensus that Israel faces a constant existential threat.[10] The implication is that national security is a built-in problem of Israel's very existence. Herzog and Shamir address this phenomenon in their analysis of the discourse on policy toward Israel's Arab citizens as it is articulated in the Israeli press.[11] Following Gamson's frame analysis,[12] they argued that, although different conceptual approaches compete in interpreting the essence of relations between Jews and Arabs in Israel, all share the underlying security assumption:

> This concept (security), in the Jewish/Arab discursive formation, assumes almost mythical and catastrophic dimensions. The concept not only relates to basic notions of "law and order," to personal protection against harm, or to concrete threats of violence and war. In its deepest sense . . . "security" is associated with the ability of the Jewish state to remain sovereign. As such, the concept of security cannot be dismissed out of the discourse even by those who wish to do so. It compels the carriers of different frames to gravitate toward a debate which places the highest premium on the question of "security" once it is convincingly tied to "survival."[13]

The concept continues to prevail despite Israel's consolidation over the years and its military and economic resilience. Israeli Jews' awareness of their ability to repel security threats does not prevent them from maintaining the "security threat" as a basic cultural frame.[14]

That the existence of a security threat is a taken for granted, irrespective of the disputes over the scale and immediacy of the threat, renders it an element of Israeli life. However, it is simultaneously an object of social political negotiations, which determines its boundaries and implications. Security has a powerful cultural resonance in Israel. It is thus, accessible and amenable to mobilization in order to justify social reality, policy decisions and/or indecisions. There is perhaps no term more charged in the Israeli lexicon; even if its evocative power has declined a bit over the years, it remains virtually a self-evident presence. Proof that security is both a given and an object of negotiations is found in Arian's conclusion that the Jewish public has generally been predisposed to support the government in the initial stages of a security event, regardless of the party in power. While this support may then fade to be replaced by polarization that closely follows the political contours of the public debate, the innate reaction is to stand firm against the threat. The public-political debate over the scale of the threat begins only after the spontaneous first support. Threat or, alternatively, security is the culturally presupposed mindset starting point in the public discussions that determine policies and positions.[15]

Most studies that address security do so from the Israeli Jews' perspective. Arguably, a mirror image is found among the Palestinians in Israel. Their basic secondary status in Israeli society stems from, and is legitimized by, the security threat. They are expected to prove "loyalty" whenever they express a political view or participate in public activity. To cite one example, in Salman Natur's introduction to a paper entitled "Tries to Think Out Loud" which he wrote for a leftist political journal, he says:

> I begin with assertion of intention, or more precisely with a declaration of loyalty, as recommended for an Arab who comes to tell about himself or to discuss questions that relate to his existence, identity and status in the State. . . . As an Israeli citizen I declare that I recognize the existence of the State of Israel and the rights of the Jewish people to live in this country as free and sovereign people, and as a son of the Palestinian Arab people I declare that I support the just struggle of my people and the establishment of their own state next to the State of Israel in the West Bank and Gaza.[16]

Smooha's findings show consistent Israeli Arab recognition of the State of Israel and acknowledgment of their status as citizens. Indeed, this approach is the basis of their intensifying politicization and their demand for equal treatment. The consensus among Jewish and Palestinian citizens of Israel on the principle of Israeli security is the foundation for the social negotiations between Palestinians and Jews in Israel.[17] Security and the security discourse are thus prime factors shaping identity, political positions, and policy within both-the-Jewish and Palestinian communities in Israel. They are the progenitors of social and political disputes, but there is no dispute over one fundamental assumption: the centrality of security. It is the basis of the conflict but also the bond that closes the rifts in the Israeli society. No differences have been found between men and women in the perceived need to unite around security and around the disputes to which it gives rise.[18]

My purpose is to examine how the centrality of the security discourse affects the status of Jewish and Palestinian Israeli women. The institutionalization of the security threat as a cultural and political frame is a major mechanism that reproduces gendered divisions of labor and, consequently, gender inequality in both Jewish and Palestinian Arab communities in Israel. The presumption of a security threat expresses itself in two contradictory directions: one has created a social discourse and concomitant practices that include women in the public sphere if needed, while the other has operated simultaneously to their exclusion. Both have had, and continue to have, the inadvertent effect of reproducing and reinforcing the public/private dichotomy and hence traditional gender-specific roles. Certainly the broad consensus within Israel's Jewish community vis-à-vis national security and its acceptance as a legitimate claim by Israel's Palestinian community, perpetuate gender inequality; but by blunting perceptions of the issue's depth, this consent dilutes protest actions geared to reverse the situation.

Security, Army, Soldiering: Bastion of the Male Discourse

In the last two decades, a growing number of scholars have indicated that civil discourse in Israel is subordinated to the security discourse, and that social reality has been shaped in no small measure in its shadow.[19] In many societies, as in Israel, the concept of "national security" has been used to define the social order that was considered necessary to ensure national security. National security can mean protection of citizens from external enemies and, perhaps primarily, maintaining the social order.[20] The social order includes the gendered binary world. This discussion aims to present several components of the security discourse and the gendered assumptions that are taken for granted in this discourse.

Army and Soldiering

The army is a central component of the security discourse. This is not unique to Israeli society; Cynthia Enloe claims that, in all societies, the close identification of the military with the state gives the military influence and privilege that is rarely enjoyed by any other corporation or Ministry.[21] Compulsory military service, reserve duty, and Israel's recurring wars have made the Israel Defense Forces (IDF) a staple of the Israeli experience and a key to Israeli identity. Exclusion of Palestinian citizens from military service demarcates the social borders between Jews and Palestinians. The male Israeli fighter symbolized the New Jew, in radical contradistinction to the *galuti* (ghetto mentality) Jew of the Diaspora; and female soldier embodied the rejuvenation and egalitarianism of the Zionist ethos. In Israel, military service is perceived as both an obligation and a right, but above all as the basis of civil equality.[22] Women's service is a mechanism by which they are included in the civil order, and it places them on a par with men in contributing to society. This attitude was reflected in the enactment of the Defense Service Law.[23] It is also articulated by many women who want to enhance gender equality in the IDF and, consequently, oppose the abbreviation or elimination of military service for women.

As an institution, the IDF is a major reproducer of the gendered division of roles, despite the laws governing the induction of women; for example, women are automatically exempted due to marriage, pregnancy, or parenthood.[24] The prime illustration of the predominantly masculine character of the military culture of the IDF is the hierarchical distinction it makes between fighters (*lohamim*, members of combat units) and nonfighters, and its explicit exclusion of women from the battlefield as combatants. Many IDF options are closed to women from the outset. Women have recently been assigned combat-related tasks, such as instructors in the Armored Corps, but they are absolutely barred from operational activity.

While the IDF always makes new missions available to female soldiers on a need basis—generally to offset manpower shortages—it does not pursue this policy in order to promote gender equality. Only a legal battle finally compelled the Air Force to allow women to enter pilots' training courses, at least formally. The Military Advocate General's office did not oppose the attempt by the plaintiff, Alice Miller, to take part in the course on the grounds of a principle against women pilots, which would have been sexist, but instead cited "defense expenditures." The military's logic was that the investment involved in setting up a special course for women would be incommensurate with the high costs of maintaining the Air Force's preparedness and combat capability, given Israel's security situation. Gender equality is perceived as a luxury.

Professional gender segregation is rampant in the IDF, especially in the different promotion possibilities for each sex. Most regular female soldiers provide clerical and similar services, almost always to male commanders. Even when women serve in the same units as men, the commanders tend to assess their contribution primarily at the social level; as feminine by nature and hence as the military equivalents of the cheerleaders.[25]

Women in the IDF have limited options for promotion because of the type of work they do and because they are excluded from combat. A condition for achieving high rank in the IDF is field and combat service; women, therefore, by definition are denied the possibility of achieving seniority. On these grounds, the Chief Officer of the Women's Corps—the highest position available to a woman in the IDF—cannot attend General Staff meetings and is not consulted on questions of policy, appointments, or other major decisions.

The preferential treatment accorded males in the military bolsters sexual stereotyping and, moreover, reaffirms the masculine-macho culture. In Israel, as in other countries, the military plays an important role in constructing "manhood" identity.[26] A significant portion of the socialization of Israeli youngsters is related to preparations for military service. Consciously or unconsciously, these often include the cluster of gender stereotypes. Such attitudes are intensified during army service and are further honed upon discharge.

Palestinian men's identity is also determined by the role of military, but in a different way. Their masculinity is determined by their role in resisting the occupation, or by the humiliation they suffer as a result of the occupation, which often divests them of their manhood.[27]

Military service as the essence of the Israeli experience goes a long way toward conferring social prestige and determining the hierarchy between servers and non-servers, women and men, Israeli Jews and Diaspora Jews, and more acutely, between Jews and Palestinians. The army is a distinct border marker within the Jewish community, and for many years the secular and national-religious groups enjoyed preferential status in defining the community's boundaries and essence. But army service, as the quintessential Israeli experience, did more than just set group boundaries and determine their internal hierarchy; it also had pragmatic expressions. Military service became a means for granting benefits to the Jewish population to army veterans, according to the agreed code. By the same token it became a method of discriminating against the country's Palestinian citizens, men and women alike.

Military service is a convertible resource in civilian life. Women's service, however, has a lower conversion rate than men's in the civilian market. The IDF is a source of recruitment for managers in business and industry, and a channel of political mobility-but primarily for males.[28] Women are not part of the old boys' network that coalesces in the army and is carried over into civilian life. Women are also strongly predisposed to accept men's superior status. The consensus on "security needs" results in acceptance not only of the IDF's discriminatory structure, but also of the gender-specific conversion rate of military service into civilian assets.

Besides its stratifying influence, the unhindered transition from army to civilian life also has a cultural impact. Men succeed not only in translating their military service into better positions in the labor market, they bring with them military ways of thinking and organizing. The gendered military order is reproduced in civil society and it augments pre-existing sexist stereotypes.

The Security and Hyper-Security (Bitchonism) Frame

Scholars in Israel are divided over the depth of the IDF's involvement in politics and the nature of army-society relations.[29] Deciding which of the competing views better describes the involvement of the military in civil life requires more than an analysis of formal or informal structures of relations, or the decision-making process on a particular issue. Army-society relations are fashioned within the broad context of security problems and they create an entire social culture. This diffuse culture both permeates and defines every aspect of life. It bears a saliently masculine character, with all that this implies. The following examples will illustrate the point.

Israeli society tends to blur demarcation lines between politics and army, not least because some political decisions are related to the army and its operations. Politicians tend to abnegate their autonomy in the face of security considerations, leaving the stage open to the representatives and interpreters of security. The melting of boundaries has been made still more acute by the close ties between political and military elites, and the entry into almost universal approbation-of senior officers into politics immediately after concluding their active service. A military mentality and an army rationale were perceived as qualities highly suitable for managing the country, and they were the foundation of decisions to go to war and implement settlement policies, and even of domestic priorities and allocations. This mindset was represented by males and identified as a male preserve; women barely had any influence. Few women achieved senior-officer rank, and because of the IDF's gendered character, they were not considered true participants in the security discourse. The military's identification as a male world extends to all males, but only males, thus excluding women qua women.

The dominance of the security discourse in Israeli politics is well reflected in the hierarchy that prevails among ministerial portfolios. Defense is considered the most important portfolio and is awarded to the senior minister, or may be held by the Prime Minister himself.[30] By the same token, until 1992 no women could be found on the Knesset's most prestigious body, the Foreign Affairs and Security Committee.[31]

Retired male career officers often turn to politics as a highly accessible second career, but this is not an option for women. Never has a female senior officer been "parachuted" into national politics from the IDF, that is, moved directly to the leadership group of a national political party following an army career. Even at the level of local government, where few female officers have made the direct transition, none have been selected as mayoral candidates or given high places on their party's list.[32]

The subordination of all other considerations to perceived security needs is highly characteristic of Israeli discourse.[33] Palestinian citizens of Israel, men and women alike, have paid the highest price. Major policies, such as confiscation of land, military rule until 1966, political limitation and security inspections, were conducted and justified in terms of the security needs.[34]

The security flag accounts for the marginalization of social issues in which women usually play a prominent role: health, education, and welfare. These areas have always occupied a low place on the Israeli public agenda. A symbolic case in point is again found in the Knesset. Women in the House are disproportionally represented on committees dealing with subjects that are perceived to be feminine; which are also considered less prestigious committees.[35]

Army and security also figure prominently in various aspects of the Israeli economy. The security threat is a lever for economic development, employment, and for the conversion of economic resources. More people are employed per capita by the Israeli military and the security sector than in any other country, and Israel also has the world's highest per capita security expenditure.[36] Military service and a security classification have become prerequisites for entry into a range of occupations. Experience in security institutions is also a convertible resource for a second career in the economic sphere. A new entrepreneurial arena has emerged which is wholly connected to military experience: companies that provide guards and other security services, and security training in Israel and abroad.

This, too, is an all-male world; women have virtually no access to economic positions that convert security experience into financial resources. The security industry only broadens the existing gap between men and women in the labor market.

The prestige associated with army and security, and the infiltration of security considerations into many areas of life, creates a civilian culture that is deeply influenced by the masculine-military mindset. One of the most striking examples of this phenomenon is the general belief that former military personnel are fit to manage municipal governments and administer schools. The natural conclusion is that the civilian managerial-organizational culture tends to accept the military mentality, and military techniques of administration, as the preferred model. This approach is inherently detrimental to women. Local governments are directly concerned with areas that pertain to women's interests, especially since women are the principal consumers and in most cases the providers of services at the municipal level. Yet, men with security experience are perceived to be best suited for municipal management. The appointment of retired army officers as school principals reflects a similar tendency: even though most teachers are women, males who have concluded an army career are preferred as candidates to administer educational units. Women are thus excluded from the decision-making process even in feminine realms.[37]

The security rationale has created a situation in which collective considerations take precedence. Consequently, demands for civil equality and individual rights, including gender equality, are shunted aside. Indeed, gender equality is not only seen as a luxury, but as conflicting with, or even harming, security needs. Consider how the prestigious daily *Ha'Aretz* reported a women's demonstration urging the legalization of abortion. The report was headlined "The Battle Front Has Shifted to the Home Front" and stated, "Israeli men will soon have to defend a third front. It's not enough that they have to man the trenches and the tanks on the borders, defending our towns and cities against terrorists. In the future they will also have to defend themselves at home, against their wives."[38] Besides delegitimizing women's demands, the quotation takes the public/private = male/ female dichotomy for granted and reinforces the gendered division of roles against the background of the continuing conflict. Yizkhak Mordechai, as Israeli Defense Minister, reproved women who demonstrated for the army withdrawal from Lebanon: "Mothers would do better if they use their energy to support the IDF officers and security ability of the army in Lebanon" (*Yedi'ot Aharonot*, 3 June 1997). In the shadow of the security threat, women are expected to fulfill traditional roles-provide support, show concern, and nurture the family, not open civilian "fronts" that will hinder men folk in carrying out their central role as fighter-defenders. This mindset is so taken for granted that even female scholars tend to accept it uncritically. In her book on women in Israeli politics, *Between the Flag and the Banner*, political scientist Yael Yishai claims that the national flag and feminist banners are incompatible if not mutually exclusive.[39]

Her Home is Her Castle
and the Castle of Israeli Society

Security, army and soldiering dominate the public sphere and are the bastions of male discourse. Nevertheless, the gendered binary world is also reproduced by the importance of the family in Israeli communal and private lives; Israel is a family-oriented society. Throughout the West, the family has changed and social pressure to marry and have children has weakened, but in Israeli society (Jewish and Palestinian), the family continues to occupy a central place and preserve traditional patterns.[40] The Israeli family, even in the secular community, is on average larger than its counterpart in the West, the divorce rate is lower, the network of ties among blood relatives is broader, and many laws take the existence of an intact family for granted.[41] In some cases, the family's centrality has enabled Israeli women to achieve gains for which Western feminists are still fighting, such as maternity leave and a maternity grant, legislation forbidding employers to fire a woman who has given birth, day nurseries from an early age, and other benefits.

On the surface, women need not necessarily suffer because the institution of the family is so solidly entrenched. The two spheres of life (public and private) are equal, each fulfilling different needs and functions in the life of the individual and the society. But in reality, inequality is inherent in the assumptions which create dichotomy and in the organizational and social arrangements that derive from those assumptions. The contemporary family functions on the basis of a gender-driven division of roles.[42] In the hierarchical, dichotomous order of the private/public world in which the family operates, women and women's roles take second place to men and their roles. More trenchantly, women are made to depend on men (the breadwinners). The traditional family pattern is a mechanism that perpetuates gender inequality Thus, there is no need for discriminatory legislation or direct bias against women; gender inequality will persist as long as the family's centrality, and women's fulfillment of their traditional roles, are taken for granted. The feminist challenge to the institution of the family does not entail criticism of the private sphere and what it contains. On the contrary, it is a call to incorporate that sphere into the public sphere. The protest is against the hierarchy that exists in practice between the private and the public worlds, against the subordination of the domestic to the public, and against the perception that family roles are women's roles.

At the heart of patriarchal social order lies gender inequality, in both the public and the private spheres. This notion suits the nationalist underpinnings of the nation-state, as well as both Jewish and Arab traditions [43] Even though each community has its own distinctive thrust and each contains a range of subgroups, they are, nonetheless, very much alike in their approach to the family and in their belief that it is society's linchpin. Arguably, the encounter between the traditional world and the modern capitalist industrialist world, which is powered by nationalism, was not in a conflict over gender role. Indeed, the family's position in the patriarchal social order, and the traditional gender divisions implied therein, was universally strengthened.

By a similar process, the Arab-Israeli conflict gradually helped to entrench the institution of the family in Israel.[44] The invocation of "security" not only encourages gendered arrangements, it functions almost as a shamanist incantation against attempts to change or defy the existing order. The family's centrality has become a powerful mechanism that incorporates women into the collective group—but as subordinate to male dominated structure. The family reproduces patriarchal, hierarchical relations; it also stifles attempts to reorder the hierarchy as its roles are esteemed and revered in the shadow of the security discourse. This shadow has affected women in both Jewish and Palestinian communities. However, it has resulted in more extreme social arrangements within the Palestinian community. The different positioning of each community vis-à-vis the Arab-Israeli conflict and the superior status of the Jewish community within Israel affect women's status within each community and within Israeli society as a whole.

Jewish Families and Women's Status

Besides tradition, life under the specter of war encourages larger families than the Western average. Raising a family, preferably with many children, became one aspect of the national enterprise in Israel.[45] Ben-Gurion declared as much in the 1950s, when he announced a prize for large families, citing the national mission of "few against many."[46] The importance of family as a "war weapon" is exemplified by the strong tendency among Jewish settlers in the West Bank to have many children in order to create a Jewish majority, or, as it often called, "the demographic problem." The monthly children's grant that every family in Israel receives from the National Insurance Institute shows the same spirit. In the early 1990s, the grant for the first and second child was abolished. Although this was done as an economizing measure, it exposed the state's wish to support large families, with three or more children. Having more children increases women's dependence on men, and the preservation of this traditional mothering role places an excessive burden on working women.

The Arab-Israeli conflict has reaffirmed the role of the Jewish Israeli family as the connecting link between the collective group and the individual who defends the nation in a crisis. Women, identified with the family, are expected to give full support to their men who are called up for military duty (in the public sphere) and, if necessary, to sacrifice their spouses or sons for the cause. Life in the shadow of war enhances the family's importance. In Western society, the primary role of the mother concludes when the children leave home, usually after high school, to attend college. The Jewish Israeli woman extends her function as a mother by two years if she has daughters and by three or more years if she has sons. The children's period of military service reinforces the woman's traditional roles: expressions of caring for the soldier-son or soldier-daughter take the form of laundering and ironing uniforms, preparing good meals for their visits, "to give them a taste of home," baking cakes for them to take back to the army, and/or traveling the length and breadth of the country to see the soldier when he or she does not have weekend leave. [47] The family's role vis-à-vis its mature sons is extended. Researchers note that the children's military service injects new content into the family, which otherwise often enters a critical phase as the children leave and the bond between the spouses weakens. [48]

The family is perceived as a source of support for its soldier(s). The IDF's need for legitimation, which the family provides, became more acute following the 1973 Yom Kippur War. With the decline in the public's sense of security and its loss of faith in the military and political establishments due to the war's disastrous incipience, the IDF decided in the late 1970s to encourage parental involvement. The goal was to recruit family support for soldiers during the basic training, the period of transition from civilian to military life. The opening of the Army's doors to family involvement was broadened after the Lebanon War (1982–1985), and became a veritable floodgate when the Intifada (Palestinian uprising) erupted at the end of the 1980s. The army opened its bases to parental visits, initiated special parents' days, and created direct lines of communication between parents and commanders. The parents, for their part, mobilized vigorously for their new role, at times going beyond what the army expected or could tolerate. [49]

Katriel maintains that parents' visits to bases in the wake of the Lebanon War and the Intifada shifted their channel of activity from political controversies to family. Strong family ties, she argues, solidified support for the army, so that in practice the parents became partners to the politics of consensus. [50] This form of cooperation—parental intervention, in alternative terminology—was accompanied by negotiations on the boundaries between army and family, and between army and civil society.

Questions such as the extent of the family's penetration into the army and the demarcation of the army's boundaries are outside the scope of this article, but it should be stressed that boundary negotiations place the family at the center of the social arena. The importance of the family and its resilience are heightened by this social reality, but so is its impact within the society. As the Kibbutz experience teaches us the reinforcement of the family undoubtedly enhances women's status, but primarily within their traditional role, as mother and as wife, responsible for the home, provider of emotional sustenance, as giver, but also as one who sacrifices her personal agenda.[51] The paradox, then, is that women's inclusion in the nation's collective process of coping with security is confined mainly to traditional feminine realms. They enter the public arena by not challenging their traditional place in the society or the stereotypical conceptions of their roles.[52] The result is that the family's centrality becomes an affirming, regressive means of sustaining gender inequality.

Israeli-Palestinian Families and the Status of Women

The Arab-Israeli conflict has also given the Palestinian family a boost beyond the traditional cultural sources, ensuring that women's inferior status is preserved in that community as well. Political marginality and barriers to integration in Israeli society make the Arab family the locus of social solidarity and nationalism. Sami and Mariam Mar'i have shown that changes in the status of Arab women society are intertwined with intra-community processes engendered by the conflict. The events surrounding Israel's establishment severed continuity in the Palestinian community. Virtually all of its political and organizational institutions collapsed, its economic structure was shaken to the foundations, and the social order crumbled.[53]

In the first two decades of the Israeli state, Palestinian men became vulnerable due to loss of livelihood, lengthy absences from home (to find work), displacement within a foreign culture, encounters with Jewish women whose behavior they could not fathom, dependence on Israeli authorities, and threats to their national identity. Traumatized, Israeli-Palestinians clung to their traditional culture. The central concept of family honor assumed an additional dimension. Insecurity produced greater social supervision over women: control of women became the yardstick by which the Arab society measured its resilience and distinctiveness.[54] Upholding traditional values underscored the community's selfhood vis-à-vis the Jewish society, and displayed significant identification with the surrounding Arab world. Women were given the role of preserving and transmitting the culture, and the community's ethnic identity was strengthened by defending their honor.

Ibrahim describes how, under the claim of upholding family honor Palestinian women work in cucumber fields under the watchful eyes of the men folk, who also relieve them of their wages.[55] Radical adherence to tradition finds expression in the phenomenon of murder of women for family honor, which has persisted under the rule of Israeli law. Close family members (father, brother, uncle or son) are allowed according to Arab tradition to punish, and even to murder, a woman who is suspected of sexually immodest behavior. According to Hassan, the term "family honor" actually serves as a kind of fortress wall behind which are mustered all the forces that restrict women's freedom, keep them economically and socially inferior, and attempt to perpetuate male privilege—both by ideological means and through coercion up to and including murder. [56]

Israeli authorities encouraged the tendency toward insularity and the reinforcement of traditional family patterns. In many cases, this encouragement has been an unintended consequence of the security frame. Seeing the country's Palestinian citizens as a security threat, the state kept them under efficient, tight control.[57] Though this control has been loosen with the years, it has not disappeared. By setting up chieftains of the *hamulot* (clans) as mediators between the Israeli-Palesanian public in Israel and the government, and as representatives of the Palestinian community, the authorities created defined channels of communication through which they were able to maintain effective rule.[58] Competition among the chieftains made them vulnerable to divide-and-rule tactics, and the system also neutralized various attempts at nationalist organizing. The result was reinforcement of the traditional clan structure, and the superior status of sheikhs and notables. The system also prevented any direct, effective approach by ordinary Palestinians to Israeli government agencies. Women paid the highest price for this form of rue: they were unprotected from the custom of murder to preserve family honor. Hassan analyzes thirteen cases of such murders; in some cases the women's "offenses" consisted of displaying an independent attitude and refusing to obey men. The only explanation she found for Israeli police ineptitude in investigating complaints in such cases—indeed, for what might appear to be their tacit collusion with the perpetrators—was the policy of preferential treatment to clan leaders. Hence the brazenness of one sheikh who declared, in an interview to Military Radio, "The custom of murder for family honor must be preserved. If a girl dishonors her family's name, the family is obliged to punish her, perhaps even to kill her. This principle is accepted by all honorable families."[59] In any other social context in Israel, such a statement would be considered incitement to murder.[60]

The official Israeli justification for the authorities' understanding of this practice is related to cultural tolerance. For years the Israeli government tried to stifle the emergence of Palestinian national identity, while showing understanding for traditional cultural patterns. That "understanding" often came at the expense of women. Many Palestinians in Israel link traditional identity with national identity. In this situation the men's privileges represent the Palestinian way, entailing the suppression of women and a preference for tradition over nationalist or democratic values.[61] Most likely, the prevailing masculine mindset among the Jewish authorities who interact with the Palestinian population helped blind the latter to the heavy price paid by the community's women. The security concept engendered the Military Government that was imposed on Palestinians in Israel until the end of 1966. Some restrictions still exist today, formally or informally, on the integration of Palestinians into the labor market, and have produced a relatively high rate of unemployment among the Palestinians in Israel. Given the constant aspiration to raise standards of living, pressure has grown to send more Palestinian women into the labor market in order to help provide for the family. Because of scarce employment opportunities in their villages and low levels of education, many of these women enter the unskilled market; consequently, they work for low pay in an economy subject to fluctuations and/ or seasonal work (for example, agricultural employment). Above all, the market is subject to male control.[62] At the same time, the level of education among Israeli Palestinian women has been on a general rise. This has given them access to new areas of employment, such as teaching, law, welfare, and social work. Still, tradition remains a potent constraint on Palestinian women the preference is for them to work in the village, where scant employment opportunities then thrust them into competition with men—a contest in which the latter generally prevail. Teaching, for example, which in the Jewish sector is considered a female occupation, is a field dominated by males in the Arab sector.

Women, particularly the educated, who have entered the labor market have found their way to women's organizations. Although traditionally perceived as the preservers and transmitters of tradition, women have become agents of social change. The adoption of modern ways of life undermines the traditional family structure. Until 1967 these processes were identified with assimilation into the Jewish society, and therefore they generated fierce opposition. After 1967, following the Israeli-Palestinians encounter with the Palestinians of the territories, awareness of women's equality ceased to be a Jewish problem which had infiltrated the Arab arena, and became a general problem of the Arab nation.[63] This was a watershed in terms of building of Israeli Arab identity as Palestinians. The new developments improved women's standing within their society but also upset the Israeli authorities, who looked askance at the growth of Palestinian identity. Until recently, they were pleased that Palestinian women remained at home and did not enter the public sphere, particularly politics. Ironically, the authorities' interests intersected with the interests of the conservative forces in the Arab community: both sought to preserve women's traditional, unequal status.

The intended or unintended support for traditional social forces proved counterproductive when the state wished to intervene or promote certain policies. For example, authorities found themselves sometimes stymied in trying to apply the Compulsory Education Law to Palestinian girls because the girls' fathers had a different agenda. Some sought to place their daughters into the labor market as soon as possible and marry them off young. Others wanted them home to run the household and look after the younger siblings so their mothers could work. Israel's attempts to introduce family planning, which might have eased women's family burden, also encountered sharp resistance in the name of tradition. The Palestinian community further made nationalist claims that the state wanted to reduce the birth rate among Palestinians as a means of national control and suppression. Again, women pay the price. Yet women themselves often look at the situation differently; the fact that they are considered the prime carriers of the traditional/national identity locates them within the Palestinian collectivity, even if this entails marginalization and dependence.[64]

Recent years have seen more Palestinian women trying to carve an independent road. After acquiring education and professions, they refuse to abide by family marriage arrangements, preferring to choose their spouses themselves. Such stands can be socially costly: Some women exile themselves to Jewish locales to pursue an independent way of life, cutting themselves off from their community but not finding acceptance from the Jewish surroundings. Life in the shadow of security fears means that it is more difficult for Palestinians to find a flat to rent or a place to work, not to mention the difficulty of developing social networks and intimate relations with Jews. Some remain single because they refuse to compromise, or else because there are few men willing to marry women who deviate from the norm. Others, eventually, give up their independence, marry, and return to their villages where they resume the traditional functions of mother and wife.

Concluding Comments

In Israel, life in the shadow of protracted conflict has developed a "security" framework that molds the basic structural and cultural patterns of Israeli society. Moreover, this framework sharpens the division of roles between the sexes. The analysis presented in this article shows that the same cultural mechanisms operate in both Jewish and Palestinians communities in Israel, and that the security frame casts a heavy pall over society's efforts to improve women's standing in Israel.

At the same time, security is also a broad umbrella under which both Jews and Palestinians gather separately, ostensibly with no gender differences. The demand for collective mobilization to counter the security threat not only makes women equals in the survival effort, it enables them to make a unique contribution as reproducers of the collective. With security at the top of social priorities, every other issue becomes of secondary importance. Women's attempts to expose the cynical manipulations of the security banner encounter resistance from men but also from other women, which attests to the deep acceptance of security as a transcendent concern.

LIFE IN THE SHADOW of the security threat has thrown up cultural walls between Jews and Arabs. The national solidarity demanded of women on both sides has blocked the emergence of understanding that women of both national groups have much common ground on which to cooperate in an effort to better their situation. In the past decade, as the feminist movement has become stronger, awareness has grown that there is a connection between the security justification and women's status. This approach has spawned numerous women's peace movements involving cooperation between Israeli-Jewish and Israeli-Palestinian women.[65]

With the beginning of the peace process a new common agenda in other social spheres has begun to emerge. Yet those activities have been vulnerable as the peace process has shown to be fragile. Finally, the security threat framework has become a fertile seed-bed for feminist ideas too. The central place of the family institution in Israeli consciousness has led to increasing politicization of motherhood and mothering. On the left side of the political map, it enabled a number of attempts to challenge the absolute force of the security rationale. Bereaved parents have banded together to protest IDF training accidents and to demand harsher punishments for those responsible. Groups such as Mothers/Parents Against Silence and Parents Against Attrition have organized protest movements against the Lebanon War and against service in the Occupied Territories, respectively.[66] On the Right side of the political spectrum, religious women have taken their own independent initiatives to establish new settlements.[67] These developments might lead to the emergence of Israeli feminist versions that rely primarily on family and ideas of mothering.

Notes

1. For a more detailed discussion of this issue, see Dani Rabinowitz, "Oriental Nostalgia: The Transformation of the Palestinians into "Israeli Arabs"; *Theory and Criticism-An Israeli Forum*, No. 4 (1993) 141–151 (Hebrew), whose paper deals with Palestinians who are citizens of Israel (called in the past, Israeli-Arabs).
2. See, Carole Pateman, *The Sexual Contract* (Stanford, Calif., 1988); Linda J. Nicholson, "Feminist Theory: The Private and the Public," in L. McDowell and R. Pringle, eds., *Defining Women* (Cambridge, UK, 1992); Nancy Fraser, "What's Critical about Critical Theory?" in Johanna Meehan (ed), *Feminists Read Habermas-Gendering the Subject of Discourse* (New York and London, 1995), 21–55.
3. Janet Siltanen and Michelle Stanworth, "The Politics of Private Woman and Public Man," *Theory and Society*, 13 (1984) 91–118; Margaret Stacey and Marion Price, *Women, Power and Politics* (London and New York, 1981).
4. George L. Mosse, *Nationalism and Sexuality: Middle Class Morality and Sexual Norms in Modern Europe* (Madison, WI, 1985).
5. Nira Yuval-Davis, "Woman/Nation/State: The Demographic Race and National Reproduction in Israel," *Radical America*, 21 (1987) 37–59.
6. Dafna N. Izraeli, "Women In the Labor Market," in D.N. Izraeli, A. Friedman and R Schrift (eds), *The Double Bind, Women in Israel* (Tel-Aviv, 1987), 113–71 (Hebrew).
7. Hanna Herzog, *Realistic Women: Women in Local Politics* (Jerusalem, 1994) (Hebrew).
8. See Note 3 above.
9. See various detailed analyses in Avner Yaniv (ed), *National Security and Democracy in Israel* (Boulder and London, 1993).

10. Asher Arian, *Security Threatened: Surveying Israeli Opinion on Peace and War* (Cambridge and Tel-Aviv, 1995); Daniel Bar Tal and Dan Jacobson, "Structure of Security Beliefs among Israeli Students;" *Political Psychology*, 16 (1995), 567–90.

11. Hanna Herzog and Ronen Shamir, "Negotiated Society? Media Discourse on Israeli Jewish/Arab Relations," *Israel Social Science Research*, 9(1&2) (1994) 55–88.

12. For Gamson's methodology see William A. Garrison and Kathryn E. Lasch, "The Political Culture of Social Welfare Policy," in S. E. Spiro and E. Yuchtman Yaar (eds), *Evaluating The Welfare State: Social and Political Perspectives* (New York, 1983) 397–415; William Gamson, *Talking Politics* (Cambridge, 1992).

13. Herzog and Shamir, "Negotiated Society?" 82.

14. Arian, *Security Threatened*, 24–53.

15. Ibid., 54–90.

16. *Politika*, 21 (1988) 2 (Hebrew).

17. For similar claim see Hanna Herzog, "Was it on the Agenda? The Hidden Agenda of the 1988 Campaign; in Asher Arian and M. Shamir (eds), *The Elections in Israel-1988* (Boulder, CO, San Francisco and Oxford, 1990) 37–62. And compare to Smooha's findings, Sammy Smooha, *Arabs and Jews in Israel: Conflicting and Shared Attitudes in a Divided Society* (Boulder, CO, 1989).

18. See Arian, *Security Threatened*, 114–19.

19. Baruch Kimmerling, "Militarism in Israeli Society," *Theory and Criticism: An Israeli Forum*, No. 4 (1993), 123–40 (Hebrew); Uri Ben-Eliezer, "A Nation-in-Arms: State, Nation, and Militarism in Israel's First Years," *Comparative Studies in Society and History*, 32 (2) (1995), 264–285; Yaron Ezrahi, *Rubber Bullets-Power and Conscience in Modern Israel* (New York, 1997).

20. Cynthia Enloe, *Does Khaki Become You? The Militarization of Women's Lives* (London, 1988), II.

21. Ibid., II–12.

22. Ultra-Orthodox religious groups do not do military service, and for years they were considered marginal groups.

23. Nitza Berkovitch, "Motherhood as National Mission: The Construction of Womanhood in the Legal Discourse in Israel." Paper presented at a conference on Israeliness and Womanhood: Feminist Scholarship and National Discourse (Jerusalem, The Van Leer Jerusalem Institute, 1993).

24. Nira Yuval-Davis, "Front and Rear: The Sexual Division Of Labor in the Israeli Army," *Feminist Studies*, 11 (1985), 649–75; Simona Sharoni, *Gender and the Israeli-Palestinian Conflict-The Politics of Women's Resistance* (Syracuse, NY, 1995); Dafna N. Izraeli, "Gendering Military Service in Israeli Defense Forces,' *Israel Social Science Research*, 12(1) (1997), 129–66.

25. Naomi Chazan, "Gender Equality? Not in a War Zone!" *Israeli Democracy*, 3 (1989), 4–7.

26. Eyal Ben-Ari, "Masks and Soldiering: The Israeli Army and the Palestinian Uprising," *Cultural Anthropology*, 4 (1989), 372–389.

27. Ronit Lentin, "Women, War, and Peace in a Culture Of Violence: The Middle East and Northern Ireland; in Rada Boric and Kasic Biljana (eds), *Women and the Politics of Peace* (Zagreb, Serbia, forthcoming).

28. Daniel Maman, *The Second Career of Top Military Officers and the Civilian Elites in Israel 1971–1984*, published by The Levi Eshkol Institute for Economic and Political Research and the Center for Study and Documentation Of Israeli Society (Jerusalem, 1988) (Hebrew).

29. Compare for example, Ben-Eliezer, "A Nation-in-Arms"; Dan Horowitz, "The Israel Defense Forces: A Civilianized Military in a Partially Militarized Society," in R. Kolkowitz and A. Korbonski (eds), *Soldiers, Peasants and Bureaucrats* (London, 1982).

30. Golda Meir, however, did hold the portfolio of Minister of Defense; nonetheless, she is the exception and not the rule.

31. Hanna Herzog,"Why so Few? The Political Culture of Gender in Israel," *International Review of Women and Leadership* no. 2(1) (1996), 1–18.

32. Herzog, *Realistic Women*, 80–82.

33. Mordechai Kremnitzer, "National Security and the Rule of Law: A Critique Of the Landau Commission's Report," Yaniv (ed), *National Security and Democracy in Israel*, 153–72; Pnina Lahav, "The Press and National Security," in ibid., 173–95.

34. Ian Lustick, *Arabs in the Jewish State* (Austin, TX. 1980); Yoav Peled, "Ethnic Democracy and the Legal Construction of Citizenship: Arab Citizens of the Jewish State," *American Political Science Review*, 86(2) (1992),432–43; Elia Zureik, "Prospects of the Palestinians in Israel: I," *Journal of Palestine Studies* , 22(2) (1993), 90–109; Elia Zureik, "Prospects of the Palestinians in Israel: II," *Journal of Palestine Studies*, 22(4) (1993) 73–93.

35. Herzog, "Why so Few?" 7–10.

36. Kimmerling, "Militarism in Israeli Society."

37. Some jobs are classified, since they are connected to military affairs. However, in many cases, the requirement for military service is a way to exclude Palestinians.

38. Marcia Freedman, *Exile in the Promised Land* (Ithaca, NY, 1990) 50.

39. Yael Yishai, *Between the Flag and the Banner: Women in Israeli Politics* (Albany, N.Y., 1997), 6.

40. See for example, Robert N. Bellah, Richard Madsen, Ann Swidler and Steven M. Tipton (eds), *Habits of the Heart: Individualism and Commitment in American Life* (Berkeley, CA., 1985).

41. Yochanan Peres and Ruth Katz, "The Family in Israel: Change and Continuity; in Lea Shamgar-Handelman and Rivka Bar Yosef (eds), *Families in Israel* (Jerusalem, 1990) (Hebrew); Baruch Kimmerling, "Yes, Back to the Family," *Politika* (1993) 40–45 (Hebrew); Majid Al-Haj, *Social Change and Family Processes* (London, 1987).

42. Nancy F. Cott, *The Bonds of Womanhood: 'Women's Sphere' in New England, 1780–1835* (New Haven, CT., 1977); Cynthia Fuchs Epstein, *Deceptive Distinctions: Sex, Gender, and the Social Order* (New Haven, CT., London, New York, 1988).

43. Nira Yuval-Davis, "Gender and Nation," *Ethnic and Racial Studies*, 16 (1993), 621–32; Haleh Afshar (ed), *Women, State and Ideology: Studies from Africa and Asia* (London, 1987).

44. Families in Israel vary in their traditional hierarchical structure. See for analysis, Shamgar-Handelman and Bar Yosef (eds), *Families in Israel*. Nevertheless, my analysis, which describes mainly the majority, secular families, fits the traditional and religious families even more.

45. Nira Yuval-Davis, "The Bearers of the Collective: Women and Religious Legislation in Israel," *Feminist Review*, (1980) 15–27.

46. Though the prize was given to all the families, including Palestinians, its intention was to prevent the decrease in family growth among the Jewish population.

47. Tamar Katriel, *Communal Webs: Communication and Culture in Contemporary Israel* (New York, 1991); Dafna N. Izraeli, "Culture, Policy and Women in Dual-Earner Families in Israel," in S. Lewis, D.N. Izraeli, and H. Hootsmans (eds), *Dual-Earner Families-International Perspectives* (London, 1992) 19–45.

48. Gita Soffer, Lea Kacen and Tamah Shochat, "The Family as 'Launching Pad': When the First Child Enters Army Service, *Society and Welfare-Quarterly for Social Work*, 13 (1993), 351-65 (Hebrew).

49. Reuven Gal and Ofra Maisles, *Parents and Youngsters*, published by The Israeli Institute for Military Studies (Zichron Ya'akov, Israel, 1989) (Hebrew); Michal Shavit-Fradkin, "The 'Involvement' and 'Intervention' of Parents in the Military—The IDF and the Israeli Family: Parents' Complaints Filed to the Military Ombudsman,

1972–1994." M.A Dissertation, Department of Sociology, Tel-Aviv University (Tel-Aviv, 1996) (Hebrew).

50. Katriel, *Communal Webs*, 71–91.

51. Eliezer Ben-Rafael and Sasha Weitman, "The Reconstitution of the Family in the Kibbutz, *European Journal of Sociology*, 25 (1984), 1–27

52. Hanna Herzog, "Enlisting Mom: Military-Family Relations as a Genderizing Social Mechanism—The Case of Israel" (in preparation).

53. Mariam M. Mar'i and Sami Kh. Mar'i, "The Role of Women as Change Agents in Arab Society in Israel," in Barbara Swirski and Marilyn P. Safir (eds), *Calling the Equality Bluff: Women in Israel* (New York, 1991), 213–21.

54. Moshe Shokeid, "Ethnic Identity and the Position of Women among Arabs in an Israeli Town," *Ethnic and Racial Studies*, 3(2) (1980), 188–206.

55. Ibtisam Ibrahim, "The Cucumber Pickers," *Nogah*, No. 26 (1993), 34–7 (Hebrew).

56. Manar Hassan, "Murder of Women for 'Family Honour' in Palestinian Society and the Factors Promoting its Continuation in the State of Israel," M.A Dissertation, (Department of) Gender and Ethnic Studies, University of Greenwich (Greenwich, UK, 1994).

57. Lustick, *Arabs in the Jewish State*.

58. Majid Al-Haj and Henry Rosenfeld, *Arab Local Government in Israel* (Boulder, CO., San Francisco, London, 1990).

59. Interview, 13 July 1991, quoted in Hassan, "Murder of Women for 'Family Honour' in Palestinian Society," 37.

60. The police, however, took vigorous measures to eradicate the phenomenon among Jews who practiced it.

61. Hassan, "Murder of Women for 'Family Honour' in Palestinian Society," 71.

62. Ibtisam Ibrahim, *The Status of the Arab Women in Israel*, published by The Association for the Advancement of Equal Opportunity (Jerusalem, 1994) (Hebrew).

63. Mar'i and Mar'i, "The Role of Women as Change Agents . . ."

64. Nabila Espanioly, "Palestinian Women in Israel: Identity in Light of Occupation, in T. Mayer (ed), *Women and the Israeli Occupation: The Politics of Change* (London and New York, 1994) 106–120.

65. Naomi Chazan, "Israeli Women and Peace Activism, in Swirski and Safir (eds), 152–61.

66. Nurit Gilath, "Women against War: 'Parents against Silence,'" in Swirski and Safir (eds), 142–146; Sara Helman and Tamar Rapoport, "Women in Black: Challenging Israel's Gender and Socio-Political Orders," *British Journal of Sociology* (forthcoming).

67. Tamar El-Or and Gideon Aran, "Giving Birth to Settlement Maternal Thinking and Political Action of Jewish Women on the West Bank," *Gender and Society*, 9(1) (1995), 60–78.

War and Peace

SIMONA SHARONI

Homefront as Battlefield

Gender, Military Occupation, and Violence against Women

There is a strong connection between violence against women and violence in the Occupied Territories. A soldier who serves in the West Bank and Gaza Strip and learns that it is permissible to use violence against other people is likely to bring that violence back with him upon his return to his community.

—OSTROWITZ IN INTERVIEW WITH SHARONI 1990

IN APRIL 1989 Gilad Shemen, a twenty-three-year-old Israeli-Jewish man doing his military service in Gaza, shot and killed a seventeen year-old Palestinian woman, Amal Muhammad Hassin, as she was reading a book on her front porch. The Regional Military Court convicted Shemen of carelessness in causing Hassin's death, but he was released after an appeal. Two years later, on June 30, 1991, Gilad Shemen shot and killed his former girlfriend, nineteen-year-old Einav Rogel.

In an interview right after her death, Einav Rogel's parents recalled that their daughter had supported Gilad Shemen unconditionally during his military trial, trying to convince everyone around her that he was not guilty. Yet during that entire period Einav did not tell anyone that Gilad also had been violently abusing her. She did not recognize the connections between Gilad's shooting of a Palestinian woman and the violence and fear that Gilad brought to her own relationship with him. Einav Rogel lived and died in a society that draws clear distinctions between us and them, and usually doesn't even record the names of Palestinians who are shot. At the same time, she did not realize that, like many other Israeli women and most Palestinians, both women and men, in the West Bank and Gaza Strip, she belonged to a high risk population since she lived in the line of fire of an Israeli man who had learned to use his gun to deal with crises and difficult situations.

This tragic story underscores the complex relationship between sexism, militarism, and violence against women. This relationship has been explored at length by feminist scholars and activists (Accad 1990; Morgan 1989; Jeffords 1989; Ruddick 1989; Cooke 1988; Enloe 1988; Cohn 1989; Reardon 1985). It is extremely important, however, also to situate the tragedy of Gilad Shemen within the specific sociopolitical context of the third decade of Israeli occupation of the West Bank and Gaza Strip.

This essay deals with the impact of the Israeli Occupation of the West Bank and Gaza Strip on women's lives, by highlighting the connections between, on the one hand, the social construction of gender identities and gender relations in Israel and, on the other, the use of violence in the occupied territories and on the Israeli home front. Although the focus is primarily on the origins and manifestations of men's violence against women, it does not treat violence as a set of practices with which men are born. Rather these practices are used as a means of coping and they are acquired by and reinforced in Israeli men through education and social interaction. This essay will critically examine the dominating role of the Israeli military in all spheres of Israeli society, and the social and political implications of militarization and violent conflict for women's lives both in Israel and in the West Bank and Gaza Strip. The central argument here is that violence against women is intimately related to other forms and practices of violence, especially in the context of the Israeli occupation of the West Bank and Gaza Strip.

Much of the recent literature on the ways women cope with the violence inflicted upon their lives by war and conquest tends to remain caught between two opposed, stereotypical images: the image of woman-as-victim and woman-as-heroine (Sharoni 1993; Abdo 1991). To move beyond the constraints of these dominant representations, this essay will focus on particular stories which demonstrate the range of women's daily experiences of violence and the diverse strategies women have employed in resisting violence. In addition to drawing attention to the multifaceted struggles of Palestinian women in the Israeli occupied West Bank and Gaza Strip, the chapter will explore recent attempts by Israeli Jewish feminists and peace activists to connect, on the one hand, their own resistance to the violence inflicted upon Palestinians in the West Bank and Gaza Strip by the Israeli military and, on the other hand, their own struggles to end male-inflicted violence in the lives of women in Israel.

Military Occupation: Implications for Women's Lives

The pitchforks in local women's hands are brown:
nails and nails,
rust and rust in their edges
and a long wooden handle
intended to pierce

the flesh of our faces,
to pluck.
Our women,
pluck their eyebrows.

(Sternfeld 1988, quoted in Ben Ari, 1989:375)[1]

This poem dramatizes the intersection between sexist, militaristic, and racist discourses. Three particular distinctions are at play here: between men and women; between *us*, the local-patriots, and *them*, the enemy; and between *our* women and *their* women. These configurations reflect particular power relations grounded in and reinforced by the reality of military occupation. The poem calls attention to the fact that Israeli soldiers have used the pretext of cultural and moral superiority to justify their use of excessive power over Palestinians, both women and men, in the West Bank and the Gaza Strip. While he treats both Palestinian and Israeli women as objects with no political agency, Sternfeld maintains a clear distinction between them by using Orientalist depictions of Palestinian women.[2] Moreover, Sternfeld uses his portrayal of Palestinian women as vicious enemies, ready to pierce and pluck the flesh of Israeli soldiers' faces, to resolve the tension between the Israeli army's self-portrayal as a humane army that has tried at all costs to prevent women and children from suffering (Gal 1986) and the reality of military occupation which has been sustained through an indiscriminate use of violence against Palestinians as a whole, including women and children.

The indiscriminate use of violence and oppressive practices against Palestinians in the West Bank and Gaza Strip, especially since the outbreak of the *Intifada* (Arab uprising) in 1987, has had particular implications for women's lives. Palestinian women have had to confront violence on two intimately related fronts: as members of the Palestinian community and as women. Their homes and bodies have become the battlefields for these confrontations.

Rita Giacaman and Penny Johnson's gendered examination of the first year of the Intifada (Giacaman and Johnson 1989) highlights these multidimensional confrontations in relation to the ongoing struggles of Palestinians against the Israeli occupation. Giacaman and Johnson's retelling of the story of Umm Ruquyya (mother of Ruquyya), the mother of a young Palestinian woman activist in the West Bank, captures the harsh reality of life for women under occupation: "We went to visit her on November 6, 1988, when we heard that the family house had been demolished by the Israeli army. Hers was one of more than one hundred houses destroyed in the northern Jordan Valley, leaving about one thousand persons homeless and devastated" (Giacaman and Johnson 1989:155). Ruquyya was the first among both men and women in her community to mobilize resistance in response to the demolitions of family homes by the Israeli military, thus serving as "one of many women forging a new chapter in the history of the Palestinian women's movement" (Giacaman and Johnson 1989).

The Israeli military has used multiple strategies to suppress the unprecedented political mobilization of Palestinian women. During the first two years of
the Intifada, the Israeli military used tear gas, which was found to cause miscar-
riages, to suppress demonstrations and to deter women from future participation
in public political events. In addition, by declaring the Palestinian Women's
Working Committees and any other form of social and political organizing by women
illegal, the Israeli military authorities created a pretext for massive arrests of
Palestinian women. Women were arrested and interrogated not only because of
their political activities but also in order to put pressure on their families and to
get incriminating evidence against family members (Strum 1992). Sexual harassment and sexual violence, in addition to other means of torture and humiliation,
have also been used as weapons against Palestinian women (Rosenwasser 1992;
Strum 1992).

To live under military occupation is to live in a permanent state of war, with
no place to hide and no ceasefires. Palestinians have lived with the oppressive and
violent reality of occupation since 1967. Only with the outbreak of the Intifada
in December 1987 have these circumstances begun to be exposed and subjected
to public scrutiny, as abuses such as sexual harassment and sexual violence against
Palestinian women have been added to the agenda of human rights and women's
peace groups in Israel. Since the beginning of the Intifada, the Women's Organizations for Women Political Prisoners (WOFPP) in Tel Aviv and Jerusalem have
received numerous complaints of sexual violence committed by Israeli military forces
against Palestinian women in the occupied territories. Such incidents occur not
only during interrogation but also in connection with street patrols and the suppression of demonstrations.

The case of thirty-six-year-old Fatma Abu Bacra from Gaza, who was arrested
in November 1986, is a representative example of the sexual abuse and humiliation which Palestinian women have suffered during interrogation by the Israeli
Security Services. One Israeli male interrogator touched her face and breast,
while another showed her a picture of a naked man and told her that the picture
was of him. He then took off his clothes and threatened to rape her. Abu Bacra
reported the torture to her male lawyers, but only submitted a detailed affidavit
about the sexual abuse later on when she had a woman lawyer. In this affidavit,
Fatma Abu Bacra describes further how she was removed by one of her interrogators
to a separate room, with no policewoman present (in violation of regulations), and
forced to sit in a corner with her head wedged between the interrogator's legs while
he touched her, verbally abused her, threatened her with rape, and eventually reached
sexual climax (WOFPP Report 1992).

This affidavit was accepted on November 22, 1988, by a military judge as the
basis for a pre-trial hearing on the validity of admissions which Abu Bacra had
made under sexual torture. In the spring of 1989, the pre-trial hearings began and

during the proceedings a plea bargain was reached: under pressure Abu Bacra agreed not to challenge the way in which her confession had been obtained. In return, she was promised that her sentence would not exceed five years. However, in June 1989, Fatma Abu Bacra was given a seven-year sentence. She appealed and the sentence was reduced to six years. The Israeli authorities later used this unfulfilled bargain to claim that Abu Bacra had retracted her statement about the torture and sexual abuse during her interrogation. Since the minutes of these proceedings remained classified, Abu Bacra's lawyer appealed to the High Court of justice demanding the right to publish them. Finally, in order to circumvent publication of the interrogation minutes, the authorities decided to release Fatma Abu Bacra a year earlier than her sentence had stipulated, in November 1991, on the condition that her appeal will be withdrawn (WOFPP Report 1992).

Although the Palestinian uprising has not broken the silence and denial of Israeli society in general, it has served as a turning point in the political awareness of many Jewish women in Israel. The Israeli Women's Organizations for Women Political Prisoners, for example, have been documenting particular cases, like Fatma Abu Bacra's, of torture and sexual violence experienced by Palestinian women. Like other Israeli women's peace groups, they gave begun to expose the connections between the excessive use of sexual violence as a weapon against Palestinian women, the sharp increase in violence against women in Israel, and the politics of the Israeli Palestinian conflict.

Especially since the outbreak of the Intifada, many women in Israel have begun to challenge the marginal, passive roles assigned to them in Israeli society and politics. For the first time in the history of the state, women have organized and taken clear positions against state and military policy. Israeli women have voiced strong dissent against the occupation and against the brutal violence used by Israeli soldiers against Palestinian civilians in the West Bank and Gaza Strip. New women's protest groups such as Women in Black, Reshet, the Israeli Women's Peace Net, Women's Organizations for Women Political Prisoners, Shani—Women against the Occupation, and The Women and Peace Coalition have emerged, providing opportunities for women to step out of their socially assigned, politically peripheral roles (Sharoni 1993a; Deutsch 1992; Chazan 1991).

Israeli women's political interventions have not found widespread acceptance among Israeli men. Women in Black groups throughout Israel have become targets for verbal and physical violence that is almost always laced with sexual innuendo. The epithets some men shout at women protesters—"whores of Arafat" or "Arab lovers"—reflect the culture of militarism and sexism within which Israeli men are socialized. But while many Israeli men find it difficult to understand what has motivated women to protest weekly for more than four years against the occupation, for Women in Black the interconnectedness between militarism and sexism remains a tangible, experienced part of their struggle to find a political voice for themselves and to express their opposition to the continuing occupation of the West Bank and Gaza Strip.

The image of the brutal occupier who commits daily violence against Palestinian women and children and brings the violence home to his family and friends does not fit the national image of the brave Israeli soldier who has no choice but to fight in order to protect Israeli women and children. But, slowly, the message is starting to become clear: the violent patterns of behavior that are used by the Israeli army against Palestinians in the West Bank and Gaza Strip are part of a culture of unchallenged sexism, violence, and oppression which women face daily on Israeli streets and in their homes.

Every Woman is an Occupied Territory

They bombarded us
they shoot one salvo after another
Directing toward us
strafing and guns.
Nurit,
I have encircled the Third Battalion,
Now I want
to encircle you.[3]

In this love poem, the heroic/erotic discourse fuses militaristic metaphors as expressions of love and lust, violence and sex. Women—like the enemy—are to be encircled and occupied by Israeli heroes.[4] This particular poem is but one representation of the perverse relationship between militarism and sexism that surfaces in most spheres of Israeli society. That relationship is clearly inscribed in the Hebrew language as well. The multiple meanings of the word *kibush* represent a striking case in point. It is the most commonly used Hebrew term for the Israeli occupation of the West Bank and Gaza Strip—and is also used in Hebrew to describe conquest either of a military target or of a woman's heart. This conflation of women and military targets is not merely linguistic, it also informs numerous practices in Israeli society in general and in the Israeli military in particular. During military training exercises, for example, the strategic targets are quite often named after significant women in the soldiers' lives: women, like military targets, must be protected so that they will not be conquered by the enemy; while men must fight, occupy, and protect. These examples suggest interplay between gender, language, and politics in Israel, which has been grounded in and reinforced by particular social and political conditions.

Israeli men soldiers constantly have to prove their readiness to sacrifice their lives on the battlefield; while Israeli women are left with no other choice but to sacrifice their lives, freedom, and independence on the home front. Israeli women's bodies, hearts, and identities have been conquered, occupied, and objectified in numerous ways. Language further reflects the state of Israeli gender relations and cultural politics. The common word for husband in Hebrew, for example, is *baal*, which also means both owner (noun) and "had intercourse with" (verb), indicating that women are perceived as their husbands' property. Israeli men's private ownership of their women has in fact been extended to the state.

The treatment of Israeli women as occupied territories also manifests itself in numerous practices of control over women's identities, roles, and bodies, which have been reinforced by the escalation of the Arab-Israeli/Israeli Palestinian conflict. Three practices are of particular relevance here: the steep rise in violence against women in Israel since the outbreak of the Intifada, and particularly in the aftermath of the Gulf War; the mobilization of women's reproductive work in the service of the state under the pretext of demographic war, a pretext that has been used to justify impediments on women's reproductive rights in general and restrictions on abortion in particular; and the mobilization of gender identities in service of the state.

VIOLENCE AGAINST WOMEN

The connections between sexism and militarism, and between violence against the enemy on the battlefield and against women on the home front are by now considered old feminist themes (Enloe 1988; Woolf 1977; Brownmiller 1975). Women peace activists in Israel have become particularly aware of these connections since the outbreak of the Intifada. Rachel Ostrowitz, editor of the Israeli feminist magazine *Noga*, calls attention to the similarities between the ways in which both Palestinians and women are treated by Israeli men: "The similarity in the treatment of oppressed human beings is clear to us. When we read every day about nameless dead Palestinians, we remember that women are often treated as persons without names. 'Women are all the same,' they tell us; 'all Palestinians are the same.' The voices merge" (Ostrowitz 1989:14).

The dehumanization of both Palestinians and women legitimizes the discrimination, the humiliation, and the oppression and violence inflicted daily upon them. Rachel Ostrowitz further delineates the connections between the use of violence against Palestinians in the West Bank and Gaza Strip and the steep increase in violence against Israeli women on the home front: "Oppression is oppression is oppression . . . There is a strong connection between violence against women and violence in the occupied territories. A soldier who serves in the West Bank and Gaza Strip and learns that it is permissible to use violence against other people is likely to bring violence back with him upon his return to his community. This has direct implications for our lives as women" (Ostrowitz in interview with Sharoni 1990).

The structures which Ostrowitz sees as responsible for the oppression and humiliation suffered by Palestinians and by Jewish women are grounded in and reinforced by the unchallenged acceptance of national security as the top priority in Israel: "The twisted priority that land is more important than human life reminds us of other twisted priorities—military equipment instead of equal pay for women, or better education for the future generation" (Ostrowitz 1989: 14–15). Such twisted priorities have served as pretexts in the recruitment of women's bodies in the service of the state.

WOMEN'S BODIES AS NATIONAL BATTLEFIELDS

In virtually all societies, the military maintains a major role in the shaping of gender identities and gender relations, especially in war zones. Focusing on the army as a major agent of socialization for men, Cynthia Enloe points out how the juxtapositions of masculinity against femininity and of men against women serve as important ideological frameworks in the military:

> Military forces past and present have not been able to get, keep, and reproduce the sorts of soldiers they imagine they need without drawing on ideological beliefs concerning the different and stratified roles of women and men. Without assurances that women will play their proper roles, the military cannot provide men with the incentives to enlist, obey orders, give orders, fight, kill, re-enlist, and convince their sons to enlist. Ignore gender—and social construction of femininity and masculinity and the relations between them—and it becomes impossible adequately to explain how military forces have managed to capture and control so much of society's imagination and resources.
>
> (Enloe 1988: 212)

Enloe's powerful critique demonstrates how women, and strategies for controlling women, have been used to support military campaigns around the world. This has been definitely true in the case of Israel.

In direct relation to men's wars on the battlefield, Israeli Jewish women have been 'recruited' on more than one front. Since the early 1950s, Israel has used one myth in particular—that of a nation under siege—to justify political practices such as the demographic war. Prime Minister David Ben Gurion actually raised the issue of women's fertility to the level of national duty, when he argued: "Increasing the Jewish birthrate is a vital need for the existence of Israel, and a Jewish woman who does not bring at least four children into the world is defrauding the Jewish mission" (quoted in Hazleton 1977:63). In the 1980s, that old myth was once again invoked to fit the political agendas of the time. The Efrat Committee for the Encouragement of Higher Birth Rates linked the public debate on abortion to the demographic war, for which women's bodies had served as the designated turf. Utilizing the rhetoric of religious anti-abortion groups, the Efrat Committee called on

Jewish women to fulfill their national duty by bearing more children in order to replace the Jewish children killed by the Nazis (Yuval-Davis 1987).

An extreme example of how this ideology was put into practice is a narrowly defeated proposal by then-advisor to the Minister of Health, Haim Sadan. Sadan proposed to force every Jewish woman considering abortion to watch a slide show which would include, in addition to horrors such as dead fetuses in rubbish bins, pictures of dead Jewish children in the Nazi concentration camps (Yuval-Davis 1987). This shocking example is not unique. In fact, the Holocaust has been mobilized in this way by the state and its dominant institutions not only to justify hardline political positions and military campaigns, or racist and sexist policies such as demographic war, but also to clearly mark the borders between what it means to be a woman and what it means to be a man in the Jewish state.

BENDER IDENTITIES IN THE SERVICE OF THE STATE

In order to have a place in the Israeli collectivity and to share the patriotic ethos of national security, Israeli women have to enter the narrow doorways marked "mother" or "wife" through their affiliation with a male soldier. Former Knesset Member Geula Cohen, the founder of the extreme rightwing Tchiya party, utilized the rhetoric of national security and her platform as a political woman to remind Israeli women of this national obligation: "The Israeli woman is a wife and a mother in Israel, and therefore it is her nature to be a soldier, a wife of a soldier, a sister of a soldier, a grandmother of a soldier. This is her reserve duty. She is continually in military service" (cited in Hazleton 1977:63). It is in this light, according to former Israeli Knesset Member Marcia Freedman, that women's liberation in Israel is deemed a threat to national security (Freedman 1990:108).

In addition to the reserve duties articulated by Geula Cohen, Israeli women have to mediate the relationship between Israeli male soldiers and their motherland. The word for homeland in Hebrew is *moledet*, which is a feminine noun derived from the verb to give birth. Moreover, homeland is almost always presented in Israeli popular culture as motherland, and men are portrayed as sons who return home to the warmth, love, and support of their beloved mothers. But Israeli men are socialized to understand that in order to be worthy of homecoming, they must accept the need to sacrifice their lives for the homeland as a national duty and an honor. The national narrative of heroic sacrifice is constituted from early childhood onward through mythologized stories such as those of Masada and Tel-Hai, and becomes the major model for measuring loyalty to the state and its ideology (Zerubavel 1990, 1991). This erotic/patriotic complex informs politics not only on the battlefield but on the home front as well. For example, the funerals of Israeli soldiers are usually broadcast on radio and TV, and become politically charged as top government officials are shown comforting weeping mothers and commending them for raising sons who are ready to sacrifice their lives for their homeland.

In sum, the institutionalization of Israeli Jewish women's roles as the primary caretakers of a nation of soldiers would not have been possible without certain dominant interpretations of the Israeli-Palestinian and the Arab-Israeli conflict. Similarly, the recruitment of Israeli women's reproductive organs into the service of the state depends upon the prevailing myth of Israel as a nation under siege, the underpinning of political practices such as the demographic war. The linkages drawn between the Nazi Holocaust and Israel's anti-abortion campaigns further reinforce a particular order of gender relations in Israel, revolving around militarized men who fulfill the sacred task of protecting women and children on the home front.

Zionism, National Security, and the Construction of Militarized Masculinity

The centrality of the military among Israeli social and political institutions has often been taken for granted. However, this centrality is not natural. It has been constituted and reinforced through specific ideologies and practices. The establishment of the Israeli state and the elevation of its hegemonic Zionist ideology made national security a top priority, designed to secure the survival not only of the country but of the Jewish people at large. This view of the priority of Israel's national security is grounded in a particular historical narrative concerning the birth of Israel, a historical narrative whose core is formed by several unchallenged myths. The notion of Palestine as the "land without people for the people without land," and the claim that the Zionists welcomed the partition of Palestine while the Palestinians rejected it belong to one sort of myth. Another is that the Palestinians fled Palestine in 1948 despite Jewish leaders' efforts to get them to stay, or that after the 1948 war Israel extended its hand in peace to all neighboring countries, but not a single Arab leader responded (Segev 1986; Flapan 1987; Morris 1988).

Through such self-legitimating myths, the state's dominant historical narrative regarding the birth of Israel has hardened into an ideological shield that has been projected on to Israeli society as well as the Jewish Diaspora. The Israeli military has become the major agent for facilitating this process of ideological projection. Since the establishment of the state, the declared objectives of the Israeli doctrine of national security have always been to build a cohesive, unified front. Accordingly, as discussed earlier, Israel's dominant conceptualizations of national security have been constructed around unchallenged representations of Israel as a nation under siege, surrounded by enemies that threaten to throw the entire population into the sea; and this myth has been reinforced through constant invocations of the Holocaust and through political manipulations of facts concerning the 1948, 1967, and 1973 wars. In recent years, a new generation of Israeli historians such as Benjamin Beit-Hallahmi (1992), Simcha Flapan (1987), Benny

Morris (1988), Anita Shapira (1992), and Tom Segev (1986) have begun to challenge the conventional belief that in all the wars it has fought Israel's actions have been just and inevitable, guided by the principles of human dignity, justice, and equality. However, despite compelling evidence presented in this scholarship, most Jews in Israel and in the Diaspora still cling to the illusion that Israeli domination and repression have been inevitable; essential to the survival and security of the nation. Simcha Flapan reflects on the rigidity of these myths and their centrality in Israeli society and politics by sharing his own experience: "Like most Israelis, I had always been under the influence of certain myths that had become accepted as historical truth. And since myths are central to the creation of structures of thinking and propaganda, these myths had been of paramount importance in shaping Israeli policy" (Flapan 1987: 8). Yet, what remains missing even from revisionist accounts, like Flapan's, of Israeli history is a gendered understanding of dominant historical narratives and myths, exploring the particular conceptions of masculinity and femininity that these historical narratives present.

By making national security a top priority, by grounding it in specific interpretations of Zionist ideology and of the history of the Jewish people, and by turning military service into a national duty, the state has offered Israeli Jewish men, especially those of European or North American origin, privileged status in Israeli society. Furthermore, since one of the primary objectives of the Israeli doctrine of national security has always been to build a cohesive, unified front, national security has been used to justify Israeli militaristic and expansionist policies and political practices, and also to neutralize and thus to legitimize and reinforce existing inequalities among Israel's citizens along lines of gender, ethnicity, class, and political affiliation. Israel's disenfranchised populations have in effect been asked to understand that until the Arab-Israeli conflict is resolved they must stand united against the external enemy (Swirski 1989; Shohat 1988). Attempts by grassroots social movements representing Israel's second-, third-, and fourth-class citizens— women, Jews from Arab and North African countries, and Palestinians who hold Israeli citizenship—to protest against discriminatory state policies have been dismissed under the premise of national security. What remains particularly concealed in most existing critiques of Israeli national security is the fact that the rhetoric of national security depends on the preservation of the status quo not only with respect to Israeli-Palestinian/Arab-Israeli conflicts but also with respect to the social construction of gender identities and roles. Israeli feminists and activists are gradually coming to terms with the ways in which the construction of Israeli masculinity is linked to the militarized political climate in Israel and in the region. More specifically, many women peace activists in Israel have recently argued that the institutionalization of national security as a top priority in Israel contributes to gender inequities and legitimizes violence against Palestinians and against women.

The Israeli state's doctrine of 'national security' depends both upon men who are ready to serve as soldiers, as fighters on the battlefield, and upon women who are ready to adjust to the needs of the Israeli collective experience. On one hand, women are socialized into the roles of unconditional supporters, exceptional caretakers, and keepers of the home front; on the other hand, they are expected to remain vulnerable and in need of protection. While these contradictory messages no doubt result in major problems in the construction of Israeli women's identities, Israeli popular culture has attempted to resolve the contradiction by subordinating both roles to the primacy of national identity and by utilizing both images as pretexts for wars. It is important to note that the practical and symbolic mobilization of gender identities, roles, and bodies in the service of the Jewish state would not have been possible without engaging the mythologies of Israel "as a land with no people for the people with no land," as the only safe place for Jews in the aftermath of the Holocaust, and as "a nation under siege." These narratives, sanctioned by some of the major tenets of Zionist ideology, have been used to justify the masculine and militaristic practices associated with the establishment of the state of Israel; through them Israel's reassertion of masculinity has been explained in terms of the need to end a history of weakness and suffering.

The symbol of the *Sabra* can stand as an exemplary metaphor for this reassertion of masculinity. Named after the indigenous cactus fruit, *sabar*, which is tough and prickly on the outside and soft and sweet on the inside, the image of the Sabra has played an important role in the construction of the identity of the new generation of Jews born in Israel. This generation has been portrayed as the antithesis of the weak, persecuted, and helpless Jews most commonly associated with collective traumatic memories of the Holocaust. The image of the Sabra as the antithesis of the Diaspora Jew is used to reinforce the notion that Israel's offensive operations and military campaigns are a matter of national survival (Sharoni 1992a). In turn, the Sabra's offensive and aggressive codes of behavior are justified through the historical appropriation of the motto of "never again." Yet, exploitation of the Sabra image is grounded not only in the juxtaposition of the image of the Sabra against the image of the persecuted Jew in the Diaspora, but also in the juxtaposition of masculine and feminine identities. In the terms of this gendered juxtaposition, men must be offensive on the battlefield in order to protect vulnerable women on the home front. The underlying model of relations between strong, possessive men and weak, helpless women serves not only as a pretext for continued male domination on the home front and as justification for the use of violence on the battlefield but also, more generally, as justification of violent behavior by men. Thus the dominant juxtapositions of the invincible Sabra man with the weak and helpless Diaspora Jew, and of men as protectors and women as needing protection, have been strongly informed and reinforced, even justified by Zionist ideology and by the unchallenged centrality of national security in Israel.

The Sabra has become a common metaphor in Israeli literature and popular culture for Israeli men, who are thus characterized as strong and brave, pragmatic, aggressive, and emotionally tough. Few have noticed, however, that only the tough and prickly outside part of the cactus fruit has been incorporated into readings of this metaphor. There are no references in Israeli popular culture to the soft and sweet inside part of the fruit, which might be deemed feminine. The Sabra metaphor may therefore shed light on the ambiguities embedded in Israeli society's expectations of women. On one hand, when Israeli men are on the home front, women are relegated to conventionally gendered roles: they have to be inside, soft, tender and sweet. On the other hand, during wartime when men are on the battlefield, women are expected to step out of their traditional roles and to enter, if only temporarily, the public political arena. During such periods pragmatic, assertive, and tough behavior on the part of women is praised as a significant contribution to the collective national effort.

Conclusion

This essay explored the social construction of gender identities and gender relations in Israel in the context of the Israeli-Palestinian conflict and, especially, in relation to the third decade of Israeli Occupation of the West Bank and Gaza Strip. The chapter focused primarily on the relationship between sexism and militarism and its implications for Israeli and Palestinian women's lives, and on the connections between violence on the battlefield and violence on the home front.

The murders of Amal Muhammad Hassin and Einav Rogel by Gilad Shemen are but one symptom of the strong link between militarism and sexism; sexual abuse and violence used against Palestinian women political prisoners is another manifestation of this pathological relationship. However, Israeli society on the whole has so far refused to address the interconnectedness of militarism and sexism. In particular, it has ignored the relationship between the escalation of violent practices by Israeli soldiers against Palestinians in the occupied territories and the steep increase in men's violence against women in Israel.

Journalist Gabi Nizan was among the few Israelis who have tried to situate the murders of Einav Rogel and Amal Muhammad Hassin in the social and political context of military occupation. A few days after Einav Rogel's murder, he wrote in the Israeli mass circulation newspaper *Hadashot*: "In a country without wars, Einav Rogel and Amal Muhammad Hassin could have been good friends. In such a world Gilad Shemen could have been a good friend of both of them. But in our society, Shemen met both of them with a gun in his hand. This is very normal for an Israeli his age and it is normal that a gun shoots. This is what weapons are for." (*Hadashot*, 4 July 1991,16)

Gilad Shemen will probably be sent to a mental health institution and not to jail; other Israeli men like him will continue to use violence as a means of dealing with problems both on the battlefield and on the home front. At the same time, even the more liberal sectors of Israeli society hesitate to link publicly the use of violence against Palestinians in the West Bank and Gaza Strip with the increase in violence against Israeli women at home. When the Israeli media finally took note of the tremendous increase in incidents of violence against women, including murder, over the years of the occupation, the reports lacked any reference to the broader historical and political context within which such incidents of violence emerge and are tolerated. There has been hardly any mention of the impact of the Gulf War on the masculine self-image and national identity of Israeli men, or on the increasing vulnerability of Israeli women. The Gulf War was the first time that Israeli men were not drafted during wartime. Men remained on the home front, confronted with their families' fears, with their own fears, and with the vulnerability and helplessness of being locked in a sealed room. The image of the invincible Israeli soldier ready at all costs to protect women and children was endangered. Israeli men became increasingly uncomfortable with this unfamiliar role; many used the word "impotent" to describe their feelings. Unable to express themselves violently against Arabs, as they have been trained and conditioned to do, and confronted with the fact that the separation between violence on the battlefield and violence on the home front existed only in their minds, many Israeli men cured their feelings of impotence and longings for the excitement of the battlefield by projecting their aggression on to women (Sharoni 1991).

Separating one set of inequalities from another reduces possible threats to the often unchallenged regimes of power and privilege. But such connections do exist nonetheless. Many of the same Israeli men who carry out violent practices against Palestinian men and women in the occupied territories with an official license from the state treat the significant women in their life as their occupied territories. The murders of Amal Muhammad Hasin and Einav Rogel by the same man in military uniform is not a tragic coincidence, but a direct result of the Israeli-Palestinian conflict. In a context where every man is a soldier, every woman becomes an occupied territory.[5]

Feminist scholars and activists who are committed to social change need to challenge the silences and gaps in the conventional scholarship on the Israeli-Palestinian conflict and examine further the relationship between militarism, violence, and the social construction of gender in Israel and elsewhere.

Notes

1. This poem appeared first, in Hebrew, in "Intifada Diary." *Iton* 77 (1988):106–107, 93–95, and was later cited in Ben Ari, "Masks and Soldiering" (1989):375.

2. "Orientalism" refers to a view of the Near East as antithetical to and radically different from the West. For an in-depth examination of the social and political implications of Orientalism see E. Said, *Orientalism*. New York: Vintage Books, 1979. For an excellent discussion of these questions as they are represented in Israeli cultural politics see E. Shohat, *Israeli Cinema: East/West and the Politics of Representation*. Austin: University of Texas Press, 1989. For more information on the representation of Middle Eastern women see Z. Hajaibashi, "Feminism or Ventriloquism: Western Presentation of Middle East Women." *Middle East Report* 172 (1991): 43–45; and Judy Marbo, *Veiled Half Truths: Western Travellers' Perceptions of Middle Eastern Women*. New York: St Martin's Press, 1991.

3. This poem is included in the preface of Meir Shapira's 1973 war journal *Written in Battle: A Battle's Journal of the Yom Kippur War*. Tel Aviv: Alef Publishing House 1976. The poem appears after the author's short introduction along with two other war poems written by Chaim Nachman Bialik and Natan Alterman, icons of Israeli poetry. The term "Third Battalion" refers to an Egyptian military battalion that participated in the 1973 war. This war journal was published in Hebrew; the English translation is mine.

4. The reference in the poem to women as territories to be occupied and as military targets echoes the interconnectedness between sexism and militarism in Israel. For more on this topic see my article "Every Woman is an Occupied Territory: The Politics of Militarism and Sexism and the Israeli-Palestinian conflict." *Journal of Gender Studies* 1, 3 (1992): 447–462.

5. This reference to women as occupied territories is discussed in R. Metzger, *The Woman Who Slept with Men to Take the War Out of Them*. Culver City, Calif.: Peace Press, 1985.

References

Abdo, N. (1991) "Women of the Intifada: Gender, Class, and National Liberation." *Race & Class* 32 (4):19–34.

Accad, E. (1990) *Sexuality and War: Literary Masks of the Middle East*. New York: New York University Press.

Beit Hallahmi, B. (1992) *Original Sins: Reflections on the History of Zionism and Israel*, Concord, MA: Pluto Press.

Ben-Ari, E. (1989) "Masks and Soldiering: The Israeli Army and the Palestinian Uprising." *Cultural Anthropology* 44, 372–389.

Brownmiller, S. (1975) *Against Our Will: Men, Women and Rape*. New York: Simon and Schuster.

Chazan, N. (1991) "Israeli Women and Peace Activism." In B. Swirski and M. Safir, eds., *Calling the Equality Bluff. Women in Israel*. New York: Pergamon Press.

Cohn, C. (1987) "Sex and Death in the Rational World of Defense Intellectuals." In L. Forcey, ed., *Peace: Meanings, Politics, Strategies*. New York: Praeger; Cooke, M. (1988) *War's Other Voices: Women Writers on the Lebanese Civil War, 1975–1982*. Cambridge, U.K. and New York: Cambridge University Press.

Deutsch, Y. (1992) "Israeli Wwomen: From Protest to a Culture of Peace." In D. Hurwitz, ed., *Walking the Red Line: Israelis in Search of Justice for Palestine*. Philadelphia: New Society Publishers, 44–55.

Enloe, C. (1988) *Does Khaki Become You? The Militarization of Women's Lives*. London: Pluto Press.

Flapan, S. (1987) *The Birth of Israel: Myths and Realities*. New York: Pantheon Books.

Freedman, M. (1990) *Exile in the Promised Land: A Memoir*. New York: Firebrand Books.

Gal, R. (1986) *A Portrait of the Israeli Soldier*. New York: Greenwood Press.

Giacaman, R. and Johnson, P. (1989) "Palestinian Women: Building Barricades and Breaking Barriers." In Z. Lockman and J. Benin, eds., *Intifada: The Palestinian Uprising against Israeli Occupation*, Boston: South End Press and MERIP, 155–169.

Hazleton, L. (1977) *Israeli Women: The Reality Behind the Myths*. New York: Simon and Schuster.

Jeffords, S. (1989) *The Remasculinization of America: Gender and the Vietnam War*. Bloomington and Indianapolis: Indiana University Press.

Morgan, R. (1989) *Demon Lover: On the Sexuality of Terrorism*. New York: W. W. Norton Co.

Morris, B. (1988) *The Birth of the Palestinian Refugee Problem*. Cambridge, U.K. and New York: Cambridge University Press.

Ostrowitz, R. (1989) "Dangerous Women: The Israeli Women's Peace Movement." *New Outlook* 35 (6/7):14–15.

Reardon, B. (1985) *Sexism and the War System*, New York: Teachers College, Columbia University.

Rossenwasser, P. (1992) *Voices from a Promised Land: Palestinian and Israeli Peace Activists Speak their Hearts*. Williamantic, Conn.: Curbstone Press.

Ruddick, S. (1989) *Maternal Thinking: Toward a Politics of Peace*. New York: Ballantine Books.

Segev, T. (1986) *1949: The First Israelis*. New York: The Free Press.

———. (1992) *The Seventh Million: The Israelis and the Holocaust*. Jerusalem: Domino Press (in Hebrew).

Shapira, A. (1992) *Land and Power*. Tel Aviv: Am Oved (in Hebrew).

Sharoni, S. (1991) "Silenced by war." *New Directions for Women* 20 (3):1–4.

———. (1992) "Women's Alliances and Middle East Politics: Conflict Eesolution through Feminist Lenses." Paper presented at the Annual Meeting of the Association for Israel Studies (AIS), Milwaukee, Wisconsin.

———. (1992a) "Militarized Masculinity in Context: Cultural Politics and Social Constructions of Gender in Israel." Paper presented at the Annual Meeting of the Middle East Studies Association, Portland, Oregon.

———. (1993) "Middle East Politics through Feminist Lenses: Toward Theorizing International Relations from Women's Struggles." *Alternatives* 18 (1):5–28.

———. (1993a) "Conflict Resolution Through Feminist Lenses: Theorizing the Israeli Palestinian Conflict from the Perspective of Women Peace Activists in Israel." Unpublished Ph.D. dissertation, George Mason University.

———. (1994) *Gender and the Israeli-Palestinian Conflict: The Politics of Women's Resistance*. Syracuse, N.Y.: Syracuse University Press.

Shohat, E. (1988) "Sepharadim in Israel: Zionism from the Standpoint of its Jewish Victims." *Social Text* 19/20, 1–35.

Strum, P. (1992) *The Women Are Marching: The Second Sex and the Palestinian Revolution*. New York: Lawrence Hill Books.

Swirski, S. (1989) *Israel: The Oriental Majority*. London and New Jersey: Zed Books.

WOFPP (1992) Women's Organization for Political Prisoners Newsletter. Tel Aviv.

Woolf, V. (1977) *Three Guineas*. Middlesex: Pergamon Books [London: Houghton Press,1938].

Yuval-Davis, N. (1987) "The Jewish Collectivity." In *Khamsin, Women in the Middle East*. London and New Jersey: Zed Books.

Zerubavel, Y. (1990) "New Beginning, Old Past: The Collective Memory of Pioneering in Israeli Culture." In L. Silberstein, ed., *New Perspectives on Israeli History: The Early Years of the State*. New York: New York University Press.

———. (1991) "The Politics of Interpretation: Tel Hai in Israel's Collective Memory." *The Journal of the Association for Jewish Studies* 16 (1/2):133–160.

AYALA EMMETT

Citizens of the State
and Political Women

This is not a war
It is only a chapter in the history
Of the powerless
Against themselves
Who cannot see
The rainbow from above
Stretching with abundance of color
Across borders.
  —ESTHER YERUSHALEM, 1990

A Women's Public Event:
Making Peace Politics on a Friday Afternoon

Friday afternoon is a time in Israel when the public domain, stores, businesses, and offices, close down in preparation for the Sabbath, and roads teem with cars heading home, making their way through narrow streets and overcrowded highways. The Women in Black—Nashim Beshahor, as they are known in Hebrew—headed in the opposite direction, not toward home and domesticity but to the public square to gather between 1 and 2 P.M. for a protest against the state's occupation of Palestinian territories.

The Women in Black in Jerusalem chose Paris Square as a site to transform talks about peace and coexistence into political acts. Paris Square is one of several squares intended by architects to grace the city. Once a week this stagelike square, elevated above street level, looked like a theatrical performance. A group of women dressed in black, holding signs that say "Stop the Occupation" in Hebrew, Arabic, and English, stood silently around the square. In the strong yellow and orange hues of early afternoon in Jerusalem, the women's deliberate silence was answered by a raucous and aggressive counter-demonstration that displayed the national colors of white and blue. The Women in Black were surrounded by pedestrians dressed in bright colors and by cars whose drivers shouted insults, curses, and obscenities. Even just passing through this busy intersection, it was impossible to miss the vigil. Standing in the vigil, it was hard to ignore the hostility of the opposition.[1]

Every Friday the women displayed a fact on the ground—a vigil—a citizen's call to their government to end the occupation. The women's silent Friday vigil, which originated in Jerusalem in 1987, shortly after the onset of the Intifada, quickly spread to other parts of Israel. In 1990 there were about twenty-six places around the country where the Women in Black kept a Friday vigil (*Women in Black National Newsletter* 1, January 1992). During my fieldwork in 1990 I spent almost every Friday with the Women in Black. I was often in Jerusalem but have also been to various other vigils. The vigils spread from Eilat in the south to Rosh Pina in the north. They took place in major cities such as Jerusalem and Tel Aviv and in cities such as Haifa, Nazareth, and Acre with large numbers of Israeli-Palestinians. Though I will pay closest attention here to the vigil in Jerusalem, I also draw on material from a number of other vigils around the country.

On any given Friday the groups varied in size from under ten in some places to over one hundred in others. Women of all ages joined, from young girls in their early teens to women in their eighties. Often mothers and daughters stood together, and occasionally three generations of women joined the vigil. While a number of the women in each vigil in 1990 were Israeli-Jewish Ashkenazi (of European descent) and educated women, it was still a varied group. There were religious and secular women, young and old, urban and rural; the vigils differed from one location to another. Thus, in some places most of the women in the vigil were Israeli born and from kibbutzim, while in others, such as Jerusalem, there were also a number of women who were born in other countries but have been in Israel for most of their adult lives. In the Haifa vigil, for example, there was an active and vocal feminist core that included *Ashkenaziot* (of European or Western descent), *Mizrahiot* (of Middle Eastern descent), and Israeli-Palestinian women. On special occasions, such as Women's International Day, Palestinian women from the occupied territories have joined the Israeli women.

Each group of women was autonomous and decided locally on procedures. Whether women were prepared to advocate in a vigil all three principles of peace—end the occupation, talk to the PLO, and two states for two nations—would depend on how far from the national consensus, forged by the Likud government, the women wanted to move. In Jerusalem, the largest and most stable vigil in 1990, the women have agreed to display only a hand-shaped sign saying "Stop the Occupation." In other locations women carried signs like "Talks with the PLO" and "Two States for Two Nations." In May 1990 the Jerusalem Women in Black produced a document to outline their political position that stated: "We are women of different political convictions, but the call 'End the Occupation' unites us. We all demand that our government take immediate action to begin negotiations for a peace settlement. Many of us are of the opinion that the PLO is the partner for peace negotiations based on the principle of two states for two people— while others are of the opinion that it is not for us to decide who the Palestinian partner for negotiations is nor the exact solution on which peace will be based. We are unified in our belief that our message is powerful and just and will eventually bring peace."

Drastic Political Shifts but Continuing Divisions

It seems that the women's call for a peace process in 1990 has become the Labor government's policy. Since the change of government in 1992, Israel has experienced an extremely rapid official shift from the politics of the Right, which denies Palestinian nationhood, to the peace policies of the Left. The shift of official policy, however, did not eliminate, nor did it diminish, the division between those who support a peace process that includes Palestinians and those who oppose it. Because of these deep and continuing disagreements, a peace process that includes Palestinians—and ultimately the future of the Jewish settlements— is still controversial in Israel and is threatened by those who oppose it. In its far-reaching progress—the two agreements signed in Washington, D.C., and one in Israel in the presence of the President of the United States—the peace process has already drastically altered political conventions in the Middle East. Yet within Israel the Right's opposition to the peace process regarding Palestinians, Jewish settlements, and the Golan Heights persists. When violent acts take place between Jews and Palestinians—the killing of Palestinians in Hebron by Jewish settlers, the kidnapping and killing of an Israeli soldier by the Islamic *Hamas*, the bombing of a bus in Tel Aviv-all in 1994—opposition to the peace process is publicly rekindled.[2] Whenever the peace process encounters problems, particularly when killings take place, this divide takes on sharper turns. The Likud, which opposed a comprehensive peace policy when the Right controlled the government, still objects to it.[3]

The women's Friday vigils and the counterdemonstrations of those who oppose the Women in Black provide one expression of these acrimonious political divisions among Israelis.[4] Opposition to the vigils displays the scope of the divide and the emotions that surround it. The counterdemonstration also foreshadows the uphill struggle for Israelis—leaders and ordinary citizens—who continue to seek peace with Palestinians. The violence expressed by the opposition in 1990 indicates how difficult it has been to take a public peace position. Not too many people on the Left chose to do it collectively and consistently. Women in Black has been the most visible group within the peace camp. In 1990 it was also the steadiest public challenge to the Likud government's official policy regarding Palestinians. Women in Black was the single peace group that, every week, publicly transformed talks for peace and for an end to Israel's occupation of the West Bank and the Gaza Strip into a consistent political act. In the Jerusalem document the women stated: "We, Women in Black, citizens of Israel, have been holding a weekly protest since the beginning of the Intifada. This protest vigil is an expression of Israeli society and expresses our need to actively and strongly oppose the occupation."

This statement in which the women evoke their citizenship as the ground for political protest is more than a gesture to address the state collectively. In this deliberate insistence on citizenship the Women in Black lift the veil of democratic rhetoric that proclaims citizens' equality in the state and reveal an ongoing and heated Israeli debate on the nature of citizenship. In forging gendered peace vigils, the Women in Black address several issues. They question whether all citizens— Israeli Jews and Israeli Palestinians, women and men—are equal. The vigils also test the right of citizens to dissent from a national consensus in a society that places high value on the collective. Moreover, the women raise questions about citizens' relationship to the law, specifically, whether political citizens can break the law or whether they should stay within its bounds. In the Friday vigils the women offer their view in this critical debate on citizenship; those who oppose them present a very different one.

The Counterdemonstrations: Questioning Women's Citizenship

The counterdemonstrations were not organized independently but came into being in reaction to the Women in Black. They therefore entered a discourse on peace with Palestinians and on gender already framed by the vigils, and they responded to both themes. They called into question the women's loyalty as citizens and cast them as (female) traitors. Accordingly, they took on the mantle of patriotism and appropriated key national symbols, such as the Israeli flag, and made much use of the national colors of blue and white to deny the need for black. The counterdemonstration, which represented the Likud government's vision of a Greater Israel—a state that includes the West Bank and the Gaza Strip—and an "only-by-force" political approach to the Middle East conflict, expressed vehement opposition not only to the call to end the occupation but also to the women's very right to make a political statement as female citizens. The women in the vigil were well aware of this double objection; even a fourteen-year-old girl, such as Roni, recognizes what is at stake: "They don't want us to stand here. They are angry because we are women. They think that women should not interfere in politics."

In 1990 the counterdemonstrations were organized by people from the ultra-Right political fringe, including Kahane's Kach group and small, extreme Right political parties, such as Tchiya and Moledet. While most, though not all, of their participants were Ashkenazi males (predominantly boys), the counterdemonstrations, like the vigils, do not fall into a tidy category; differences exist across the country. In Jerusalem, for example, at the time of my fieldwork the counter-demonstrations included Kach supporters (many wearing Kach shirts or carrying identifying posters) and religious boys. In other places, such as Ra'anana in the center of Israel, the counterdemonstrations were composed of Ashkenazi and secular adults and youngsters, male and female, who identified themselves as Tchiya and Moledet supporters.

To deny the women's political act, physical and verbal threats were quite common. In most locations, attempts were made by the opposition to either force the women to leave or to obscure the vigil by standing in front of them. In Jerusalem this opposition took on a struggle over territory, when the counterdemonstrators forced the women to leave Paris Square for several weeks and stand on the street while the counterdemonstrators occupied the square. In occupying the square and forcing the women out, there was a covert threat that those who strayed from the national consensus could be exiled, sent away. National vulnerabilities such as the Nazi Holocaust were invoked against the women to mark the fact that they were betraying the Jewish collective: "The Women in Black are longing for Auschwitz" (Galili 1989), and more direct accusations of treachery were made; for example: "The Women in Black-A Knife in the Back of the Nation" on a poster that shows a knife dripping with blood. Women as killers are portrayed in a statement handed out by the counterdemonstrators, such as "We 'recognize' Black Widows. We recognize that they can kill, and we recognize that they are insects."

Going against an Official Consensus

Only two years before the signing of a peace agreement between Israel and the PLO, the vigils of the Women in Black were a dangerous business; women felt vulnerable and outsiders recognized that the women were exposed to violence. Even Israelis who were not necessarily sympathetic to the vigil acknowledged that for women to take an extremely unpopular political position and to call for an end to the occupation required courage and determination. Around the country the Women in Black stood perilously close to the traffic at extremely busy and highly congested intersections, protesting the Likud government's occupation of the West Bank and the Gaza Strip. In summer the blazing sun was beating down on them; in winter the cold chilled them. In every season they faced an aggressive ultra-Right counterdemonstration. Because the vigils publicly questioned a consensus on the issue of occupation, there was an ever-present violent response.

The women's political act in a public event was also clear to those who did not join the organized counterdemonstration but who opposed the vigils' peace position. Opposition to the vigils was thus displayed by drivers and pedestrians who were predominantly, but not exclusively, male. They hurled verbal abuse, curses, and sexual insults, and made physical threats, such as pushing, spitting, and throwing food. The response to the Women in Black in 1990 indicates not only the degree of opposition to peace and coexistence by the Likud government but also the extent to which citizens' dissent in a public event was perceived as a threat. The ultra-Right counterdemonstration expressed, and was joined by, a disapproval of the women by the more moderate right wing, which supported the government's settlement and occupation of the West Bank and the Gaza Strip.

The encounter between the vigil and the counterdemonstration brings forth tensions between the Likud government's insistence on a national consensus and peace groups, who in 1990 opposed the state Middle East policies. The degree to which the peace camp departed from the state's policies in 1990 was made visible every week in the women's vigils; their distance from official politics could be measured by the fact that the ultra-Right groups were empowered, at least covertly, by the Likud to speak for the government's policies of occupation. The counter-demonstrations, which were composed of members of these groups, were aligned ideologically with the Likud government's position of a Greater Israel. The alliance between the Likud and ultra-Right groups was expressed in the fact that members of these groups who were found guilty of crimes against Palestinians, includ-ing murder, received light sentences and favorable terms of imprisonment and were pardoned by Israel's president.[5] Since these facts were well-known in Israel, the ultra-Right's opposition to the Women in Black in the form of threats of verbal and physical violence was meant to warn women peace activists that their step-ping outside the national consensus could have detrimental consequences.

Gendered Contentions

Within each local vigil, women had to decide on how far they, as a collective, were willing to place themselves outside or opposite the national consensus. The vig-ils of Women in Black around the country displayed differences in the degree to which a local group was willing to be contentious, reflected in the signs—"End the Occupation," "Two States for Two Nations," "Talk to the PLO"—that groups chose to display. For the Women in Black, as for all women peace groups in Israel, activism is forged in social spaces between adherence to the consensus, to tradi-tional gender roles (convention), and forging new roles, shifting domestic/pub-lic boundaries, and distancing from state policies (contention). The vigils as public events become sites in which cultural conventions are employed by women to create political facts of contention. Women defied convention by choosing Fri-day afternoon (domestic time) to protest as citizens (in a public space); at the same time, they used conventional roles (of wives, mothers) as the ground for their defi-ance as political demonstrators.

It would be easy to assume that the Women in Black's gendered defiance was a statement on women's position in the state but not on their position in the peace camp. It would, however, be a hasty assumption. In challenging gendered roles, women faced not only the state, the Right, and the ultra-Right but the peace camp as well. A Left position on peace with Palestinians did not necessarily mean support for women's equality. The Women in Black challenged a position that peace politics is not gendered, or egalitarian, and formed their own independent peace group. As the women tell it, the conception of the vigil happened almost by accident, but it struck an immediate chord for the women who were there. Sarit, one of the founders of the Women in Black, noted the vigil's roots in the joint (male and female) peace organization End the Occupation, *Dai Lakibush*, and described an event that in her view was the launching point for a women's peace vigil.

> We had a man in Dai Lakibush who was a theater director and he and one of the women, who was a graphic artist, had decided that we should have a group of men in white and women in black and we would stand there to dramatize the situation. Well, the women showed up in black but the men never got together to come in white. It was very dramatic. Not a car went by without stopping and looking. So we decided to have it as a separate women's demonstration. At the beginning there were eight of us. We stood in a different place every Friday between 1 and 2. At that stage the men from the group were around giving out leaflets but not demonstrating. And then it became a separate entity; other women started joining and eventually it separated off from Dai Lakibush and became what it is now, a national and international women's peace group.

Within the peace camp, Women in Black insisted on their right to participate in political debates as an autonomous group and to engage with the state as a collective of women. To insist on women's groups goes beyond a demand that women participate equally in the peace camp. Women claimed their own collective voice—the vigils and other women's groups—as female citizens in speaking to other collectives—the state, the peace camp. Sarit offered her view of a conjunction of the politics of peace—demonstrators as citizens—and the politics of gender in the vigils—demonstrators as female citizens: "Some of the women who joined the Women in Black in the beginning, not from the Dai Lakibush days but once it got a little bit beyond that, were politically active in the feminist movement here and they very much wanted it to be a women's thing. And it seemed to us logical that it would be. Part of the vigil's attraction and part of the reason why it has kept up the impetus is that it is women. We decided on the name Women in Black. So that was it. It was done for dramatic purposes; we did know the symbolism of black."

The vigils weave conventional female roles of wife and mother into a fabric of political peace protest. By embracing, yet subverting, customary gender roles, the vigils define women citizens at the confluence of the politics of peace and the politics of gender. The social good is invoked as members of the vigil say that they are fulfilling their social duty to guard the well-being of husbands, brothers, and children. Gender is mobilized to forge a peace position as women self-consciously remove conventional boundaries between the domestic and the larger social good; the domestic, rather than being merely enfolded by the political, contains and encompasses political concerns. Rachel, one of the women in the Jerusalem vigil, said: "Some of the accusations and the nastiness that we get thrown against us are, 'How can we, as women, possibly spend time on Friday afternoon demonstrating when we should be home, we should be cooking, we should take care of the children?' Yet I am here taking care of my child."

Women citizens mobilize conventional gender expectations for political contention. Culturally encoded gender elements such as femaleness, motherhood, and domesticity were deployed by women in the vigils to shift the relationship between themselves—as politically passive or powerless citizens—and the state and between the political and the domestic. In the women's version, the political and the domestic were closely linked. Sarah, a religious Jewish woman who stood in the Jerusalem vigil, said: "We get ready for the Sabbath. We are under the same pressures as everyone else. But we say that it is not possible to forget at any moment, including our busy preparation for the Sabbath, what is going on around us. And it is important enough to us that we try to be heard and do something about it and make a difference." Women like Sarah reconstituted traditional Jewish roles as compelling elements in the politics of peace. Domestic roles entailed political obligations and compelled women to act politically—the kitchen spilled over to the public square, to the vigil; conventional domesticity, the women seemed to argue, now pointed toward public spaces.

While the Jerusalem Women in Black accommodated different political views on the details of the peace process, the women saw themselves as unified on ending the occupation. Gender provided the glue of the vigil, which was marked by the color of the black clothes, the structure of a vigil (a weekly protest), and the time of Friday afternoon. The only requirements for joining a vigil were gender and dress code: any female, young or old, dressed in black could become part of the group. When men joined, they did so as guests, on special occasions, and did not necessarily observe a dress code. Some wore black; others did not.

Collective and Transnational Grief

While Jewish mourning customs do not require women to wear black, the women in the vigil did refer to black as a symbol of grief. Those who saw their weekly vigil recognized it as a symbol of mourning. At the same time, black is a sign of mourning in much of the Middle East, where black clothes are gender specific and

highlight mourning customs that apply to women but not to men. Gender, therefore, is emphasized in the black of the dress. The Women in Black were aware of
women's groups around the world who use black in their respective protests, such
as Black Sash in South Africa and the Madres of Plaza de Mayo in Argentina, but
they claimed that their use of black was conceived locally.

The significance of black thus was self-consciously and readily articulated by
the vigils' participants. The official statement of the Women in Black in Jerusalem
(1990) says, "The black clothing symbolizes the tragedy of both nations, the
Israeli and Palestinian." Daphna, an Israeli-Jewish woman, offers her understanding of it: "The black symbolizes our sadness and mourning. We have lost many,
many Israelis in the war. But the other side has also lost, and so the black is a sign
of mourning. We want this to stop. That is why we wear black." A woman at a
vigil in the Gilat intersection emphasizes the tragedy of the conflict for women
and men: "I have a husband who is in the military reserve and two sons in the Israeli
army. How long will they have to go to wars and the women will have to wear black?"
(Bar Meir 1989).

The women's frequent use, in conversation and official statements, of the plu-
rals we, they, and women is important. Citizens in Israel are expected to be concerned with the social good. Emphasis on a women's collective signifies that the
grief articulated in the vigil concerns the larger collective. This concern is displayed
in their emphasis on their mourning for the nation and is anchored in a tradition
of mourning concerning collective grief.[6] The grief expressed in the women's black
clothes is collective and transnational, concerned with both Jewish and Palestinian
national suffering.

At the same time, the vigils reveal the ways in which the collective is also
concerned with the loss of individual life. The grief that marks the vigils is also
consonant with the high value that Jewish tradition places on each person's life.[7]
It is precisely because the women extend this Jewish value to Palestinians, because
they construct it to have universalistic, transnational applications to include
Palestinians, that their vigil is strongly contested by the counterdemonstrators.
The vigils' expression of grief enraged the ultra-Right opposition, which cast
itself as the guardian of the Jewish nation, precisely because the symbolic implications of the women's mourning are anchored in Jewish tradition but across national
and gender boundaries.

In the discourse on citizenship and who has a right to act as a political citizen, those who opposed the Women in Black attempted to challenge their right
to act as citizens and to diminish the collective nature of their actions. To undermine the vigil as apolitical entity (a collective) to deny that the women (female
citizens) can make demands on the state, the opposition deliberately addressed
individual (domestic) women and used the singular when talking to them. The
counterdemonstrators recognized the political significance of the women's clothes

as a transnational sign of mourning and made mocking references to the black clothes
to deny the grief articulated by the vigils in comments such as "Tell me who are
you mourning for?" and by using the singular pronoun in Hebrew in angry curses,
as, for example, "May your husband die so that you will really be a widow, *almana*."
Using the singular was meant to indicate that women were mere individuals; evoking their domestic roles meant to delegitimate them as political citizens and to cast
them as just women. Since public events in Israel are political spaces in which collectives transform ideologies (talk) into political facts on the ground, the use of
singular pronouns was meant to deny that the women were there as a collective.
The implication of the use of the singular was that individual women lacked the
necessary attributes to act as political citizens.

Collective Emotions: Grief and Rage

The vigils and the counterdemonstrations display tensions not only between two
political positions but also between two groups, each expressing collective emotions surrounding these political positions. The women's vigil expresses grief for
tragedies in both nations; its ultra-Right opposition expresses rage toward Palestinians and by extension toward the women, who are seen as representing them.
In the Friday vigils, grief and rage represent neither individual sadness or anger,
nor are they about the mourning of individual deaths; instead, they are the collective emotions that represent political relations between two groups.[8] These two
emotions ar e each expressed by a political collective, grief by the Women in Black
and rage by ultra-Right groups. Rage and grief at the Friday vigils are about politics and are located in a social interaction between women peace activists and
ultra-Right opposition. These collective emotions articulate two drastically different political positions about Palestinian nationhood. While the Women in Black's
grief recognizes and embraces a Palestinian nation and its entailed rights, the opposition's rage denies such an entity for either Israeli Palestinians or for Palestinians in the occupied territories.

In 1990 Israelis were fiercely divided on the question of the occupied territories; no peace demonstration that included men, however, elicited such violent
reactions as the all-women vigil of the Women in Black. Though some demonstrations expressed much sharper political messages, such as the call to refuse military service in the occupied territories, none elicited the kind of violent response
that the Women in Black have faced. The intense response to the vigil has to do
with the intersection of the politics of gender and the politics of peace and the
particular discourse that it creates about *gvulot*, a Hebrew word meaning, among
other things, borders, boundaries, and limits. In the Friday confrontations, collective emotions of rage and grief articulate the divisions over the borders of the
state of Israel—with or without the occupied territories—over the boundaries

between Israeli Palestinians and Israeli Jews, and over the relationship between women and the state. The rage and grief are about all of these.

The vigils displayed an Israeli debate on the state's borders, and the grief and rage were about the presence or absence of political boundaries and borders. In the Friday public event, collective emotions displayed a dramatic reconstruction of boundaries: grief-mourning (the Women in Black) stood on one side of the street, representing Israeli borders without the occupied territories, and rage-violence, the counterdemonstration representing the borders of a Greater Israel, stood on the other. They faced each other, spatially divided and in fierce political contestation.

Given the close links between gender and peace in women's groups, grief and rage, as collective emotions that accompany the vigils, may seem to be articulations of gender. Given the attribution of emotions to women and rationality to men that has dominated Western philosophical ideas from the Greeks to Freud, it would be easy to assume that the vigils reveal that men are associated with vengeance and rage and women with peace and grief. This is not the case, however. On the side of the counterdemonstration there are women, albeit few, and the right-wing parties include women; the Tchiya Party had a prominent, active, and vocal woman leader in 1990.

As for the vigil, men periodically join the Women in Black. There are men who would do so on a regular basis but for the women's insistence on keeping it a gendered vigil. While it is obvious that the women choose to emphasize mourning in a way that joint peace demonstrations do not, when men join the vigil they become part of the collective grief. The incorporation of men in grief can be seen in a notice issued by the Women and Peace Movement that called on women and men to wear black and join in a silent memorial service for Palestinians who were killed by Israeli police in October 1990 in Jerusalem.

Women, as the vigils make clear, are not associated with emotions any more than men are associated with rationality, and in this political confrontation both women and men articulate emotions.[9] Insults leveled at the women do not imply the absence of female rationality. Emotions in the Friday vigils are about politics: grief in this context is a political statement about two national rights of Jews and Palestinians, while rage is about exclusive nationalism.

Rage Politics and Mourning Customs

The confrontation between the women's vigils and the counterdemonstrations reflects a larger political dispute in Israel regarding both the law of the state and Jewish laws of mourning. It became prominent in the last decade as ultra-right-wing groups publicly defied state laws and Jewish mourning customs. These ultra-Right groups, for example, have invaded funerals of soldiers and civilians killed by Palestinians, calling for revenge and randomly attacking Palestinians who happened to be in the street on the day of the funeral. These groups, who see themselves as guardians of the nation, claim that Jewish national interests supersede state laws and override notions of democracy (Gal-Or 1990). Yet bringing rage into grief is considered by bereaved families to be a breach of customary Jewish rules of mourning and a violation of proper behavior at funerals. Rage is not part of Jewish mourning customs, and the Kaddish, the mourner's prayer, is recited in public to signify the bereaved's acceptance of death and the justification of God's will in the midst of grief. A number of Israelis, among them family members of the victims, express their dismay that the extreme Right's call for violence toward Palestinians has invaded the families' mourning and have politicized their grief. An Israeli-Jewish widow whose husband, a taxi driver, was killed in retaliation for the killing of Muslims at the Temple Mount area on October 8, 1990, noted the rules for proper mourning conduct and rejected the politicization of grief by those on the extreme Right who call for revenge: "While the murder of my husband was motivated by revenge I don't want revenge visited on Arabs. I have not changed my views after my husband was murdered. I am glad that his funeral was peaceful, without the participation of extremists, like Kahane's people and others. We did not want them. I have never thought of, and will not think of, taking revenge on all Arabs" (Al Hamishmar, October 14, 1990).

The opposition to the women's Friday vigil reveals this politicization of rage by ultra-Right groups. It also reveals that in the discourse on convention and contention, the opposition breaks conventions, such as the law, that the women uphold. In this context grief can be seen as a representation of convention, while rage represents the defiance of religious and legal conventions. A letter to the editor speaks to politically motivated intrusions at funerals, which disregard the law and mourning customs: "Whenever there is an attack, one immediately notices the political gamblers, the variety of 'blood consumers,' those who never allow the mourners to be with their sorrow in a quiet and dignified fashion" (Al Hamishmar, October 31, 1990).

While the women's grief certainly takes on some gendered traditional properties, like the black of mourning, in other respects it stretches the bounds of customary rules of mourning in several ways. The vigils have shifted the focus of mourning from that of the particular (the death of an individual) to the collective (many deaths) and from the specificity of nationality (Israeli or Palestinian) to a transnational, inclusive one (both). The intensity that in traditional mourning diminishes with time here remains unabated. Where it is usually time bound—for Israeli Jews it is marked by the funeral, seven days, one month, one year, and so on—it is here politically bound: the women intend to mourn for as long as the occupation lasts.

What Kinds of Citizens Are Women?

The vigils display different positions on the relationship between citizens and the law of the state. The Women in Black represent a political position that promotes protest within the bounds of the law; the counterdemonstrators challenge the law of the state in their threats, which at times border on the dangerous. The extreme Right position, which regards Palestinians as outside the protection of the law, is also evoked in the threats made against the Women in Black, threats that disregard their civil rights. In some locations drivers have tried to run over the women (Keshet 1989). In Jerusalem a soldier pointed a gun from a car window at the women, and a young man in army uniform went from one woman to the next cursing each one of them. The threat shouted in a number of vigils, "We will transfer you first," refers to the threat of Right extremists to transfer all Israeli Palestinians and Palestinians from the occupied territories to Arab countries. A middle-aged man in Jerusalem kept shouting, "We will visit Der Yassin on you," and made a throat cutting gesture. Der Yassin was a village in which Palestinians were massacred by Jews; by invoking the village, the threat could not be clearer. Placing the Women in Black outside the state and the community is also expressed in politicized threats such as "Go to Iraq" and "Saddam will take care of you," and in curses such as "I hope you die of cancer, slow, Palestinian cancer."

The Women in Black challenged the government's occupation of Palestinian territories, but, unlike the opposition, upheld the law. To underscore this position and in response to the violence of the counterdemonstration, the Women in Black's vigils have called for and receive police presence and protection. Calling for police presence is also the women's statement that they are citizens of the state. While the opposition casts the Women in Black outside the state by accusing group members of being disloyal—"You are all PLO"—the women chose to highlight their position as citizens who speak for the social good.

The women's vigils are one way in which citizens forge a collective to challenge the government's policy of occupation in a public event. Moreover, it uncovers how gender matters in this kind of a political challenge. As Women in Black insist on their right as citizens to make a claim that they are an expression of Israeli society, they uncover a contested understanding of citizenship. They provide their version to a question about the politics of gender in Israel: What kinds of citizens are women? Women's peace groups such as Women in Black position themselves against a more conventional version of Israeli women as nonpolitical citizens. This version can be seen, for example, in a newspaper cartoon featuring a couple: the woman wears an apron, holds a cooking spoon, and has tears in her eyes; the man holds a pistol and grins mischievously. The woman asks him: "Why are you grinning?" and the man replies: "Next week it is our turn" (*Hadashot*,

October 22, 1990). Like the vigils, the cartoon alludes to the themes of violence and counterviolence and brings to the fore a conjunction of Middle East conflict and the politics of gender. But, unlike the vigils, the cartoon constructs different social identities for women and men regarding this conflict: men are the warriors, the fighters, and the protectors; women are the domestic, the protected, worried, and distressed. This conventional version presents Israeli women as passive, domestic, and protected citizens.

The vigils and the opposition bring forth a discourse on women's roles. While the women insist on their right to challenge domestic and political convention, the opposition deligitimates this very right. It links peace politics to both female domesticity and sexuality; women's peace position is equated with domestic negligence and sexual transgression. Verbal assaults on the group's legitimacy included inserting conventional domesticity into the discourse to depoliticize the vigil in comments, such as "Go back to the kitchen," reminding the women of traditional definitions of the good mother. Personalized questions in the singular were often asked: "Why don't you go home? My mother is home right now, and she is cooking. How come you have time to stand here?" And some hecklers attempted to flatter individual women as objects of desire: "Not all of you are ugly. Some of you are really beautiful. So why are you standing here?" Female indecency and a peace position (contra the government) were joined in insults that sexualize not only the women but Palestinians as well: "Whores," "You like to fuck Arabs," "Arafat's whores," "Saddam's whores," and, since at that time the Right dominated the government, "This government will fuck you."

Struggles for Women's (Equal) Citizenship

The women's vigils contest this construction of women as domestic and protected beings. The Women in Black's insistence that they are political citizens concerned with the social good is grounded in political debates on gender equality in Israel. These contemporary debates on women's relationship to the social good have critical local antecedents; they are homegrown products, so to speak. The roots of these indigenous debates go back to the very early days of the Yishuv, the early settlement pre-state period of 1880–1947. Struggles for women's equal citizenship, such as that of the Women in Black, were sown on the native ground of the Yishuv. Despite the promise of equality made by Theodor Herzl and the Jewish liberation movement, women time and again fought to be equal citizens of the Zionist collective and struggled for political representation in Palestine (Friedman, Shrift, and Izraeli 1982). Women's accounts from the pre-state period reveal that they objected to what they saw as a systematic exclusion from organized politics within the pre-state structure (Azaryahu 1980; Trager 1984). Documents written by women pioneers about women's efforts to become full members of organized politics as it existed in the pre-state structure reveal a gap between the ideology of equality for women and its implementation in social reality. Women of the First Aliyah, the first wave of Jewish immigration to Palestine, demanded the right to vote in local elections in an effort to define themselves as equal citizens in the collective.[10] Women demanded to share political power because they had shared in social projects, working equally and side by side with men in building the community, and had shared the hardships of the early settlements. In using phrases such as "We the daughters of this settlement" and "We take part in building a new society," they created a female collective that could claim political equality and engage in a dialogue with the Yishuv official collective because of their work for the social good."[11]

The vigils of the Women in Black express similar concerns with the relationship between the state and its female citizens. The vigils reveal the scope of the marginalization of women peace activists. Women are on the political margins not only because they distance themselves from state politics; they are mostly absent from organized politics and from positions of power in Israeli society. The difference between mere talk—an ideological position—and a fact on the ground is reflected in the state's position regarding women's equality. In its Declaration of Independence the State of Israel espoused gender equality. In 1951 it reaffirmed its commitment in a Women's Equal Rights Law, which proscribed discrimination against women and introduced a number of laws to correct inequitable practices (Bowes 1989; Karp 1989). Women's peace groups came into being because, among other things, the reality of organized politics does not reflect equality for women. The birth of groups like Women in Black takes place alongside, and in response to, women's negligible representation in organized politics. While there are 120 seats in the Knesset, women have held no more than eleven of them in any one term.[12] The change in government and in Middle East politics is not matched by a similar gender change. The current Knesset, elected in June of 1992, has eleven women, the exact same number of women as in the first Knesset. While the present government includes two women ministers and two elected women who are members of the Foreign Affairs and Security Committee, Israeli women by and large are not part of the political decision-making process. Moreover, their domestic roles as wives and mothers are used to exclude women from public and political positions of power and authority (Sharfman 1988). The absence of women from Israel's organized politics is so pervasive that it is perceived by many Israelis as a natural phenomenon rather than as a cultural product of the politics of gender.[13] While the women's vigils take place in a political context that excludes women from organized politics, they also indicate an increasing politicization of women beyond and around organized politics. The vigils provide one way in which Israeli women establish themselves as citizens/protectors and political persons.

Notes

Yerushalem dedicated this poem to a meeting between women peace activists from Israel and Palestinian women from the occupied territories.

1. Every time I went to the vigil I had to make a choice between demonstrating and taking ethnographic notes, taping and photographing. When I joined the women I wore black; experience with violence (I was physically attacked by men from the opposition, and my camera and tape recorder were almost destroyed) taught me that when I acted publicly as an ethnographer I should not wear black.

2. Israeli political analysts describe the fragility of the peace process in terms of threats to derail it by groups on both sides. After the kidnapping of the Israeli soldier in October 1994, the journalist Nahum Barnea wrote in *Yediot Ahronot*: "The agreement is hostage in the hands of its opponents: Arafat is fettered by enemies of the agreement on his side, and Rabin is fettered by security needs of the settlers. If he redeploys the army he will abandon their security. If he resettles them he abandons Eretz Yisrael, the land of Israel" (Barnea 1994).

3. Because of this serious disagreement, the rivalry between the two parties has implications for the peace process. Recent surveys, in September 1994, show the prime minister running neck-and-neck with the Likud's leader. Surveys indicate strong support for the peace process, 65 percent said that was going well to very well and 34 percent thought that it was going badly (Hillel Halkin, *Forward*, September 23, 1994).

4. After the signing of the agreement with Jordan in the Arava in October 1994, Ariel Sharon explained in *Yediot Ahronot* (October 28, 1994) why he refused to participate in the ceremony and outlined his objections to the actions of the Labor government, which include relinquishing what he considers sacred Jewish land and the possibility of recognizing the right of Palestinian refugees to return to the West Bank and the Gaza Strip.

5. See Gal-Or 1991.

6. While most of the women in the vigil do not follow traditional Jewish practices, they are culturally familiar with them. A story in Jewish folklore highlights the import of women's mourning for the collective and the significance of black as a sign of mourning for women. It recounts that the prophet Jeremiah saw a woman in black sitting at the top of Mount Zion in Jerusalem. He went over to find out the reason for her grief and to comfort her. When he realized that her grief was not personal but that she was the Mother of Zion mourning for the nation, Jeremiah went down on his knees and blessed her (Zmora 1964). Grief for the collective is also the theme of the ninth day of the month of Av, in the Jewish calendar, which is a day of fasting and mourning for national tragedies. The Fast of Esther, *Ta'anit Ester*, on the thirteenth of the month of Av, while in support of Queen Esther, is related to her plea to the Persian King to save the Jews. The Women in Black, like the Mother of Zion and the mourners of the Ninth of Av and on the Fast of Esther, mourn for the collective.

7. That tradition is expressed in a famed Talmudic statement which equates the worth of an individual life with that of a whole world (Yudelson 1986, 23).

8. Emotion as an analytic category has drawn both interest and criticism in anthropology. Some consider the discussion of emotions as outside the bounds of the discipline (Rosaldo 1989), implying a division of labor between anthropology and psychology. Recently, however, anthropologists, such as Catherine Lutz and Lila Abu-Lughod, have called attention to the social features of emotions and particularly to "the role of emotional discourse in social interaction," to the "construal of emotion as about social life rather than internal states," and to the "close involvement of emotion talk with issues of sociality and power" (1990, 1).

9. Elsewhere I have discussed this tradition of associating women with emotions (Gabriel 1992). See also Coole 1998.

10. The claim to equal rights and the grounds on which women made the claim are expressed in Hannah Trager's account: "A young woman spoke up: 'Now is the time that we the daughters of this settlement, *moshava*, will insist on our right to participate equally in public affairs. We take part in building a new society in Eretz Yisrael, a society in which we should all be free. But is this society going to be built on equality between women and men? Did not our mothers suffer as did our fathers, did they not know the same hardship and dangers? And we, the daughters, did we not take on any job at home or in the fields? Did we not weed the vineyards under the blazing sun? Did we not gather the harvest? Did we not milk the cows? And did we not do anything that we could in times of sickness and in trouble? Therefore, let us all go together. Not men against women, but men with women.' 'You should know,' another woman turned to the men, 'that in the next public meeting we plan to bring up the question of our vote. We expect your support'" [1923] 1984, 133).

11. Women's struggle to become equal citizens is noted by Sarah Azaryahu, who worked to advance the status of women in the Yishuv days. She offers a historical comment on the genesis of a hiatus between noble promises to women and harsh social reality: "In 1897, at the dawn of the political Zionist movement, Theodor Herzl declared that there would be equality for the daughters of Israel . . . the fact is that the political liberation movement of the Jewish people was founded upon the principle of equality. The Zionist woman had good reason to assume that when her turn came to immigrate to Israel, thereby fulfilling a lifelong ambition, she would be able to work and to create in a society in which she had full and equal rights in all spheres of activity. Reality, however, was a slap in the face. Upon arrival in Palestine, women were faced with the necessity of beginning the struggle for political and civil rights and this at a time when they had been certain that this issue had already been resolved" ([1948] 1980, 1, 2).

12. The highest percentages of female participation in parliaments are found in Norway, 32.4 percent; Finland, 32.5 percent; and Sweden, 32.5 percent.

13. As Wolfsfeld notes, "Israeli children learn . . . that politics is a predominantly male concern" (1988, 42). His view is that "even those women who do want to participate find it difficult to take part in institutional action. . . . The political parties may recruit from a variety of social classes, but it seems that they prefer men" (1988, 67).

References

Azaryahu, Sarah. [1948] 1980. *The Union of Hebrew Women for Equal Rights in Eretz Yisrael*. Haifa: Woman's Aid Fund (Hebrew).

Bar Meir, Oded. 1989. "Exposed to Curses and the Blazing Sun." *Davar*, October 19 (Hebrew).

Barnea, Nahum. 1994. *Yediot Ahronot*, October 14 (Hebrew).

Bowes, A.M. 1989. *Kibbutz Goshen: An Israel Commune*. Prospect Heights, Ill.: Waveland Press.

Coole, Diana H. 1988. *Women in Political Theory: From Ancient Misogyny to Contemporary Feminism*. Hertfordshire, U.K.: Harverster Wheatsheaf.

Friedman, Ariela, Ruth Shrift, and Dafna Izraeli. 1982. *The Double Bind: Women in Israel*. Tel Aviv: Hakibbutz Hameuchad (Hebrew).

Gabriel, Ayala H. 1992. "Living with Medea and Thinking after Freud: Greek Drama, Gender and Concealments." *Cultural Anthropology* 7, 346–374.

Gal-Or, Naomi. 1990. *The Jewish Underground: Our Terrorism*.Tel Aviv: Hakibbutz Hameuchad (Hebrew).

Karp, Judith. 1989. "The Legal Status of Women in Israel Today." *Israeli Democracy* (summer):8–11.

Keshet, Silvi. 1989. "To Run Over." *Yediot Ahronot* , February 2 (Hebrew).

Lutz, Catherine A. and Lila Abu-Lughod. 1990. *Language and the Politics of Emotion*. Cambridge, U.K.: Cambridge University Press.

Rosaldo, Renato. 1989. *Culture and Truth: The Remaking of Social Analysis*. Boston: Beacon Press.

Sharfman, Dafna. 1988. *Women and Politics*. Haifa: Tamar Publications (Hebrew).

Trager, Hannah. [1923] 1984. "The Women's Right to Vote." *Stories of Women of the First Aliya,* edited by. Yaffa Berlowitz. Tel Aviv: Zahal, 132–135 (Hebrew).

Yudelson, Larry. 1986. "Raising a Religious Voice for Compromise on the West Bank." *Religious Zionism: Challenges and Choices*. Jerusalem: Oz Veshalom Publications, 5–15.

Wolfsfeld, Gadi. 1988. *The Politics of Provocation: Participation and Protest in Israel*. Albany: State University of New York Press.

Zmora, Israel, ed. 1964. *Women of the Bible*. Tel Aviv: Dvir (Hebrew).

Gender Performance in a Changing Military

Women Soldiers in 'Masculine' Roles

THE STATUS OF WOMEN IN THE ISRAELI MILITARY has been undergoing structural and conceptual changes in recent years. For most of its existence, the Israeli army has maintained a rigid gendered division of labor which reflected a dichotomous essentialist perception of gender (Enloe 1988; Yuval-Davis 1985; Izraeli 1997). However, there is a growing awareness in Israel that women are not perceived as equal citizens, due, in part, to their unequal military service. Therefore, some Israeli feminists, like their counterparts among U.S. liberal feminists (Feinman 2000; Peach 1996), have called for equal military service, including drafting women for combat roles. Since 1995 the military has complied with intervention of women parliament members and the Supreme Court and integrated women into a few select combat roles, such as pilots, border police, anti-aircraft and the naval commando. In September 1999, Chief of Staff Lieutenant General Shaul Mofaz unveiled a plan to widen the number of roles for women and to open to women high officer positions previously occupied only by men. In January 2000, the Knesset approved a law stipulating the acceptance of women soldiers to any military job, depending on military needs. This reform reached a new stage when the Women's Corps (Chen) was dismantled in June 2000 and its commander, Brigadier General Suzi Yogev, given the new title Chief of Staff Consultant on Women's Issues. The rationale for this move was that women soldiers should be under the direct authority of their respective units instead of a separate, special system for women only.

The reform in women's military roles received concrete expression when two women pioneers made the news in July 2001: Roni Zuckerman, the first woman to become a combat pilot—the other two women graduates of the pilot course are aircraft navigators—and Hani Abramov, the first border police woman soldier wounded in action. The media coverage of these occasions simultaneously reflected the structural changes the military is undergoing and portrayed these two women as "unique species" deserving special attention as representative of all women and not as signifying a general phenomenon.

A backlash, however, might come sooner than expected, not from the military but from religious Zionist rabbis who claim that religious male soldiers who serve alongside women will be prevented from observing the modesty laws.[1] The rabbis reject the suggestion that religious soldiers serve in separate men-only units, saying they "will not be ghettoized" in the military. Thus, their fear of what they term gender "friction" on the one hand, and their insistence on participating in the mainstream of Israel's military (and society) on the other, might preserve binary gender organization and perpetuate women's lower status in the military.

This ongoing debate, crucial as it may be for women's status in Israel, tends to view women soldiers as pawns in a bigger game. The religious leaders, and often the military as well, regard women in combat roles as hindering the military gender system and damaging the efficiency of the war machine (Mitchell 1989). Various feminist observers, on the other hand, argue whether military service is a venue for equal citizenship for women (Peach 1996:174–178; Stiehm 1989) or a reinforcement and reification of masculine concepts of martial citizenship (Feinman 2000; Enloe 1988). Hence, both liberal and radical feminists tend to view women soldiers as either serving or harming women's interests in general. The contemporary debate on women in the military therefore tends to remain on the macro level, ignoring the women soldiers' subjective experiences and their meaning for both the women's lives and the military and state "gender regimes" (Connell 1990). This essay seeks to add the subjective, phenomenological dimension to this contemporary debate. Through interviews with women soldiers serving in masculine roles, I explore the ways gender identities are constituted within a changing structure of gendered organization.[2] The analysis of how subjective meanings are created at different locations within structures of inequality (Lamont 2000:605) focuses on the interaction between state institutions and identity practices, and exposes the consequences of the structural changes for the women themselves, for the military system in particular, and the social gender order in general.

My primary thesis is that women soldiers in masculine roles adopt various discursive and bodily identity practices characteristic of male combat soldiers, which signify both resistance and compliance with the military gender order. From the women soldiers' perspective, these identity practices subvert the military gender regime in that women are refusing to accept military definitions of femininity and masculinity as essentially and naturally dichotomous identities (Butler 1990). At the same time, women's adoption of masculine identity practices can be interpreted not as subversion but as collaboration with the military androcentric norms, thereby strengthening rather than challenging the military gender order. Women's integration into combat roles thus neither challenges the male hegemony in the military nor threatens the ideology that links masculinity and combat and thereby contributes to the legitimization of Israeli militarism and its gender regime without altering women's lower civil status.

Military, Citizenship, and Gender

Military identity practices are of special significance because the army is not just another patriarchal institution (Enloe 1988:10). Rather, it is the one most closely identified with the state, its ideologies, and its policies. Functionalist and critical sociologists both agree that in the West, military service and war have become integral to the definition of citizenship and to the development of the nation-state (Janowitz 1976; Tilly 1996). Armed forces indicate the sovereignty of the state, and service in it delineates the boundaries of the political collective (Helman 1997).

This has changed in the last thirty years when, following the transition to voluntary professional armies in Western nation-states, the military lost some of its power to shape the meaning of citizenship. In Israel, however, the link between military service and citizenship still holds special meaning due to the prolonged Arab-Israeli conflict and the development of civilian militarism (Ben-Eliezer 1988; Kimmerling 1993). Military service is still perceived in Israel as the fundamental expression of the individual's commitment to the state, and civic virtue is constructed in terms of military virtue (Helman 1997). Rank and position in the military shape a hierarchy of belonging and allegiances to the state and determines one's access to concrete and symbolic social resources in civilian life.

Militarism is, of course, not gender blind. According to Cynthia Enloe (1988), the relationship between militarism and patriarchal masculinity is characterized by mutual interests because of the great significance of combat in the construction of masculine identities and in the justification of masculine superiority. In Israel, the military, as a central institution of both the state and of patriarchy, constructs the Jewish combat soldier as the prototype of hegemonic masculinity (Lomski-Feder and Ben-Ari 1999), which is identified with good citizenship and used as a major criterion in shaping differential modes of belonging to the state. Groups that do not or cannot meet this criterion, such as women or Israeli Palestinians, are not integrated as full and equal citizens.

Thus, the Israeli military vividly exemplifies the contradictory nature of women's citizenship. On the one hand, Israel is the only Western state with compulsory conscription for both men and women, which could signify an egalitarian and universal citizenship. However, despite recruitment and promotion policies purportedly based on universal and achievement-based criteria, the Israeli army is still a male-dominated territory where masculinity is the norm (Robbins and Ben-Eliezer 2000; Levy 1998). The conscription law grants priority to women's roles as wives and mothers (Israeli 1997; Berkowitz 1999) with women easily exempted on grounds of marriage, pregnancy, or religious beliefs. Women comprise only 32 percent of the regular army; they serve a shorter term than men and are usually excluded from combat roles.[3] These structural and organizational differences limit the range of roles available to women and constitute a definite barrier to their advancement in the military (Cohen 1997). Indeed, the majority of women soldiers serve in traditional feminine jobs, at least 30 percent of which are secretarial and administrative. Women's other military roles—as social workers, nurses, or teachers, for instance—reflect the feminine professions in the Israeli labor market and the perception of women as caretakers.

Thus, women's military service carries a double significance. While it enables Jewish Israeli women to enter the public sphere of citizenship and contribute to the country's security, which is perceived as Israel's most urgently existential problem, the military's rigid gender division of labor and chauvinist culture creates and preserves dichotomous, hierarchical, and essentialist perceptions of femininity and masculinity (Enloe 1988). As Izraeli put it: "The military intensifies gender distinctions and then uses them as justifications for both their construction in the first place and for sustaining gender inequality" (1997:129).

Identity Practices of Women Soldiers in Masculine Roles

Women who serve in masculine roles are in an ambivalent position within the military. They hold the most prestigious positions available to women soldiers, yet the military's structure, culture, and policies continue to emphasize their inferior place within it. Against this ambivalent background, women soldiers in masculine roles describe their service as a period of personal growth and empowerment. My argument is that their empowerment and autonomy derive, in part, from the construction of alternative gender identities, which are shaped according to the hegemonic masculinity of the combat soldier, through three related practices: 1) mimicry of combat soldiers' bodily and discursive practices; 2) distancing from traditional femininity; 3) trivialization of sexual harassment. As the following analysis will show, these three identity practices have a dual meaning within the military system, signifying both refusal to accept its essentialist definition of femininity and masculinity, and collaboration with its androcentric thinking.

MIMICRY OF COMBAT SOLDIERS' BODILY AND DISCURSIVE PRACTICES

If as Judith Butler (1990) says a "true gender is a fantasy instituted and inscribed on the surface of bodies," then the fantasy of women soldiers in masculine roles is clearly that of the combat soldier. "I used to look like a man," said Shiri, who was an officer commanding men in basic training. "In what sense?" I asked. "Well," she answered "first of all, you wear this big uniform, so it's very gawky; you don't wear a uniform that is tight on your body. And you walk with a rifle, and then your voice drops. I won't talk to him like this [in her own voice]; I'll talk to him like this [in a low voice]."

Through "a stylized repetition of acts" (Butler 1990:140) such as lowering their tone of voice, using foul language, wearing a big and dirty uniform, and carrying a weapon, these women soldiers mimic the identity practices of the combat soldier. In this behavior, which combines both feminine and masculine elements, the women soldiers assert their own identity and shape it to their liking, and thus reveal the fluid and performative nature of gender identities.

The shaping of the self according to the patterns of the (male) combat soldier entails serious investment in learning how to do gender. Often, women soldiers learn how to do masculinity directly from their male and female commanders, as Yardena, an infantry instructor said: "In the infantry instructors course, the commander teaches you how to do a masculine walk, a fast walk." On some bases women soldiers are ordered to "conceal their femininity" and are forbidden to wear perfume, makeup, or jewelry. These orders reflect the military perception that women cannot command as women. The women soldiers adopt these masculine practices in their totality, and add other, similar practices. At times, the mimicry of men is a reaction to mockery from male soldiers. Many of the women soldiers told stories of men who ridiculed their voice, walk, or uniform, insinuating that they did not adhere to the military's masculine norm.

The unstable and temporary nature of gender identities was evident when I met these soldiers, a year after their release from the army, and noticed that none of these masculine practices, so dominant during their military service, were apparent in their behavior or appearance. Yiska, a religious soldier who served as a commander for male soldiers from the Center for Advancing Special Populations (CASP), described the changes in gender practices through her use of language: "You go through these stages. When I just arrived at the army, I was shocked by the curse words. Then all of a sudden I got used to it, it didn't bother me. Then I noticed that I also used these words. When I was released, there was a reverse process. In the beginning I cursed, then I didn't but it didn't bother me, and then, all of a sudden, it's starting to bother me again" (Cohen-Tuati, 1999 cited in Sasson-Levy 2000).

Not only is the mimicry of the combat soldier temporary, it is also not unified, and is expressed in varied ways in different military units. For example, infantry instructors are known to use lower voices and take fewer showers "for ideological reason" than tank instructors. What is common to all these soldiers is their pride and joy in their personal weapon. Associated as it is exclusively with masculinity, they perceive the weapon as symbolic of their privileged military position, a meaningful achievement, a privilege that attests to their military value, and a source of self-confidence. Yonat, an infantry officer, explained: "It really made me feel good. And safer. Also, it's nice to see the jealous looks of others; it does something to your ego. But you also feel that you've earned it, because not every girl carries a weapon, not even every officer. You feel you worked hard for this."

And Dorit said: "The weapon symbolized first that I've come a long way and that I got it rightfully . . . that I've done a lot of things to earn it. The weapon was a symbol of my status, of my role, of me being equal." The weapon was represented as an object of desire in the media coverage of Hani Abramov, the injured border police officer, who told all her visitors in the hospital: "All I want is to get back to the unit. Just promise me that I will get a short M-16."[4] Abramov's yearning for the weapon, which is typical of women in combat roles, portrays it as a status symbol, as attesting to her proximity to the hegemonic masculinity, and ignores its function, which is to threaten, injure, and kill. Perceiving the weapon as if it had only a gendered meaning contributes to the normalization of means of violence and to the perpetuation of the militaristic culture (Robbins and Ben-Eliezer 2000).

Mimicry is not, however, always dangerous and can have a parodic potential (McClintock 1995). When women embrace male norms, they participate in what can be termed a "drag show," a show that ridicules the idea of gender as inner constant identity. Nadav, a male soldier who served in an elite unit described such a drag show: "We arrived at early dawn at the training base. We had no idea where we were or where we should go. Just then a course of women infantry trainers woke up. They went out of their tents with only towels wrapped around them, stood in a row about 25 meters away from us with their weapons between their legs, barrels pointing up, and yelled "we want to fuck."[5] We were embarrassed. We were shocked. We didn't understand where it came from. It was like seeing ourselves in the mirror, to see how embarrassing our behavior had been at other times. There was something so masculine about them, it was really shocking to see.

Nadav's story of the stunned and wounded male, testifies to the female soldiers' strength as they combine masculine and feminine practices. Military culture allows men to behave in aggressive and chauvinistic ways that are unacceptable in civilian society. In their exhibition with towels around their chests and guns protruding between their legs, the women soldiers mock Israeli military constructions of masculinity as ridiculous, almost pathetic. The women soldiers' "subversive citation and redeployment" (Butler 1990:124) of military/masculine behaviors can be interpreted as their way of resisting the military's masculinist ideology.

At the same time, the women's performance held a mirror before the men soldiers, confronting them with their own abusive behavior. This time, if only for a moment, it is the men who are the sexual objects, exposed to the women's violent and invasive gaze. "Gender sameness is a violation of masculinity," notes Susan Bordo (1994: 290); and the women's drag show certainly violated the men's sense of gender order as natural or authentic. The female soldiers' ability to play, to change and transform gender identity practices, is revealed as a means of resistance, personal power and pleasure within the repressive military organization, allowing them to challenge the dichotomous perceptions of the military.

DISTANCING FROM TRADITIONAL FEMININITY

Though the mimicry practices seem to empower women, the integration of masculine practices within their gender identities is not only subversive, it simultaneously complies with the army's androcentric norms. The identification with the military's gender regime leads women soldiers to distance themselves from identities and practices they perceive as traditionally feminine. Roni, a medic's instructor, explained why she didn't want to serve at a women's basic training base: "I didn't want to be with girls all the time, because I didn't like girls, I just didn't like them, I would call them females, they would get on my nerves[6] . . . I used to think that girls, and I was not necessarily wrong, are hypocrites and liars, and I just can't stand these characteristics in a person. All their showing off and putting on make up and everything, it got on my nerves."

Roni's words are symptomatic. Like Roni, Shiri thought women "don't function well under pressure, not just in the army, you can also see it driving on the highway." And Naama, who served in the air force, complained that women are pathetic and care only about make-up. Shachar, an army police investigator, said women are spoiled, weak, and vindictive.

In their words, these women soldiers articulate a misogynist viewpoint, characteristic of the hegemonic ideology of patriarchal societies. Using Gramsci's terms, the power of hegemonic ideology is preserved when social institutions and practices construct meanings and values that create "spontaneous" consent (Holub 1992:6) to the patriarchal status quo. The army, via its gendered division of labor and its chauvinist culture, produces spontaneous consent with hegemonic masculine ideology among men and women alike. Thus, like their male counterparts, women soldiers in masculine roles identify with the military, masculinist ideology and express anti-feminine attitudes. In order to differentiate themselves from what they perceive as traditional, weak, and submissive femininity (as defined by the military), they speak with condescension and disdain about most other women whom they regard as being inferior to men.

Like postcolonial subjects, they feel they must differentiate themselves from other women in order to construct a positive self-perception (Fanon 1963). Hence, they present themselves in opposition to what they perceive negatively as traditional femininity and construct their identities by way of negation. In a way similar to that of the combat soldier, the traditional woman is the other against whom they construct their identity. Thus, despite personally subverting the military's construction of masculinity and femininity, they ultimately identify with the military's ideology, laws and rules. By linking military power with masculinity, women soldiers reproduce and reaffirm masculinity as the only source of military authority.

TRIVIALIZATION OF SEXUAL HARASSMENT

The ongoing dilemma of constructing subversive feminine identities within a male organization is most salient in the women soldiers' reactions to sexual harassment. Many of the women soldiers I interviewed described incidents involving what could be termed sexual harassment but only a scant number labeled these events as such. More often, they were called "jokes," "just kidding," etc. Rutti, for example, told me that when the NCOs of her platoon were annoyed with her, they would sing: "Rutti is a whore, Rutti gives head to the whole company." Her reaction was mild: "Obviously it wasn't fun. It's annoying, but you can't take it too hard. It's a trivial song, nobody notices it, nobody pays attention to it." Tali, an intelligence officer told me about her commander: "One day, when I went into his office to get some documents, he opened his drawer and started showing me pictures of naked women that people had faxed him. I said to him: is this what you do in your spare time? It looked so dumb to me, I didn't even get angry."

Ignoring or interpreting it as "just something that happens" is women's most prevalent reaction to sexual harassment (Thomas and Kitzinger 1994). Yet research has shown that women with high status, high-skilled jobs and high self-esteem respond to it more assertively (Gruber and Bjorn 1986). Women, then, in masculine roles would be expected to react more assertively to sexual harassment, so we must look into the military context in order to understand why they disregard or ignore it.

Sexual harassment is primarily a way of reinforcing male power over women (Farley 1978) and thus may be one way for men to keep women "in their proper place" (MacKinnon 1979) and preserve male exclusivity in the top echelons of the military. The women's masculine roles allow them to be "mini-men," almost "one of the guys" (as they told me), whereas sexual harassment relates to them as sexual objects. An insulted and hurt reaction would confirm the discourse that the harassment itself is trying to create, which constitutes women as sexual objects. Thus, by ignoring the insulting character of the jokes, women do not allow the harassment to attain its intended exclusionary power. The women worry that if they label and act upon an event as sexual harassment they will be seen as constituting a gender problem within the army and therefore will not be treated as an integral and equal part of it.

Furthermore, complaining about sexual assault would associate the women soldiers with the identity of the victim. In their eyes the victim is defenseless and vulnerable, with no place in an army whose duty is to defend the weak. In that context, women soldiers stand at the center of the inherent contradiction between the discourse of the victim and that of equality in the military. The trivialization of sexual harassment, then, is a challenging response that expresses a refusal to submit to the military's definition of femininity.

Yet at the same time, one cannot ignore the fact these soldiers do experience sexual harassment, and that choosing not to call it such does not necessarily end it. Ignoring sexual harassment might be an effective strategy in the soldier's immediate environment, but it can also be interpreted as consent and might validate it as normative behavior and allow its continuance.

Conclusions: Gender Performance and Military Gender Regimes

In summing up the identity practices of women soldiers in masculine roles, I believe that in their immediate environment, the mimicry of combat soldiers seems to be a means of resistance and a strategy for overcoming the military gender barrier. However, often resistance is not merely undercut but utilized in the maintenance and reproduction of existing power relations (Bordo, 1993). While the mimicry of masculine patterns undoubtedly expresses subversion of the military norms of femininity, it also contains an element of obedience and acceptance of the military system's central values. Mimicry, as Scott (1990) argues, expresses an idealization of and ingratiation to the powerful group and "is bound to be futile . . . precisely because it reaffirms the superiority of the dominant group" (Scott 1990:39). Thus, mimicry practices should be understood as multivocal acts that empower women soldiers while strengthening the androcentric military norm. Hence, while their identity construction might be subversive locally, it does not alter the military's gender regime.

And indeed, when the focus is turned from the women themselves to their place in Israeli society, it is clear that adopting masculine combat norms does not ensure them the hegemonic status of the combat soldier. Their military careers are blocked at a very early stage and their advancement and promotion are limited. After their release from the army, they are not entitled to the same economic privileges as combat soldiers' or to their political voice and power and thus are not endowed with the same recognition and respect (Burk 1995) of the good citizen (Raday 2000:215).[7] The power acquired by women soldiers through their military service is revealed as temporary and localized, as it does not lead them to positions of power in either military or civilian life.

Thus, it seems that the close link between combat, masculinity, and citizenship in Israel makes the conversion from military to civilian resources almost irrelevant for women (Levy 1998). This rupture between women's military service and their status as citizens is the result of their limited inclusion in the military, in which they are enlisted but placed for the most part in peripheral positions. Through this partial participation, the military ensures women's loyalty and identification with the militaristic culture, while at the same time maintaining their marginalization within the army and the state.

True, the women soldiers in masculine roles do not perceive their location within the army as marginal. On the contrary, they see themselves as the ones that made it in the prestigious realm of militarized masculinity. The illusionary prestige the military confers on them engenders their allegiance to the military system, and as they internalize its masculine ideology and values, including those that debase women, they become loyal citizens of the existing gender regime. They strive to change their own place within the military, but accept its policies regarding women. Thus, while they are viewed as symbols of feminist achievement, they emphasize individual gender-blind equality and meritocracy and do not call for a general transformation of gender relations. Ironically, then, women's achievements in the Israeli army might work to legitimize the military's gender regime, which is based on the subjugation of women.

If military service, despite its universal compulsory nature, does not contribute to an egalitarian citizenship for women, it validates the claims of radical feminists that women's participation in the military institution merely reaffirms masculinity as a universal and normative model (Enloe 1988). However, as long as the army remains central in shaping the contours of society and citizenship in Israel, any attempt to repeal women's compulsory enlistment would further weaken them. Ending women's military service would lead to their exclusion from the central discourse in Israeli society and diminish even the modest benefits that women gain from military service. Thus, an unsolvable conundrum is posed. A solution will be found only with advances of a peace process which will create a fundamental change in the relationship between the army and Israeli society (Cohen 1992) and offer new, nonmilitary definitions of Israeli citizenship.

Notes

1. See for example "Because of the combatant girls, the IDF is risking a Psak Halacha against military service," *Ha'aretz*, 16 July 2001; "A woman officer with soldiers in army vehicle— improper situation," *Yediot Ahronot*, 9 August 2001.
2. The data for this essay are drawn from a larger study of identity constructions in the Israeli military, which was based on in-depth interviews with fifty-two male soldiers and forty-seven female soldiers within a year of their release from the army. Out of the forty-seven women, twelve were serving in masculine roles, that is, in positions that were formerly occupied only by men, but not in combat roles, as the research was done in 1995–1997, before there were actually women in combat roles. Note that their relative share in the study does not represent their percentage in the military, which is much lower. All of these women are from middle class background and graduated academic high schools with honors. Their military occupational distribution was as fol-

lows: three infantry instructors, three commanders in men's noncombat basic training, one headquarters officer, one tank instructor, one medics instructor (for male soldiers on reserve duty), one army police investigator, one intelligence NCO, and one
intelligence officer.

3. Women serve one year and nine months as opposed to men's three-year service. The
   new law of January 2000 requires women who volunteer for combat roles to serve three
   years like the men.
4. See for example, "I am willing to sacrifice my life for the state," *Ma ariv*, 1 August 2001.
   Carrying a short M-16 (as opposed to a regular one) is the privilege of commanders,
   and is considered to be military status symbol.
5. A common behavior among Israeli male infantry soldiers.
6. "Females" is a derogatory term in Hebrew, especially in military language.
7. Combat soldiers receive higher salaries during their service and are entitled to a "warrior certificate" which confers on them different benefits such as discounts at movies
   and theatres. When they are released from the army, they receive larger discharge grants
   and public campaigns such as "adopt a warrior" finance their higher education.

References

Berkowitz, Nitza. 1999. "Women and Citizenship in Israel." *Israeli Sociology* 2 (1):277–318
    (Hebrew).
Ben-Eliezer, Uri. 1998. *The Making of Israeli Militarism*. Bloomington: Indiana University
    Press.
Bordo, Susan. 1993. *Unbearable Weight*. Berkeley: University of California Press.
Bordo, Susan. 1994. "Reading the Male Body." In *The Male Body*, edited by L. Goldstein.
    Ann Arbor: University of Michigan Press, 265–307.
Butler, Judith. 1990. *Gender Trouble: Feminism and the Subversion of Identity*. New York: Rout-
    ledge.
Burk, James. 1995. "Citizenship Status and Military Service: The Quest for Inclusion by
    Minorities and Conscientious Objectors." *Armed Forces and Society*, 21 (4):503–529.
Cohen, Stuart. 1995. "The Israel Defense Forces: From a People's Army to a Professional
    Military—Causes and Implications." *Armed Forces and Society* 21(2):237-254.
Cohen, Stuart.1997."Towards a New Portrait of the (New) Israeli Soldier." *Israeli Affairs*
    3 (3/4):77–117.
Connell, Robert. W. 1990. "The State, Gender and Sexual Politics." *Theory and Society*
    19:507–544.
Enloe, Cynthia. 1988. *Does Khaki Become You?* London: Pandora.
Fanon, Frantz. 1963. *The Wretched of the Earth*. London: Penguin.
Farley, Lin.1978. *Sexual Shakedown: The Sexual Harassment of Women on the Job*. New York:
    Warner Books.
Feinman, Ilene Rose. 2000. *Citizenship Rites: Feminist Soldiers and Feminist Antimilitarists*.
    New York: New York University Press.
Gruber, James, and Lars Bjorn. 1986. "Women's Responses to Sexual Harassment: An Analy-
    sis of Sociocultural, Organizational and Personal Resource Models." *Social Science
    Quarterly* (129):814–826.
Helman, Sara. 1997. "Militarism and the Construction of Community." *Journal of Politi-
    cal and Military Sociology* 25 (winter):305–332.
Holub, Renate. 1992. *Antonio Gramsci: Beyond Marxism and Postmodernism*. London:
    Routledge.
Izraeli, Dafna. 1997. "Gendering Military Service in the Israeli Defense Forces." *Israel Social
    Science Research* 12 (1):129–166.
Janowitz, Morris. 1976. "Military Institutions and Citizenship in Western Societies."
    Armed Forces and Society 2 (2):185–204.

Kimmerling, Baruch. 1993. "Patterns of Militarism in Israel." *European Journal of Sociology* (34):196–223.

Lamont, Michel. 2000. "Meaning Making in Cultural Sociology: Broadening Our Agenda." *Contemporary Sociology* 29 (4):602–607.

Levy, Edna. 1998. "Heroes and Helpmates: Militarism, Gender and National Belonging in Israel." Dissertation submitted to the University of California, Irvine.

Lomsky-Feder, Edna and Eyal Ben-Ari. 1999. "From 'The People in Uniform' to 'Different Uniforms for the People': Professionalism, Diversity and the Israeli Defense Forces." In *Managing Diversity in the Armed Forces: Experiences from Nine Countries*, edited by Joseph Soeters and Jan van der Meulen. Tilburg, Netherlands: Tilburg University Press, 157–186.

MacKinnon, Catherine. 1979. *Sexual Harassment of Working Women: A Case of Sex Discrimination*. New Haven: Yale University Press.

Mitchell, Brian. 1989. *Weak Link: The Feminization of the American Military*. Washington, D.C.: Regency Gateway.

Peach, Lucinda Joy. 1996. "Gender Ideology in the Ethics of Women in Combat." In *It's Our Military Too!*, edited by J. H. Stiehm. Philadelphia: Temple University Press, 156–194.

Raday Francis. 2000. "The Military- Feminism and Citizenship." *Plilim* (9):185–216 (Hebrew).

Robbins Joyce and Uri Ben-Eliezer. 2000. "New Roles or New Times? Gender Inequality and Militarism in Israel's Nation-in-Arms." *Social Politics* (fall):309–343.

Scott, James. 1990. *Domination and the Art of Resistance: Hidden Transcripts*. New Haven: Yale University Press.

Stiehm, Judith H.1989. *Arms and the Enlisted Woman*. Philadelphia: Temple University Press.

Tilly, Charles. 1996. "The Emergence of Citizenship in France and Elsewhere." *International Review of Social History* 40 (3):223–236.

Thomas, Alison, and Celia Kitzinger. 1994. "It's Just Something that Happens: The Invisibility of Sexual Harassment in the Workplace." *Gender, Work and Organization* 1 (3):151–161.

Yuval-Davis, Nira. 1985. "Front and Rear: The Sexual Division of Labor in the Israeli Army." *Feminist Studies* 11(3):649–667.

Literature
and Culture

Amalia Kahana-Carmon and Contemporary Hebrew Women's Fiction

THE HEBREW LITERARY ESTABLISHMENT traditionally has most valued works that can in some way be seen as allegories of the nation's political predicaments and collective identity crises. As a result, fictions about women are deemed important only to the extent that they can be conceptualized as archetypal dramas of a Neumannesque "great mother," representing the land of Israel.[1] This association of great work with national metaphors and the consequent celebration of the fathers of modern Hebrew literature—the current critical consensus is that there have been no mothers—perpetuates the Israeli critical establishment's longstanding association of creativity with masculinity.

Thus writers like Amalia Kahana-Carmon, the most highly respected woman author in Israel, who writes about the lives of women, are under siege from all sides, excluded from the androcentric critical establishment of their own culture and excluded from the Anglo-centric focus of Western feminist critics. As one of a handful of prose writers who has ventured to write in a language reserved, until the turn of the century, for men, Kahana-Carmon's struggle to write in this hostile environment is both institutional and psychological. She must face not only a suspicious, male-dominated literary establishment and tradition but also her own doubts about the legitimacy of her literary activity. Even woman authors who expect, as Kahana-Carmon puts it, an automatic dismissal of their work as "wasted on the peripheral, on the ultimately unimportant, and on the trivial," even they are not exempt from the "value judgments that are [so] destructive to them."[2]

Such expectations, Amalia Kahana-Carmon suggests, can be a hindrance, for "they [women writers] recognize a priori without a doubt that even at their best, [theirs] will be an identity and a perception, and an order [of priorities], and a voice, that are less weighty and go less far, and answer a need that is less deep than those men writers may achieve when they are at their best." Even though Kahana-

Carmon so sensitively articulates the predicaments of the Hebrew woman writer, she is not exempt from the impact of phallic criticism. She likens the Hebrew woman writer to a mutilated fish: "And the fish is advancing [after they tied its torn tail back to its body] and is making all the turns and moves. But instead of the harmony in the motions, and the wonderful graciousness, there appears an uncertain, slipping, wretched movement."[3]

Against the hostility of the environment in which she writes, Kahana-Carmon's artistic sensibility is a miracle of stubbornness that deserves attention both for the quality of the stories it engenders and for what it says about women's ongoing efforts to create art and inner life in the face of patriarchal resistance. Best known as the author of the collection of stories *Under One Roof*, and of the novels *And Moon in the Valley of Ajalon*, *Magnetic Fields*, and *Up in Montifer*, Amalia Kahana-Carmon received the 1985 Brenner Prize for belles lettres.[4] She was awarded the prize, according to the panel of judges, for her "sensitivity to [literally, the sense of] the word, the rigor, the precision, the scrupulousness in the choice of the word, the word in its widest narrative meaning."[5]

Amalia Kahana-Carmon is, notably, the first woman Hebrew fiction writer to be honored with the Brenner prize, which bears the name of one of the most respected fathers of Hebrew literature. However, it is not surprising that the critical establishment failed to call attention to the precedent, for Amalia Kahana-Carmon is appreciated for her style and poetics, not for her thematic, in which she explores the lives of traditional women.[6] Critics have talked about everything from the archetypal conflict between the Saint and the Dragon in her work to the anatomy of human encounters and the mystical desire to transcend life through self-sacrifice.[7] However, they did not discuss Kahana-Carmon's interest in women and the ways in which her themes shape and are shaped by her unconventional narrative forms.[8]

In *Under One Roof*, Amalia Kahana-Carmon destabilizes in very unique ways the traditional privileging of heterosexual bonding as a locus of supreme meaning in Western romance.[9] She avoids what the poet Natan Zach calls "the romantic doublebind" that plagues so much of male-authored modern Hebrew literature with its visible susceptibility to acts of violence, betrayal, divorce, and such catastrophic endings as suicide, fatal diseases, and accidents, murder, death in battle, and death in childbirth.[10] Shunning both the conventions of the euphoric story, leading to the heroine's marriage, and the dysphoric story, leading to her death, Kahana-Carmon constructs alternative narratives that both reflect and disrupt conventional narrative forms.[11]

Moreover, Kahana-Carmon consistently avoids the simultaneous reciprocity which is at the heart of the traditional romantic mythos of the phenomenology of unrequited love by capturing how the participants in the romantic event emote at cross purposes, at the wrong times, at the wrong places, whenever their partner seems least interested, aware, or accessible. The romantic moment is atomized into ever-shifting flashes of attraction, paralysis, and flight in order to question the solidity or stability implied in the concept of "love" and in the notion of "relationship." Nevertheless, the author celebrates the romantic encounter as a revitalizing experience of "enchantment."[12] Despite their romantic defeats, despite their helplessness, her heroines emerge as princesses, as queens who know what they have lost and continue to hope anyway. Love, despite its instability, seems to bring out the noble, the royal sensibilities even in the most victimized partner. Thus Kahana-Carmon challenges the happily-ever-after euphoric paradigm but, nevertheless, displays her belief in the dignifying aspects of the ability to love.[13]

The heroine of the story "Neima Sasson Writes Poems" in *Under One Roof* is an adolescent student at an Orthodox school for girls. The "one of a kind" (meyuhad bemino) man in her life is her married teacher, Yehezkel da Silva. The specialness of the beloved man is an issue for many of the heroines in Kahana-Carmon's stories. Neima Sasson asks da Silva if she only imagines that he is special: "I have a recurrent chimera: Usually, I know that you are like everyman. But sometimes, and this is the chimera, it seems to me that you are different. Apart. One of a kind. Another question. Only one more. Teacher Yehezkel, tell me, are you at all a one of a kind person?" (*Roof*, 143). Neima is desperately trying to draw Yehezkel's attention: "I, in the new summer dress for which I had so many hopes. The teacher Yehezkel is already sitting without motion. . . . And I knew once again that everything is lost" (*Roof*, 136). But Neima is not deterred by her failures. Again and again she tries to make contact with her beloved teacher. She takes "everyday the wrong bus" so as to be able to sit or stand by him (*Roof*, 137–138). She walks by his house, watches his wife, and spends all her evenings at the back balcony of her parents' house waiting for him to show up, but "the teacher Yehezkel does not come. He never comes" (*Roof*, 140). Despairing of verbal communication, Neima turns to writing: "I do not know how to express in words. I therefore tried to convey in writing" (*Roof*, 144). But the poem, "My Dear Teacher," which is accepted for publication by the school paper, is coldly shrugged off by da Silva, as are the other poems Neima entrusts to him: "The poems. I opened to read. I read about two pages. And I fell asleep" (*Roof*, 146). "Neima Sasson" thus affirms that love "happens" in one's consciousness or perhaps in poetry rather than in "real" life events.

Yet it is never too certain that da Silva is completely indifferent to Neima's pleas for attention. Shortly after the teacher admonishes his pupil—"One Neima Sasson, one Yehezkel da Silva will fit themselves to the rules please—he turned around. He returned to me." The zigzagging dance that ensues epitomizes the fluctuating emotional movement alternately distancing and bringing together the participants in what the author constructs as both chimerical and real moments of love. "He went. I hurried. He went. Stopped. Went. I did not move. I hurried. He stopped. He went. I stood. He is going, turning around. He came back" (*Roof*, 149–150). The lack of directional markers increases the indeterminacy of the fragile and ever-shifting relationship. What emerges from this confusing dance is the possibility that the teacher has been holding back out of fear rather than lack of interest. The recognition that Neima's willingness to be rejected and hurt again and again—"humiliating myself for the millionth time" (*Roof*, 140)—is in fact a kind of courage that may point us in the direction of "the secret that turns the weak one into a hero" (*Roof*, 144, 149). For despite Neima's ultimate failure to create real contact with da Silva, Kahana-Carmon celebrates her self-conscious willingness to make herself vulnerable.

The same confusion and fragility characterize the encounter between Mrs. Amsterdam and the Yeshiva student in "If I Found Favor," also in *Under One Roof*. Here, however, the movements are larger. Like Neima, Mrs. Amsterdam hesitatingly initiates contact by offering to walk her nameless student home, making small talk, inviting him to a film, and haltingly confessing to him that she thinks him "a mysterious man," soon after which she is rudely rejected by him (*Roof*, 104–108). Like da Silva, the nameless Yeshiva student leaves Mrs. Amsterdam midway and decides abruptly to go home alone: "I always go this way. Good night" (*Roof*, 108). But unpredictably he, too, returns. When she reaches her home, Mrs. Amsterdam discovers him "standing on our steps and I ran towards him. How didn't I notice? Wet. Because of me. For me. Without his books" (*Roof*, 111). "The man living on a star," as Mrs. Amsterdam calls him, returns without any explanation, and only after he is pressed by Mrs. Amsterdam to communicate with her on the bus, they both take toward his home, he says: "You said it yourself. I felt I was like Cain. After the deed with Abel. Abel is not you. It is you and I" (*Roof*, 114). Shortly after this confession, however, he gets off the bus, abruptly, to walk the rest of the way to his home, which marks the end of their zigzagging dance.

A narrative structure that atomizes the plot line into infinitesimal moments of enchantment and disenchantment challenges the happy ending, as well as the climactic moments of intimacy and reciprocity. Within this subtle subversion, the romantic moment, or at least the potential for one, is affirmed. Where reality fails, memory and art reshape it. Neima Sasson transforms her failure into translucent memories, into poetry. Realizing that the magic moment between them has passed forever, Mrs. Amsterdam imagines herself offering a cool response to an imaginary reporter about her mysterious partner: "Ah, this one. Well, yes. Why not, a good opinion." But the narrative does not end on this disillusioned note. The concluding sentence validates the mystery of the evanescent encounter and reaffirms the image of the beloved man as an unforgettable memory: "And I, forever, forever will remember how he sat, not here, and with a chin resting on his chest as if reciting something" (*Roof*, 115).[14]

The heroine's ability to win over reality through the mnemonic and imaginative powers of her consciousness gives a structural and thematic logic to Kahana-Carmon's narratives that questions catastrophic endings of violent separation, death, or suicide. The prioritization of subjective drama explains not only the serenity of the single woman when the reader expects that only marriage will yield happiness, but also the strength of the lackluster wife in stories that are seemingly tragic.

The nameless heroine of "To Build Herself a Home in the Land of Shinar" is a lower-middle-class housewife who feels deeply alienated from her husband: "Her marriage did not turn out well. But life continued in its tracks. Her husband used to come at night, a stranger, taking no part in the domestic life, sinking into the sofa by the radio, turning the receiver's knobs and finally falling asleep there in his clothes and shoes, until he would wake up and go to bed. His world he did not share with her" (*Roof*, 95). The heroine, a Sephardi immigrant, visibly disconnected from the modern Westernized environment of the new Israeli development town, is disenchanted: "Real neighbors she did not have either. Only the old Mr. Azulai and his daughter, Yochebed" (*Roof*, 95).[15]

The nameless heroine does not accept the pragmatic solution to her alienation offered by her guest, the big, blue-eyed, "beautiful and independent" (*Roof*, 96) woman specialist for nutrition and home economics who suggests that the heroine might "find work outside the home. Perhaps a part time job." The heroine counters: "After sixteen years of marriage I need courage." She seems to imply, however, that pragmatic solutions are incompatible with life's real problems: "No. This is life. Fate." After all, a similar move, immigrating to a new country, did not stop the inevitable deterioration of her marriage: " 'A new country, a new life, ha?' she said with empty hands" (*Roof*, 99).

Although the heroine's resignation initially seems to remove her from reality, action, and control of her own destiny, in the structure of Kahana-Carmon's narrative, it shows the heroine's recognition of the relativity and instability of objective constraints, and the precedence of her subjective life. While physical actions may be followed, unpredictably, by tragedy or fortune, emotional disenchantment is inevitably preceded and followed by new hope. The heroine experiences the childhood memory of her visit to a phantasmagorically bright hospital—"And all three nurses united into one figure, burning in a white fire" (*Roof*, 96)— more intensely than the bitter regret she feels when she compares herself to the "perfect" specialist. She notices the subtle overtures of her long-estranged husband: "As a swift arrow the words went through her. After all, he had not addressed her in a very long time. . . . It was not easy for him to speak to me but he is making an effort nonetheless—a kind of fear, hesitation she heard in his voice. She waited to see what would happen. She was wondering if the specialist was noticing. And her heart was beating inside her like a hammer" (*Roof*, 98). Shortly after the protagonist confesses to the specialist—"Nobody knew how stunning this confession was"—that she had lost interest in cooking, she remembers an epiphanic moment of great beauty, when her children showed her "a white boat gliding on the clear blue sea" (*Roof*, 98).

The narrative's intermittent flashbacks and attentiveness to the invisible drama of the heroine's subjective life undercut the elegiac tone of the dysphoric convention. It becomes clear that her resignation to her restrictive life and her refusal to rebel against it stem from an unconventional strength. Here the secret that turns a weakling into a hero is her ability to embrace with gratitude the little joys of life and to open herself up to the hidden significance, even mystery, couched in what appear to be pedestrian, routine events.

The valorization of this strength renders the catastrophic resolution of this seemingly dysphoric narrative superfluous, even unthinkable. Noticing her husband's efforts to serve dinner, the heroine is overcome with unspeakable joy. Having been complimented by the specialist and her husband for the cleanliness of the house, "the heart of the mistress of the house was consumed inside her, as after great deeds" (*Roof*, 100). What makes this conclusion plausible is the sympathetic focus on the heroine's consciousness and the sketchy presentation of the public world of events, which implies that the really great deeds are not those referred to by the director of the town's council at the beginning of the story, or by the specialist for nutrition and home economics, but those performed by the confined, powerless housewife. The accomplishments of a nameless, traditional, and unsuccessful woman overshadow the pioneering achievements of the new development town.

Kahana-Carmon's poetics is inseparable from her interest in the female condition. Her focus on the consciousness of her introspective characters becomes sharper as she de-emphasizes, even obscures, action and plot sequences. Her strategic use of "the moment before the action" or the "longing for, or recoiling from, or the gentleness surrounding one's relationships," as articulated in "Primary Premises" (*Roof*, 238), points to her fascination with the woman banished from the public sphere of action. By avoiding the linear, causal plot progression—beginning, climax, denouement—and focusing instead on the drama of consciousness, Kahana-Carmon redefines the meaning of narrative action. By including desires, intentions, plans, as well as fears, misgivings, or doubts in the category of action, Kahana-Carmon expands the meaning of action to include the perceptual and emotional events shaping, even as they disrupt, the lives of her otherwise passive characters. Her "strobe light technique" which illuminates single moments in the continuum of the character's daily routine, enables us to perceive the uniqueness and even sacredness of the traditional woman's activities.[16]

Despite their weaknesses, or perhaps in recognition of them, her characters emerge as heroic. Mr. Hiram, Kahana-Carmon's poetic alter ego in *And Moon in the Valley of Ajalon*, answers an imaginary question about the weakness of his characters thus: "It depends on how you interpret them. I do not think that they [my characters] are weak people. They are exposed. They lack a certain cortex. To permit themselves not to develop it testifies ultimately to another strength. A strength they essentially had. But one which became eroded, due to the circumstance."[17]

Kahana-Carmon's unique use of metaphor and simile; her euphuisms, biblicisms, and archaisms; and her unconventional use of grammar and syntax—all of which make her work difficult to translate—allow her to elevate, dignify, and even mystify what has traditionally been trivialized. Moreover, her use of a solemn, nuanced, and allusive Hebrew is an integral part of her attempt to give literary shape to the mundane routines of daily life that are so unimportant to Israeli critics. Although in reality the women her heroines represent may not speak or think in such precise subtle terms, the power of Kahana-Carmon's stories depends on the reader's belief that the character's sensibilities—implied by the author's careful use of narrative and dialogue—do exist.

Not only are Kahana-Carmon's poetics and thematic artfully intertwined, they also demonstrate her indebtedness and her contribution to a women's literary tradition in Israel that has gone largely unnoticed by the critics. Kahana-Carmon's presentation of traditional women is reminiscent of Nehamah Pukhachewsky (1869–1934), the foremost woman writer of the first Aliyah (immigration wave), who described the struggles of female pioneers in Palestine, and of Dvona Baron (1886–1956), who depicted the victimization of women in the traditional, male-dominated Jewish European shtetl.[18] Although they differ much in their artistic and stylistic sensibilities, Kahana-Carmon's predecessors, as well as her contemporaries, such as Naomi Fraenkel, Yehudith Hendel, Miriam Schwartz, Rachel Eytan, Shulamith Hareven, Ruth Almog, Yael Medini, and Shulamit Lapid, share an intense interest in giving poetic articulation to the plight of women in a male-dominated society.[19]

The tradition represented by these women writers challenges the generational demarcations of the canon acknowledged by the Hebrew literary critical establishment.[20] According to this formula, suggests critic Nurith Gertz, Amalia Kahana-Carmon fits neither the Palmach generation of the late 1940s and 1950s, characterized by the tendency to exemplify socialist Zionist ideas, nor the generation of statehood, characterized by the tendency to criticize these ideals and which has dominated the literary scene since the 1960s. Kahana-Carmon's thematic world lies outside the critical questions posed by most contemporary critics. Like earlier women writers, she has little to say about the traumas and crises of living in a state of national siege, but she has much to say about the perpetual crisis of living in a state of patriarchal siege. She does not use her strife-torn couples as symbols for the love-hate relations of people and country.[21] Her female characters have little in common with the treacherous wives of Yigal Mossinsohn and Amos Oz, the unreachable beauties of S. Yizhar and A. B. Yehoshua, the vapid sex objects of Moshe Shamir and Pinchas Sadeh, or the hysterical nymphomaniacs of Yitzhak Orpaz, Yitzhak Ben Ner, or David Shutz.[22] Yet, even though Kahana-Carmon's poetics and thematic defy the literary traditions that give precedence to the public over the private realm, the gender-determined polarization of these two spheres and the dichotomy between romantic love and the marketplace continues to be maintained in her work. In this sense, rather than "reinventing womanhood," Kahana-Carmon re-inscribes the dominant Western interpretations of what it means to be a woman.[23]

Kahana-Carmon's valorization of women's sacrifice of the external world in order to enrich the life of the mind romanticizes feminine imprisonment. The heroine's escape from a hostile social world into the poetry of daily routine, her escape from the world into her consciousness, is ultimately an escape into "a prison of sensibility."[24] To the extent that this inner beauty constitutes a heroic core, she can be seen as an extension of the perfect beauty of romance, for as Rachel M. Brownstein argues in her study of English novels:

> The fiction of the heroine encourages aspiration and imposes limits. Paradox is at its core: probably that accounts for its power. The beautiful personal integrity the novel heroine imagines and stands for and seeks for herself is a version of the romantic view of woman as a desired object; as the image of the integral self, she is the inverted image of half of a couple. The literary associations that halo the heroine keep her in a traditional woman's place. That self-awareness which distinguishes her from the simple heroine of romance ends by implicating her further in fictions of the feminine.[25]

Kahana-Carmon's sympathetic treatment of women involved in destructive or hopeless heterosexual relationships may, thus, be interpreted as an idealization of feminine vulnerability and dependence, as an affirmation of women's traditional enclosure within a male-dominated economy. Moreover, Kahana-Carmon's insistence on the heroine's intellect implies a paradoxical validation of the Victorian idealization of female asexuality.[26] Thus, even though Kahana-Carmon's image of the good heroine challenges the image created by male authors of voluptuous and treacherous helpmates, at the same time the central role of men in her heroine's lives may reinforce the androcentric notion that men are indispensable to women. Similarly, Kahana-Carmon's tendency to present her heroine's romantic involvements as quasi-religious experiences endorses the vision of heterosexual love as redemptive. The presentation of male lovers as potential redeemers underwrites the mystification of phallic power, as expressed, for example, in the work of D. H. Lawrence.[27]

Nevertheless, by focusing on the heroine's consciousness, Kahana-Carmon challenges the androcentric interest in the physical and physiognomic attributes of female characters. Her attentiveness to the heroine's fluctuating perceptions, hopes, fears, reflections, moral principles, and psychological struggles endows the female character with what contemporary Hebrew male authors have denied her: conscience and consciousness. By combining in a female character the ability to love a man, and/or be loved by him, with a creative susceptibility, Kahana-Carmon defies the literary tradition which declares these qualities mutually exclusive.[28] Thus she makes an important contribution to reclaiming the female Other in Hebrew literature.

Notes

1. One of the most distinguished examples of the tendency to allegorize the land of Israel as the maternal or female principle can be found in the collection of essays *Between Right and Right* (Tel Aviv: Schocken Books, 1980; in Hebrew), in which A. B. Yehoshua diagnoses the "neurosis of the Diaspora" as the result of the lack of balance between the land of Israel, or the mother, and the religious tradition, or the father (55–73). The book is available in English, trans. Arnold Schwartz (Garden City, N.Y.: Doubleday & Co., 1981). See also Erich Neumann, *The Great Mother: An Analysis of the Archetype*, translated by Ralph Manheim (New York: Pantheon Books, 1955). The recent revival of Neumannesque and Jungian approaches to Hebrew fiction rarely shows any awareness of basic critiques of androcentric stereotyping, such as those outlined in Simone de Beauvoir's *The Second Sex*, edited and translated by H. M. Parshley (New York: Vintage, 1974; first published 1949); or Kate Millet's *Sexual Politics* (New York: Ballantine Books, 1969).
2. Amalia Kahana-Carmon, "Brenner's Wife Rides Again" (in Hebrew) *Moznayim* 59, 4 (October 1985):13. On the place of the woman author in the Hebrew canon, Kahana-Carmon comments: "To be the outsider: the one who is not a member of the club. Brenner's wife [i.e., the woman writer] is the one whose work is predestined to remain outside any labeled drawer. She sees herself as one who was miraculously chosen, or doomed, depending on the point of view, to be totally outside the system" (Kahana-Carmon, 13). This and all subsequent references to her texts are based on my translation.
3. Ibid., 12–13.
4. Amalia Kahana-Carmon, *Under One Roof* (Tel Aviv: Hakibbutz Hameuchad, 1977 [1966]; in Hebrew), hereafter cited in the text as *Roof*; *And Moon in the Valley of Ajalon* (Tel Aviv: Hakibbutz Hameuchad, 1971; in Hebrew), *Magnetic Fields* (Tel Aviv: Hakibbutz Hameuchad, 1977; in Hebrew), and *Up in Montifer* (Tel Aviv: Hakibbutz Hameuchad, 1984; in Hebrew).
5. Quoted from the panel of judges in *Iton* 77, 64-65 (May-June 1985):5. The Brenner Prize ranks third after the more prestigious Bialik and Israel prizes. Opening with a reference to "one great [male] author" who said that "in the short story . . . almost every word must be completely right," the judges not only complimented Kahana-Carmon for her obedience to rules set down by her literary fathers but also hinted that her greatest achievements are in the genre of the short story rather than the novel. The judges referred to her as one "who knows intuitively its wished [goal] and searches and looks for it and often finds it and creates out of it a delicate filigree of a story." The implicit references to sensibility and intuition—the agreed-upon staples of "feminine writing"— and the metaphor of "a delicate filigree" re-encode the traditional perception of women's art.
6. Even the most severe critics of Amalia Kahana-Carmon's allegedly confined thematic world are careful to note her stylistic achievements. See for example, Shimon Sandbank, "To Be Wasted on the Peripheral" (in Hebrew), *Siman Kri'a* 1, 1(1972):326–328.

See also Gershon Shaked and Nissim Calderon, "Magnetic Fields: Two Opinions" (in Hebrew). *Yediot Aharonot* (March 18, 1977):38–41; Amnon Navot, "Up in the Montifer of the Rococo" (in Hebrew). *Ma'ariv* (June 15, 1984):45. For an introductory discussion of Kahana-Carmon's poetics in her early fiction, see Gershon Shaked, *A New Wave in Hebrew Fiction* (Tel Aviv: Sifriat Poalim, 1974; in Hebrew), 168–179, 205–223. See also Nissim Calderon, "A Work of Art" (in Hebrew). *Siman Kri'a*, 1, 1(1972): 321–326; Galit Hasan-Rokem, "Like a Man Encountered with a Mirror: On *And Moon in the Valley of Ajalon*" (in Hebrew). *Hasifrut* 30-31 (April 1981):184–192. For quick surveys in English on Kahana-Carmon's style, see Warren Bargad, "Elements of Style in the Fiction of Amalia Kahana-Carmon." *Hebrew Annual Review* 2 (1978):1–10; and Leon I. Yudkin, "Kahana-Karmon [sic] and the Plot of the Unspoken." *Modern Hebrew Literature* 2, 4 (1976):30–42. See also my interview with Amalia Kahana-Carmon in Esther Fuchs, *Encounters with Israeli Authors* (Marblehead, Mass.: Micah, 1982),7–14.

7. See, for example, Avraham Balaban, *The Saint and the Dragon* (Tel Aviv: Hakibbutz Hameuchad, 1979; in Hebrew); and Imanuel Berman, "The Desire to Be Sacrificed" (in Hebrew). *Siman Kri'a* 7 (1977):431–436.

8. Kahana-Carmon commented that the woman author's "place will be determined by, and she will be complimented for, her great writing talent, but not for the contents, for the ideas: for the closer the values and questions will reflect her own as a woman, the more the mainstream will disengage from it." See Amalia Kahana-Carmon, "To Be Wasted," *Yediot Aharonot* (September 15, 1985): 23.

9. For a larger discussion of this phenomenon in women's literature, see Rachel Blau DuPlessis, *Writing beyond the Ending: Narrative Strategies of Twentieth-Century Women Writers* (Bloomington: Indiana University Press, 1985), in which she explores the alternative fictions created by women authors in defiance of "the mechanism of social insertion of women through the family house, the private sphere, and patriarchal hierarchies" (xi).

10. See Natan Zach, *Air Lines: Talks on Literature* (Jerusalem: Keter, 1983; in Hebrew), 11–28. See also Esther Fuchs, "Is There Humor in Israeli Literature and If Not Why Are We Laughing?" In *Jewish Wry: Essays on Jewish Humor*, edited by Sarah Blacher Cohen (Bloomington and Indianapolis: Indiana University Press, 1987), 216–233.

11. Euphoric and dysphoric texts are defined and discussed in Nancy K. Miller, *The Heroine's Text: Readings in the French and English Novel, 1722–1782* (New York: Columbia University Press, 1980). Miller is correct in noting that these literary paradigms transcend the limits of the eighteenth century (ix–xii).

12. Kahana-Carmon speaks of "the enchantment with the primordial forces" as the principal theme of "High Gambles," the title of two stories published in 1980. Both are included in *Up in Montifer* (n. 4 above).

13. Describing Rembrandt's paintings, for example, Kahana-Carmon says: "What we are seeing is some recognition of the simple nobleness and the courage of the human condition. You [feminine) are not an angel, I am not an angel. You are not a queen, I am not a king. But you are an angel and a queen nonetheless. And I am an angel and I am a king, nevertheless." See "A Piece for the Stage in the Grand Style" (in Hebrew). *Siman Kri'a* 5 (February 1976):245–246. Similarly, the image of the demoted Russian Princess Anastasia of the House of Romanov is evoked throughout *Ajalon* (n. 4 above) as an allusion to the heroine Mrs. Talmor's defeat and pride, hopelessness, and nobility.

14. Memory also overrides the grim contours of what is presented as reality in the stories "Winning from What Is Free," "From the Sights of the House with the Staircase Painted Bright Blue," "Beersheba the Negev's Capital," and "Painted Postcards," all in *Under One Roof* (n. 4 above).

15. The sense of disconnectedness and exile also characterizes the consciousness of Mrs. Peretz (in "The White Light"), an Israeli woman who finds herself in a provincial British

village, where her husband is professionally employed (*Roof*, 37–43). This is also the case with Bruria in "A White Goat, a Bindtree, a Road of Casuarines," who has given up a career as an artist to stay with her husband, Iov, in a provincial Israeli settlement (*Roof*, 116–136).

16. The term "strobe light" for this technique is inspired by Kahana-Carmon's description of Rembrandt's typical picture as "always dark. When the darkness is broken by illuminated regions. . . . Only the climactic points, where the silent drama of the picture is taking place, only they are the center of the lighting" (see Kahana-Carmon, "A Piece for the Stage, in the Grand Style," 246).

17. Kahana-Carmon, *And Moon in the Valley of Ajalon* (n. 4 above), 201.

18. See, for example, Nehamah Pukhachewsky, "Sima Ruskin" (1911), "Regret" (1911), "Afya's Disaster" (1925), included in *Stories by Women of the First Aliyah*. edited by Yafa Berlowitz (Tel Aviv: Tarmil, 1984; in Hebrew), 90–117. Dvona Baron, *Stories* (Tel Aviv: Davar, 1927; in Hebrew), and the short stories *Trivialities* (Tel Aviv: Omanut, 1933; in Hebrew).

19. See, for example, Naomi Fraenkel's trilogy *Saul and Johanna* (Tel Aviv: Sifriat Poalim, 1956–1967; in Hebrew); Yehudith Hendel, *The Street of the Steps* (Tel Aviv: Am Oved, 1958), translated by Rachel Katz and Steven Segal (New York: Herzl Press, 1963); Rachel Eytan, *In Fifth Heaven* (Tel Aviv: Am Oved, 1962; in Hebrew), and *Pleasures of Man* (Tel Aviv: Am Oved, 1975; in Hebrew); Miriam Schwartz, *The Story of Eve Gotlieb* (Tel Aviv: Am Oved, 1968; in Hebrew); Yael Medini, *Arcs and Traces* (Tel Aviv: Hakibbutz Hameuchad, 1977; in Hebrew); Ruth Almog, *The Stranger and the Enemy* (Tel Aviv: Sifriat Poalim, 1980; in Hebrew), and the short stories *Women* (Jerusalem: Keter, 1986); Shulamith Hareven, *Loneliness: Short Stories* (Tel Aviv: Am Oved, 1986; in Hebrew); Shulamit Lapid, *Gai-Oni* (Jerusalem, 1982; in Hebrew); Hadara Lazar, *From Now On* (Tel Aviv: Hakibbutz Hameuchad, 1983; in Hebrew).

20. For general background on these categorizations, see Shaked (n. 6 above), 11–70. See also Nurith Gertz, *Generation Shift in Literary History: Hebrew Narrative Fiction in the Sixties* (Tel Aviv: Hakibbutz Hameuchad, 1983; in Hebrew).

21. "The people" is usually symbolized by a male character, the country by a female character. When the inner turmoil and conflicts of the state are the issue, they tend to be represented as the psychopathology of a female character. For further discussion, see Esther Fuchs, *Israeli Mythogynies: Women in Contemporary Hebrew Fiction* (Albany: State University of New York Press, 1987), 24–33.

22. Ibid., 13–23. See also Esther Fuchs, "Women as Traitors in Israeli Fiction: Steps toward Defining the Problem." *Shofar* 4, 1 (fall 1985):5–16, and "Gender and Characterization in the Palmach Narrative Fiction." In *Proceedings of the Ninth World Congress of Jewish Studies* (Jerusalem: World Union of Jewish Studies, 1986), 179–184.

23. Carolyn G. Heilbrun notes that the failure to re-conceptualize what it means to be a woman is common in contemporary women's writing: "In a world where such [antifeminist] judgments continue to be made, it is scarcely surprising that women writers have not attempted the struggle to present their own accomplishment as women fictively." *Reinventing Womanhood* (New York: W. W. Norton & Co., 1979), 90. See also Mary Poovey, "Persuasion and the Promises of Love." In *The Representation of Women in Fiction*, edited by Carolyn G. Heilbrun and Margaret R. Higonnet (Baltimore and London: The Johns Hopkins University Press, 1983), 152–180.

24. For further discussion of this term, see Mary Jacobus, "The Difference of View." In her *Women Writing and Writing about Women* (Totowa, N.J.: Barnes & Noble, 1979), 15.

25. Rachel M. Brownstein, *Becoming a Heroine: Reading about Women in Novels* (New York: Viking Press, 1982), 295.

26. For an analysis of the Victorian ideology of female propriety, see Mary Poovey, *The Proper Lady and the Woman Writer: Ideology as Style in the Works of Mary Wollstonecraft, Mary Shelley, and Jane Austen* (Chicago and London: University of Chicago Press, 1984). For

a semiotic analysis of the female body, its significance and interpretations in Western culture, see Susan Rubin Suleiman, "(Re)writing the Body: The Politics and Poetics of Female Eroticism." *Poetics Today* 6, 1–2 (1985):43–65.

27. For a critique of D. H. Lawrence's mystification of phallicism, see de Beauvoir (n. 1 above), 242–252; or Millet (n. 1 above), 333–411.

28. This opposition recurs in male-authored Hebrew fiction. See for example Amos Oz, "All the Rivers." In *Where the Jackals Howl* (Tel Aviv: Am Oved, 1982 [1965]; in Hebrew); Pinhas Sadeh, *Life as a Parable* (Jerusalem and Tel Aviv: Schocken Books, 1968; in Hebrew); and A. B. Yehoshua, *Late Divorce* (Tel Aviv: Hakibbutz Hameuchad, 1982; in Hebrew).

Making the Silences Speak
in Israeli Cinema

THE MYTH OF EQUALITY fostered by Zionist discourse, in which feminism has generally been marginalized, is reflected in Israeli cinema. The Israeli film industry has not only been dominated by men but has also catered to privileged, male-oriented concerns, addressing women's issues only insofar as they seem relevant to nationalist rhetoric. One can hardly speak of a feminist alternative discourse for reasons which have to do not only with the militarization of Israeli culture but also with the history of the nationalist Sabra (native-born Jew associated with European origin) ethos: the mythological Sabra, the prototype of the newly emerging Jew in Eretz Israel/Palestine, constituted the masculine antithesis of the Zionist image of the "feminine" Diaspora Jew. The Sabra was created by the immigrant generation of pioneers, who viewed their children as the hope for Jewish salvation and therefore endowed this first generation with the proud status of a kind of moral aristocracy.

In a reversed oedipalism, the Sabra was born into a vacuum in which the ideal figure was not the father but the son. Hebrew narratives were therefore premised on the absence of the Diaspora parent. The heroes—there was very little space for heroines—were celebrated as eternal children devoid of parents, as though born by spontaneous generation. Zionist parents raised their children to see themselves as historical foundlings, worthy of more dignified, romantic and powerful progenitors. The mythological Sabra, posited in gendered language as the masculine redeemer of the passive Diaspora Jew, also signified the destruction of the Diaspora Jewish entity. Incarnating the same nationalist features that oppressed the Diaspora Jew, the Sabra hero was portrayed as healthy, tanned, often with blond hair and blue eyes, presumably cleansed of all Jewish inferiority complexes, a kind of child of nature, confident, proud and brave. Ironically, this conception was partially influenced by Gustav Weinken and the youth culture fashionable in Germany at the turn of the century, especially in the German youth movement, Wandervogel (Elon, 1981). The Zionist stereotype of the Diaspora Jew as a passive victim and the Sabra as an active redeemer has subliminally perpetuated a gendered discourse in which masculine toughness has been highly cherished, undermining the possibility of a revisionist feminist perspective.

Already during the Yishuv (the pre–1948 Jewish settlement in Palestine), the pioneer genre of films such as *Sabra* (1933) suggested the superiority of Jewish over Arab society through the comparative portrayal of the status of women in the two communities (Shohat, 1989). As equal members of the collective, women pioneers are portrayed working alongside the men. They demonstrate—in accordance with a positive female stereotype—an enhanced mental capacity to continue the struggle in the face of adversity. Images of women working the land and, in later films, wielding weapons, further strengthened this egalitarian mystique. In fact, however, even in the socialist communes, women were still largely limited to traditional roles. In the pioneer films, female equality is directly correlated with conformity to Zionist pioneering ideals: the hard-working pioneer is portrayed as a Madonna, the hedonistic bourgeois as a whore. *Sabra*, for example, contrasts the hardworking pioneer woman who sacrifices her beauty and comfortable life in Europe with the provocatively dressed Jezebel-like woman who refuses to abandon her hedonistic ways and spends her time drinking and listening to the gramophone in the pioneers' tent. The film enforces identification with her boyfriend's puritanical censure, culminating in his final expression of contempt: "The only thing you know how to do is drink, while we go hungry. You would dance all your life, but here dancing is death."

In *They Were Ten* (1961), produced decades after the early pioneering films, the pioneer woman as Madonna is exalted, even mythologized, into the status of a veritable great mother. The film portrays Manya, the only woman among nine men living in overcrowded conditions, who is unable to find the privacy to fulfill her function as wife to her pioneer husband. An exemplar of self-abnegation, she is characterized as a substitute mother who takes care of all the pioneers' needs. When one of them desires her, however, she rebuffs him, evoking an embarrassed confession of moral weakness. The only lovemaking between Manya and her husband during the film takes place outdoors and leads to her pregnancy. Fulfilling her ultimate woman-mother role of giving fruitful birth, she dies shortly thereafter, suffering the fate of the frontier woman in many Western films.

While pioneer women are granted few roles and little dialogue, no dialogue is accorded the Arab women who appear but briefly in the pioneer and post–1948 heroic-nationalist films. The few sequences with Arab women reduce their image to the exotic Orientals familiar to Western imagination. A rather improbable mélange in *Sabra* features a belly dancer with a ring in her nose, a dot on her forehead, and a jar on her head, thus condensing several third world female stereotypes. The dot on the forehead is usually associated with women from India; the ring in the nose is more common in Africa, while a jar is usually carried on the head by Arab women for practical rather than exotic-artistic purposes. The Hollywood-style "mark of the plural," to borrow Albert Memmi's terminology (1967:85), flattens a diversity of third world cultures in an unlikely synthesis. While the belly dancer in Sabra leaves the screen when an Arab man signals for her to go, the equally brief appearance of a noble Arab woman is associated with one of the pioneers. She shyly exchanges affectionate glances with him early in the film and later succors his wound and gives him water as in the classical biblical figure of the worthy woman.

In films such as *Rebels against the Light* (1964) and *Sinaia* (1964), the positive portrayal of a noble, exotic Palestinian or Bedouin woman entails her devotion to the Israeli cause. The representation of the Arab woman is, in many ways, subordinated to romantic fascination with the other. Arab women, as pointed out by literary critic Gershon Shaked (1983) with regard to Hebrew literature of the twenties and thirties, tend to assimilate with Jews, as though their origins were in the East but their heart in the West, that is, as represented by Israelis. The Orient, as suggested in Edward Said's *Orientalism* (1977), is regarded as mute and powerless, available for European plunder, in complete disregard of the desires and resistance of the indigenous population. In the Israeli heroic-nationalist films, the traditional Western male fetishization of Oriental women takes the form of a virtually silent Arab woman behind whose melancholy eyes seems to lurk a desire for rescue by the Western male. The minor Arab woman character in *Sabra* is granted no dialogue, and Naima in *Rebels against the Light* mouths only a few sorrowful words of mourning.

In *Sinaia*, the noble Bedouin mother who hides an Israeli pilot (who has bandaged her wounds) from Egyptian soldiers, even though it was his crashing airplane that caused the destruction, is marginalized within the film's narrative. The Hebrew title *Sinaia* is taken from the actual Hebrew name given to a Bedouin baby girl rescued by an Israeli pilot during the 1956 war—the inspiration for the film. Set during the same war, the film presents the Bedouin woman as an object of ethical debate between the Israeli pilot and the infantry. Although there is no room in the helicopter, the pilot insists on taking the Bedouin mother and her two small children. The infantryman argues that in wartime soldiers must have first priority. His mean-spiritedness is explained as a product of traumatic memories of Arab terror (a massacred sister) as well as the recent loss of his best friend in the war. Gradually, however, he adopts the pilot's morally superior stance, even saving the life of the woman's son from a threatening Egyptian soldier. While the Egyptian soldiers torture the Bedouin woman to extract information about the Israeli pilot, the Israeli soldiers rescue her. Here the narrative-ideological role of the Bedouin female character is to contrast the humanism of the Israelis with the barbarism of the Egyptians. The infantryman agrees to stay behind to facilitate the rescue. When the helicopter crashes, only the baby girl survives. The depiction of the Bedouin woman as almost silent, expressing, through gesture, primal emotions of motherhood and fear, forms a striking contrast with the portrayal of the Israeli soldiers' free stream of expression. Close shots emphasize the beautiful, light eyes of the Bedouin woman, but otherwise she forms part of the desert scenery, a perfect embodiment of nature. The actress, painted dark with makeup, literalizes the notion of a Western soul beneath an Oriental surface, allowing the film to construct her as positive, an exotic woman on whom an expansive and eroticized generosity can be projected. Arab women, in other words, can be seen as analogizing the Hebrew settlers' relations to the alien land and culture, via a metaphor that links the Orient and sexuality. The Middle East is subliminally conceived as fallow land, waiting to be ploughed, as a resistant virgin coyly waiting to be conquered.

Like the Arab woman, the Oriental Jewish woman—also referred to as "Sephardi" (Jews who came to Israel mostly from Arab and Moslem countries, who form the majority of the Jewish population yet have been denied access to political, economic and cultural power)—is also typically denied a voice in Israeli films. In *Hill 24 Doesn't Answer* (1955), for example, the ethnic "inferiority" of the "exotic" Oriental Jewish woman is compensated for by her heroic sacrifice for the country. Set during the 1948 war, *Hill 24 Doesn't Answer* revolves around the personal stories of four (in fact three) fighters: an Irishman, an American Jew, and two Israelis, one an Ashkenazi Sabra and the other an Oriental woman, assigned to defend a strategic hill outside Jerusalem. On the way to their last mission, the three men recount, in lengthy flashbacks, the roots of their Zionist conviction and their previous combat experiences. *Hill 24 Doesn't Answer* chronicles the evolving Zionist consciousness of the protagonists and, through them, of the spectator. The device of focalizing the narrative through an ethnically and nationally diverse gallery of characters enables the film to maintain the facade of a democratic distribution of points of view. The merging of the three stories into the brief final episode on Hill 24 reflects the final integration of perspectives within the mold of a national collective history. A reductionist view of the Arabs as a kind of synecdoche for violence and menace is accompanied by European paternalism toward the friendly East of the Druze and the Oriental Jews, as epitomized in the character of the woman fighter. The only detail she provides about herself concerns her place of birth, Jerusalem, but her accent and appearance make it clear that her country of origin is Yemen. Although one of the four protagonists assigned to defend Hill 24, she is granted no episode of her own, as if she had no particular story to tell. It is up to us, therefore, to make the text's silences, and hers, speak.

Within the film's Zionist Eurocentrism, the history of Jews from the Middle East is eliminated or subordinated to the European Jewish memory. The Arab historical memory of the Yemenite Jewish woman is elided, an absence forming an integral part of her definition as one of the four Zionist heroes. The film thus reflects the official view that the Arab culture of Oriental Jews was fated for extinction, in accord with general colonialist assumptions about what was regarded as the twilight cultures of the East, an idea expressed by various Zionist leaders, on both the right (Ze'ev Jabotinsky and the Revisionist movement) and the left (David Ben-Gurion and the Labor movement). In the context of the mid-1950s, following the mass immigration of Arab Jews, the creation of a Jewish national identity came to imply the melting of Orientals with the hegemonic Euro-Israeli culture based on the assumption of a single official, European Jewish history. It is scarcely surprising, then, that the film stages an encounter between the Ashkenazi Sabra man and his European history, condensed into the image of the Nazi soldier-oppressor who fights with the Egyptians against Israel, while never offering any equivalent encounter for the Yemenite woman. Not only is the Israeli-Arab political conflict projected onto an imaginary Arab-Nazi nexus, but also all other Jews are grouped, inappropriately, under the sign of the Nazi Holocaust. The Oriental Jew does not look to her own historical roots in the East, or to those with whom her ancestors shared what was essentially a life of coexistence, that is, the Arabs, even though the film, like Israel, is set in the Middle East and not in Europe. While European Jewish history is referred to in all three episodes, Asian and African Jewish history is totally excluded from representation.

Hill 24 Doesn't Answer also intimates the price paid by Oriental Jews for redemption from their primal sin of belonging to the Orient—the waging of war against the Arabs. The climactic United Nations decision that Hill 24 belongs to Israel—even though the four fighters do not survive to claim it—is a consequence of the Israeli flag being clasped in the hand of the dead Oriental woman. The sequence inadvertently suggests the ironic nature of her equality and redemption; through her self-sacrifice, she is accepted (as a martyr) even though, as the film implies, she has no story to tell. Her (hi)story begins here, with the Zionist act, not before it, and will only be told through the agency of male western, Jewish and non-Jewish, narrators.

In other films, Western altruism saves the Jewish Orient from its social, moral, and sexual obscurantism In the melodrama *Fortuna* (1966), an Algerian Jewish family, from a development town near Sodom, forces their daughter Fortuna to wed a rich old man to whom she was promised at an early age, while sabotaging her love for a French engineer. The tyranny of what is presented as a typically patriarchal Oriental family leads to the heroine's death. The critique of the inferior culture brought from underdeveloped countries is reinforced by the topographical reductionism of the Orient to desert, and metaphorically, to dreariness. The desert, a frequent reference in the dialogue and a visual leitmotif throughout the film, is presented as essential to the history of these third world Jews. The

Oriental is associated with images of underdevelopment, poverty, and back-wardness, in implied contrast to the Sabra, generally portrayed as the very antithe-sis of the Oriental desert: an active, productive, and creative pioneer, the masculine redeemer who conquers the feminine wilderness. In Fortuna, the Orient becomes a world immersed in death, a theme emphasized by shots of circling birds of prey, and by the association of Fortuna's family with Sodom, the biblical city of evils. The dichotomy of Orient (death) and West (life) structures the film. The Orient appears as the enemy of Eros and the partisan of Thanatos, both in the attempts to kill the French lover and in the forced marriage which indirectly leads Fortuna to her death. The West, meanwhile, is personified by the handsome Frenchman, the savior of the oppressed daughter and the bringer of technological advancement. Salvation for the Oriental woman must come from the West, or from the west-ernized, modern Sabra world.

The victimization of the Oriental woman by Oriental men and her implicit salvation by the Western Ashkenazi world, particularly by a Western man, is pre-sented in other Israeli films as well. In *Queen of the Road* (1971), the narrative pro-motes an opposition between the gentle kibbutznik, who gives the protagonist, a Moroccan prostitute in Tel Aviv, warmth and affection, and the rough Oriental men, especially those of the development town in the South, who brutally rape her during her first months of pregnancy. Her involvement with the kibbutz-nik, her pregnancy by him, and her visit to the enlightened kibbutz, where she sees his well-ordered family, make her decide to give up prostitution and raise the child herself. While visiting her mother in the South of Israel, she is violently raped, leading to the birth of a retarded child. Rape, retardation, and even death, caused in these films by Oriental male mistreatment of Oriental women, stimulate a kind of rescue fantasy in the progressive male spectator.

A similar representation of sexual tensions between Oriental men and women is extended to the present day in the comedy *You're in the Army Now* (1985). The film recounts four weeks of boot camp training for women soldiers in the Israeli artillery. From the very beginning, the film develops a structural contrast between its major characters, an upper-class Sabra woman, Niva, and a development-town Oriental woman, Shula. Already in the credit sequence, the film cuts from Niva's separation from her father to Shula's separation from her family, underlining their opposing class and ethnic backgrounds. The film betrays a differential attitude toward these backgrounds that permeates the entire film. Whereas the camera fore-grounds Niva and her handsome, protective father, revealed to be an insider in relation to the establishment, Shula's large family remains more or less anonymous as the camera pans over their shoulders to record the daughter kissing them good-bye, while she censures their overly emotional, that is, non-Israeli, reaction to her departure. Shula is dressed in colorful, cheap clothing, while Niva is dressed in expensive, fashionable togs acquired in the boutiques of Paris and New York. (The contrast in their appearance and manner, translated into a North American context, would correspond, roughly, to the stereotypes of the refined [perhaps repressed] Wasp and the sexy Latina.) Acknowledging that her situation at home is unbearable and rebelling against the (presumably Oriental) prospect of ending her life "at the age of thirty with fifty children," trapped "between the grocery store and the laundry," Shula joins the army. Once in the army, however, she becomes the object of prejudice. Perhaps in reaction to the treatment accorded her, she runs away from the army and encounters her Oriental boyfriend, depicted as stuttering, weak, and unintelligent, but also good hearted. Out in the brutal Oriental world, she finds herself forced to smoke dope and about to be raped by three Oriental men. Unable to save her, the weak and pitiful boyfriend calls Shula's women's unit for help. The Sabra women's unit collectively performs a private military mission to save their comrade from the Oriental sexual vultures, thus compensating for their previous lack of ethnic sensitivity. In a heroic action, they release the Oriental woman and humiliate the surprised and frightened Oriental machos. The unit's patriotism is expressed in an additional act of generosity toward the culturally deprived Oriental woman. With her father's help, Niva gets the musically talented Shula into the prestigious army entertainment troupe, while she herself gets another (equally prestigious) position in military radio. The army, metonymic of Israel and its Ashkenazi elite, then, together save the Oriental woman from her backward, violent world and give her the opportunity to develop her talents and resolve the sexual conflicts presumably endemic in Oriental society, in a way that intimates a peaceful transcendence of the ethnic, class tensions of Israeli society.

The violence of Oriental men toward Oriental women and their rescue by the Israeli establishment, or Ashkenazi men, function ideologically to explain away the exploitation of Oriental women within the Israeli system (Oriental women are the lowest paid sector within the Israeli Jewish population) as well as the exploitation of working class Oriental men, while at the same time eliding Ashkenazi men's oppression of Ashkenazi women. These films reproduce the hegemonic male discourse whereby gender relations are blamed on the Orientalism of Sephardi Jews. The position of women within Israeli society, as well as the fact that the Sabra ethos is based on nationalist-macho ideals, is ignored.

Such a vision is at times internalized by Oriental Jews themselves, as in *Coordania* (1984), a short film made by an Oriental director. Set in a transit camp of the 1950s, it opens with the rape of an Oriental woman by her husband. The problem is not the realism of the scene, but the fact that it was created in an interpretive context in which the notion of sexual violence within the Oriental family has been used to rationalize Euro-Israeli male power. The rape of women has not been limited to particular classes, ethnicities and nationalities and in Israel, Ashkenazi men have raped Oriental women; therefore the political drift of such representations is obvious, especially considering the history of Israeli cinema, in which rape is never performed by Ashkenazi men, but always restricted to Oriental men.

More often, however, in the comic *bourekas* genre—the name derives from a popular Oriental pastry and came to refer to comedies and melodramas which deal with Ashkenazi-Oriental ethnic tensions—gender relations are subjected to a more implicit nationalist ideology in which young mixed couples allegorically unite conflicting communities. Social integration is dreamed via eroticism, and the wedding which presumably bridges the gaps, celebrates national-familial harmony, as expressed in the song "We are all Jews" used in the movie *Casablan* (1973) or the song "To the Life of this Nation/People" used in *Salomonico* (1973). Most bourekas films give expression to the dominant attitude that cultural differences and class distinctions will be eliminated by the younger generation, especially through marriage. The Israeli-Arab conflict remains latent, an unspoken presence in bourekas films, and is suggested only through the context of Jewish unity in the face of Arab animosity.

With the decline of the mythic heroic Sabra in the 1970s, the new movement of personal cinema focused on sensitive, vulnerable male characters, thus indirectly opening up some space for women protagonists. As in much of personal cinema, *My Michael* (1974) focuses on alienated outsiders, this time with female protagonists. But even the political *parti pris* of personal cinema is not completely untouched by national context and Orientalist ideology. The Arab twins in *My Michael*, for example, presented within the woman protagonist's stream of consciousness, serve little narrative function beyond mirroring and metaphorizing the repressed Dionysian inner self of the protagonist and her romantic frustration with her humdrum and unimaginative existence. In this sense, the Arab presence penetrates the hallucinatory space of Jewish-Israeli subjectivity, but is silent as a national, political voice.

The late 1970s also witnessed the emergence of women filmmakers, who, like their male colleagues, tend to highlight themes of alienation and the search for identity. The personal films present a closed world that is centered in the West, spurning any authentic dialogue with the East. Moreover, the focus on women is rarely an explicitly feminist one. Depicting the world of upper-middle class Ashkenazi women, women's personal films tend to reproduce the hegemonic national, ethnic, and class perspective. For example, *A Thousand Little Kisses* (1982) fosters identification with the elegant and sophisticated bourgeois Euro-Israeli widow facing a crisis in her life. Through the visually precious and sophisticated *mis-en-scène* and complex camera movements, the spectator is led to identify with the complex world of the widow against that of the petty, intrusive, and materialistic maid, who is merely interested in taking food and clothing from her employer and is totally insensitive to the widow's emotional state. Due to their conspicuous and unnatural exclusion from a film shot in a well-known Oriental neighborhood, Orientals (other than the maid) form a "structuring absence" in the film. A *Thousand Little Kisses* consistently maintains a hygienic and self-conscious atmosphere of artistic beauty, exploits the old local architecture of the neighborhood but eliminates almost all traces of its inhabitants.

The superficiality and passivity associated with Oriental women has been challenged in a few films made by Oriental producers, notably *The House on Chlouch Street* (1973) and *Light out of Nowhere* (1973). In the former, the protagonist's mother, Klara, works as a housemaid, and this is one of the rare cases in Israeli cinema where the Oriental female laborer is treated with understanding, largely through mechanisms of identification. Her portrayal contrasts with numerous Israeli films in which the maid is depicted as a symbolic ornament for the upper class and presented from the vantage point of her employers (and her producers), whether she is a marginal character or a central one. *The House on Chlouch Street* devotes most of Klara's narrative time to events in her home, showing her on her own terrain, where she is independent and even a boss to her children. This film's portrayal of the maid's emotional depth not only eschews all condescension, but also reinforces identification with her struggle as a widowed working mother. When Klara is first seen scrubbing the floor, the act is not presented from the employer's point of view, but from the point of view of her son, the protagonist, who intensely identifies with her feelings of shame and hurt, an identification underlined by a close shot of his face. His humiliation is exacerbated when Klara's employer, Mrs. Goldstein, enters the house, for her remarks call attention to a painful situation of dependency.

Similarly, in *Light out of Nowhere*, the oriental woman is significant even though she is not a central character. When, for example, establishment representatives break into an Oriental underclass neighborhood to carry out their mission—the implementation of harsh social policy—the Oriental woman is the one who expresses protest. In a sequence in which the inspectors and the police execute an order to destroy a home, the protagonist's female neighbor becomes the representative of the Oriental community, whose rebellion is expressed by the words she hurls at the authorities: "It's OK for our kids to fight the Arabs, but nobody gives a damn where they live! What does this government care! Go on, bring those *Vuzvuzim* [pejorative term for Ashkenazim] from Russia." This was a period of large-scale immigration from the Soviet Union. The Soviet immigrants were given preferential treatment, which angered Oriental Jews, who had never been the recipients of similar governmental largesse. In *Light out of Nowhere* and *The House on Chlouch Street*, the Oriental woman fights within the limited framework of her possibilities. Furthermore, her oppressor does not take the form of a monstrous Oriental man, but rather that of an oppressive establishment. *Light out of Nowhere* does not ignore the macho behavior of street youths toward women; it demonstrates

that Oriental women and men, whatever their differences, are nonetheless victims of the same policy. The woman's violence is presented within the context of
a violent policy and, as a consequence, takes on significance different from the
stereotype of Oriental irrationality. This woman expresses the anger and violence
of a subjugated group which is first and foremost a reaction and rebellion against
violence, the violence rooted in the asymmetries of power.

References

Elon, Amos (1981). *The Israelis*. Jerusalem: Adam (Hebrew).
Memmi, Albert (1967). *The Colonizer and the Colonized*. Boston: Beacon Press.
Said, Edward (1977). *Orientalism*. New York: Vintage Press.
Shaked, Gershon (1983). *No Other Place*. Tel Aviv: Hakibbutz Hameuchad (Hebrew).
Shohat, Ella (1989). *Israeli Cinema: East/West and the Politics of Representation*. Austin: Texas
    University Press.

The Woman as Other in Israeli Cinema

ONE OF THE DRAMATIC HIGHLIGHTS of Michal Bat Adam's film *Moments* (1979) occurs when the underlying sexual tensions between Yula (Bat Adam) and Ann (Brigitte Catillon) hover at the breaking point on a hotel bed in Jerusalem. After touring the unfamiliar city together, the two women, one a Tel Avivian, the other a French tourist, laze indulgently on the bed, opening up emotionally to each other and, perhaps, lightly touching.

The scene develops into a love scene but not before another, apparently necessary, element is introduced—Yula's boyfriend, played by the definitive male of the Israeli cinema, Assi Dayan. What began as the prelude to an intentional and dramatic climax of intimacy and sexual love between two women turns into a trite display of pornography. It begins with the most basic of all situations in this genre: a man observing two passionately aroused women, partially undressed, about to make love. The act becomes pornographic as it is performed before the penetrating gaze of a man who derives sexual gratification from observing the scene. He is using the women for his voyeuristic pleasure. They are thus transformed from subjects of love into objects of exploitation. The scene continues as Dayan sleeps with both of them—another model in the genre. As a result of this form of intercourse—and the film does not offer any (lesbian) alternatives—the ultimate connection between the two women is achieved by means of the male organ: the movement of the phallus from one woman to the other. Only the phallus, we are being told, has the power to constitute female and interfemale sexuality.

Moments is a film in which the main characters are women, and the main theme is women's experience. The constitution of the female subject is the heart of the narrative and the subject of the dialogue between the women: everyone has told Yula that she has no talent; her boyfriend has told her that she wrecks everything important; Yula goes to Jerusalem to try to fulfill herself by writing, and there she meets Ann.

The film was written by a woman, directed by a woman, and a woman stars in it (and in this specific case, the viewer/critic is also a woman). Yet despite this, the constitution of women's sexuality is achieved through the "penetrating gaze" of the voyeuristic "peeping Tom"—the reifying male. Thus, the representation of women in this film is no different from that of most other films in which women are not the main subjects, are not central to the narrative, and have no part in its creation.

In film theory, the concept of the penetrating gaze has been used to describe the apparatus both for film enjoyment in general and for representing the female in particular. Expounded by Laura Mulvey (1975) in an article that is regarded as a classic, the concept has been discussed, criticized, and updated by, among others, Mulvey herself (1981). According to this concept, woman's specific "otherness" differs from the otherness of other minorities in that the core of her otherness consists in her being subjected to a penetrating gaze. This gaze reifies her as it turns her into the object of the male's voyeuristic pleasure. Under the penetrating gaze of the male, women are not experienced as active flesh-and-blood persons. Whether under the penetrating gaze of the man in the film, the male viewer in the audience, or the male camera/director on the set, the woman becomes a thing, a displayed object to be used. This is the dominant mechanism through which the cinema marginalizes women as the Other.

In films, as in culture in general, the marginality or otherness of women is not simply the result of specific moments or situations. Rather, the text constructs a normative world in which the woman is always perceived as inferior. Lacking any position at the center, she does not function as an autonomous, coherent self. Instead, her entire existence depends on and is marginal to that which lies at the center, that is, the normative phallocentric system that sees that which the phallus represents as perfection. Thus, the female (margin) is not a counterpart of the male (center), but an object to be used by him. She exists solely to fulfill a function for him: to be the object of his sexual voyeuristic gratification.

The problem raised by feminists scholars is, how is it possible for women to enjoy films like Garry Marshall's *Pretty Woman* (1990) or Luc Besson's *Nikita* (1990), two modern Pygmalion-like tales in which the women are tamed and shaped to fit precisely into the molds required by patriarchal society, or Howard Hawks's *Gentlemen Prefer Blondes* (1953), in which, as in so many other films, the woman's body is commercialized and put on permanent display—the very display of which becomes thematicized—for the enjoyment of the viewer?[1]

Mulvey, in her later article (1981), formulated her psychoanalytic explanation, comprised of three components: Freud's concept of masculinity in woman; the identification triggered by the logic of a narrative grammar; and the ego's desire to fantasize itself in a certain, active manner (in Penley 1988, 72). Of course, this explanation presupposes a Freudian view in which woman is defined in terms of absence as *un homme manqué*, as devoid of or lacking a penis. However, this Freudian view has been severely criticized through feminist readings of the case of Dora (see Bernheimer and Kahane 1985) and critiques of the Oedipus complex.

A film like *Moments* seems to indicate that women do not necessarily position women in a different way and that the female gaze is not necessarily different from that of the male. It is not the sex of the filmmaker that determines the positioning of the women characters (or the women viewers), but rather the normative world created by the text. The most potent factor in defining the woman's position in the normative world built by a text is the depiction of the character of women in it. The way the text positions and judges the female characters transmits to me, the female viewer, my position and the way I am to be judged in the real world. Through this positioning, I become aware of my otherness. Thus, just as women can create a text in which women are marginal, it is theoretically (and not only theoretically) possible for a man to create a text in which the woman, constituted as an autonomous subject, is positioned at the center. The opinions of some feminist theoreticians notwithstanding, women do not necessarily read texts differently than men. Reading and viewing are acquired skills and not functions of biological differences. Insofar as women, like men, learn to read and view within the hegemony, any difference between the way men and women read/view can only emerge within the context of that system.

Therefore, a possible mechanism for a non-patriarchal form of reading/viewing is the technique of subversive reading, which becomes, ipso facto, feminist reading. In such readings, the woman reads against the grain of the text. Such readings, which challenge the plain meaning of the text, permit the woman a coherent autonomous existence. Nevertheless, just as there are many women who do not write subversive texts, so there are many women readers who, contrary to the opinions of some feminist theoreticians, do not perform subversive readings (Lubin 1993). A hegemonic text, adhering to a set of norms defined by the center, situates woman at the periphery. A feminist text is not simply a text that focuses on woman's experience but is one in which I, the female reader, can constitute my subjectivity as I read without having to struggle against it. A text can also be subversive. While establishing a hegemonic set of norms, it can simultaneously, through the same words, expose their hegemonic character. Thus, by exposing the norms as humanly constructed rather than naturally given, it can provide the female reader with the means to resist them. Similarly, a text that purports to be feminist can actually be hegemonic.[2] While seeming to position women at the center, it can subvert this positioning through negative judgments and negative consequences. The focus of this analysis, therefore, is twofold: first, the devices employed by the text, such as the penetrating gaze and the positioning of women, that reify women and establish the otherness of the female character and, through her, the female viewer; and, second, the appropriation and use of these devices by the Other—the female camera/director—in those instances where they, subvert the hegemonic norms. The number of full-length feature films produced in Israel—three hundred eighty— permits a fairly accurate generalization concerning the way in which women are represented in them (Schnitzer 1993). Virtually all of these films were made by men. While women have made a large number of short films, the number of feature films made by women is quite small—only fourteen (six of them by Bat Adam).[3]

The device of the penetrating gaze is employed in almost every Israeli film in which there is a female character. In almost all such films, women's sexuality is displayed—not as a central theme or a plot catalyst, but as a contingent prop. However, careful analysis reveals that despite the recurring use of this mechanism to position women as inferior, it is not the dominant one. In Israeli films, the dom- inant mechanism is not the penetrating gaze but rather social positioning— women's professional standing, their place in the community, and their role in the family: the war widow in Gilberto Toffano's *Siege* (1969), the soldier's wife in Yossi Somer's *Burning Memory* (1989), the girlfriend of the soldier who is killed and who then marries his best friend in Shimon Dotan's *Repeat Drive* (1982), the prosti- tute and the housewife in endless films, and the helpmate in Shmuel Imberman's *Don't Give a Damn* (1987), and in Amos Gutman's *Himmo, King of Jerusalem* (1987), or women in such stereotyped female professions as teaching or nursing. Frequently, however, no mention is made of a woman's vocation: either she has none, or her working only occurs off-screen. Even when the woman has a profession—for example, the physical training teacher in Uri Barbash's *Where Eagles Fly* (1990)— it is irrelevant to the plot and inconsequential to her life and to her relations with the world. Furthermore, as is the case in this film, her profession is only used as an excuse for displaying her body. Even when the woman fulfills an economic func- tion equal to that of her husband—as in Jacob Goldwasser's *Over the Ocean* (1991), where both run a family business—her main function, in terms of plot and theme, is as the sister of a fallen soldier. While her husband, who is responsible for the financial well-being of the family, is anxious to emigrate, she feels prevented from doing so because of her responsibility to visit her brother's grave. Thus, while the husband's actions are based on his central function as a provider, her actions derive from her role as a man's sister.

In short, most Israeli films construct a normative world in which the woman is positioned, socially and professionally, at the margins. There are, however, a few films in which a woman is positioned at the center of the action. These include *The Summer of Aviya* (1988), a joint enterprise of the writer and leading actress Gila Almagor and the director Eli Cohen which deals with a child (marginal) and a mentally disturbed woman (also marginal) whose heroic past is mentioned and then forgotten; Isaac Zepel Yeshurun's *Noa at Seventeen* (1982), in which strong women deride and emasculate the men; and Avraham Heffner's *Laura Adler's Last Love Affair* (1990), a film about the Yiddish theater and its star actress, both in a state of decline. There are also films in which the women are less stereotypical, such as Eitan Green's *American Citizen* (1992), where, in addition to a stereotypical nymphomaniac groupie, there is a serious career woman, a pianist who initiates all of her professional and romantic pursuits, creating her own world. But in most Israeli films, as already pointed out, women are not central and their marginal positioning is determined by their place in the community.

In Hollywood films, the mechanism of the penetrating gaze dominates the portrayal of women. In these films, the objectification of women by using them for sexual pleasure is the dominant mode of marginalizing women on screen and, by extension, in the audience. The mechanism of social positioning is also actively used but is not dominant. In Israeli films, on the other hand, the mechanism of social positioning is dominant, although the penetrating gaze is very active as well. This circumstance results primarily from mainstream Zionist culture's suppression of the sexual body and the privileging of the body of the worker attached to the hoe or the plow.[4] Thus, sexuality and eroticism are subordinated to the national project. When the sexual body again appears in Israeli culture, it functions as an act of subversion. Unable to constitute an autonomous female subject in the spheres privileged by Zionism—that is, community and work—poets, writers, or those filmmakers discussed here who seek to represent female experience will often have to turn to the sphere of sexuality.[5] However, in the very act of rendering the sexual body as Other, Zionism has provided women artists with a space in which to constitute the female subject. Whereas the power of Zionist culture renders difficult any effort to position women at the center socially and professionally, its silence regarding the sexual body leaves a space into which women artists can move. And, in the case of film, the move to place the sexual body at the center entails the mechanism of the reifying penetrating gaze. Only now, the penetrating gaze serves to subvert the hegemonic, patriarchal culture by representing the woman as a sovereign and autonomous being with her own center. This is a subversive rather than a revolutionary act. A revolutionary act would be to represent the sovereign autonomous woman functioning professionally and socially. Restoring women to the center by focusing on the sexual body is, rather an act of subversion—that is, an action that subverts but does not overthrow the hegemonic system.

A film in which the sexual body and the penetrating gaze are used subversively is Dina Zvi-Riklis's 1984 short film *Coordania*. This film tells the story of two families left behind in an immigrant transit camp (*ma'abara*, from the 1950s). The heart of the film is the experience of a female adolescent and the story is told from the young girl's point of view. The young heroine witnesses her mother being raped by her father and her mother's pregnancy and difficult childbirth, and she experiences the loss of childhood love and her first menstrual period. Desire and its absence, sexuality and the beginning of puberty, and the significance of female sexuality fill the world of the young heroine. The mechanism of the penetrating gaze—which is basically sexual—is evident in a scene showing the awakening of desire between the girl and a boy. In that scene, the girl, bathing alone in her underwear, is unaware of the presence of the boy on a hilltop overlooking the sea. The boy gazes at the girl and, in an act that literalizes the metaphor of the penetrating gaze, uses his hands like binoculars. The camera also literalizes the metaphor as it thematizes the penetrating gaze: no longer an abstract description, the penetrating gaze is now an actual event. This transition from metaphor to literalness uncovers and subverts the power mechanism of the gaze. It is as if the film were saying: If, in order to constitute the female subject, one must abandon the social scene and operate in the realm of the body—constituting a sexual subject and introducing the penetrating gaze—we shall subvert the power of this mechanism—the gaze—by exposing it.

The camera, however, does not focus on the girl from the boy's vantage point, that is, from above to below. Instead, it persistently views the girl at eye level. Furthermore, the camera does to the boy exactly what he is doing to the girl: it gazes on him from below rather than from the height of his eyes. This twofold act—showing him as observer and as the object of observation—exposes the penetrating gaze as a power mechanism. Moreover, Zvi-Riklis integrates the ethnic issue into the film alongside the gender issue. The boy, an Ashkenazi, concentrates his gaze on the girl, a Sephardi.[6] By intersecting the gender-sex axis with the ethnic axis, the camera exposes the penetrating gaze as nothing but a power mechanism, a human construct that can be used to oppress any minority or group. In thematizing the penetrating gaze, the film also reveals its inherent limitations.

Zvi-Riklis uses a similar juxtaposition of axes—this time nation/gender—in another short film, Lookout (1991). An Israeli soldier, posted on a roof in a refugee camp in the occupied territories, is preoccupied with a young Palestinian woman living across the street with her family. He follows her fortunes obsessively as she is forced into a marriage and becomes pregnant. Moreover, her father is jailed by the occupation authorities and her husband, involved in radical activities, uses her young brother to carry a grenade, concealed in a shoe box, to another radical outside. Upon seeing his father return from prison, the boy drops the box and is killed by the explosion. Appalled, the soldier shoots the husband. From the beginning, the camera follows the soldier manning the lookout as he observes the surrounding area. Besides the family across the way, he also watches people in the street. By using the penetrating gaze simultaneously on a Palestinian woman in the street and another Israeli soldier patrolling the area, the camera/director positions them on the same plane. This thematization of the gaze exposes it as a device that can be turned on whomever the power behind it chooses. The camera thus maintains its own position of power, filming the world from the soldier's vantage point, and filming him as well. In this way, the camera, in the act of photographing him, subjects the soldier to its own gaze. Thus, the position of power simultaneously lies in the hands of the soldier, who holds both the gun and a pair of binoculars, and those of the director, both of them white Israelis —that is, citizens of the occupying nation—and apparently heterosexual, bourgeois Jews. On the other hand, one is a man and the other a woman. And the woman, despite her being a citizen of the occupying country, observes the soldier from an alienated position. The overriding, oppressive power of the gaze derives from its capacity, as already noted, to reduce and reify the object it is observing. If that gaze is turned on me and I stand naked before it, I am both my physical body and an object, as I cannot return the gaze: powerless, I lower my eyes. The gaze represents established power, as Foucault (1977) has pointed out, while I am transformed into an object of gratification. The female director's subversive act is to thematize the subject. As a result, the film is not about the occupation but about the mechanisms for controlling others. Turning the mechanism of the gaze into the subject thus exposes it as a mechanism, discloses its limitations, and reveals ways in which one can defend oneself against it.

The film presents the major alternative modes for dealing with the penetrating gaze. The first, the simplest and most common, is to continue living under it, aware of its presence but ignoring it. The second is to block the gaze. Thus, in *Lookout*, the shutters of the family's apartment across the way are closed twice in the face of the soldier's binoculars, once by the young Palestinian woman who has aroused the soldier's interest and once by her husband. A third and more rebellious mode of coping with the gaze is to return it, refusing to lower one's eyes. This is done by the young Palestinian woman in an obvious and determined manner at least twice in the film. But above all, the film exposes the inner contradictions of the colonialist's position of power. The soldier, who apparently occupies an Olympian position of power, seeing and controlling everything, is ultimately revealed as someone who knows nothing and does nothing. In the middle of the film, Israeli troops break into the apartment that has so absorbed the soldier's attention. Having no advance knowledge of the break-in, he contacts the troops to find out why they are doing it. Helpless, he neither takes part in the break-in nor is able to prevent it, although it appears that he would have liked to. Later he has neither the foreknowledge of, nor the power to prevent, the blast that kills the young woman's small brother. Similarly, he lacks the power to prevent the girl from being married off against her will. The only power he has is the power to react after the fact. Not having generated the events, he can only react to them. Thus, he reacts to the death of the young boy by killing the husband who gave him the grenade. He reacts, just as the soldiers who broke into the apartment react, to something that has apparently happened somewhere else. Thus, the occupying Israeli can only react to that which others around him have caused to happen. The thematization of the penetrating gaze is a subversive act that reveals the gaze as a mechanism of oppression while at the same time exposing its limitations. One is thus given the prescription for surviving it, even if one is unable to expunge it, cancel it out, or undermine it. When the soldier kills the person responsible for the child's death, he is making a twofold statement: he is not responsible for the boy's death—"they" kill each other, he had no part in it—and he is the one who restores the moral order by killing in the name of universal justice.

The order that he has restored is that of the Zionist ethos, the ethos of selective killing. While soldiers (the occupation) are responsible for the situation that results in the killing, it is not, the film asserts, the occupier who has bloodied his hands. The occupier can distinguish, even in the heat of battle, between justified and unjustified killing and between moral and immoral killing. It is this order, this code, which the soldier seeks to restore. From the heights of the lookout, surveying everything except himself, he—and with him the camera—observes the world through a closed, coherent moral system that refuses to consider the Palestinian native's own moral system. The positioning of the native-born Israeli in this lofty moral position thus precludes any criticism of the occupation. Not only is there no discussion of the roots of the situation that led to the killing, but the occupation is presented as providing a foundation for implanting a superior system of moral norms—a traditional position of the colonialist toward the inferior native. But the absence of concrete political criticism does not diminish the criticism of the mechanism, the unmasking of the limitations of the power mechanism.

This absence of political criticism is linked to the one power position that cannot be avoided but is in no way subversive—that of the penetrating gaze of the camera. The power of the camera's eye cannot be nullified. True, the thematization of the penetrating gaze neutralizes its force, subversively exposing the mechanisms of power and oppression contained in the penetrating gaze of the soldier. Nevertheless, the fact that the camera remains with him all the time, seeing everything from his viewpoint alone, never taking the position of those who are subjected to his gaze, makes it into a full partner in the restoration of the Zionist moral order. This is the hegemonic side of this subversion. The subversive stance in Lookout does not, therefore, challenge the Zionist moral or communal ethos. Instead, it works in the space left by Zionism, the space of the sexual body. Although not focused on the sexual body, Lookout nevertheless uses the related apparatus, the penetrating gaze, for its subversive ends.

A good example of the subversive use of the sexual body to constitute the female subject while leaving the hegemonic norms intact is the film A Thousand and One Wives (1989), adapted by Michal Bat Adam, who also directed the film, based on the story of Dan Benaya Seri (1987). In this film, a woman filmmaker adapts a story written by a man about male experience into a film about female experience. The film centers on the sexual awakening of Flora, Naftali Siman-Tov's third wife. In both the story and the film, Naftali's two previous wives have died before bearing any children (he has apparently murdered them). Anxious about the fate of his third wife, Naftali decides that his dead wives were poisoned by his sperm. With

Flora, therefore, he only masturbates into a towel that she brings him every night. Afterward, she wraps herself in the towel, laundering it the next day. Into Flora's life comes Hamedian, a textile merchant, who gets Flora pregnant, although Flora herself is not entirely aware of what is happening. The rabbi points out Flora's pregnancy to Naftali, who, realizing that he is not the father, murders Flora too, thus restoring order. Although Seri's original story centers on Naftali, there are also allusions to Flora's desires. Bat Adam's film, on the other hand, centers on Flora's sexual awakening and her subversive actions. In the transition from story to film, the point of view does not change. Both Naftali's and Flora's points of view are represented in each. The difference, as noted, lies in the thematic emphasis. In the film, the transition in focus from Naftali to Flora is made by the camera alone, without dialogue. We do not hear Flora's voice: the camera merely observes her actions, her face, her movements. And silence is precisely what Naftali wants of Flora: "Why are you never quiet?" he asks. "Shut up!" (Seri 1987, 64). Lacking a voice, Flora cannot tell her own story. Thus, it is not she who constructs her biography but Naftali, and her attempt to digress from the lines of his story brings about her punishment. It is the camera that makes it possible for Flora to tell her own story—that is, to constitute her own world—and, in so doing, to subvert the original story's intention. However, the camera is used subversively, not rebelliously in a revolutionary manner. The only voice the film gives to the woman—aside from a few irrelevant pieces of scattered dialogue—is through her singing. The film opens and closes with a woman singing. Although the song also provides her with a voice, it is not a speaking voice, a logical voice, a voice that can formulate grievances against the world. It is simply sound. The change of focus achieved by the camera, the transition from the *telling* by Seri's omniscient and authoritative narrator (as shown by Hever 1990) to the *showing* in the film, endows the characters with more authority. Insofar as Flora is the film's dominant character, this narrative device enhances her authority. It now becomes her story rather than the narrator's even though it is told wordlessly. The omniscient narrator, whose irony in the story is pitted against Flora's naiveté, is replaced by a camera which, by providing a visual and authoritative presence for the woman's perspective, privileges it over that of the man. Herein lies the essence of the subversive act: in both the story and the film. Flora, even though she does not fully understand what she is doing, seeks sexual satisfaction with another man and becomes pregnant by him. At the same time, the film enhances this subversion by visually representing both the sexual awakening as well as the crystallization of a model of subversive female sexuality—thus bypassing the voicelessness of the heroine.

Flora's first act of subversion is to limit the effectiveness of the penetrating gaze. As Flora undresses on her wedding night, Naftali peeks through the keyhole. But Flora has placed a towel over the handle, thereby blocking his view. It is this same towel that will later absorb his semen. Moreover, Flora gazes at Naftali while he is asleep. Finally, a moment before her death, even as she cries out, she refuses to avert her eyes from his penetrating gaze. Flora's second act of subversion is to go to another man in order to fulfill her sexual desires. In the story, her sexuality is described in only a few words. Her sexual desire is awakened after the wedding when, on a walk, she finds Naftali's appearance pleasing and notices "that strange superfluous motion in his pants." "A dense smell filled her nose" (Seri 1987, 16), a smell that becomes the main metaphor for male sexuality, which is concretized in the smell of Naftali's semen: "The strange smell which so engrossed her the whole night again filled her nostrils. She believed, without knowing quite why, that this was the sticky smell of aged trees and indeed, when she brought the towel to her nose, all her hopes were realized [!]—carob jelly" (35). Naftali quickly hides the towel, "her new possession," under her clothes. The towel becomes a substitute for sex: "She never tired of looking at it . . . she only wanted to stretch out her arm and touch. Each time, excited by her loathsome craving, she would secretly draw the towel across her belly and rush off to the steam of the bath" (37). She demonstrates her strength through a penetrating gaze, and in place of the desired sexual contact she clings to the towel, which smells of carobs and which she takes with her to the bath—to do what? It is the camera that executes this action: the combination of laundering the towel and masturbating with it provides the main sexual scene of the film. Here Flora vents her sexual desires in a semi-masturbatory simulation of the sexual act. When she meets Hamedian, she feels "in her heart the sticky taste of carob jelly" (46). From that moment until she faints after apparently having had intercourse with him, the story presents her point of view: from her joy after the first meeting to her agitation at home in anticipation of the second meeting to her thoughts and her attempts to please Naftali retroactively, and through numerous images of rain, downpours, and droughts that, from the beginning, are constructed as an analogy to intercourse and fertility.

The film builds a much more complex story than the text, introducing an important event that does not occur in the story: Flora's act of injuring herself in anticipation of her second meeting with Hamedian. The act itself is an allusion to a story from the traditional text, *Sefer Hayashar* (Book of the Righteous), which recounts the attempted seduction of Joseph by Potiphar's wife, Zuleika. In the film that story is introduced through the character of Zuleika, a spinster who once gave up her lover and subsequently died, an allusion to Potiphar's wife. After falling ill out of longing for him, she invited her friends in to explain her actions: "She gave them citrons and knives to peel them and eat them with. And she gave the order and they dressed Joseph in fine clothes and brought him before them. And Joseph came before them and all the women looked at Joseph and saw his beauty and were unable to take their eyes from him. And they all cut their hands with the knives they held and covered all the citrons they had in their hands with blood." (Dan 1981, 200).

At the center of this story is the female penetrating gaze. A group of women (a group, and not a singular woman) gazes at a man who has been brought before them as a displayed object. While the text alludes only to Potiphar's wife's name, the film alludes to the entire story: Flora takes a sharp instrument and, intentionally cutting herself, draws blood. Her maddening desire connects her with Zuleika and her friends. Her desire must be satisfied. Whereas the book alludes to fertility, the film stresses sexuality and desire, thereby undermining the story through images, again, without sound. After the subversive act of constituting the sexual body comes the act of abolishing the body's limits, annihilating the distance between the body and what lies outside of it by mutilation, by the eruption of the body fluids. At this point one can contrast the positioning of the woman in the story and in the film. In the story it is her social position that is emphasized. In the film it is the sexual body.

Both texts, the written and the visual, are based on commonality and seriality. The title "The Thousand Wives of Naftali SimanTov" (changed in the film to *A Thousand and One Wives*) indicates an undifferentiated and serialized mass of women. The number one thousand is equivalent to unlimited (the thousand wives of King Solomon) or unparticularized. "In a thousand tongues people lay in wait for him [Naftali] under the bed" (Seri 1987, 24). And "even if you wait a thousand years you will never see her [Flora] dead," Naftali consoles himself (27).

In the story, Flora attempts to end the cycle, whereas Naftali seeks to thwart this attempt by restoring order by destroying her. Seriality is at the heart of woman's social positioning. To be a good woman means to be one of Naftali's wives, one of a group of undifferentiated women all of whom fulfill the same role, one in a chain of objects designed for his sexual satisfaction and for the constitution of his social position. "You are a good woman," says Naftali to Flora—until she becomes pregnant—and he repeats this before the murder. Flora disrupts this seriality by going to another man, thereby breaking the chain of good women and emerging as a woman undifferentiated from the mass, but her subversive attempt fails. Even the seriality itself is a simulation, a substitute, a transformation: all of the women in the series are interchangeable. The very act of placing them in a row is a simulation. The subversive—not revolutionary—act of female survival is an act of substitution: substituting sex for a towel, one man for another, a fetus for the anti-Christ. However, by turning to the body, the singular, the particular, the film brings this process of simulation to an end. Thus Flora, unable to overcome the power of social positioning, subverts it by choosing the sexual body for self-fulfillment. The film, acknowledging the impossibility of overcoming the force of social positioning, chooses, instead, to subvert it through the suppressed region of sexuality. But the film's subversion is much greater than the story's. Whereas the story focuses on the restoration of order, the film focuses on the sexual body; whereas the story focuses on the positioning of society and family—and, ipso facto, fertility—the film focuses on sexual awakening. In the story, the only threat to seri-ality is Flora's act of going to another man. In the film, the threat is greater, involv-ing the constitution of the sexual body and sexual awakening.

But the greater the subversion, the greater the failure. First of all the story, unlike the film, leaves open the possibility that the cycle will be broken, if only after the death of Flora. In the story, following the funeral, the rabbi says, "This interest in women, Mr. Naftali, even though the Torah demands it from us, per-haps it would be better to let them alone a little" (Seri 1987, 78). This sentence was cut out of the film, thereby eliminating the hope that the seriality would end. Furthermore, the fact that the film—though not the story—opens and closes with a funeral gives one a feeling of unending repetition: everything that happens after the first funeral will happen after this one, too, ad infinitum. The second thing that indicates the continuation of seriality in the film is the change in the posi-tioning of Zuleika. In the story, she refuses to marry any of the handsome men who ask for her hand. After her death, it is revealed that she had been in love with a Torah scholar, who loved her in return. His grandfather, however, begged her to leave him alone, and she died of a broken heart. None of this remains in the film.

In the film, Zuleika, pursuing a married man, refuses to relinquish her earthy life. Gazing at Flora like a vulture, she awaits her turn in the chain of wives. As Flora lies dying inside, Zuleika follows Naftali to his doorstep. Thus, Zuleika serves as an agent for continuing the cycle, ensuring the victory of familial and communal positioning over female sexuality. In the most subversive act of all, Flora, through her body, allegorically actualizes an act of redemption—the birth of the Messiah—whereas Naftali takes the unborn child to be the devil or the anti-Christ. Naftali notices something and, when Rebbi Duak explains to him that Flora is pregnant, Naftali tries to explain it away as something that happens among the gentiles. He tries to convince Duak that there once was a woman who conceived from a spirit and not from a man. But Duak rejects this explanation, thus denying the possi-bility that Flora could be the Holy Virgin Mother, uncontaminated by any "snake poison" (as Naftali considers his own semen). Consequently, Flora must die.

Here again, neither the character of Flora nor the film as a whole has the power to overcome the social positioning of women. Any attempt to do so is doomed to failure. If one adds to this the attempt of the film to build upon the suppressed sex-ual body, the failure is magnified: the seriality that Flora has attempted to break is destined to continue. In other words, the transition from the male text (of Seri) to the female text (of Bat Adam) is also a transition of focus from the family-society positioning to bodily subversion, from the good woman to sexual awaken-ing, which ends in the bodily concretization of the myth of redemption. The battle of the sexes thus becomes a battle between bodies: that of the Messiah and that of the woman. This intertextual element deflects the discussion to an area in which the body becomes the essential thing: it provides a structural affirmation of an ideological reading that sees the body as central to the gender plot. The female text, which attempts to crystallize a model of female sexuality, to constitute a female subject, is forced to do this in the margins, through suppressed elements: through the sexual body. It has not succeeded in successfully creating an alternative to the powerful Zionist model of social-professional-familial positioning, which is the dominant mechanism for turning the woman into the Other in Israeli cinema.

In the secular Zionist ethos, the body is mobilized for the historic event of redemption, the core of secular, messianic Zionism. Consequently, the body, valued primarily for its social-national function, is deprived of its privacy, its sexuality. However, in the subversive act of turning to the sexual body, Flora privileges a non-secular Sephardic messianism, a Sephardic otherness, which contrasts with Ashkenazi secular messianism. In this, Naftali, also a Sephardi Other, stands with her. His view of messianic redemption is also opposed to Zionism's secular version. Here, too, as in Coordania and Lookout, two kinds of otherness are portrayed, female and ethnic. Thus the focus of *A Thousand and One Wives* on the sexual body subverts the Zionist hegemony.

An attempt to challenge directly the dominant mechanism of social positioning is made in the "Divorce" episode of the film *Tales of Tel Aviv* (Ayelet Menachmi and Nirit Yaron, 1992). In earlier episodes, the women's professions are stereotypical. In "Sharona Honey," Sharona is an assistant art director in a country where this is not yet considered a real profession. In "Operation Cat," Zofit is both a reporter for a local journal who is fired from her job and a poet with a small modicum of success (one of her poems has been set to music). The first two episodes of *Tales of Tel Aviv* deal with the constitution of female sexuality ("Sharona Honey") and the constitution of an autonomous female subject ("Operation Cat"). At the end of the first story, Sharona screams "Why don't you listen to me?" at three of her four lovers, who insist on courting her contrary to her wishes. She insists on her right to choose her own sexuality and the kind of relationship she has with them. She does not want them bothering her all the time, making demands and proposals (especially for a common child) while ignoring what she has to say. She insists, in other words, on getting her own voice back, of being able to write her own story even if it does not jibe with that of her friends. And when she does not get what she wants, she leaves on the garbage truck that has come to clean up the city, ridding it (and her) of all the garbage that has accumulated. But, of course, this is a film about Sharona's sexuality and her sexual biography. Once again, in order to constitute the female subject, the film turns to the sexual body and the relevant mechanism—the penetrating gaze. Here it takes the form of the gaze of a male friend—through binoculars—on the roof across the street, and Sharona's gaze at the parade of men among whom she functions. While it is too difficult for her to challenge the social structure, she can, however, smash the binoculars, thus eliminating the male gaze and constituting herself as a sexual subject according to her own model.

This is the case in "Operation Cat" as well. Zofit is a stereotypically fragile, passive, helpless woman: she fails at a suicide attempt, loses her bank card, and finds that her job is not only not central to her life but also interferes with what has become central—rescuing a cat that has fallen through the grid of a sewer. The fact that the cat has become the focus of her life deflects her attention from far more serious matters, such as tending to her job and completing the arrangements for separating from her husband. The cat, which she succeeds in saving, is her only area of success. Zofit has applied to all the bureaucrats who run the municipal services, all male, except for the woman veterinarian of the S.P.C.A. She, by the way, is the only one whom Zofit dares to threaten. Finally, Zofit realizes that she alone is capable of saving the cat (saving herself?) and she does just that. She reaches this realization with the help of another woman, an assertive, creative career woman who is dying.

It is as if the film wants to say that such women have a place in this world only as disembodied mentors and not as real living creatures. Again, the constitution of an autonomous female subject—one who is not dependent upon or subservient to the surrounding male milieu, who is able to choose her own goals and attain them by her own efforts—cannot take place through a woman's social or professional positioning. It can only take place when this kind of positioning is nullified or at least marginalized through female solidarity or through the encouragement of a coveting male—in this case, one who not only covets her body but also appreciates her poetry. And in any event, the constitution of the female subject occurs through an act of simulation: saving the cat instead of herself. Only through the analogy of transformation can the female subject be constituted. Thus, Sharona constitutes herself as well as her biography around her sexual body and her sexuality. Zofit constitutes her subjectivity by projecting her world onto the travails of a cat. But neither of them can do it directly, just as the film itself cannot, by confronting the dominant mechanism of their marginalization-their social positioning. And then comes Tikva, the protagonist of the third episode, who tries to construct her own mechanism for obtaining a divorce. Tikva is a policewoman who does her job well, even managing to challenge the patriarchal rules of the game, which dictate sexual submission for job advancement. Tikva refuses to show favoritism in distributing parking tickets. She also performs well in her community role as a mother. Raising her children alone since her husband departed five years ago, she always keeps her promises to them. Thus, her social position is simultaneously that of a good woman—a perfect mother, holding an acceptable job—and an unflawed person—professionally honest, good parent. In short, she is a success. Tikva has not seen her runaway husband for five years. Although deserted by him, she cannot, according to rabbinical law, get a divorce without his consent. One day she spots him in a tall office building and begins to chase him. Here, too, she refuses to play by the rules. She steals a gun from a security guard and tries to force her husband to agree to a divorce. When her husband succeeds in escaping, she takes hostages and refuses to release them until her husband is brought back. Thus, she takes her destiny into her own hands and, for the first time in her life, determines her husband's destiny as well. Moreover, she is ready to accept the consequences of her action and pay the price—a jail sentence. Tikva begins her odyssey by choosing divorce, thereby remaining within the rabbinical system. When the security guard offers her another option—freeing herself from the established order by having an affair—she refuses to consider this option. She wants a divorce, to be set free not by an act of her own volition but by the rabbinical establishment that has imprisoned her in the first place. She tries to create her own mechanism for liberation by forcing the police to find her husband and bring him before the rabbinate. When that does not happen fast enough, the rabbinate—in the person of one of her hostages, a rabbi—gets the religious establishment itself to go after the husband. Returning the husband to the place where she is holding the hostages, they are now willing to perform a divorce on the spot. Although Tikva has succeeded in constituting herself as a social subject and forging the mechanism for her divorce, at the last moment she relents. She is unwilling to undergo an instant divorce and now wants her husband jailed. In the final analysis, she still needs the official sanction of the establishment, which, she feels, is preferable to her own.

The female gaze, the female camera/director, in "Divorce" attempts to constitute the autonomous female subject but stops short of challenging the dominant mechanism for the reification of woman, the mechanism of community or social positioning. A more accessible option is found in what has been suppressed, the sexual body, with its accompanying mechanism, the penetrating gaze, and its thematization. At this point, in accordance with the critical traditions of feminist theory, the question arises, how can one eliminate the penetrating gaze of the camera, considering that it is itself the active cinematic apparatus? Is, therefore, the feminist cinematic project doomed to failure, or does an alternative model exist, one that includes the power struggle as a legitimate component? One can assume that it is the second alternative that we are seeking—not to distance ourselves from the penetrating gaze but rather to internalize its operating mechanism and use it to our own ends.

Notes

1. See also Turin 1990; Seneca 1990.
2. Most recent Hollywood films in which women play leading roles are of this type. On the one hand, the woman, at the center of the movie, has some feminist traits. She has a non-stereotypical job, is autonomous and develops as a sexual being. However, these norms are subverted through the normative world of the film. This is accomplished by making negative judgments of the woman or by calling into question her professional abilities. See, for example, *Mermaids* (Richard Benjamin, 1990); *Blue Steel*

(Kathryn Bigelow, 1990); *Shirley Valentine* (Lewis Gilbert, 1989); *Always* (Steven Spielberg, 1989); and *Indecent Proposal* (Adrian Lyne, 1993).

3. The reasons for this are not certain. It may be because the number of women who fin-ish higher studies in cinema, and therefore produce short films, do not enter the film industry in as great numbers as men. Or, it may be that fewer funds, national or com-mercial, are entrusted to women directors. There does appear to be a correlation between the situation in the Israeli film industry and literature worldwide. In general, women seem to choose the short story form over the long novel. Perhaps the amount of time required by the shorter genre is better suited to women's economic and social situation resulting from family and home responsibilities. Similarly, until such time as women's artistic creativity is encouraged, they are not likely to embark on full-time film careers.

4. In Abraham Shlonsky's 1920 poem "Yizrael" (the valley), which praises the *halutz* (pio-neer) of the Third *Aliyah* (coming of the Jews to Israel for permanent residence), he transposes physical identity into the discourse of national rhetoric. And in Bialik's poetry, eroticism was almost always read in terms of national issues. On Zionism and the erotic, see also Biale (1992, 176–203).

5. For an extremely blunt, and controversial, example, see Yona Wallach's poetry.

6. On changes in the balance of the racial power structure between Ashkenazi and Sephardi in this scene, see Ben-Shaul (1987).

References

Arbuthnot, Lucie, and Gail Seneca. 1990. "Pre-Text and Text in Gentlemen Prefer Blondes." In *Issues in Feminist Film Criticism*, edited by Patricia Evens. Bloomington and Indianapolis: Indiana University Press.

Ben-Shaul, Nitzan. 1987. "The Politics of the Creator" (Hebrew), *Sratim* (Films) 3.

Bernheimer, Charles, and Claire Kahana, eds. 1985. *In Dora's Case*. New York: Columbia University Press.

Biale, David. 1992. *Eros and the Jews: From Biblical Israel to Contemporary America*. New York: Basic Books.

Dan, Joseph, ed. 1981. *Sefer Hayashar* (Book of the Righteous). Dorot Library. Jerusalem: Bialik Institute.

Foucault, Michel. 1977. *Discipline and Punish: The Birth of the Prison*. Translated by A. M. Sheridan Smith. New York: Pantheon.

Hever, Hannan. 1990. "On the Fiction of D. B. Seri" (Hebrew). *Siman Kriah* (20):394–397.

Lubin, Orly. 1993. "Women Read Women." *Theory and Criticism: An Israeli Forum* (3):65–78.

Mulvey, Laura. 1975. "Visual Pleasure and Narrative Cinema." *Screen*, 16, 3 (autumn).

———. 1981. "Afterthoughts on 'Visual Pleasure and Narrative Cinema,' inspired by *Duel in the Sun.*" *Framework* (6):15–17.

Penley, Constance, ed. 1988. *Feminism and Film Theory*. New York: Routledge; London: BFI.

Schnitzer, Meir. 1993. *Israeli Cinema: Facts, Plots, Directors, Opinions*. Jerusalem and Tel Aviv: Israel Film Archive, Jerusalem Cinémathèque and Kineret Publishing House.

Seri, Dan-Benaya. 1987. *Birds of the Shade*. Jerusalem: Keter.

Turin, Maureen. 1990. "Gentlemen Consume Blondes." In *Issues in Feminist Film Criticism*, edited by Patricia Evens. Bloomington: Indiana University Press.

Feminism under Siege

The Vicarious Selves
of Israeli Women Writers

I live on the top floors now, she summed it up to herself,
where there is a constant commotion, workrooms, children's
rooms, the kitchen, the living room, all kinds of things.
[Only] the cellar is locked, and I don't even know where the
key is [any more]. Perhaps one should not know.
   —FROM SHULAMITH HAREVEN, *A City of Many Days*[1]

IN THIS PASSAGE the age-old metaphor of the house as the image of its tenant is given an added twist. The vertical division of this dwelling, whose upper floors are full of movement and light in contrast to the locked cellar below, offers a clear analogue to Freud's topographic model of the human psyche. The female voice using this metaphor, however, seems to question the very foundation of the Freudian quest when she suggests that one may do better to leave the underground room of the unconscious inaccessible.

   This questioning of the usefulness of introspection grows out of the experience of Sarah Amarillo, the protagonist of the novel in which Shulamith Hareven reconstructs life in Jerusalem under the British Mandate, before and during World War II. Although the impulse for self-knowledge is quite palpable here, it clearly stops short of breaking into the locked psychological "cellar." Self-knowledge is thus displaced to externally observable facts, and a potential psychological exploration turns into a socio-cultural inquiry. Situated as it is a few pages before the end of the novel (184 in the Hebrew edition; 199 in the English translation), this arrested introspection functions as the author's culminating reflection on the uneasy coexistence of modern psychology within a society of collective persuasion in which female roles have been traditionally limited.

As *A City of Many Days* indicates, contemporary Israeli women novelists seemed to have shied away from telling their life stories directly.[2] While the Hebrew literary canon features a long list of women poets, until the last decade Hebrew prose was mostly the domain of male writers. The few women who excelled in fiction wrote short stories and novellas, mainly in the lyrical impressionistic mode (for example, Dvora Baron). Indeed, as early as the turn of the century, women were cast in a well-defined role by the arbiters of the renaissance of Hebrew, who declared, "Only women are capable of reviving Hebrew—this old, forgotten, dry, and hard language—by permeating it with emotion, tenderness, suppleness, and subtlety." This generous, as well as limiting, evaluation was offered in 1897 by Eliezer Ben-Yehuda, the first propagator of spoken Hebrew; and it is not easy to determine today whether the encouragement or the limitation was more effective.[3] It took more than half a century for the old barriers to begin crumbling. And it is only in the last two decades that a number of women have made the shift from short stories to novels, many of which are set in the past. Until very recently, however, none of these narratives came close to fictional autobiography, even in the arrested form found among Israeli male writers.[4] I would nevertheless argue, using the examples of Hareven and Shulamit Lapid, that it is in these apparently historical novels that one must look for the representation, however indirect, of the self of the Israeli female author.[5]

This generic choice is neither accidental nor arbitrary, for these quasi-historical novels camouflage a contemporary feminist consciousness, and express, in different degrees of displacement, their authors' struggles with questions of female subjectivity and gender boundaries.[6] In fact, one can point to a process of regression in the choice of historical settings, from Jerusalem of the 1920s and 1930s in *A City of Many Days* (1972) through Palestine of 1882 in Shulamit Lapid's *Gei oni* (1982; Valley of My Strength). However, this chronological regression is counterbalanced by a diametrically opposite progression in the feminist consciousness of the protagonists of these novels, who move from traditional gender roles in a patriarchal society to a utopian new womanhood, paradoxically projected back into the mythical past.

That they do this under siege, in a society that is fundamentally unfriendly to their quest, is part of the explanation of their literary choices, but also part of the paradox. For it is precisely those pressures that have rendered Israeli male subjectivity different from its western counterparts, that have also prevented the direct expression of Israeli female subjectivity. For contemporary European and American women, issues of selfhood and gender definition are inextricably bound up with feminism; as such, they automatically become politicized. But in Israel such an agenda would necessarily collide with the larger political issues that are always at the center of attention. Israeli women writers are therefore trapped in a double bind: unwilling to relegate themselves to marginalized women's journalism and female thematic, they are obliged to enter the mainstream in disguise, registering their social critique vicariously via their presumably historical protagonists. This phenomenon results, in part, from woman's problematic place in the Jewish tradition, which by and large excludes her from participating in man's public roles.[7] However, as in the writing of their male contemporaries, the sociopolitical pressures of Israel's reality and the major historical events of Israel's collective memory also work to inhibit psychological introspection and the quest for individual autonomy. It is precisely this embeddedness within a larger, collective order that is at odds with any feminist aspiration; and it is the slow and vicarious realization of this unavoidable conflict that is the subject of the following analysis.

For Sarah Amarillo, the protagonist of *A City of Many Days*, the pivotal historical moment is the breakdown of the Jewish-Arab equilibrium in Jerusalem of World War II. As the tension heightens, the narrative is permeated by a sense of an ending: "Something was ending, and something was about to begin" (136, 146 [see also 75, 77]). Jerusalem's oriental design, which the novel recapitulates in its lyrical impressionism, is doomed to oblivion, except in the literary reconstructions of its mourners. Jerusalem's polyphony of voices will be replaced by the "first-person plural" of the next generation, as the male protagonists wistfully observe:

> "All these men will be coming home from war now," said Professor Barzel. "They'll all have learned to fight. The country will change again. Everything will become more professional, the fighting too. The individual won't count any more-only the stupid plural. The plural is always stupid."
> "And what will be then, Elias?" asked Hulda worriedly.
> "We will be then," said Elias, so quietly that they couldn't be sure they had heard right. "For better or worse, we will be."
> (182, 197–198)

This is, the notorious "we" of the Jewish defense forces—"We are everywhere the first we, we, the Palmach," as their song proudly announced. Hareven's characters grieve this loss of the first-person singular, while rationalizing it as the unavoidable result of the political situation. Her ambivalence is further demonstrated by her treatment of Sarah's interior monologue quoted above. On one hand, she allows Sarah a measure of self-awareness, the admission that she lives "on the top floors." But then she lets her state flatly, without any change of tone, that "the cellar is locked, and I don't even know where the key is any more" (184, 199). Moreover, the attentive reader may note not only what is marked as "locked" but also what is marked by its absence: the curious omission of a bedroom from the list of rooms on the top floor, which passes unremarked.

Apparently, to join the war effort, Sarah must, like Professor Barzel before her, "skip over her own self" (ibid., see 122, 130). Barzel, the German-born physician who had trained her as a nurse in her youth, now insists that she help him prepare paramedics for the insecure, threatening future. It would seem that in this society under siege, male and female share the same lot. But this is not quite true, since it is Sarah and not Professor Barzel who registers the loss in psychological rather than social or intellectual terms. While he is reported to "have lost the key" to his hobbies and philosophical ideas (122, 130), Sarah is aware that what she misses is nothing less than the key to her own "underground room," to the cellar of her psychic apparatus (184, 199).[8] Yet this insight does not lead to any action. Neither the protagonist nor the authorial voice shows any signs of rebellion— "Perhaps one should not know." On the contrary, despite the great losses, the novel closes on a poetic note of mystical transcendence:

> A silent presence, the whole city spread at her feet, and [she] looked at the lambs wool light out over the mountains, over the houses drowning in radiance, as if once this city, long, long ago, soon after Creation, had burst from some great rock and its truth flown molten and shiny over the hills. She could feel the moment to the quick. Now this is me, she told herself, now this is me, here on this hill, with this feeling of great peace [reconciliation] that will never last, or standing in the street, people know [recognize] me: I have three sons and so little time. Now this is me in this moment of hers. Tomorrow I'll be gone and the street will be gone. Or another street and another time. And always, forever, this fleecy pile of light, that rock tumbled halfway down the hill to a lonely stop, a terraced alley, a dripping cypress tree, a caper plant in a wall. A place to walk slowly. A place to touch the sky: now it is close. To breathe in mountain-and-light. Now.

It is hard to exaggerate the contrast between this reconciled woman and the spunky girl that Sarah once was. Described by herself and others as a chip off the strong and feisty (mostly male) Amarillo block, those who "are always quarreling with life" (36, 113; 36, 119). This "big" emancipated woman now takes a turn toward submission, "lying low in realities, the wick trimmed all the way down" (179, 194). The woman who prided herself on her sharp tongue and unabashed "meanness" is now growing emotional over her motherly duties. And the daughter who as a young girl vented her rage against her absent father by screaming "No father! No mother! No grandpa! No grandma! No nothing!" (16, 14) is now processing poetically her discovery of his helpless insanity: "I went down into a garden of nut trees [to see the fruits of the valley]. Down down down. To the rockbottom beauty of madness" (187, 202; cf. *Song of Songs* 6:11). Again, the anguish is camouflaged by the indirection of metaphor. And again, both protagonist and narrator stop on the brink of the abyss: "Sarah looked at him for a long while, the great question that had haunted her for so long, now a spent little answer cast mindlessly before her." This is all Hareven grants her protagonist by way of self-scrutiny. Staged as it is two pages before the end of the novel, this encounter loses its potential force as an all-embracing psychological explanation.

Even Sarah, whose education is at the core of the plot, is rendered only by brief surface brush strokes. Moreover, she does not occupy center stage by herself; as the lyrical fusion of her last narrated monologue makes clear, she shares it with another female, the city of the title of the book. It is Jerusalem who is the strongest presence in this novel, because, ironically, it is "she" who embodies the powers of history: "This city abides no one's decision about who they are. She decides for them, she makes them, with the pressure of stones and infinite time. She teaches humility" (121, 129). In the final analysis, it is history rather than psychology that circumscribes human action in this novel, subsuming both anguish and pleasure under its impersonal workings. Yet the closing statement of the poetic coda makes clear that there is a place for the female subject. Despite the constant effort of the authorial voice to decentralize its focus, to multiply its points of view, Sarah emerges as the central consciousness of the narration. The more the rich mosaic of the past disintegrates, the more her introspective voice usurps that of the ironic narrator, culminating in her final monologue.

It is perilous to see in Sarah any sort of direct self-representation. For Shulamith Hareven has not followed the lead she herself suggested. She never adopted the autobiographic modality in her writing, and except for one collection of stories partially addressing women's issues (*Loneliness*, 1980; available in English as *Twilight and Other Stories*, 1992), she has shunned female protagonists altogether. *A City of Many Days* stands alone in her oeuvre, written after two books of poetry and two collections of stories (1962–1970), and followed by more collections of poems, essays, short stories, and two possibly allegorical novellas whose narrated time is the biblical past.[9] Moreover, Hareven is notorious for her refusal to participate in any forum dedicated to women's literature; she does not believe in women writers as a category, and she has often claimed that a writer is a writer regardless of gender. At the same time, she is politically active, voicing her ideological positions in her oral pronouncements and excellent essays.[10] But when critics tried to read her political convictions into her latest biblical novellas, she vehemently protested that art is art and should not be confused with one's worldly preoccupation.[11]

In other words, the woman behind the novel is an engaged person of clearly drawn convictions and priorities. Feminism, however, is not among them, as *A City of Many Days* complexly demonstrates. On the one hand, cross-gender equality as a realistic possibility is an unquestioned premise of this novel, for without it the characterization of Sarah would be totally spurious. In fact, in her independence of spirit, intolerance of weakness, and provocative sexual freedom, she is almost a parody of the typical male adolescent. On the other hand, by equipping her with a weak father who is easy prey for false female charms and a victim of mental

illness, and a strong paternal aunt, the colorful, single but happy Victoria (no less),
Hareven seems to exaggerate the feminist cliché of transcending gender roles.

Sarah starts from a non-gendered dichotomy, rejecting one model and adopting another without any problem. Yet it is marriage and motherhood that pose
the real test. How would this male-modeled, autonomous woman function as a
wife and mother? Superbly, of course, but at a cost. After giving birth to her first
son, Sarah for the first time allows weakness to penetrate her hitherto armored
psyche. The self-centered, unrelational ego restructures itself, but reacts with a
sense of loss and fear: "Help me, Grandpa," she prays from her maternity bed,
"because a frightening vulnerability has opened up in me today" (111, 118). But
if we think that motherhood is the end of androgyny, we are mistaken, at least
as far as this novel is concerned. It is the father, not the mother, who verbalizes
the effect of parenthood on the self: "The first child forces you to define yourself.
When the second comes you are already defined. Not just as a parent. Whatever
you are and aren't, you can be sure that's what your child will learn to demand
from you" (112, 119).

At this point of the narrative, just past the midpoint of the story, the myth
of male/female equality still holds. But not for long, as in the following pages we
witness the deterioration of Arab-Jewish relations and the palpable echoes of World
War II. Life is disrupted, individual destinies get farcically and hopelessly entangled
in plots they do not comprehend. The dichotomy of weak/strong, so hopefully deconstructed in the human sphere, ominously sneaks back into people's political
discourse. Against this background, Sarah slowly emerges to her difference only
to realize that under these circumstances she cannot take this difference anywhere.
The motive power behind her emergence is, predictably, a chance rekindling of
a youthful love. But just as predictably, this emotional reawakening is painfully
cut off, undermined by the historical moment of underground activities and military voluntarism of men at war. All that she has left is acceptance of her unexamined
inner life. So that when her self-conscious "I" is finally vocalized, it is only to be
defined in terms of others: "They recognize me: I have three sons and so little time."
The irony could not be any greater: Sarah Amarillo, the paradigm of the new,
Jerusalem-born Jewish woman—echoes of the social-Zionist ethos of the "new man/
Jew" not unintentional here!—falls back on the most traditional and often
maligned Jewish definition of womanhood. Like the biblical Sarah, she gains
status through motherhood, and more significantly through the recognition of
others. In the Hebrew phrase *makirim oti* (they recognize me), she is clearly the
passive receptor of the action.

In this novel, the celebration of the self, feminist or not, is temporarily com-
promised by the historical circumstances dramatized in this novel. The sociopolitical
conditions that have given rise to the ideology of "we," the "stupid first person plural," have also dictated the suppression of the Freudian quest and the throwing

away of the key to the psychic underground room. But all this is historically, not universally or essentially, determined.[12] And if the female subject of this narrative cannot be privileged with a fully autobiographical voice, she is allowed the empowerment of existential transcendence. It is the eternal female Other, Jerusalem, that offers a moment of ecstasy, of metonymic submersion: "Now this is me, she told herself, now this is me, here on this hill, with this feeling of great peace [reconciliation]. . . . Now this is me in this moment of hers. . . . A place to touch the sky: now it is close. To breathe in mountain-and-light. Now."

The uniqueness of Hareven's position on feminism among Israeli writers is paralleled by the splendid isolation of her heroine among Israeli female protagonists. In no other novel has the gap between lofty ideals—authorial and Zionist, intratextual and contextual—and the limitations of reality been so sensitively, if ambivalently, dramatized. In some sense, this novel was ahead of its time. In the early seventies, the horizon of expectations was not yet ripe for a literary discussion of feminism, even in its moderate, selective form. It is not surprising, then, that *A City of Many Days* was received as another nostalgic tale about Jerusalem, "lacking highly significant themes and conceptual contents."[13] That the issues of gender and female subjectivity, as well as their conflict with the historical constraints, are central to the novel passed totally unnoticed. It goes without saying that the potential critique of Zionist ideology implied by this material was not even surmised.

It would take a whole decade, and the stimulus of the Yom Kippur War (1973) and its aftermath, for the next attempts at female self-representation to materialize. Although Shulamit Aloni's treatise on women's deplorable status within the Israeli legal system, *Women as Human Beings*, appeared in 1973, the 1978 report of a Knesset commission on the status of women still concluded that "their contribution to society was marginal and supportive by nature . . . a reflection of their political status and the inclination of the Labor Movement elite to view them as voters but not as decision makers."[14] In the following decade and a half only a gradual and incomplete change has taken place.

Still, the distance traveled by Hebrew readers in the 1970s can be readily measured by the openness with which Shulamit Lapid's *Gei oni* (1982), a highly popular historical novel, tackled the very issues upon which Hareven had circumspectly touched a decade earlier. Here we do not find metaphoric indirection and nuanced play of voices. On the contrary, in a realistic, rather coarse style, in which dialogues and interior monologues are stylistically indistinguishable, the third-person narration weaves its way through a maze of relationships that would easily rival those of any Hollywood or television romantic melodrama. Nothing is implied here, not even the characters' most intimate reflections. Thoughts, emotions, ideology, and popular psychology are all evenly spread out as if illuminated by the bright Israeli sun. Yet despite its limitations, Gei oni caught the imagination of Israeli

readers in an unprecedented manner. In the first place, it played into the wave of
nostalgia that swept the country in the 1980s, when the first centenary of the earliest Jewish Aliyah (wave of immigration) to Palestine was celebrated. Indeed, Shulamit Lapid, until then a rather obscure short story writer, wrote her first novel
in anticipation of this anniversary.[15] In that year the Galilean settlement Rosh Pinah,
whose earlier name was Gei Oni, celebrated one hundred years of its existence.
Judging by the reception the book enjoyed, the timing was right. Readers exhibited great hunger for the richly documented panorama of that distant past filtered
through a fictional prism. And this was not the only reason for the novel's success. Readers were no doubt responding to the novelty of being introduced to a
serious historical reconstruction through the eyes and mind of Fanya, a young Russian immigrant who joins Gei Oni in the opening scene and remains the central
consciousness through which the narrative is vocalized throughout the novel.

Yet one must inquire why a strong independent female settler was considered
such a novelty. Wasn't the pioneer movement, indeed the Zionist ethos in general, supposed to have promoted the equality of women? In fact, wasn't the
woman question one of the basic issues debated, and deemed solved, by the early
communes and kibbutzim?[16] The answer is, of course, yes to all of the above, but
only as long as we remember to add the qualifier "in theory." For what recent research
has shown is that in practice, neither the early settlers nor the second wave of immigrants at the turn of the century had transcended the patriarchal norms of their
home communities in Europe.[17] And as Shulamit Lapid herself has recounted, she
could find no historical model for her heroine in the archival records of Gei Oni/
Rosh Pinah.[18] As the jacket of the book states, the names of those "giant women"
who were part and parcel of the early settlement wave "are absent from history
books because the records of the saviors of the motherland list only men." Even
among the figures of the Second Aliyah, Lapid could make use only of one exceptional personality, Manya Shohat (1879–1959).[19] Fanya had to be invented; here
is a woman who "did not know she was a feminist," but whom the contemporary
reader recognizes as such.

Gei oni succeeds in creating a narrative frame that authentically preserves the
patriarchal way of life of the 1880s while at the same time accommodating a fictitious protagonist whose own norms would satisfy contemporary feminist expectations by piecing together two novelistic genres: the settler epic and the romantic
melodrama. On one level, *Gei oni* is a typical settlement drama, realistically
depicting the struggles against all odds of the small Galilean group in the early 1880s.
The chief antagonist of this plot is nature itself, the mythic Mother Earth. In this
story she is no welcoming bride; as we join the narrative, she has been holding
back her gifts for two consecutive years. Severe drought has chased away most of
the pioneers, leaving behind just a few tenacious, idealistic families, including that
of Yehi'el, the male protagonist.

On another level, this is a typically euphoric heroine's text, a predictable love story whose models are not only the canonic texts adored by Fanya—Tolstoy's *Anna Karenina* and the novels of Jane Austen (161)—but also popular modern romances.[20] Fanya is the self-conscious budding young woman, who struggles to preserve her independent spirit while falling in love with her enigmatic "dark prince." The latter, for his part, is "handsome like the Prince of Wales" (34, 69, 85) and "wise like King Solomon" (117); he falls in love with Fanya's looks the moment he sees her but keeps the secret to himself. Since neither the reader nor Fanya gets to know the truth before half the story is over, a chain of romantic misunderstandings and jealousies constitute the better part of the plot.

One must ask whether Lapid has not wandered too far afield from founding mothers, since the conventions of the romantic novel cannot contain a fighting, independent spirit like Manya Shohat. Lapid could not have sustained her model and satisfied her feminist quest had she kept the model intact, nor could she write a true historical novel and stay as close to Fanya's consciousness as she did. She resolves this problem, however, by splicing the two genres together; from this intersection a new model emerges, one that generously accommodates contemporary expectations. To begin with, Fanya's romance deviates from the romantic model in one crucial detail: its denouement does not coincide with the closure of the novel. Nor does its culmination lead to a proposal or an engagement, since her love affair takes place within the boundaries of a marriage. And our two protagonists are atypical as well: Fanya is not only an orphan, she is a sixteen-year-old survivor of a Russian pogrom (the infamous pogroms of 1881/82, especially devastating in the Ukraine, that are credited with having inspired the first wave of immigration to Palestine), who finds refuge in the Promised Land, accompanied by an old uncle, a deranged brother, and a baby, her initially unwanted fruit of rape in that pogrom. Yehi'el, who happens to see her upon her arrival in Jaffa, is a twenty-six-year-old widower and a father of two, one of the few courageous souls still left in the nearly desolate Gei Oni.

As the narrative opens, we are privileged to hear Fanya's reflections after a hasty betrothal in Jaffa. While Yehi'el's motives are not disclosed, it soon becomes clear that for Fanya this is not just a marriage of convenience but also a marriage of appearances. On arriving in Gei Oni, she insists on separate sleeping arrangements, a rather unexpected turn within the conventions of the romance but a perfectly plausible step for a psychologically conceived character still in pain from her traumatic past. The attentive reader, however, will notice a structural and symbolic analogy in this otherwise realistically motivated action. It is not only the human bride who denies her husband her favors; with the drought continuing, the fertilization of Mother Earth is also prevented.

There is a perfect symmetry, then, between the two plots: the psychological and the mythic, the romantic and the historical. In both, the male principle is initially defeated and no consummation is possible. This symmetry does not escape Yehi'el himself, who, unaware of Fanya's trauma, reacts to her refusal by saying: "When you change your mind, let me know. I ask for favors only from the land" (45). To get the story rolling again, both female protagonists must give in; it is against the background of the long-awaited rains (117, 121, 123) that the passionate (and confessional) reunion between Fanya and Yehi'el finally takes place (119–128) and the euphoric plot seems to have reached its happy ending.

But not quite. For in the second part of the narrative, the settlement plot comes back with a vengeance and leans down heavily on the delicate balance of the new romantic attachment. Not unlike Hareven's Jerusalem, the Galilee, or Mother Earth—or perhaps the pioneering quest itself—exerts pressure on the human subjects of this story, limiting their freedom of choice and forcing them into its mold. But unlike Hareven, Lapid seems less willing to accept the verdict of the historical moment, of the Zionist "dream of redemption, burning like fire in the bones" (103–104, 144, 175). She does not have Fanya "skip over her own self," as Sarah did in A City of Many Days, but rather lets her develop her female subjectivity despite and against the pressures of the collective vision, with all its tragic consequences. By so doing, Lapid unwittingly blends her two models into a third, a novel of experience and education that may be rather fanciful for the 1880s but is totally satisfying to readers one hundred years later.

Predictably, Fanya achieves her independence through a series of tasks that she undertakes in order to save her husband and home from the devastation wrought by Mother Nature. We find her breaking into the male-dominated worlds of commerce, political discussion, even armed self-defense. At the same time, she does not deny her difference from the male world around her (104, 144, 175). Her personal code is defined, then, as the freedom to choose the best of the two worlds, to move freely from one to the other. More than her predecessor in Hareven's novel, this heroine fully embodies cross-gender equality as she shuttles between home and world, Gei Oni and Jaffa, taking care of husband and children, and conducting business. Yehi'el turns out to be just as exceptional. Although he does not fully approve of Fanya's "androgynous" tendencies, he does not stand in her way, which is more than can be said of any of his peers (109, 172–173, 188, 236). The result is a virtual reversal of conventional gender roles, with Yehi'el staying close to home and Fanya going into the world, and more importantly, the transformation of Fanya from a child-bride into a mature wife-companion, fully aware of her choices, sexual as well as social.

It is only natural, then, that as the novel comes to a close and Yehi'el succumbs to exhaustion and malaria, the reader is ready to embrace Fanya's experience as a necessary training for her ultimate task in the perpetuation of the mythical male quest. But in an ironic twist, Fanya, though ready to take up the role, perceives it as something alien, not her own script: "Should she sell their home?

Driving Yehi'el out of his dream? This home and this land were the purpose of his life. Once again fate has decreed that she realize others' dreams. Has she ever had her own dreams? But perhaps everyone is like this? Everyone realizes someone else's dream?" (256). Is this a feminist protest lamenting the lot of women in general, or a specific charge against the androcentric Zionist dream? And who is the "everyone" of the final questions: women? all people? The lines seem to blur here, leaving the reader with a sense of unfocused grievance. For what is read throughout the novel as a critique of a male-engendered ideology— "Her father's dream of rebirth has turned into sacred madness that now consumes her youthful years, her life" (102)—is now taking an existential turn, possibly hiding behind the human condition.

We should not be surprised, then, that Lapid does not give her heroine the chance to try to make it on her own. On the last page, the plot of the romance prevails. Sasha, an old acquaintance, himself a survivor of the Russian pogroms in the Ukraine, reappears, asking permission "to help and be helped." With this new beginning, the novel reverts to its original two models: the historical and the romantic. Subjective experience is embedded again in Jewish collectivity— "This is what we Jews do. Start all over again. Again. And again. And again"— only to be taken over by an old/new romance closure: "'I need you, Fanya! Will you allow me to help you?' Fanya looked at him wondering. Then she thought that if he hugged her, her head would barely reach his shoulder. And then her eyes filled with tears" (266).

It is evident that this quasi-historical, quasi-feminist romance set a century ago may be read as a vicarious representation of a contemporary female quest. Lapid's lack of distance from Fanya (ironic or other), as well as the narrator's narrow point of view, undermine the work's claim to being a historical novel. Rather, the reader receives the impression that the development of the historical heroine represents the concerns and expectations of a contemporary consciousness that present-day Israeli reality cannot satisfy. In some sense, *Gei oni* is a feminist novel of education masquerading as a more acceptable genre, the historical novel. Lapid obviously felt that Israeli society of the early 1980s would accept a feminist identity as a historical projection but would find it difficult to digest it as a realistic proposition for the here and now.

This impression is further reinforced by the unmistakably contemporary feminist protest of one of Lapid's earliest stories, "The Order of the Garter," and by the totally female orientation of her oeuvre in the last few years.[21] Although, like Hareven, she does not consider herself a feminist, she has been limiting herself, by her own confession, "to women's thematic," and perceives herself as "small, delicate, and becoming more and more aggressive" at the "ripe age of fifty-four."[22] Thus, her recent novel, *Local Paper* features Lisa, a lower middle-class woman journalist in a contemporary provincial town (Beer Sheva).[23] In this popular quasi detective story, Lapid does what she did not dare to do in *Gei oni*. She imagines a female character more common in contemporary America than in Israel: an unmarried woman who is proud of her work ethic, of her professionalism, and whose priorities are working and being in love. Yet despite this daring move, Lapid's penchant for romance is operative here as well, although from a more ironic perspective. For if matrimony has totally lost its appeal ("I have seen my sisters," Lisa explains), the romantic attachment has not. Like Fanya, Lisa gets her reward in the form of a "dark prince," updated for the 1980s: a tawny, handsome, rich, and worldly divorcé, whose timely information rescues Lisa from the imminent danger of losing her job.

Working within the conventions of the popular romance, Lapid has created female subjects whose identity seems to be much more seamless and unconflicted than those created by Hareven and other women writers. While Hareven, for example, consciously questions the place of individual autonomy, gender difference, and psychological determinism in a society under siege, Lapid uses the historical and ideological materials as a setting against which her protagonists reach toward their optimal development. By the same token, she does not subject her own premises about gender to a serious scrutiny. Motherhood, for example, is never really problematized. Lisa rejects it out of hand, and Fanya just weaves it into her busy schedule, although it is never clear how. Nor does she indulge in a true psychological exploration of her characters. In a curious way, the wealth of information we accumulate about them, even about their past, does not allow any meaningful conceptualization. Lapid is content to follow their present entanglements to their happy endings without delving into the larger questions posed by the issues she has dramatized.

These deeper concerns are explored in the latest work of other writers, including Amalia Kahana-Carmon and Ruth Almog, who attempt to overcome the state of historical siege so convincingly demonstrated by Hareven and Lapid.[24] In doing so they uncover new sets of limitations and other kinds of psychological and existential states of siege for women, an inevitable ironic consequence, perhaps, of the artistic endeavor and the human experience it attempts to represent.[25]

Notes

A more extensive version of this chapter appeared in *Prooftexts* 10 (1990):493–514.

1. Shulamith Hareven, *Ir yamim rabim* (Tel Aviv, 1972), 184. Subsequent references appear in the body of the text. The second page numbers given refer to the English version, *A City of Many Days*, translated by Hillel Halkin (New York, 1977).

2. This is not to say that women do not use autobiographic materials—Naomi Fraenkel, Rachel Eitan, Amalia Kahana-Carmon, Dahlia Ravikovitch, Hedda Boshes, and Yehudit Hendel do—but rather that their narratives generally do not take the shape of autobiographical retrospection. On the obvious exception, Netiva Ben Yehuda's *Bein hasfirot* (Between the Calendars, 1981), see my article, "Gender In/Difference in Contemporary Hebrew Fictional Autobiographies." *Biography* 11, 3 (summer

1988):189–209; reprinted in *Sex, Love and Signs: European Journal for Semiotic Studies* 1 (1989): 435–456.

3. It was also easier to write verse without the training in classical Hebrew traditionally reserved for males. It is no coincidence that the first modern Hebrew prose writer, Dvora Baron, had been raised "as a son," instructed in the sacred sources by her father who was a rabbi. On the emergence of women's poetry see Dan Miron, "Founding Mothers, Stepsisters" (Hebrew). *Alpayim* 1 (June 1989): 29–58; and see a translated excerpt from this work, "Why Was There No Women's Poetry in Hebrew Before 1920?" In *Gender and Text in Modern Hebrew and Yiddish Literature*, edited by Naomi B. Sokoloff, Anne Lapidus Lerner, and Anita Norich (New York and Jerusalem, 1992), 65–91.

4. See my "Living on the Top Floor: The Arrested Autobiography in Contemporary Israeli Fiction." *Modern Hebrew Literature* 1 (fall/winter 1988):72–77.

5. Shulamit Lapid, *Gei oni* (Tel Aviv, 1982). Page references will appear in the body of the text, with quotations in my translation.

6. Another example of this is Amalia Kahana-Carmon, "The Bridge of the Green Duck" (Hebrew). In her *Lemalah bemontifer* [Up on Montifer]. (Tel Aviv, 1984), 59–184.

7. See *On Being a Jewish Feminist*, edited by Susannah Heschel (New York, 1983).

8. Although the precarious position of Freudian psychology is most palpable in the language and plot of this narrative, it is not easy to determine whether it derives from the historical materials themselves (the 1930s and1940s), or from the personal ambivalence of the author, who expressed her contempt of classical Freudian psychology in conversation with me (16 August 1989). The problematic reception of psychoanalysis in Hebrew literature is the subject of my "Freudianism and Its Discontents" (work in progress) and is partially presented in my "Back to Vienna: Zionism on the Literary Couch." In *Vision Confronts Reality*, edited by Sidorsky et al. (Rutherford, N.J., 1989), 310–335.

9. *Sone' hanissim* (Jerusalem and Tel Aviv, 1983) was published in English as *The Miracle Hater*, translated by Hillel Halkin. (Berkeley, Calif., 1988); *Navi* [A Prophet]. (Jerusalem and Tel Aviv, 1988) was also translated by Hillel Halkin. (Berkeley, Calif., 1990).

10. *Tismonet Dulcenea* [The Dulcenea Syndrome]. (Jerusalem, 1981).

11. See, for example, her essay "The First Forty Year." *The Jerusalem Quarterly* 48 (fall 1988): 3–28, especially 25–26; and an interview with Helit Bloom in *Bamahaneh* (March 1, 1989).

12. See on this point the succinct analysis by Naomi Chazan, "Gender Equality? Not in a War Zone!" *Israeli Democracy* (summer 1989): 4–7.

13. Gershon Shaked, "Imbued with the Love of Jerusalem." In *Gal ahar gal* (Wave after Wave in Hebrew Narrative Fiction) (Jerusalem, 1985), 13.

14. See Dafna Sharfman, "The Status of Women in Israel: Facts and Myth." *Israeli Democracy* (summer 1989):12–14.

15. Lapid's earlier collections of short stories are *Mazal dagim* [Pisces]. (Tel Aviv, 1969); *Shalvat shotim* [Fools' Paradise]. (Tel Aviv, 1974); *Kadahat* [Malaria]. (Tel Aviv, 1979).

16. See, for example, Elkana Margalit, *Hashomer hatsa'ir me'adat ne'urim lemarksizm mahaphani* [Hashomer Hatsa'ir: From Youth Movement to Revolutionary Marxism]. (Tel Aviv, 1971).

17. See Dafna Izraeli, "The Labor Women Movement in Palestine from Its Inception to 1919" (Hebrew). *Cathedra* 32 (1984):109–140; and Deborah Bernstein, "The Status and Organization of Urban Working Women in the 20s and 30s" (Hebrew). *Cathedra* 34 (1985):115–144.

18. Private communication, 1984. Literature does not score much higher on this point, the few exceptions such as Rivka Alper's *Hamitnahalim bahar* and Moshe Shamir's *Hinumat kalah* notwithstanding.

19. Rachel Yanait Ben Zvi's fascinating biography of Shohat, *Before Golda*, was recently published in English, translated by Sandra Shurin (New York, 1988); it was also the

basis of a documentary film. See also Shulamit Reinharz, "Toward a Model of Female Political Action: The Case of Manya Shohat, Founder of the First Kibbutz." *Women's Studies International Forum* 7, 4 (1984): 275–287. On the situation of women in this period, see the essays in *Pioneers and Homemakers: Jewish Women in Pre State Israel*, edited by Deborah S. Bernstein (Albany, N.Y., 1992).

20. Nancy Miller, *The Heroine's Text* (New York, 1980).

21. In Lapid, *Mazal dagim*, 1969.

22. See interview with her in *Lilith* (summer 1989): 20. The same issue also includes a translation of one of her new "aggressive" stories, "The Bed."

23. Shulamit Lapid, *Meqomon* [Local Paper]. (Jerusalem, 1989).

24. Ruth Almog, *Shorshei avir* [Dangling Roots]. (Jerusalem, 1987). For Kahana-Carmon see above, n. 6. See my "The 'Other Within' in Contemporary Israeli Fiction." *Middle East Review* 22, 1 (fall 1989): 47–53, for a discussion of some of these issues.

25. See my "Feminism and Its Discontents in Israeli Literature." In *Voices of Postmodernism in Israeli Fiction 1973–1993*, edited by Alan Mintz (Hanover, N.H., 1994).

About the Editor

ESTHER FUCHS is professor of Near Eastern studies and Judaic studies at the University of Arizona in Tucson. Born in Tel Aviv, she graduated from the Hebrew University in Jerusalem in the history of Jewish thought and English literature and completed her Ph.D. at Brandeis University. She authored books in Hebrew and numerous essays on S.Y. Agnon, Israel's Nobel Prize Laureate in literature, and a first book of interviews with leading Israeli authors in the early 1980s. She also published a Hebrew volume of poetry on being the daughter of Holocaust survivors (1983). She was assistant professor at the University of Texas in Austin, 1979–1985, and became associate professor at the University of Arizona in 1985. Her first book on gender and writing in Israeli literature, *Israeli Mythogynies: Women in Contemporary Hebrew Fiction* was published in 1987. She has authored several essays on the representation of women in Holocaust films, and edited a book of interdisciplinary essays entitled *Women and the Holocaust: Narrative and Representation* in 1999. In 2000 she has collected some of her pioneering essays on gender and biblical literature in a book entitled *Sexual Politics in the Biblical Narrative: Reading the Hebrew Bible as a Woman*. As professor of Near Eastern studies, she has taught undergraduate and graduate courses on such topics as Israeli women, women and Judaism, and feminist approaches to the Hebrew Bible and gender issues in Middle Eastern studies. Most recently she has published essays on the politics of Jewish Women's studies.

About the Contributors

DEBORAH S. BERNSTEIN is professor of sociology and anthropology at Haifa University. She is the author and editor of several publications on gender and Israeli society, among them *The Struggle for Equality: Urban Women Workers in Pre-State Israeli Society* (1987) and *Pioneers and Homemakers: Jewish Women in Pre-State Israel* (1992).

JUDITH BUBER AGASSI is professor emerita of sociology at the Research Authority of Tel Aviv University. She is the author of several pioneering essays on the status of women in Israel and is currently at work on a study of the women's concentration camp Ravensbrück.

TAMAR EL-OR is professor of sociology and anthropology at the Hebrew University and head of the Lafer Center for Gender Studies. Among her publications on Israeli religious women are: *Educated and Ignorant: Ultraorthodox Jewish Women and their World* (1994) and *Next Year I Will Know More: Literacy and Identity Among Young Orthodox Women in Israel* (2002).

AYALA EMMETT is associate professor of anthropology at the University of Rochester. She is the author of *Our Sisters' Promised Land: Women, Politics and Israeli-Palestinian Coexistence* (1996).

YAEL S. FELDMAN is the Abraham I. Katsh Professor of Hebrew Culture and Literature and professor of comparative literature and gender studies at New York University. She is the author and editor of several publications on gender and literary theory, among them *No Room of Their Own: Gender and Nation in Israeli Women's Fiction* (1999).

MANAR HASSAN is a Ph.D. student in the department of sociology and anthropology at Tel Aviv University. She has published several articles on the status of Palestinian women in Israel.

HANNA HERZOG is associate professor of sociology at Tel Aviv University. She is the author of several publications on gender and politics, among them *Realistic Women: Women in Israeli Local Politics* (Hebrew, 1994), and *Gendering Politics: Women in Israel* (1999).

DAFNA N. IZRAELI (1937–2003) was professor of sociology and head of the department of sociology and anthropology at Bar Ilan University in Tel Aviv. She is the author and editor of numerous publications on gender and society in Israel, among them *The Double Bind: Women in Israel* (1982; Hebrew) and *Sex, Gender and Politics* (1999; Hebrew).

ORLY LUBIN is associate professor of comparative literature at Tel Aviv University. She is the author of several essays on gender and literary and film theory, and most recently of *Women Reading Women* (2003; Hebrew).

TAMAR MAYER is professor and chair of geography at Middlebury College. She is the author of several publications on gender and the Israeli-Palestinian conflict, and editor of *Women and the Israeli Occupation: The Politics of Change* (1994) and *Gender Ironies of Nationalism: Sexing the Nation* (2000).

ORNA SASSON-LEVY is senior lecturer in the department of sociology and anthropology at Bar Ilan University. She is the author of several articles on women and the military in Israel.

SHULAMIT REINHARZ is the Jacob Potofsky Professor of Sociology at Brandeis University and director of the Women's Studies Research Center. She is the author and editor of several publications on gender and social theory, among them *Feminist Methods in Social Research* (1992) and *American Jewish Women and the Zionist Enterprise* (2004).

SUSAN SERED is senior research associate at the Center for Women's Health and Human Rights at Suffolk University in Boston. She is the author of numerous publications on gender, culture, and religion, among them *Women as Ritual Experts: The Religious Lives of Elderly Jewish Women in Jerusalem* (1992) and *What Makes Women Sick? Maternity, Modesty and Militarism in Israeli Society* (2000).

SIMONA SHARONI teaches in the department of political science at Evergreen State University. She is the author of *Gender and the Israeli-Palestinian Conflict: The Politics of Women's Resistance* (1995).

ELLA SHOHAT is professor of cultural studies at New York University. She is the author and editor of several publications on gender, ethnic studies, Middle Eastern Studies, and postcolonial theory, among them *Israeli Cinema: East/West and the Politics of Representation* (1989) and *Talking Visions: Multicultural Feminism in a Transnational Age* (1998).

YAEL YISHAI is professor emerita in the political science department at the University of Haifa. She is the author of *Between the Flag and the Banner: Women in Israeli Politics* (1997) and *Civil Society in Israel* (2003; Hebrew).

NIRA YUVAL-DAVIS is professor of gender, sexualities, and ethnic studies at the University of East London. She is the author and editor of several publications on gender, race, ethnicity and nationalism, among them *Woman-Nation-State* (1989) and *Gender and Nation* (1997).

Index